Fil Bufalo has been writing for a lifetime—on the sand, on slate and in shorthand. An animated storyteller and accomplished raconteur, she has gathered all her thoughts, philosophies and musings on life into a bonfire of words and taken the plunge with a match.

For Nino, Gaye and Marg, who would've had a laugh, had they not been in heaven at the time.

Fil Bufalo

## A Suitcase Full of Koalas

AUSTIN MACAULEY PUBLISHERS™
LONDON * CAMBRIDGE * NEW YORK * SHARJAH

Copyright © Fil Bufalo 2021

The right of Fil Bufalo to be identified as author of this work has been asserted by the author in accordance with section 77 and 78 of the Copyright, Designs and Patents Act 1988.

All rights reserved. No part of this publication may be reproduced, stored in a retrieval system, or transmitted in any form or by any means, electronic, mechanical, photocopying, recording, or otherwise, without the prior permission of the publishers.

Any person who commits any unauthorised act in relation to this publication may be liable to criminal prosecution and civil claims for damages.

A CIP catalogue record for this title is available from the British Library.

ISBN 9781528915687 (Paperback)
ISBN 9781528922081 (ePub e-book)
ISBN 9781398462502 (Audiobook)

www.austinmacauley.com

First Published 2021
Austin Macauley Publishers Ltd®
1 Canada Square
Canary Wharf
London
E14 5AA

Acknowledgements to everyone who agreed to inclusion. Thank you!

# Chapter 1
## Airport and Boarding

If it hadn't taken me so long to learn how to operate the 'camera component' of my new iPhone 7, I would not even have attempted a video filming of the Passport Control department of Melbourne Airport. The video component of the iPhone was easy. A blind parrot could not have failed to press play! There I stood, all dolled up in my Sunday-best in the hope of scoring an upgrade from premium economy to business class. My feet protested vehemently – obviously acutely distressed at being overdressed in my once-a-year shoes with the killer stiletto heels. As I tottered towards the zig-zagging queues in my quest towards the passport control booths, I glanced around with well-practised nonchalance, and noted that all the passport officials were busily shaking out bags – in search of heaven knows what!

Good. No one within cooee. Out with the phone!

Quick as a flash I whipped out the rose-coloured appendage, flicked on video, and began furiously filming the snaking hordes of holiday-makers bound for passport control booths. Alas, I didn't even make it to the voice-over. I was disturbed almost instantly by a heavy, hairy hand which seemed to be decompressing my left shoulder into pulp. This was no airport massage! From the look on the face of the owner of the hand, iPhones were decidedly not the flavour of the month.

"Put that phone away immediately or it will be destroyed."

I looked up into his face and then looked away immediately. Too brutal to view. Lazy-crocodile eyes, stunted double chin, wide cavernous mouth and greasy black curly hair framing his face like a golliwog wig. Oh yes, and yellow cracked teeth, jutting out from pink cracked lips. Not a pretty sight. Not one I wanted to gaze into for any length of time – that was for sure!

"I'm sorry," I managed to blubber, "I just wanted to make a short video of the beginning of my trip for my family and friends. Please don't destroy my phone – I've just signed up for the $10 per day phone home deal, and I intend to make the most of it." I was rewarded with a laugh (more like a bellow) at my vain attempt at using humour to diffuse the situation. At least he got it. His whole unsavoury face had changed when I'd cracked the joke, and I seized the moment and my phone, and ducked under the rope to the security of the adjacent aisle. Of course, I met with immediate procrastination from the groups of families who had already spent the last twenty minutes weaving their way up to that point but at least I had escaped the clutches of airport security. I looked behind me to see if I was still being pursued, but there was no sign of the hairy handed gentleman.

Must have moved on to his next video victim. Just to be on the safe side, I deleted the footage.

Moving aisles turned out to be a fortuitous move. It was there that I met 'Robbie' – on his way to Cambridge for his mother's 80th birthday.

After a quick introduction, Robbie told me that he had been watching me in the line. That he'd watched me casing the joint, that he'd watched me whip out the iPhone, and that he'd watched me squirm and protest at the mercy of the Customs official. I played my nonchalant card for the second time, but he took my acting like I didn't care about what had happened, to mean that I didn't care for his concern for my welfare, and he looked sad and rejected. Robbie had such a wholesome earnest boyish face that I could not bear to let this stranger think I was shunning him. Robbie was one of those ageless genderless people Lady-fate often throws at you, and I had an instant affinity with him.

I turned towards him with my best beaming smile. "No Robbie please, I'm really interested in your story, I love meeting new people and hearing their stories. Tell me about where you are flying to, and why." And so, the floodgates were opened. Robbie talked his way onto the tarmac with tales of England and Cambridge University. He told me about his dear old mum and the rest of his family in Cambridge as we were shuffling towards Passport Control. As soon as we arrived at the head of the queue, a booming voice echoed out, "Stand perfectly still on the yellow dot and look straight at the camera."

I would have been pleased to have obliged, only this time a miniscule camera replaced the beady eyes of the passport control giant with the hugely bushy eyebrows I had come eyeball-to-eyeball with on my last big O.S adventure. I have to say I pretty much struggled with finding the lens of that camera. Then, to top it off, I was surged on forwards with the crowd to complete my own auto-regulated passport control dealings with a faceless machine. I detest grappling with these machines. I avoid the self-service lines at supermarkets and department stores like the plague because of my declining eyesight, and inability to retrieve my reading glasses at the exact time of need. Now, I was being faced with no choice but to line up in the queue to serve myself in this passport scrutinising ritual. It was madness! I knew who I was. Why did I need to get the machine to verify my identity?

It was obviously no use procrastinating. The deed needed to be done before I could advance much further in this over exhausting ritual pilgrimage to my designated seat on the plane. Even further along there were more surprises in store for me and my hapless tribe. All of our hand luggage had to be heaped out onto the belt, made to suffer the undignified, scathing scrutiny of the laser beams (or whatever they were) hell-bent on identifying liquids, white powders and other banned substances. It would have been easier to escape the clutches of a hungry pack of lions than to avoid this gum chewing, overworked border patrol pack, all screeching out at the top of their lungs, "Oo owns this ear case?" I saw my cherished case in one of the scrutiniser's sweaty hands and felt instantly compelled not to betray my luggage.

"That's my case," I mumbled incoherently, with acute embarrassment, and a fast-reddening face. "I need all those pills and potions and creams for a personal medical condition." My lame excuse at carrying copious amounts of medication did not seem to go down that well, as the overly efficient patrol person gave me a look of life-long contempt, and spitefully emptied the entire contents of my case higgledy-piggledy onto the counter, ruffling through all of my personal items with the tenacity of a deranged robber delving into the depths of drawers for hidden jewels and diamonds. Naturally, all he found were multiple boxes of tablets and assorted travelling paraphernalia. He lost interest pretty quickly after that.

"Move on ven," he barked at me. "Yer olding up vu queue!"

What a cheek! I had not voluntarily requested this embarrassing pit-stop. In true Aussie spirit, I was about to feistily backchat him, but then thought the better of it. The crowd of travellers in the line I had unwittingly held up were on the verge of an uprising, and I really couldn't be bothered with their jeering and pointing at me as someone with a massive medication fetish. I moved quickly onwards, diligently following the thick yellow line towards the Duty-free perfume.

Out of all the shop attendants and spruikers outside restaurants and sporting venues vying to entice potential customers – the class of vendors I feel most sorry for are those unfortunate individuals who spend their days hauled up in international airports dishing out little white cards with the tiniest, miniscule hint of scent sprayed sparingly on them (mostly the scent smells like fly spray). These people are those unfortunates you do not ever look in the eye on your seemingly never-ending yellow brick road to your departure lounge. Over the decades I have mastered the trump card of the intrepid traveller, to keep one's head down and mumble manically to oneself, pretending to commit the departure gate and seat number to memory, and to keep on walking in a straight line. Never look up, never meet their eyes, and most importantly, never stop dead in your tracks. These seasoned traders are trained to attack. They take bartering back to its pre-stone-age roots, where Adam and Eve kicked it off with an apple for paradise. At the slightest falter or diversion on your part, these spruikers will pounce on you like a pack of hungry Venezuelan Cheetahs. Unfortunately for me, I stumbled at the first hurdle, due to an errant shoelace on my brand spanking new black and silver Sketchers shoes, which had come undone. Without thinking, I bent down to tie the lace, and when I raised my head, it was at near-perfect eye level with an expertly trained, perfectly coiffure-perfume whisperer. He was unconcerned that I had almost tripped over headfirst due to an errant shoelace. No. He just thrust a suite of little white cards into my face and asked me to choose the one which smelt the best. Frankly, the spray imprint was so feint that I couldn't smell anything on any of them. But I sure could smell him! Olfactory purgatory was where I had landed.

My note to self and new Confucius saying was, "always keep walking even with untied shoelaces."

"Oh yes, thanks! I'll study and smell them and get back to you if I am interested."

There! Pacified him! That comforting little phrase, 'I'll get back to you' worked a treat every time. He probably knew in his heart-of-hearts that he was never going to clap eyes on me ever again, but he smiled graciously, and turned abruptly to the next unsuspecting shoe lace tier in the surging airport crowd. I was gleefully (and rightfully) granted a type of diplomatic immunity at the next five or so perfume shops en-route to the Gate lounge. All I needed to do was to flash my suite of little white cards at the would-be sellers, and I was waved on. Handy little blighters those cards turned out to be.

In no time at all, I was at the departure lounge hours early, but still cashed up enough to buy a coffee and a snack as a treat to myself for having outwitted the perfume peddlers. I settled down in one of the comfy, funky airport lounge chairs, and struck up a conversation with a Buddhist monk – on his way back home to England. Even though he was wearing standard monk-type sandals, I guessed immediately that he had been unsuccessful in avoiding the plethora of perfume shops which lined the route to the departure lounge. A friend had once told me that she believed me to have been a sniffer dog in a previous life. In between the coughing and spluttering over the sweet-smelling monk – I was beginning to believe her. The monk and I weren't the only people in the lounge to have been infected. It was practically perfume plague territory in the departure lounge. Even the babies smelt of Chanel Number 5. I looked around at my 'soon-to-be' companions for the next twenty-four hours, and I just couldn't believe that one plane would transport us all to London. It was incredible to think that in less than an hour we would all be packed in like pilchards, and the enormous plane would somehow heave itself into the bright blue sky and disappear over the horizon. For a second, I panicked and wanted to run from the scene. It was just a micro panic attack though, because in the next breath I was jumping around in excitement at the prospect of boarding the plane and ending up in England. I felt eyes boring into me, heard giggling and tittering, and I realised with dismay that I had not dreamt the jumping around on the carpet like a Mexican bean bit. I decided to skip the anticipated last meal on solid ground, as I wanted to have an empty stomach for the late-night evening meal which I knew would be served on the plane.

Soon enough it was time to board. My cabin class was to be Premium Economy for the first time ever in my flight taking career. Securing the ticket had not been all smooth sailing, and I had spent many an hour on the phone to Qantas arranging my seat and flight details. The first part of the boarding went like a dream. The announcement came over that those passengers holding a Premium-Economy seat ticket were to board first, closely followed by the masses in Economy class. This was my moment to spring up – smooth down my clothes and proceed forward. The smiling crew, fresh as daisies in their immaculate uniforms ushered all of us with premium economy tickets toward the wide stairs which wound their way up to the top of the airbus. It was like walking into a whole new world at the top. Soothing quiet music wafted through the empty cabin with minimalist seating. I instinctively knew to turn left – the unwritten law of airline travel. This was the gold class of airline travel for me. More room, luxurious seating and a promised gourmet menu to come. The welcome packs were branded 'Country road' and they contained all that I needed for the long flight ahead. I thought that the socks were a trifle on the thin side, but I wasn't bothered as I had come well prepared with personal footwear.

Everything was going so well, until the flight attendant stopped short at the middle row of three separate seats and indicated to me to take the middle seat. A young man was already seated on the aisle seat on one side and in the seat on the other side there appeared to be a high pile of blankets and plastic apparatus. I quickly turned back to the flight attendant. "Excuse me (I began politely), excuse me, but this is not the seat I booked. Mine was an aisle seat so that I would be assured of direct access to the bathroom."

"Uh," replied the monosyllabic flight attendant. "This is the seat on your ticket and I'm afraid the seats are all strictly allocated. You will just have to squeeze in there in the middle!" I looked around in a panic for an empty seat that I could persuade him to escort me to, but the know-all flight attendant was entirely correct. All the seats were indeed taken. What was I to do?

What I did was cause a fair dinkum fuss!

I struggled over the knobbly knees of the gangly gent with the heavy Ray-Ban sunglasses entirely closeting his face. Perhaps he was a member of a sect? Or maybe a rock star? He was too big for a boy band, too young to be a crooner, and too surly to be a real-estate agent. Then again, maybe he was just an arrogant little sod who couldn't be bothered moving to let me clamber into my designated seat. Whatever the reason, he would not budge! (Little was I to know that he was not going to open his mouth the entire trip to London.) When I finally contorted my body into the middle seat, I found that there really was quite a lot of room after all. I swung my body around into an upright position and boldly surveyed the lay of the land. There were three people in front of me, and three people behind me. That meant three seats in each row. What I couldn't understand was why no one was sitting in the seat next to me on my left. Well. No one human that is. There was only that big amorphous lump of blankets, cushions, plastics and a metal box of some sort. The whole conglomeration was fastened in with an expanded seatbelt.

"Excuse me." I managed to tag the flight attendant as he rushed past balancing a tray of champagne and orange juices. Of course, he faltered as I tugged on his shirt, and of course one of the orange juice glasses wobbled and fell ceremoniously onto the ground. The flight attendant had really had enough of me by now. I could tell by the furious spluttering and hissing sounds he was making. "I'm so sorry, I was just trying to get your attention."

"How can I be of assistance madam?"

This was a lucky turnabout. Him, assisting me? Might as well make the most of it.

"Well, since you're offering, I wouldn't mind a glass of bubbly, and perhaps you could tell me about this great lifeless lump next to me, and why it is lumping in the very aisle seat I booked six months ago?"

He couldn't or wouldn't answer me. Just stared at the lump as if he was trying to recall a name or a reason for it to even exist. He finally stammered out, "I'll just go and summons my supervisor and get him to explain the situation." He hesitated, and then added, "You know it is a good thing to have a vacant seat next to you on a plane?"

I shot him the 'you are a blithering idiot' glance.

What vacant seat?

The big gun never appeared. What did come (over the loud speaker) was the authoritative, definitively Aussie drawl of the Captain, informing the crew to prepare for take-off. There was a long-winded message for passengers as well. "Could all passengers please ensure that their seats are upright, their tray tables stowed, mobile phones are switched off and seatbelts fastened tightly low around your hips." I methodically checked off these steps and then sneaked a look at Roy Orbison to my right. He hadn't taken the slightest bit of notice at the announcement, and his tray table was still out of its socket in front of him, laden with champagne glasses (well two actually), a huddle of cords and mini headphones, and wrappings from packets of chips. Oh well. I swivelled around in my seat until I was almost sitting in his. Might as well make the most of it. Surely, he could talk!

"So, I'm travelling all the way through to London, is that what you're doing, or are you getting off in Dubai?" I deliberately made my tone off-handed and with just a slight hint of curiosity. I learnt that trick when I was coaching young teachers and was aghast at something they had just said to their students. Like, "any student who can't answer the riddle will stay in at recess until they come up with the answer."

Mr Orbison didn't move, didn't flinch, didn't even register that he was inhabiting the same universe as the rest of us. I decided to refer to him as the 'green goblin' after the newly discovered planet which was able to expertly hide itself. OK, so he was in at recess. In for the count and the duration. I tried a second time to get him to respond. Again, I failed, although I swear, I saw his head move. It could have been the sudden jerking of the plane as it began to taxi down the runway. I suddenly remembered how much I love to feel the sheer power of the big airbuses as they magically become air borne. It is a soft, surging mighty uplifting. Like expelling air from filled-up lungs. Satisfying and stirring. It was touching me and making me feel as if I myself were flying through the air, engulfed in soft white fluffy cumulonimbus clouds (disregarding the pitch-black night sky outside the plane of course). Yes. It was touching me, and I was touching him. Not on purpose of course. And surely my subconscious hadn't propelled me to this encounter. What had actually happened was that when the plane ascended, I lurched sidewards, and grabbed the closest hand. What was with this guy? Surely a perfect stranger grabbing your hand and squeezing the blood out of it would rouse you from your inertia?

That was my last straw. I came quickly to my senses, and hastily extracted my hand from his. I was categorically not going to spoil my intense pleasure of the lift-off coaxing this elective mute to verbosity. I wasn't in England yet – and I had no Henry Higgins in my ancestry.com profile. I probably could have persisted a little longer, but three strikes meant that he was out! Great! A lump to the left of me and a lump to the right. I was in for a long night. I remembered that the cabin steward was going to get his supervisor to explain the lump to my left. Where was he? He had been ages, and I was a little uneasy about sitting next to the lifeless pile of pillows, blankets and leather straps. It was fine whilst I was awake, but since we had boarded the plane at eleven pm, I was already getting a little sleepy, and we'd only been airborne for about 20 minutes. Maybe if I just rested my eyes a little…

I was awakened to the sound of a rattling tray and someone bending over me asking if I preferred beef or chicken. I was still half asleep, so I didn't really get the meaning of the question. Was this a 'Monkey-Survey' of plane food preferences?

"Chicken I guess," I managed to stammer out, and as if that word was the Rumpelstiltskin of airline food, my tray table was lowered with one swift encroaching hand and a tray full of food thrust at me with the other. Chicken it was! I glanced at Mr Mute-head, but he was still playing possum (did not move in Aussie slang). The flight attendant had not even attempted to rouse him. Some lucky steward buddy of his was surely headed for a gourmet meal of beef or chicken once all the other passengers had been served. Actually, maybe two or three meals for the gleeful flight attendants if they chose to ignore more of the non-cooperative passengers. I reached for the luxurious, thick white napkin – the size, but thankfully not the texture of a baby nappy, and delicately dabbed the corners of my mouth before I tucked in (think Poirot). The smell of the chicken was mouth-watering, and I drooled in anticipation of the taste.

It was a feast all right!

Oodles of tender looking chicken, expertly cooked vegetables and a fresh bread roll on the side. The white wine I had opted for was delicious and fruity, and the dessert sweet and creamy. I polished it all off in record time, carefully wiping my hands and face with the crisp white napkin. It felt good to be an upper-class citizen for once. The food was top notch! The seat was super-sized and soft, the pillows were plentiful and the whole row was very, very quiet – the mute to the right of me – the lump to the left! Serendipity at last!

The next thing I knew I was being roused again by the flight attendant – my old sparring partner. This time he was dangling a steaming hot face cloth in my face, urging me to take it and refresh myself. I was reminded of an incident (quite a few years back) when I had needed to visit a chiropractor, as I'd slipped whilst mopping the floor. The chiropractor was a friend of a friend, and I was given an emergency appointment. My friend drove me to the chiropractor, who turned out to be a very engaging man about my age.

"Put this towel around you and lay face down on the massage table," was all he had said to me, as he'd handed me a folded towel. He then disappeared into the next room – giving me time to cover myself with the towel. Except, the towel wasn't a towel at all. It was a face washer. A tiny little white face-washer, which went about a quarter of the way to covering my exposed chest. I needed to hurry as I knew that Brendan (the chiropractor) would be back any minute. In a panic, I jumped up on the table and flung myself face down on the padding. There was a large gaping indentation in the table, about the size of a large orange, so I was able to position my mouth and nose over the hole and breathe normally. I just wanted it to be all over, and the pain in my neck, shoulders and back to dissipate.

"Ready are we?" Brendan was back and hovering over my back kneading my neck and shoulders with both hands. He had applied some sort of strong-smelling massage oil, and I was beginning to relax. Not enjoy, but definitely relax.

"That should do it, I'll just need to do the front of your neck and shoulders, and we'll be all done. Turn over now."

Instant alarm bells! How was I to turn over when I only had a small white face-washer to cover me? I hesitated for too long, and Brendan spoke again, this time with a hint of impatience in his tone.

"You can turn over now, just put the towel over your chest. In your own time."

I tried, I tried very hard to stretch that face washer to cover my chest from side to side. It was never going to stretch though! I had no alternative but to turn quickly onto my back and then just try desperately to cover at least half of myself.

"Oh, my goodness, where is your towel? Cover yourself!" Brendan was aghast. I tried to reach the fresh bath towel which had miraculously appeared on the chair next to the table. I managed to grab it and fling it across my chest. Brendan was amused now. Laughing, in fact, that I had thought a face-washer could ever replace a bath towel. But the bath towel hadn't been there when Brendan left the room. So, you can sympathise with me when I was reluctant to accept the steaming hot face cloth. I really didn't think it was going to be big enough to wash my hands, face, and arms – all of which were quite sticky and sweaty. I took the outstretched towel and immediately regretted it. The towel was scorching hot and I couldn't hold onto it. I threw it up into the air for momentary relief – but my aim was bad, and it veered to the right and landed smack bang on the protruding nose of the elective mute beside me.

Well, he suddenly came to life!

Off with the sunglasses, fist flaying and generally unhappy about having a steaming hot cloth thrust in his face just about wrapped up how he reacted.

"I'm so sorry!" I began to apologise, "I am just terrible at throwing and catching."

He gave me one of those contemptuous looks saved for the lowest of the low, and quickly contorted his body (a clue to his profession?) so that his curved back was towards me. He was beginning to look and act more like the lump to my left – as the journey unfolded.

Air travel does something to your psyche and exaggerates your sense of self-importance. I rummaged around in my over-laden newly purchased combination-locked black handbag and lugged out the heavy novel I'd brought with me to impress the other passengers on the long plane journey. 'Ulysses' courtesy of James Joyce. I had always wanted to read 'Ulysses', but I had never had the time or real inclination. Now I was really motivated to do myself proud. Although, there was the lure of the headphones and the promised new releases that I again, never had time for in the busy months leading up to the big trip. I tried to find the socket for the headphones on the left-hand side of my seat, but the lump was covering the arm rest as well, and I dared not disturb for fear of implosion. I also dared not to disturb the even bigger lump to my right – for fear of an explosion! I clearly couldn't win this one, so I opted for Ulysses. All seven hundred and thirty pages of it! I felt quite smug with my book propped up on my knees, as well as quite snug in my oversized seat – an unwelcoming back to my right, and a still to be explained conglomeration with the soft pillow anatomy to my left. Would that chief in charge ever appear?

# Chapter 2
## On the Plane – Up, Up and Away!

As they say in the classics, "careful what you wish for". I wished for the chief in charge to appear, and when he finally did so, I immediately wished to reverse my wish. This was no normal flight attendant. He was genetically linked to one of those enormous black genies who had spent the last century or so locked in a long-nosed bottle. No Ancestory.Com needed to make that connection! On the other hand, surely this massive towering man leaning over the lump to my left was a confused passenger on his was to participate in a rugby match somewhere in the heartlands of Africa? The man was magnificent in stature, but I could see all top and bottom rows of gleaming white gritted teeth as he flashed me a winning grin which clearly read: "Oh great, another time waster on my hands!"

I instantly turned to aeroplane jelly. Morphed from being an assertive, grumpy, cantankerous, whining passenger to a blubbering mass of a deep river rhino – this man was definitely not someone to be upsetting.

"There seems to be some sort of misunderstanding over seat allocation here, is that right?" Even his voice was of mammoth proportions. Growly with a side order of disdain. Too right there was some sort of problem! My mind was doing all the brave banter, but nothing was escaping my quivering lips. What I actually ended up saying – whispering – miming – was that everything was fine. Totally OK. So what if there were lumps to my left and right? I was just perfect wedged in between them both, and I was quite thrilled at the prospect of spending the next 20 hours encased in this very position. Suited me just fine!

I must have convinced him, because, with a final look of air-born authority mixed with supreme distaste, he lumbered off down the aisle to find someone who obviously did not suffer from the bizarre behaviour I was exhibiting. I felt that I should breathe deeply and count my lucky stars that I had escaped unscathed. I began breathing softly, building up to a crescendo as I became more comfortable with the endeavour. I suddenly noticed that people in the seats in front of me were up on their haunches, turned around, and looking at me with intense frustration. I guessed astutely that these were not accolading looks. It had never occurred to me that I might be disturbing my fellow passengers with my over exaggerated breathing. It couldn't have been that loud though, because nobody in my own row was reacting. Typical!

I stopped abruptly as I felt fingers drumming angrily into the headrest of my seat. So, the people in the seats behind me could hear me breathing as well. It just wasn't worth taking advice from people. The 'sweet-smelling monk' from the airport departure lounge had impressed upon me to breathe deeply and I would fall into a natural meditation – if things got a bit heated on the plane. The monk must have had a sixth sense. Either that, or he was one of the rear kickers. I dared not crane my neck to look for my old buddy. I did see a flash of orange cloth as I quickly bobbed my head up and down, but I couldn't be sure that it was the monk. Besides, what would a poor penniless monk who couldn't even afford to buy shoes be doing in Premium Economy class? It just didn't add up!

All the commotion and uneasiness had made me quite thirsty. The grand (fake leather) covered menu, had boasted that drinks would be readily available throughout the journey. Time to press the handy buzzer again. This time they were wise to me and sent one of the pretty young stewardesses. She tiptoed up to me after about five minutes and shone her little pink flashlight into my face. The cabin lights had only just been dimmed, but it was already quite dark. The torch was very effective, because Mr Ray Ban to my right decided that it was probably morning already and time for him to make his escape to the restrooms. Once he had vacated his seat, the stewardess slipped stealthily into his spot, and whispered to me that someone in this row had pressed the buzzer. "Yes." I whispered back. "That would be me. I'm the only one with a voice in this row. The others don't talk at all. Well, one because it can't, and the other because he won't. So, obviously, I'm the one who rang the buzzer. Do you have Coke?"

The young attendant looked at me as if I was quite stark raving mad, as there was obviously a heap of blankets and pillows, seatbelt still fastened to the right of me – and no one else. The second strain of my potential madness seemed to alarm her even more. "What do you mean, coke? Like the white coke?" I thought immediately of the delicious Vanilla Coke they had recently brought out in Australia, so I nodded enthusiastically. "Yes, some white coke would be great. I love the effect on me. Makes me feel energised and ready to do anything." I tried to see her expression, but she had shrunk back into the seat, and seemed to be trying to work out what to say. I thought I'd made myself clear, but maybe this young lady was an English flight attendant, and coke meant something different in England? And then smack! It hit me. She thought I mean Coke as in cocaine. I stared at her and tried to think how to redeem myself, but she who hesitates is lost and the lass has disappeared into the darkened cabin.

I slumped down in my seat, hoping that I wouldn't receive a further visit from the chief flight attendant. Mr Ray Ban was still not back in his seat, so I decided to venture out to the toilets whilst I could get out without having to clamber over any one. I had it in my mind that there would be an endless sashaying, fumbling towards the toilets in this darkened cabin corridor. But it was surprisingly wide, and initially I did not stumble at any hurdle. Anticipating the cramped convict conditions of the lower deck, I felt my anxiety dissipate with each tentative, overly cautious step up here in the mezzanine floor of the giant airbus. It was so easy to walk this red carpet. I decided to take advantage of this fortuitous opportunity to stretch my aching legs, and leisurely stroll this short passageway a few dozen times. It was very dark, and very still. Mood music hummed softly in the background in perfect synchronicity with the gentle purr of the massive airbus. I could see no one up ahead of me and could sense no one behind me. Good! The coast was clear. I surged forward with this new rush of adrenaline, and in my haste and exhilaration, forgot to look down for serious errant obstacles. And there is always one isn't there? And I tripped over this offending appendage, which tuned out to be the plump puffy stocking-clad leg of a snoring businessman (well, I think I saw a wad of business cards popping out of his shirt pocket, and he had that business man look of 'I am someone of extreme importance'.

In cabin class, I would have been ever alert to the numerous legs and arms which spilled out from the seats like sporadic booby traps in a minefield. But up here in Premium Economy class I was caught off guard. And I was caught by no one, as I hurtled forward towards the cabin floor. Actually, I was saved from a more serious injury by the carpeted floor, as it was so soft and luxurious that I ended up staying there snuggled up in a foetal position for the next few minutes. A pillow had somehow ended up in the aisle, and I edged my face towards it and buried my head in the fluffy feathers. Every cloud has a silver lining, and mine was most certainly this little stretch of heaven on the carpeted floor of premium economy. For added comfort, I spitefully whipped the blanket from Mr Snoring Businessman of-the-wayward-leg and snuggled up for a five-minute kip.

It couldn't have been more than three minutes later that I felt a gentle prodding around my lower back, and I was aware that someone (familiar) was whispering in my ear. I must have drifted off into one of those micro sleeps that signs on Australian freeways are always hell-bent on promoting. It was the pretty flight attendant from before, and she was balancing a can of coke in her free hand. She was whispering in my ear that perhaps I would be more comfortable back in my seat, as I was sprawled in such a way that anyone on their way to the bathrooms would need to jump over me, and that would not have been ideal. I roused myself slowly from my slumbering position and smiled sheepishly at the cabin-whisperer. "I was just testing out the carpet. Yes. All good." The flight attendant was fussing over me like I was someone concussed on a football field. She helped me up and grabbed the blanket and pillow with her free hand. She then ushered me back to my seat and helped me to clamber over Mr Ray Ban who had returned to his seat and his silence. I gratefully accepted the can of coke and I was so thirsty that I guzzled half of it down without even waiting for the flight attendant to return with a glass, ice and a packet of promised peanuts. Exhausted with the aisle antics I closed my eyes and wriggled around in my seat trying to recapture the comfort of the carpeted aisle. I started thinking of how many sheep were involved in carpeting an airbus. It beat counting sheep for no actual purpose, and it must have sent me to sleep almost immediately because the next thing I knew it was almost daylight and I could smell breakfast and movement.

Since this was to be the first breakfast of many, and since I had no one to talk to (except the carpet whispering flight attendant who must have been hiding from me), I decided to embrace the food with a vengeance, determined to remember this as the first breakfast of the big trip. It was a new fresh-looking flight attendant who bent over me with an abrasive monotone requesting me to make the agonising choice between an omelette or scrambled eggs. I opted for the former because I preferred not to see the actual eggs on my plate. I preferred them flattened and incognito. Omelette it was. Accompanied by tiny cherry tomatoes, snappy asparagus (I tested – they snapped) and two little bread rolls with four little containers of butter. A gourmet feast! I chewed slowly and purposefully, determined to remember this ceremonious breakfast and equally determined to make as much noise chewing as possible, so as to stir Mr Ray Ban into boisterous babble. I had given up on coaxing the blob to my left into conversation hours ago. The chewing rendition went unheeded, I switched to slurping my milky tea, but no luck with that either. Right! I was done with the friendly neighbour routine. As an Australian I had been brought up to respect our neighbours, both locally and globally. Growing up in the suburbs of the Capital city, we had been one big happy street family. We had street parties, billy cart races, bonfires, and secret club meetings underneath the houses. In my later years, I had always attempted to be proactive in promoting Aboriginal rights as well as joining protest groups in support of East Timor seeking independence, and the Kosovo refugees in camps outside Melbourne. I was a global citizen, and yet I could not manage to strike up even a monosyllabic utterance with my closest neighbour on this aircraft. I yearned for the monk of the airport lounge. Flicking through the play list on the audio channel of my entertainment consoles, I found Simon and Garfunkel's "I am a rock, I am an island" and settled back with my headphones to digest the soulful lyrics. I felt homesick already and we hadn't even reached Dubai International.

Surely there would be someone willing to engage in conversation with me over a coffee or the promised steaming shower?

After breakfast things started to brighten up. It was daylight for one thing, and we only had three more hours in the air until Dubai International. I had switched from the music channel to the screen in front of me some time after breakfast, but although I am a practised channel surfer in the privacy of my own home, I reverted to a category way below novice as soon as I clasped the remote for the screen. Resolved to sitting in silent meditation for the next three hours, I was on the brink of reclining in my seat when an outstretched hand with meticulously filed bright red nails carefully and gently removed the remote from my hand, and with one savvy push managed to find the very movie I had wished for. Entitled 'I Daniel' – it was right up my alley, the storyline revolving around an unemployed fifty-something gentleman. The hand belonged to the night-time carpet whisperer flight attendant and she looked smiley, rested and refreshed. "Anything else I can assist you with madam? Another coke? Some crisps?" And there was the mother of all clues as to her heritage. Crisps was a word I knew and loved. My favourite snack of all time. It was also a word which signified big time that she was English to the core. Only in England would you consistently hear the phrase: "Like a packet of crisps with your meal?"

Although some time had passed, I was still full from breakfast, and I didn't really feel like the crisps she was offering. "No, I'm fine thanks. Maybe later – after the movie – but thanks anyway." That's what we say all the time in Australia – most of the time without realising it. We are a grateful lot. The English are apologetic.

"Sorry about that," is a much-repeated phrase all over England. That, and the phrase "All right?" which I have decided means hello. Perfect strangers often came up to me on previous trips to England and asked me if I was alright. That's all any of them said, "All right?"

Of course, I was alright, and who on earth were they anyway? I looked up to find that the flight attendant had disappeared, probably tired of waiting for me to come out of my endless daydreaming.

I really enjoyed the movie. Granted, the screen was too small and too close and too loud most of the time, but I identified with the main character and I got a few laughs in (not that I would have disturbed anyone in my row). When it finished, I immediately switched off the screen pressing the same button the flight attendant had pressed two hours before to turn the screen on. It went blank and black immediately and I just knew that would be the end of our partnership since surely, I would be relocated to another seat after Dubai, when people would have disembarked for their holidays or for whatever reason people visited Dubai.

It is the unwritten law of airline travel that you visit the bathrooms before the plane lands, to 'freshen up, wash up and generally stand up' (in a long queue since everyone had the same idea).

Well, that may have been the case in cabin class (economy) but definitely not so in Premium Economy where there was not a soul lined up when I reached the bathrooms – having taken eight whole steps to get there. I spent ages in the bathroom grooming myself and applying liquids and potions to make myself look as presentable and well-groomed as possible for when I reached Dubai and the land of the mega rich sheiks. Not that I had a lot to work with. The bathroom (toilet with basin) was so small and under stocked that I had to rummage through my enormous handbag until I found anything slightly resembling a potion or paste. I ended up with toothpaste and ponds face cream, nail polish remover, a spare packet of tissues and some runny mascara. Oh! And a stub of an eyeliner pencil. I realised in a panic that this paltry assortment was never going to do the job and that I was certainly doomed to a penniless sheik-less life.

There was a sharp banging on the door and a panicked voice called out, "All right! Are you all right?" I ignored the incessant drumming and got on with applying my makeup. Why anyone would be banging on the door calling out "hello, hello" was quite beyond me. I knew no one on the plane – except for the monk and he was most assuredly settled in the cabin class a floor below. Finally, I could stand it no longer. I hastily threw all my theatrical make up into my bag and pushed open the door.

"Oh, it's you!" The flight attendant looked relieved that I was alive and well, but she was kind of staring at me in a perplexed fashion. "It's just that other passengers were wanting to use the bathroom and the door was locked for at least ten minutes, are you OK?"

"Yes. Thanks. Fine. Just a touch of air sickness." She seemed more than satisfied with my response and I flounced past her and back to my seat. All of the passengers I passed were buckled up in their seat belts in upright positions and I realised that I must have missed the announcement advising passengers to be buckled up and the crew to prepare for an immediate landing.

# Chapter 3
## Dubai and Beyond

Arriving in Dubai International airport is like landing on the moon with about five thousand other visitors. It is a massive, heaving totally unfamiliar entity of bustle and action 24/7. The smell of this foreign country is the first thing to hit you as all five hundred passengers burst out of the air bridge and into the maze of arrival pathways open to you. True fact. Dubai International airport handles thousands of pieces of luggage every day. Headquarters for this giant operation are underground, and it is sheer luggage purgatory down there. A tangled looping freeway of conveyor belts and big glossy red stop buttons to slow down or speed up the process. I knew this to be the case as I had watched a documentary about Dubai airport on a flight to London some years ago.

The second thing to hit you is the intense heat, the oppressive stuffiness of the Arrivals lounge, and the way your clothes instantly stick to you as you gasp for fresh air. It is a heady feeling. I rather fancied plonking myself in one of the state-of-the-art wheel chairs all lined up at the end of the airbridge, but I figured that once the economy class travellers were let loose, there would be a frenzied octogenarian rush on the wheelchairs. I would just have to opt for the travelator. Or walk. Trouble was that all hand-luggage needed to be offloaded in anticipation of repeating the whole gruelling process of luggage inspections at the conveyor belts. We had landed around 2pm Dubai time, but I really had no clue as to real time for my time-zone challenged body.

I was slightly peckish, but I think perhaps the rumbling in my stomach was more uncalled for nerves at being a single, hatless woman in Dubai, than it was actual hunger. I was once travelling to a seminar with a colleague notorious for her cut-to-the-chase bluntness. I was probably just as nervous and ill at ease travelling with her in the close confines of her car, as I felt today. Halfway to our destination I blurted out to her that I was 'starving hungry'. I may well have blabbed that I was going to bomb Number 10 Downing Street or sell national secrets in London, for the lashing retort I received from her. "You're starving! Why do people say they are starving? Refugees and children are starving! Not you!" So, you can sympathise with my reluctance to admit even the slightest tremor of hunger pains. Once we reached the first conveyor-belt I relaxed my pace and anxiety levels. (One notch.) The Captain had announced that we only had a short two-hour stopover in Dubai, and that boarding for the second leg of our journey would commence fifty minutes before the actual displayed time. I checked my phone and realised that I could afford to slow down a little as it was so humid, and I was feeling flustered and exhausted. I hadn't even made it past the conveyor belts, let alone up to the Lounge, where I was sure all the sheiks would be congregating.

I really shouldn't have relaxed my pace or even slightly let my guard down. I should have sprinted to the luggage belts, flung down my hand luggage and zipped through the x-ray door frame. Had I done so, I might mercifully have escaped the totally humiliating experience which followed my exiting the x-ray section. "Move over please madam, over to the side. Now." She couldn't mean me? Clearly, she had me confused with someone who was really a drug smuggler or petty thief? Not me. I was squeaky clean, and besides, I only had two small bags of mostly water and jumpers, tee-shirts, tracksuits, books and sweets.

I didn't resist for long. The strong arm of the law really was the strong (and quite painful) arm of the law, propelling me forwards, away from the crowds at the conveyor belts. "Arms up and take off your shirt, quickly!" I looked around in horror! I was standing in a completely open area behind the conveyor belts, and there was not a partition or barricade to be seen. I had a sinking feeling that the 'Coke' incident back on the plane may have been my downfall. I tried protesting, but it was no use. The mean woman summonsed an even meaner woman, and in perfect synchronicity they tugged at my top. Two of the toughest and snarly ladies-in-waiting one could ever hope for. My top was thankfully stuck on my head, so I could not see the looks on the faces of my travelling companions. I could feel cold hands poking and prodding at my skin and patting me down, but it was quite muffled as the top was still stuck on my head. I hoped I wasn't in for a random beheading. I'd read about Oliver Cromwell whose severed head ended up on a plate, and I knew this barbaric practise was still alive and well in some countries. Luckily, I must have passed with flying colours, because there was a sudden downward yanking of my shirt, and then a flood of light. I could see again! Though the incident had cut to the core of me, no one else seemed in the least bothered. They were all hell-bent on hot-footing it towards the cafes, toilets and gift shops. The Captain with his two-hour curfew really had put the fear of God into them. I smoothed down my clothes and took some deep breaths. Well, that part was thankfully over. I hoped it wasn't only half of the ordeal and that I wouldn't be recalled for similar scrutiny on the return ritual. I looked around for some sheiks to follow, but they had all disappeared into the sterility of the airport corridors. My hopes of becoming somebody's wife number Twelve were fast fading.

Checking my watch for the tenth time, I calculated that I still had time to rush up to the QANTAS lounge for a shower and a bite to eat. Finding the right lounge was relatively easy. I just followed the signs with a Q and a picture of a QANTAS plane. The Saudis must have tired of foreigners asking for the location of the QANTAS lounge, and just gathered a bunch of street-kids to draw pictures of planes and practise their scribing, using the letter Q as a prototype. The Lounge was located on the 4$^{th}$ floor of the terminus, and up at the counter I needed to show my passport and boarding pass – which I dutifully did. I asked for the direction of the showers and although I had to walk a bit, they were also easy to find. The crew at the bathroom station were so keen and so excited to have a customer.

I had expected there to have been hordes of people wanting showers after their long flights, but it was a 'Shower Station' ghost town. In Australia we do a lot of camping and caravanning and the Ablutions blocks are nearly always the focal point of the caravan parks. Friendships are made and cemented in the shower blocks. Mostly we wear thongs to the toilets and showers, an old Aussie custom. I had, of course, packed my thongs in my hand luggage but I realised that I wouldn't be needing them, as this shower block was Five-Star, and there were literally five people on hand to assist me. They would probably carry me to the shower of my choice if I indicated that I did not wish my bare feet to touch the tiled floor. I didn't think it would come to that though, as the tiles were mosaic edged and magnificent. One of the workers spoke English. The other four were accomplished 'nodders'. Perhaps they were of Indian descent, and the nodding was genetic? Whatever the case, there was a lot of nodding and smiling going on. The English speaker was enunciating slowly. "We have four showers for you to choose from. I am Armin, I will be booking you in. This is…" and he proceeded to rattle off the names of all the workers and outline their respective job profiles. When he had finally finished, he nodded and smiled at me. "And so what time would you like to come back for your shower please?"

Now. I wanted my shower now. I only had less than an hour and a half to get scrubbed up, fed and ready to board.

"Oh no, so sorry, so many apologies, we are closed for half an hour for cleaning. The showers will be ready at 3 o'clock." I quickly decided to book in for 3 o'clock and to grab a drink and a bite to eat in the interim. Armin carefully and cautiously copied my name into the enormous Book-of-Kells-like ledger and I noticed that my name was the first and only name in the book for that day. Surely, they didn't need to clean the showers right this very minute?

I was about to mention this to Armin and his nodding flock, but I figured that would waste more time – crossing or rubbing my name out. I was hungry, and thirsty, and at least this way I would be refreshed or the plane. Off I trekked to the food lounge. Guess what the food lounge was stuffed full of? Yes, well food of course, that was a given, but it was also cramming with sheiks. Sheiks eating, sheiks drinking, sheiks smoking bongs and sheiks shrieking and holding court whilst all the sheiks groupies held onto their every word. They were meticulously dressed right down to their sandaled feet. All wore the same flowing thick white robes and an even whiter cloth with a thick rope tied around their heads to secure the head dress. And they were all men. Nor a woman in sight. Over to the side of Sheiksville, I glimpsed a group of black Birka clad women huddled around a tea pot and some knotted bread rolls. I assumed that they were women. They were slighter, and shapelier than the men, and although I couldn't see their faces, I was willing to bet that they wouldn't have looked so pretentious and self-important as their male counterparts. Probably all wives of the same man – the one who was holding court and puffing out smoke equivalent to Robert Louis Stevenson's first steam engine launch.

I remembered the occasion some years back, when a group of us had stopped in Dubai for a couple of nights on our way to England. We were a party of three, two women and one gentleman. Our pre-booked accommodation was a five-star garden hotel in Central Dubai, with a grand swimming pool, perfectly groomed swaying palm trees and a pristine to the point of sterility restaurant attached to the hotel. When we ventured out to the restaurant for something to eat, there were at least ten sheiks already seated on little carpeted stools chatting and smoking. No one else was in the premises besides us and the sheiks. Misogyny reigned supreme in this establishment. They completely ignored us (the women) but fell all over Dave. We thought they were being rude, but in retrospect, we realised they were actually being very respectful. They approached Dave first, and the expectation was for him to relay the messages on to us. It would have been extremely rude of them to have talked directly to women. But that was years ago, and I had no go-between with me today, and to all intents and purposes I was being totally ignored! It was a light-bulb moment for me. In that instant I went right off sheiks. They could keep their money and their status and their flowing white garb. I would be forever happy with my own company. I had woken up to myself! (Probably would do so now for the rest of my days). As I passed the group of huddled women, I smiled cheerfully but they all stealthily lowered their heads and turned their faces away from me. I quickened my step towards the large brown crock pot of steaming dim-sims I could see billowing away on the counter up ahead. Perfect comfort food.

All the food in the lounge was delicious and very fresh. A mixture of eastern and western dishes – quite light and appetising. I thoroughly enjoyed partaking of that meal in the Dubai lounge, and with the yearning to become a rich Sheikess now a mere shadow of a foolish dream, I switched my thoughts to the anticipated warmth and comfort of the promised shower. I felt happy, resolved and relaxed. Things were looking up.

When I re-presented myself for the shower appointment a long queue had formed, and Armin seemed not to recognise me. I knew it to be accepted etiquette to join the end of the line and patiently wait my turn, but I also knew that it had taken Armin at least 2 minutes to carefully copy the minimal letters of my name from my passport some 20 minutes before. So, I broke protocol. I played one of my traveller's diversion cards and it worked. For this trick you need to be loud and brazen and to act immediately eyes are turned. (Americans are naturals)

"Oh, look over there! A monkey, it's grabbing all the goods." Dutifully, they all looked intently over towards where I was pointing and crazily waving my arms! In a whisk, I was at the front of the queue, and flashing my passport at Armin. This time he recognised me (must have been short sighted as well as tediously slow at handwriting).

"Oh yes. It really is you. Your shower room has been ready for ten minutes." That didn't bother me as I knew I was going to have to get my skates on, if I was ever to end up in England. "No, its fine Armin, I will be very quick."

The four gangly women attendants who had been nattering in clipped low tones and leaning lazily against the gleaming counter, sprang into action. Two of them dragged me into the curtain-clad den, and a third woman carried my hand luggage. (She may have mistaken me for royalty, so proud was the expression on her face.) The fourth picked up a brush-broom and led the way to my allocated shower room, singing loudly and sweeping invisible dust as she swayed towards the shower. All we needed were the elephants and bell-ringers to trumpet out our arrival. They really had come to life with the prospect of helping me with the showering. I was trying to remember how much Dubai currency I had with me. Tipping was going to be tricky. When we reach the bevelled-blue glass door of the shower room I had been allocated, the attendants suddenly all disappeared, and my short-lived brush with royal treatment came to an abrupt end.

The shower suite was enormous, with a marbled pinkish-grey floor, and state of the art gleaming white hand basin, toilet seat and bidet. The shower itself was nothing short of magnificent, and I could have stayed in there all day and all night. The soap smelt like musk oil, and the shampoo was glorious. I was quick though. Nagging me, in the back of my mind, was the fact that time was ticking fast, and I didn't really know which direction to take towards the exit gate for my plane. I swiftly finished showering, and hurriedly cleaned my teeth with the delicious creamy white toothpaste provided on-tap-along with the shampoos, lotions and potions of all sorts. Everything was so garden-of-Eden in the shower room.

I reluctantly pulled on my second supply of travelling attire and hand-dried my 'now-silken' hair by patting down furiously with the Egyptian cotton towel (I had checked the tag and made a note to buy some similar towels when I returned from the big trip). The echoing in the room was deafening, so anyone listening at the door would have had a field day trying to work out what I was up to. Luckily there was no repetition of the furious rapping on the door the cabin-whisperer flight attendant had resorted to. Neither was there anyone calling out: 'All right, all right?' I figured I still had about five minutes of being left to my own devices. I then dragged on my leggings and a faded sloppy Joe. My feet were comfy in my well-worn jiffies. I find the tiny half-moon jiffies to be the perfect match for the tight travel socks I had stashed in my hand luggage. I did not have time to lay flat out and try and squeeze my newly waxed legs into one sock, let alone two. The socks had taken a full twenty minutes to struggle into when I had readied myself for the long flight some twenty-four hours before. I decided to leave the inevitable pantomime for the plane. It would make the time pass, if nothing else. I felt my hair, but it was still damp, and I was not one for appearing in public with wet hair at the best of times, let alone on my last five hundred metre opportunity to snare a sheik. The nodding women were still congregated haphazardly outside the shower rooms – but at a respectable distance, and as soon as they heard the hairdryer rev up, all four of them shyly entered the room and began fussing around cleaning and sweeping and drying – nodding and smiling all the while. They didn't look directly at me, but courtesy of the mirror I could see them smiling and using hand and facial gestures to communicate with each other. They seemed happy and brimming with pride and efficacy. I lingered as long as I could, as it was nice to see them enjoying themselves. It really was getting late though, and I knew that I'd have to pick up my game if I was to board the plane. After prolific nodding and bowing (on my part, not theirs) I managed to back my way out of the shower block. Armin still had his head in the ledger copying names and passport numbers. I slipped past him as silently as I could manage. I recognised a few of the lined-up shower seekers and they looked at me in surprise – possibly because I had been at the end of the line ten minutes ago, and now I was showered, changed and rushing off. I was gone before they could protest.

    At the lifts, which I discovered teleported one straight down from the Lounge to the departure lounges and luggage conveyer belts, I engaged in a conversation with a tubby, twinkle-eyed Japanese man who was struggling with his life-possessions of cameras, laptops and Gucci luggage. I offered to help even though I was quite laden down myself, and he was eternally grateful. More nodding and bowing – all the way down in the lift to departures. Once underground and settled in the lounges, he reclaimed all his assorted goods, and exclaimed to me that carrying all the hand luggage by himself had been 'hin tollelable'. So, he could speak English after all! As luck would have it, talking to Mr Komishi was my golden ticket to re-boarding the plane without harassment from the Dubai strip searchers. To be fair, they were probably only doing their jobs, but their abrasive manner, cold, bony, raking hands and lack of empathy for those unfortunates such as myself made to suffer acute humiliation and embarrassment, did nothing to endear them to any of us passengers. I kept my head down and shuffled in perfect time with Mr K. By the time we had heaved all our hand luggage onto the belt, the mean women had already pounced on their prey.

    As I stepped over the air-bridge and onto the giant plane, I stole a quick sympathetic look behind me to glimpse the unfortunate individuals who had been detained this time. It was a whole family and the baby was squealing in protest.

They appeared to be in shock and were looking around desperately for help. I wanted to go back and assist, but the rules were quite clear – once you stepped on or off a plane – no reversals! I had been caught before, trying to retrieve a forgotten pair of sunglasses.

Instead, I immediately turned left (old professional that I was at turning left), and the power and surge of the move was incredibly invigorating. I resolved to turn left in my forthcoming overseas travels whenever there was a fork in the road. Who knows where I would end up, but I thought that this decision would somehow add daily excitement to my trip. I felt better straight away and swanned up the staircase, to my old familiar seat. Mr Ray Ban had disappeared, and there was no one in his seat. Yet! The blob was still securely settled down in its seat, and it didn't look like it had been touched in the two hours I had been away from the plane. "Hello old pal," I whispered to the blob. "Good to see you looking so relaxed." Of course, inevitably, silence was the grim reply, but it didn't bother me – not one little iota. I had the whole row to myself. I could stretch, I could yawn, I could read out loud and I could even put my stockinged feet up on the blob to stretch out if I wanted to. Uh oh! What stockinged feet? One laborious job I had forgotten to do. Squeeze into the dreaded skin-tight stocking socks. But they did the job – supposedly. I'd like to see the research that supports the hypothesis that fewer plane deaths occur when passengers wear the proclaimed anti-blood clotting socks. I knew that I couldn't take the chance though. It would be just my luck to get a fast-moving blood clot and die before we even reached London if I didn't don the stockings. I still had ten minutes until seat belt fastening, and they hadn't yet brought out the pre take-off drinks – so I knew I had time on my side.

I have found with experience that it is easier to put on the plane socks (actually fawn not plain coloured) if you are lying down, so I quickly whipped them out of my travel bag and crouched down on the floor in front of my seat. That is the beauty of Premium Economy. There is plenty of room to perform whatever exercising movement you desire. I managed to get one stocking/sock on quite easily, but the second one kept coiling back into itself and I fumbled furiously. I finally managed to get it straight and folded it over my bulging calf muscle.

All done.

I was sitting up, still on the floor in front of my seat, when I was almost trampled on by a pair of gleaming red stilettos. I could also see a pair of tightly stockinged legs leading up to knees, but that was about it. Either Mr Ray Ban had changed into a drag costume or I was to have a brand-new neighbour – possibly female. I struggled to my feet and looked around for my jiffies. I was trying to inconspicuously attach the shrivelled jiffies to my nylon-covered feet, but the little blighters kept springing back in my hand. In the end I stuffed them into the newly emptied seat pocket and heaved myself up to eye level with the owner of the red stilettos.

My first thought was that I knew her. Déjà vu. That she must have been a teacher friend of mine from years ago. But she was not reacting to my over-zealous winking and smiling. Her eyes were polite but unwavering. Maybe I was confusing her with another teacher friend of mine. You know us teachers. We roam in packs, we have the widest and longest lasting friendship group in the world, and we are mostly women. "Hi, welcome to Premium economy." I extended my hand toward her, but she had already begun patting down the seat and positioning herself into a comfortable position. Great. Another mute. Must be a prerequisite for reserving that seat. I turned away and began to fidget with my jiffies. "A dancer, are you? Do you choreograph now?" I suppressed a smile and then remembered my leotard-like outfit and now slim-slippered feet. "Well, I dance with my own company. Mostly after a shower, or on a deserted walking track." She looked slightly surprised but seemed to be still of the opinion that I had an affinity with dancing. (Given my age, height and weight, it was highly unlikely.)

"No, I'm not a dancer. But I've been a dance teacher. How about you?"

"Yes, I'm a teacher too, but I've been a Principal for the past ten years."

I knew it. I just knew she was a teacher. I bet myself a hundred dollars that she was from Melbourne too, even though she'd just boarded in Dubai.

"I'm from Melbourne."

There's one hundred virtual dollars into my account!

We both settled down in our seats before we continued in our conversation. It turned out she was Principal of a small country school on the outskirts of Melbourne. I was impressed with her humility and lack of boasting about her status. Although I had recently reinvented myself as an Educational Consultant, I realised that Principal trumps Consultant every time. Margie (that was her name) seemed oblivious to her esteemed standing in the community and had really warmed to our conversation. We were discussing Aurora Borealis – the Northern Lights in Norway, which was where she was headed. I dared not mention that I was headed for the Southern lights of Barton on Sea in South England. It didn't sound nearly as glamorous a destination as when I had boasted the location to farewelling friends and family at my going away party last weekend. Margie was meeting up with two friends in Oslo, and they'd organised to travel to the Northern lights in a four-wheel drive, camping along the way. I immediately felt better and joined enthusiastically into the conversation. I would be travelling to Barton on Sea in a brand-new Mercedes and sleeping in a beautiful thatch-roofed holiday cottage in a pretty seaside village. I liked having the upper hand. As the plane pelted past most of Europe, we chatted on and on, moving from the inevitable conversations about teaching to places of National Trust and the Royal family of Denmark and how Princess Mary was Australian.

After a substantial meal bearing very little resemblance to your usual aeroplane grub, we both slumped down to have a nap, and the cabin lights were surreptitiously dimmed.

I knew nothing more until. "Wake up please Mrs Ballard, your 'welcome to Heathrow' drink is ready for you."

I opened one eye to the English-looking stewardess but it was not me she was awakening. Margie was the lucky recipient of the welcome drink. The stewardess didn't seem to notice me at all, and I did not receive a drink. It was Margie who was apologetic, and it was Margie who was attempting to share her drink with me. I politely refused her offers and took the opportunity to nip to the bathroom for the ritualistic freshening up. On my way to the bathroom (the whole ten paces), I bumped into the same stewardess. She must have recognised me and realised her mistake at not offering me a welcome to Heathrow drink. "I apologise for missing you when I was handing out the drinks, I thought you were asleep, and I didn't want to awaken you. Would you like your drink now?" She was beaming at me and waiting expectantly for my response. Of course, I could have snapped back that it was too late now and that it was back then when I wanted the drink, but I decided that this was the first real test of my turning over a new leaf with airlines. I was a regular user of the portal for customer feedback in Melbourne, and it was about time I changed my tune and cut these people some slack. No. She had just misinterpreted my closed eye for the signal that I was fast asleep.

"No, that's fine. I wasn't thirsty anyway, and I'm just on my way to the bathrooms." I made it sound like there was a whole row of bathrooms, but in fact there were only two. That's two with a queue, rhymes with view, and that was what I got as I stumbled up towards the bathrooms. A real cracker of a view. A view of at least five First Class passengers clogging up the bathrooms' clearway, trying to disentangle themselves from the airline pyjamas they had been encouraged to wear as part of the extravagant service by QANTAS to First class passengers. It was hilarious. Half of them were struggling to get the tops over their heads, and the other half were hopping about on one leg trying to set their legs free of the clinging polyester. They were so engrossed in their tasks that none of them actually realised that the bathrooms were free. I hurriedly barged past them and into one of the bathrooms. When I emerged, clean and deodorised, the 'Pyjama-game players' ensemble had vanished, and been replaced by a new crowd of bathroom seekers. I flounced smugly past them. There was a little girl about ten years old who tugged at her mother as I wafted past. I could hear her clearly as I approached my seat.

"Mummy, that lady has a towel thuck to her twackswoot." I dared not turn around. All I could do was fumble around my back to see if it was me with the towel tucked into my slacks or some other unfortunate soul. It was me alright. It had been so cramped in the bathroom where I had changed into my respectable airport clothes. The white fluffy towel must have somehow become caught up in the small of my back and was now trailing down behind me like a bridal train. It was white and long and they continued to stare. Some were sniggering, but I held out until I reached my seat and sunk gratefully into the cushioned refuge. As inconspicuously as I could, I stuffed the large white wet fluffy towel into my travel bag. Margie was nowhere to be seen. She had told me that she liked to exercise her legs just before the plane landed, so I assumed that she would be walking the width and breadth of Economy class by now.

It was just me and the blob for the next thirty minutes. I felt a tug at my heartstrings as I realised that we probably only had an hour or so left together. His/her life would end the second someone realised they were missing pillows and a steel box. "It's been nice knowing you blob." I was sincere in my sentiments. It had been nice knowing that no one was going to occupy that seat. Initially I had been uneasy and indignant, but as the trip panned out, I felt more relaxed and comforted by the pillowed conglomeration.

Margie was back, and we were all madly stowing away errant articles of clothing and tangled headphones. Once all the preparations for the landing were completed, we were able to relax a little and enjoy the image of the giant plane on the monitor in front of us as it glided towards Heathrow International. It was still very early in the morning London time, and dawn was just breaking. The mood music had been switched on, and the unmistakable rippling of Richard Clayderman echoed 'Fir Elise' throughout the cabin. Margie and I smiled a knowing smile at each other. We were of the same vintage as Richard, and the mellow music was instantly recognisable. There was a sudden bump and barely audible skidding – and we were down. Safely settled on English soil.

So many times, in the past year, I had ground myself through hectic days with one line playing over in my head, "Oh to be in England!"

Well, here I was! About to leave the familiarity and comfort of the plane and venture out into the great unknown. "I suppose this is where we part?" Margie was shaking my hand with gusto and balancing all her hand luggage on her hip with her free hand. "Yes, bye…it was lovely meeting you and chatting all the way to Heathrow – hope you get to see the Northern lights and take some great pics for your Pinterest board." Margie nodded and disappeared into the walkway. We had reached the fork in the road where we met up with Economy class, so this was it for us. Fortunately for me I was able to keep my promise to myself of turning left whenever possible. Adios Margie! A steep escalator loomed up in front of me. Onwards and upwards!

*At Heathrow*

The first strikingly different sign I noticed (well, bumped into actually, as I had not been able to locate my long-distance glasses in all the confusion of exiting the plane), was the 'UK Border' sign. Big, bold, boring, and with an indiscernible hint of stuff British upper lip. No 'Welcome to our friendly island' which would definitely have been the case in Hawaii or any of the South sea colonies. No fanfares, no floral wreaths, no smiling round-faced musicians with ukuleles. Nothing but those eight beady-eyed, heavy, black letters: 'UK BORDER.' I was squashed and slumped deliriously on one of the travelators when I first spotted the glaring black mono-brow.

The last time I had hurtled into Heathrow, I had been caught up in the midst of a surge of West Indians in flamboyant attire, in a rush to get back home to good old England. I remembered them with the acute clarity of a 5-year-old anxiously awaiting promised presents from travels abroad. All those years ago, – they had all but crushed us Aussies. So, I repeat, the last time I had hurtled into Heathrow was in 1995, and the signage had been 'Well, fick'-thickly plastered and peeling everywhere. Twenty odd years later – and this was it. No fanfare of 'Rule Britannia', no acapella Jamaican choir cousins serenading long lost rellos, and certainly not a scrap of colour anywhere within cooee.

I will be bold and assert that it was absolutely bland! Once off the travelator, it was all blacks and whites and navies. No furniture or prints anywhere. No Laura Ashley or Liberty wallpaper. Minimalist decrepit bland. I looked down to the floor to check for the typical red and green faded checked British hotel/airport carpet, but even that had disappeared, only to be replaced by copious amounts of the most tired, most faded, and most grotty linoleum in the entire universe. I craned my neck past an Asian VonTrapp family of at least sixteen, in a vain attempt to glimpse the world beyond this 1984-esque border control virtual reality. But the panels were too high, and the white light was everywhere, and I was a rat in a trap – so I gave up. Pulled my head in, obligingly shuffled forward in the conga line which appeared to be snaking for at least twenty useless turns and resigned myself to the fact that I would probably be shuffling, two, minute steps at a time, towards the passport stamper – for the next twenty odd years.

But, as sweet life would have it, just as I lifted my foot in perfect chain gang tempo and dragged my bulging hand luggage forward for the twenty-seventh shuffle of the morning, the thick coiled black rope in front of me was miraculously lifted (as if by generous casting of Harry Potter magic) and a brand-new pathway was instantly created. For an entire 10 seconds, myself and the sixteen Von Trapp family members were at the front of this brand spanking-new line. It was like a brand-new country had materialised, all because a hand had reached forward and gently shifted the border. I was now at the front of the new queue (just behind the Von-Trapps).

We were rightful heirs to the imminent passport stamping ritual, and we were about to mercifully exit this painstaking pilgrimage to the passport gods, and casually waft down this new yellow brick road.

I wasn't even particularly worried that there was one of me and sixteen of the Von-Trapps, because I knew that families could all get stamped en-masse at the one booth, and there were two booth attendants awaiting their prey. My fatal mistake, in retrospect, was that I allowed myself the luxury of a gloating, prolonged jet lagged yawn, and when I opened my eyes and closed my frog-wide mouth, I was looking straight into the beady eyes of the fiercest looking passport control lady you would ever be likely to encounter. She was eyeballing me like it was an Olympic event, and I didn't even know how to begin eyeballing back.

I felt like I was going cross-eyed, so I stopped abruptly. I quickly sized up the situation. The Von-Trapps had stolen away (as swiftly as the real Von-Trapps had scurried through the crypt in Maria's old convent.) I could see them up at the passport counter – all smiles and babbles. I could even hear the Captain calling out the names of all his children. (The family must have been from Iraq, and not Austria after all, as all their names began with the letter S.) A dead giveaway as to ethnicity with the Iraqis. Uncanny though, the connections to the real Von-Trapps. But me? What happened to me? Well, in the wink of an eye I was literally surged backwards into the body of the Guinness book of shufflers. The tiny tributary that had opened up for the Von-Trapps was still operating – but obviously not for white Caucasian Anglo Celts.

Every man and his dog were being ushered from the pack into the new line, the new exit – the fast track to freedom. The rest of us, me included, were being shouted at to move forward, to stay in the lines, and to have our passports at the ready!

I was aghast at the impropriety and injustice of it all! We have kangaroo culling in Australia, so I knew a little bit about weeding out the unwanted. But, as I looked around in shock at the sheer audacity and obvious aversion to my white complexion, I realised that everyone behind me who was white and Caucasian, was being redirected past the new opening, and forced to resume the shuffling and dragging routine.

"Hey! What about us? We were in the new line? Why did we have to keep walking?"

The words were out before I had time to think of the consequence of my actions (well, yes…there was a bit of arm wiggling and fist wagging to accompany my outburst.) For five seconds there was silence. Agonising silence. The kind of silence you can expect to experience on Remembrance Day's all over the world. People stopped chatting about the expected London rain, the location of taxis outside the airport and where in London their hotel would be situated. Squeaking babies ceased their squealing, children stopped skipping and hopping on and off the luggage, and even the older people looked up from their sunken semi-slumbering positions on their walking sticks.

The passport lady was the first to break the silence. Everyone could hear her. "You have two choices, either you keep quiet now, and wait your turn like the rest of the passengers, or you can step into the office and explain your outburst." I lowered my head quickly and nodded that I would stay forever silent. I dared not look at the passengers behind or in front of me for fear that they would lynch me. When I reached the 'passport stamper-extraordinaire', he enquired kindly if I was travelling, or in England purely for business. "Pleasure and Leisure," was my sombre response. He smiled encouragingly and pointed me in the direction of the luggage carousels. I shuffled over towards the luggage sign and quickly located the sign displaying my flight number, QF1. The absolute best thing in the world happened next.

Poetic justice at a premium. My big shiny purple suitcase was the very first cab off the rank to emerge from the bowels of the building. Thank you, thank you airport Gods!

I was out of Customs even before anyone else had claimed their luggage.

# Chapter 4
## Barton on Sea Arrival

The brand-new blue Mercedes I had boasted about to Margie was parked on Level Three in the closest car park to the International Terminal. Alice, my friend since our first day of High school, was seasoned at airport pickups. She had been picking me up at Heathrow for many years, and always made it an important and exciting occasion for myself and the other passengers, by standing at the door way to Customs with a fanciful sign displaying my name splashed across chunky white cardboard. This trip was no exception, but it was novel, in that she had replaced the white cardboard sign with an iPad with my name scrawled across the screen in the most capital of capital letters. Of course, people were looking at her, because all the other iPad holders were there to greet impeccably dressed business men and women. These drivers were similarly impeccably dressed in chauffeur uniforms and accompanying caps. Alice was a pea-in-a-pod to me, dressed comfortably in travelling clothes and sensible shoes. (Her driving outfit she later informed me.)

"Yoo-hoo Fil, I'm over here!" The last two words were shouted out at the top of her voice, and she was waving uncontrollably. Alice is a teacher of the deaf, and I think that she was using her practised, louder than usual voice, out of habit rather than an unreasonable desire to destroy the eardrums of surrounding travellers. Whatever the reason, it worked, because we all spun around to see who was causing all the commotion, and as soon as Alice spotted me, she instantly ceased her raucousness. Well, that and the fact that two airport bouncers were making their way towards her with irritated looks on their faces. It was probably unusual for anything out of the ordinary to happen outside the customs doors where long lost friends and relatives locked each other in bear hugs and chatted inanely about the length of the flight and how hungry they were.

At this point in time Alice had me well and truly encased in a bear hug to rival all bear hugs. It wasn't as if we hadn't seen each other for a lifetime. I had been over to England (arriving Gatwick that time) two years before and stayed with Alice and her husband Patrick for almost a month.

She must have missed me terribly. Or maybe she was missing my accent. I hadn't had the chance to breathe a word yet, so it was nice to be finally released from the bear hug and blurt out how good it was to see her. I thought she looked quite tired and strained, but then I remembered that she was still working full time as a teacher/consultant of the deaf, and how tiring it would be to try and make yourself understood to the deaf – especially the babies with whom she worked. All jobs are exhausting, but some more physically and emotionally draining than others. A well-deserved rest up for a week at the holiday house in Barton should perk her up. "It's really good to hear the Aussie drawl." Alice was genuinely pleased when I started relating the plane trip over, and how I had been this close to meeting a sheikh in Dubai. She was laughing already at my jokes and we hadn't even left the car park.

Once we were out on the open motorway headed toward Barton, I quizzed Alice about life in England and how things were going for her at work. She prattled on all the way to the New Forest. I knew we were close to the heart of the New Forest, as the sign had been hard to miss, and we had turned up a little winding, muddy country road with hedgerows and ditches. I was still a little surprised that we had left the motorway before we'd reached New Milton, which is the fair-sized town bordering Barton on Sea.

"Why are we turning off the motorway Alice?" I need not have bothered asking her, because no sooner had the words escaped my lips than I noticed with pleasure, that we were driving through the New Forest itself. It was breath-taking. It felt like we had turned into a whole new world in the wink of an eye We had gone through the Stargate. It was so totally unexpected. "I should have warned you that we'd be taking a shortcut to Barton." Alice was totally matter of fact about the stunning, kaleidoscopic landscape of heathland, forest trails and native ponies. The ponies fascinated me the most. Although we were only in the New Forest for about twenty minutes there were ponies everywhere, and they appeared to be quite tame and friendly. In Australia, we have wild brumbies. They are free-roaming feral horses. The best-known brumbies are found in the Australian Alps regions of Victoria and New South Wales. This terrain was definitely not mountainous – more like a flat green, flowering robe of a desert.

The landscape we were driving through was also something quite eerie and definitely other worldly. I was so excited at being there that I was jumping up and down in my plush (real leather) seat exclaiming over and over. "Oh, this is just so different."

"Hey, watch the new seat, it's the maiden voyage to Barton on Sea for this Mercedes, and if you keep jumping about it could be the last one!"

I settled down straight away then. Not a good idea to anger your host, and certainly not a good idea to do so out in the middle of nowhere in a foreign country. I reclined as far as I could back in the seat, and suddenly felt exhausted. It was starting to catch me. The dreaded jet-lag. We flew past more hedgerows and posies of ponies. I was so drowsy, yet I couldn't tear my eyes away from the beautiful landscape. There was suddenly a large field on our right. "That field used to be full of travellers caravans and campfires, but they've been ordered by the council to move on, because they'd settled on unauthorised encampments." I wondered what had become of them. The road was less bumpy now, and I could see houses and a church spire looming up in the distance. My eyes were shutting, and I could feel my head falling forwards.

When I opened my eyes, it was pitch dark. I had no idea where I was, and it felt quite chilly. As I gradually became more aware of my surroundings, I realised I was still in the car, with some sort of thick material tucked in around my lap. I tried to look out the windows, but I could only see the outline of walls on either side of me. Perhaps I was in an underground car park, and Alice had gone to get groceries for tea. It didn't feel like a carpark though, and it was so dark I had trouble finding the car door on the passenger side. There was a fraction of light slithering in from the driver's side, so I tried to sidle over the protruding handbrake in an effort to land myself in the driver's seat. (And who has never completed that particular act in their lives?) I managed to do so with little repercussion, although I got my shirt caught on a piece of protruding metal, and it ripped slightly. I thought it a small price to pay for freedom from wherever I was!

The driver's side door handle was illuminated in tiny little circles of blue light, and quite easy to open. My legs were stiff and aching, and I realised that I had forgotten to remove the dreaded airline socks/stockings. No wonder my legs ached. The socks were cutting off the circulation. It was even darker outside the car, and I fumbled my way towards the walls. There must have been a door somewhere. My head was splitting by now, and I was hungry and thirsty. Where on earth was I? And where was Alice? I felt blindly along a corrugated ridge, and finally discovered the protruding handle to a door. I half expected it to be locked, as I had watched too many episodes of Midsomer Murders and the doors were always locked in the darkened rooms when people were trying to escape (and, I knew Midsomer filming had gone on close to Barton on Sea in one of the series).

Thankfully the door opened, and I pushed forward on it for good measure. The darkness turned instantly into blinding light, and I was St Paul on the road to Damascus. I got my bearings straight away. I had been in the garage of Alice and Patrick's holiday home in Barton. Safe and sound. What a relief! I really had let my imagination go wild with thoughts of having been kidnapped and held hostage for weeks on end. I knew I was too old and too heavy to be trafficked, but maybe it had something to do with the Coke incident on the plane? Regardless no kidnapping had taken place, and I was now gingerly stepping onto the pristine green lawns of the front garden, complete with bordered cottage plants in full bloom. Very pretty and very English. There was still the nagging thought at the back of my mind as to whether I was to be welcomed as a guest for a week in Barton, or whether Alice and Patrick were so dreading my visit that they had tried to put me off by leaving me locked in the car in the dark cold garage. I was soon to find out!

I made my way cautiously around the side of the house toward the kitchen. The carefully laid out stepping pavers were a great help. Since the last time I had been to Barton, this section of the house had been scheduled to have undergone a much-needed renovation. "We just have to do something about the kitchen at Barton." Alice had confided in me on many an occasion during out monthly phone chats or 'WhatsApp' tweets. I always felt that the English are favoured in terms of who gets to talk in the depths of the night or who scores the 'wideawake' midday time slot. In Australia, we often miss out, as the United Kingdom is nine hours behind us, and the entire country seems to be awake when we are asleep. Funny about that. As the months went by Alice had kept me informed on the progress of the Barton kitchen. "The kitchen has had a whole new makeover. We've also changed the colour scheme." Alice came from the all facts and no embellished details tribes who roamed the planet. I was the complete opposite. Ludicrously fanciful, totally over exaggerating and a skilled embellisher of the truth. We had a perfect platonic friendship and were headed for our fiftieth anniversary next year.

I was looking forward to seeing the improvements and changes. The Barton kitchen was classic bespoke, and reminiscent of a bygone quintessentially English era. German spies could have set up headquarters quite comfortably for the duration of both wars in that timeless kitchen. Separated from the dining room by a thick oak door, the kitchen had been functional, but ugly. Like one of those extremely ugly oriental vases people pay a fortune for at auctions. Still, it had its charm, and I was eager to see the makeover.

Disappointingly, all the changes must have been internal, as the back door was the same shape and in the same place. It was slightly ajar. I popped my head around the open door and there was Alice singing happily to herself, busily whisking some concoction in a big blue striped bowl. As she had her back to the door, she didn't see me – or hear me, but the dogs did! Holly and Looby came rushing up to the door, yelping in delight and excitement. They seemed over the moon to see me (probably thought I'd just popped out to the off-license on the corner two years ago.) Alice spun around at all the commotion and looked surprised to see me at the back door.

"Oh, it's you Fil! Did you have a good rest? We left you asleep in the car. You were dead to the world. Are you feeling better now?" Well yes, I did feel better, but I also felt slightly embarrassed at having fallen asleep before we'd even reached Barton. "Sorry for falling asleep, I was just resting my eyes for a tick and the next thing I knew I was alone in the dark car with a thumping head. I do feel rested now though. How many days have passed?" My little joke broke the ice and potential awkwardness of the moment for me. Although she did manage a micro smile, Alice moved on quickly with the directions – as only Alice could. She is a very practical, organised neatness fanatic. It is an endearing quality, but I sometimes wish that I could suddenly super-organise my own life, and then challenge her to a bed-making competition – or something.

"Patrick's in the sitting room reading, if you want to go through and say hello. He's been pestering me every five minutes about going out to wake you up, but I just wanted to get this shepherd's pie in the oven. I've already made a little vegetarian one for you." I felt relieved that I wouldn't have to explain again why I don't eat red meat. On previous trips Alice had often forgotten about my thirty-year boycotting of red meat and had done her mother and the 'Great British bake Off' proud with scores of evening meals which always included plenty of British beef. I hadn't eaten any of the dishes, but visitors had marvelled at the carnivorous delights. I moved silently past Alice who had resumed her rhythmic stirring and manoeuvred my way around my large purple suitcase which either Alice or Patrick must have managed to drag into the middle of the dining room. "Thanks for lugging my case inside," I called back to Alice. Patrick must have heard my voice, as he was at the double doors opening onto the lounge room before you could say Jack Robinson.

"Fil! You're awake. This is marvellous." Patrick is an Englishman and a gentleman. He is the dichotomous epitome of stuff upper British lip, and boyish charm. He looked relieved to see me – probably because he'd feared having to sit up all night waiting for me to wake up in the garage. Knowing Alice as well as I did, it was a fairly safe bet that it would have been Patrick and definitely not Alice herself who would have been on stake out duties. I didn't think it be such a marvellous thing to see me again – well, not to the extent that Patrick was effusing – but perhaps it was a British thing? I played along like a natural. "Patrick, great to see you. How have you been?" I took two steps towards all six foot of him. I was genuinely pleased to see him, but I was feeling shy about hugging him, so I decided in the moment that I would just peck his check. Only one side though. None of the European profuse kissing of both cheeks, and sometimes even a double chin or two as a way of greeting. Patrick beat me to it with an extended hand, which I gratefully accepted, and began to shake with gusto.

"You look as if you haven't slept in days, was it a rough flight?"

"No, it was fantastic. I travelled Premium Economy, and I even had a shower in Dubai. It was long though. Felt very long."

Just then Alice appeared in the doorway. "Well then you'll appreciate a good night's sleep just as soon as we've eaten. Patrick, could you please carry Fil's case upstairs and put it in her room?" As I said, Alice was very good at giving the orders and taking control. So many times, over the years, she had exclaimed to me in exasperation, "Fil, you can't wear that outfit, it's all crushed!" But I'd tricked her this time. I'd been spending up big online in the weeks before I left Melbourne. A friend of mine had discovered an online-clothing store which sold only non-crushable slacks, scarves, tops and dresses. My suitcase was stuffed full of these items. Packing had never been so pleasurable. I hadn't even needed to sit on my case to close it (It was customary for me to involve the rest of the family in the sitting on the case ritual before a big trip). I couldn't wait to see Alice's face when I paraded around in one of the new outfits tomorrow morning. The labels had also promised that the clothes were highly suitable for travel, and that they would lose their creases in the course of the day. There it was. Another difference in travel convenience. No more travel irons taking up more than half your case and sending your luggage allowance into a frenzy, no more travel-kettles, no more blow-up coat hangers and definitely no more wads of Travellers Cheques stuffed into hiking boots. They were all relics from the past, when travelling had been as challenging as packing your suitcase. Of course, even without all the appliances, my suitcase was crammed full. I always bring at least sixty or so of those cute mini koalas you can buy at the markets in Australia. I love to give them out to the least expectant recipients and watch their faces as they place the miniature koala with the Aussie colours and tiny flags up on their trophy shelf. This trip I had exactly sixty and I needed to be discerning about handing them out.

So, there was poor Patrick lugging my koala filled suitcase up the stairs, one precarious step at a time. "There's nothing breakable in the case Patrick, just get it up any way you can." I tried to help him, but the stairs were narrow, and the case kept skipping backwards. Patrick was a good sport though. He took it all in his stride, and even though I had almost finished my meal by the time he reappeared in the dining room, he didn't grumble or complain. "That's all done then," was his only comment before he stuffed a steaming spoonful of shepherd's pie into his mouth. He didn't speak again until he'd scraped the plate clean, and then it was only to utter that he would 'pour himself a Port, and would we like one'. Neither Alice nor I felt inclined, so Patrick ambled off towards his little bar in the lounge room to enjoy his regular nocturnal beverage.

"Goodnight, Patrick," I called out to his retreating back. The dogs followed him in.

That left Alice and I sitting looking at each other across the table. "Do you want a cup of tea, or do you want to go straight to bed?" Alice asked the rhetorical question, although she must have already anticipated my response by the whiteness of my face and fast drooping eyelids. "Bed please." was all I could manage to utter.

Ten minutes later I was snuggled up in the glorious bulging blue quilt of the double bed in the Blue room. The room opposite mine was called the 'baby's room', even though there was no baby. I was glad that Alice had put me in the Blue room. The baby's room was the size of a small cupboard, whereas in the Blue room I was able to spread out my case (I emptied it onto the floor looking for a cool nightie) as well as open both windows and lay quietly listening to the night sounds. I heard an owl hoot, the wind whistle and the rustle of the trees in the lane opposite, and then nothing till morning.

At least I thought it was morning when I woke up. The digital clock actually read 3:10, but I felt as wide awake as I ever had in the mornings at home. Uh oh, jet lag day one! I am a notorious jet-lagger. Some people escape this peculiar pesky-phenomena altogether, whilst others must suffer the interminable nights after a long-haul flight on either ends of their journey. I fall heavily into the latter category. I had no idea what time the dawn light would creep in, so I decided to read, in the hope of falling back to sleep. Then I did that thing that all travellers do. I started counting backwards nine hours, trying to work out what time it was in Australia, and what everyone would be doing. A completely useless pastime really, as it didn't matter at all what was happening in Australia. It was a crepuscular interlude for me. Peaceful and still. The house was positioned about three blocks from the sea, and as soon as it was light enough, I would be sprinting up to the beach to watch the sunrise. My first sunrise of the big trip. Very exciting, and a little daunting as well.

Although it was only a feint light – a streaky slither in the red morning sky – it was incentive enough for me. I slipped out of bed quietly and with befuddled senses, grabbed a bundle of clothes from the overturned purple suitcase. I had left my shoes downstairs the evening before. I just wanted to creep down the stairs slowly and silently without waking Alice or Patrick. I had no idea where the dogs were, but I prayed they were heavy sleepers.

Sadly, they weren't! I had barely put my bare big toe onto the creaking first stair, when the two of them came bounding up the staircase and took a simultaneous flying yelping leap into my arms (they were only small dogs and very soft and fluffy.) I quickly seized the opportunity to carry them back downstairs, bundling them up and half suffocating them in the clothes I was carrying. Their vain attempts at yelping and barking came out all muffled as I clasped them to my chest and took to the stairs with my mission. The mission was not to awaken my hosts and to sneak out to the beach to watch my perfect first sunrise.

At the bottom of the stairs there was a powder room, so I locked myself in there and dropped my bundle of fur and clothes. The dogs were looking at me with deep suspicion and mistrust, as if they didn't quite know how far I would go next. They decided to perform. I talked soothingly to them.

"It's OK girls, I only silenced you because I knew you'd wake up Mummy and Daddy." (I had witnessed Alice repeating to the dogs on many an outing. "Who's being a good girl for Mummy?") The canine creatures seemed to accept me then. If I was a friend of Mummy's, then I must be trustworthy. Once the girls were quiet, I gathered my pile of clothes up from the powder room floor and began to struggle into them. I must have been half asleep and in a real rush when I'd picked the clothes up, because these were no walking clothes. I had, in anxious haste and semi darkness, ended up with the one decent pair of slacks I had packed for the trip (complete with gold sequinned cuffs), and a lacy, puffy sleeved purple number. I realised that I had two choices. Either I would have to put on both items of clothing, or face the stairs and the yelping dogs again, and retrieve a more appropriate outfit for an early morning beach walk.

I can sometimes be a little lazy and this was one of my lazy days. I just wanted the beach and it was still very early. I probably wouldn't even meet a soul on the walk up to the beach. If I did bump into anyone, I could always say that I'd been at a rage-party all night and that I was just on my tottering way back home. I noticed a beach-towel lying on the back of a dining room chair, so I grabbed it for good measure. I was now ready. Sequinned slacks – check; puffy sleeved purple chiffon top – check; shoes – check; money for coffee – check (ten-pound note – check).

It was cool outside, and once in the garden, I happily jumped from one stepping stone to another as I approached the side gate. We sometimes do crazy things when we think we are alone. The house was down a muddy overgrown country lane, and there were trees bordering the lane on either side. It was so beautifully still in that dirt lane that first morning. I was engulfed with memories of Tess of the D'Urbervilles and Lady Chatterley's Lover and other 'last century' strong women characters. Here was I, brave and adventurous and ready to embrace England. It felt good. Surprisingly good. Goodness never really lasts though. You can be so enthralled with something, so into it, that nothing else in the whole world matters, and then bang the balloon bursts, and the goodness is gone! On the short, twenty-five-minute walk up to the beach my balloon well and truly burst. I was chased by a fox in the lane, and then two snappy insomniac little dogs who lived in a house with no front fence, and finally by a nasty little waistcoated man, when I accidentally wandered into his field. (He looked like the angry pixie from the Enid Blyton stories.) All this happened in the first block from Alice's house.

In the course of the second block, I managed to get in the way of two paramedics who were trying to back their van into an old lady's driveway to get her to hospital I presume. (I was bending over on the side of the road tying up my shoe laces. Yes, the same lace that had come undone at the airport two days before.) To top it all off, I managed to stand smack bang in the middle of a pile of dog – or cat, or fox or whatever – poo. It settled itself smugly all over my left shoe, and I had no tissue or rags or water with which to clean it off. Thank heavens the glorious Barton beach reared its calming head over the next hill. All that activity and it was only 6:30am.

# Chapter 5
## Beach, Ian Et Al

I was panting by the time I came up over the hill and feasted my eyes for the first time (of this trip) on the glorious waters of Barton on Sea. Whenever I view large stretches of ocean, which this morning was as blue as blue could be despite the dull nearly morning half-light, my heart does a little pirouette, my spirits soar, and I feel happy to be alive. It's something about the water. We must have all come from the water, because I have yet to meet someone who does not share this exhilarating sentiment. It is part of the innate wiring of the human condition.

"Bet you're wondering why I've got odd shoes on, aren't you now?" I looked immediately down at his feet and then back up into his face. I was met with an inanely wide grin and a copious amount of head aerobics. I immediately flashed back to the nodding shower assistants at Dubai. But this man was of no Indian, or even Pakistani descent. He was a true-blue Brit. Classic pointy face, long nose, lanky body and idiosyncratic odd shoes. He even had that slight British lisp going on.

"Well, it doesn't really matter at this early hour does it?" Right back at you mister, and not a word about my own peculiar dressing habits.

"No, I s'pose not. Care to thit down here with me and take in the view?"

Not really. Not just now anyway. What I wanted was to kick off my own shoes (which, granted, looked slightly incongruous with the rest of my attire), and race down the cliff to the warm, yellow English sand. (no such thing, I know!) And paddle. I wanted to paddle. I wanted to be ten years old again – before I needed to consider anyone other than myself. We do a great deal of wading, paddling and sand storming in Australia. Most of the population are coastal inhabitants, and beach combing is the perfect pastime. It's glorified walking really, but you feel like you are exercising more strenuously, as you are constantly pushing against the tide and getting dragged down in the seaweed (and sometimes rips).

I eased my body reticently and reluctantly onto the well-worn bench next to the odd shoed man, whose name turned out to be Ian. He rewarded me with a head-to-toe smile and asked me outright if I was South African.

"No, Australian." There was loyalty in my voice, even though I knew that Australian citizenship did not hold much kudos for the British, as they supposed us all to reside in that 'Godforsaken colony bordering Antarctica'. We were the butt of many a stereotype with the British media.

"Oh, that's a stroke of luck that is. Can't abide the Souff Africans myself, ever since me faver married one, and I was landed with a Souff African stepmother. Thank Evans she's gone to God now, we're well rid of 'er."

I nodded in agreement even though I didn't really get why Evans (whoever he was) deserved thinking about, and what exactly was it that we well rid of?

Ian was happily prattling on. He told me he lived in "vat ver ouse across ve wode". I looked casually over in the direction in which he was pointing, and all I could see was a row of smart looking houses and apartments with million-dollar views. "Which house is yours, Ian?"

"Ve one wiv the pretty flowers."

Well that definitely narrowed it down! All of the houses had pretty gardens. And million-dollar views. I was in awe of Ian. He was retired and informed me that he spent his days roaming the beaches and small villages, talking to anyone who would give him the time of day – telling them the exact same tale he was now unravelling to me. I have to say, Ian had an interesting life to retell. He came from a theatrical family, and he'd been a doorman at quite a number of exclusive London clubs before turning his hand to aquatic show business. He then got himself a job as a front-man, introducing, organising and heralding the entertainment on varied famous cruise ships. Ian abruptly ceased his monologue. He was staring transfixed at his really, really old watch, and suddenly announced that he needed to get home and prepare his outfit for today's job. He was hosting a local bowls tournament, and he needed to look spick and span. There were to be two hundred geriatric bowlers descending upon the New Milton bowling club, and it was up to Ian to personally meet, greet, pacify and feed the bowlers.

"The average age will be seventy-five, and we even have a couple of centurions bowling with us today. Just imagine it, vayve already reached a century! Pity it's not cricket they're playing." Ian became quite animated as he bombarded me with the proposed details of the day. However, even though he had come up with a fairly adequate pun, he did not smile. He was much too serious and pragmatic for that. He just shrugged matter-of-factly and jumped off the bench. Then he stood quite still and stared up at the sky. I wondered if he might be beckoning a flock of birds. At that precise moment a huge flock of white seagulls flew low over our heads. The park bench we had been occupying was smack bang in the middle of a large grassed paddock at the top of the cliff. Not a tree or another bench in sight. I surmised that by lunchtime this embankment would be abuzz with holiday-makers. But now it was empty. Except for myself, Ian and…one large white husky dog which had come bounding towards the two of us at an alarming speed. I quickly jumped ship, but Ian stood his ground, and the big white furry bundle came to a grinding halt inches from his odd shoes. The dog was panting, and I could see a big wet red tongue gushing in and out of his cavernous mouth at rapid intervals. I took five hurried steps backwards, away from Ian and his over-excited canine companion. I had no idea that on this first early morning of my trip that I would encounter many, many more dogs in my travels. Possibly more dogs than people, but I could not have known that then.

"Good girl. Good dog Lucy." I was willing to give Lucy a pat and an Aussie gidday, when I realised how calm she had instantly become. At Ian's command she had dropped quickly into a crouching position and offered her neck to him whilst he slipped a silver studded collar over her huge head. The lead followed. "There you go Lucy, all done. Weady for the long journey ome." Another joke from our illustrious oblivious MC. Ian lived literally twenty metres from the park bench. The bench was directly opposite his front door, and in the course of his previous monologue, he had told me that he'd been sitting on the very same bench every morning after his morning walk for the past ten years.

"How long have you had Lucy?" I was loping the twenty metres to his house alongside of him. I figured that if I knew where he lived, I might be able to call on him tomorrow morning when I was sure to be walking again – at this ungodly hour. It would be handy to have a chaperone on the beach, and Ian did have the most amazing stories to tell. Being on a cruise ship for months on end had allowed him the opportunity to strike up acquaintances with assorted characters from all walks of life. Ian had also encountered his fair share of celebrities in his travels on the seven seas. He rattled off Tom Jones, Cilla Black, Rod Stewart and Penelope Keith to name a few. His favourite cruise ship was the 'Canberra', and since Canberra was where my whole entire family resided, I felt an even deeper affinity with this stranger on the shore.

We had completed the twenty-metre walkathon. Only I was panting, as the pace had been quite strenuous. Ian probably could've been serious competition in the one-minute mile had he been a professional runner. He told me that his legs were exceptionally strong because he walked everywhere. Mine were exceptionally weak because I shuffled everywhere.

"Lucy, come back here. Come back here at once!" Lucy, it seemed, had a mind of her own. She had been released from the lead as soon as we had reached the pretty hedgerow of Ian's house. But instead of racing into the garden, Lucy was heading straight for the front door of the house next door.

"Oh, I'll just leave her there for a while."

Ian wasn't fussed that Lucy was curled up territorially on the over-sized flower printed mat on the front doorstep next door. "She's just missing Enid. She's only gone away for the Bank holiday weekend, but Lucy is devoted to her." Back at home we have Basil and Charlie the two cats from next door. They tended to spend more of their time curled up under our trailer or foraging in our organic compost heap than they did in their own backyards. They were like teenagers we just couldn't get rid of. I was awoken every morning at dawn by one or the other of them stealthily cat-walking the paling fence outside my bedroom window. I got the neighbourly connection.

Ian was hopping about by now, over-intent to take leave of me. "Well, it was nice to meet you Ian. Will you be up again same time tomorrow morning? I usually have three days of jetlag after a big trip, so that means a dawn walk again for me." Ian looked puzzled with my information overload. "Well, I suppose it's likely that I will be on the park bench tomorrow morning." With that he turned abruptly and jogged off down the garden path towards the front door. As he was putting the key in the lock, he called back to me. "I forgot to tell you two things. Number one, Lucy doesn't belong to me. She's Enid's dog, I just walk her every morning. And number two, today is my birthday!"

With that he was gone, and Lucy must have skulked around the back of Enid's because she had also disappeared. Suddenly there was a loud hissing and revving of an engine, and I looked up to see a red Maserati flash past me and zoom off into the distance. Enid and Ian's road was located at the top of the cliff. It was as flat as a pancake, as grey as an elongated stratus rain-cloud, and as straight as an arrow. The Maserati flew past me again, and I hadn't even moved from my spot outside Ian's house. The noise was twice as deafening this time, as the engine had warmed up, and the driver looked like he was in for the long haul of deafening burnouts and laps up and down the esplanade. I started walking down the path, but I realised that at some point I would need to cross the road again. The boy in the red Maserati was so fast that I was worried I would be mowed down as I scuttled across the road. Still, I had to take the chance, if I was to reach the poky little corner shop, I could see up ahead on the beach side.

Fate is so good at intervening. Just as I positioned myself to zip across the road, who should pull up beside me and casually wind down his heavily tinted window, but Mr Maserati himself.

"Hey Chikkiicho, where ya offta at this hour of the day?" I ignored him and stared straight ahead. I hadn't realised that I was both a sexist and an ageist until that moment. He was a young twenty-something boy, with a winning grin and Daddy's expensive car. And it was red. Say no more.

He must have read my thoughts.

"Like my motor?"

I was hardly in a position to comment on his motor as the bonnet was down, and besides, I knew nothing about motors or any parts of cars really. I once had to change a tyre on a backroad in the Australian bush when I was driving by myself. Twenty-four hours later I was still sitting there waiting for help (had to sleep in the car). I was forty at the time.

'Thweer twiirh…' A high-pitched wolf whistle escaped the boy's lips (that was the second whistle I had experienced in the last half hour.)

"Pretty groovy sequinned pants and top. Last night's outfit is it?"

I looked at him in disgust. I was not in the mood for the incorrigible youth of England especially on my first morning of sightseeing, and most certainly not outside Ian's gate where I had just farewelled him. Thank heavens I hadn't given Ian a birthday peck on the cheek.

"Move yer motor yer long-haired lout!" I looked up, amazed to see that quite a crowd of oldies had congregated outside number Thirteen, which was on the other side of Ian's house (not Enid and Lucy's side.) All the onlookers looked to be at least eighty, and a couple of them had brought their sticks and walking frames along for the customary early morning Bank holiday entertainment. Most were still in pyjamas and light dressing gowns (it was turning out to be a very mild morning.) I thought instantly, of the book I had taught last year to a group of Year 6 students 'The Boy in Striped Pyjamas'. Such eloquent prose, but such a sad story line. These people didn't look at all like the ill-fated characters in the book, but I was nevertheless instantly reminded of Bruno and his young pyjama clad friend. These people were old and feisty and fed up with the Bank Holiday ritual of the pop-up speedway on the cliff top.

"Go on clear orff now!" The crowd were one!

"I'm Daniel." was all the boy could monosyllabically utter through his wound-down window. He winked and extended an extremely tanned, and meticulously manicured slim limb towards me. It was adorned at the wrist with masses of silver bracelets (he may have been in a Bollywood evening show last night and had forgotten to remove the bracelets.) Completely ignoring the disgruntled crowd, Daniel floored the red sports car and sped off down the esplanade.

"And don't come beck termorra!"

The crowds knew their lines alright.

I felt slightly sorry for Daniel, as he had little clue about picking your audience to suit your performance. Had he chosen to perform his burnouts in the evening slot, he may have attracted an entirely different demographic. But as I noted to myself, he may have been all tied up with other past times come nightfall. This morning he had presented as just plain irritating.

The grudging crowd was beginning to slowly disperse. (small, faltering steps for most of them.)

I made a dash for the road, while it was still deserted. I just wanted breakfast by now. Across the bitumen, I could see that a cosy crowd of about a dozen or so were congregating around the bright yellow double doors to the café. I wasn't wearing my long-distance glasses, but I could hazard a guess that these were not relatives of the 'oldies in pyjamas locals' but 'townies' who had descended upon Barton for the Bank holiday weekend. These were the beautiful people of the English Rivieras. There were dogs amongst them, but they were in the minority. Most probably these opulent townies had left their dogs with a dog minder in Mayfair or Chelsea or wherever they maintained their principal abode. The breakfasts must have been Michelin star, because the large sign on the door stated the 'Bank Holiday Weekend' opening hour as 8 o'clock. It was still only thirty minutes past seven and people were already queuing. I stayed for ten interminable minutes and then gave up. There was always tomorrow morning. And the next. I began to edge out of my position in the queue.

"Excuse me, but you can't do that!"

"I'm sorry. I've changed my mind, I'll come back tomorrow morning."

But the Mr Know-It-All was not to be silenced. "That information is not even remotely relevant, I meant you can't do THAT!" I wasn't sure what 'that' was, but I supposed he did. All I could think of was the fact that I'd tried to poke my head under the thick red rope that had been placed outside the café. Possibly to limit the customers? I ducked under the thick red coil barrier as quickly as I could. I had no idea what the interfering gentleman was on about. Up ahead of me I could see the welcoming sign of the Off Licence or 'the offie' on the corner' as these shops were referred to in England. I planned to buy some milk for the household, the local paper and a packet of crisps. (For me.) Whenever I'm in England I tend to eat a packet of crisps a day. It's just my little treat to myself. I realise that plenty of people have far more exotic penchants, but crisps did it for me. There is still a glut of English and Irish ancestry in Australia, and potatoes in some form or other would have to be our national food.

"I'm pleased to see you're open nice and early."

The Pakistani shopkeeper rewarded me with a bedazzling beam, possibly because of my compliment to his business time-management skills, but more likely because he was delighted by my accent. He nailed it immediately. "You are from Australia! From which place in Australia?"

"Melbourne," I announced proudly.

"I have not heard of that place. Is it big?"

"Fairly big." I was enjoying the banter. "Big for Australia that is."

"Is it near Summer bay?"

"Probably."

He nodded knowingly, "Oh, I see! I have not visited Australia. Actually, I have not visited anywhere. Only Brighton for the fun fair for my kids. We had to travel so very far. I was born in Barton and we have had the shop for a long time. We work long hours. My whole family is sleeping upstairs."

There you had it. He was English. In the course of my travels, I was to meet many people from many different cultural groups, but surprisingly enough they would mostly be English – their ancestors having settled in England generations ago. David – that was his name, was explaining to me that all of his six children attended the local Catholic Primary school, and that his wife and parents would be upstairs now getting them ready for school, had it been a school day. But it wasn't a school day until tomorrow. Today was the Monday Bank Holiday, and in a couple of hours, the shop would be crowded out with holiday-makers. The kids were allowed the luxury of a sleep-in and by default, that meant his parents sleeping in as well. His wife was in the back of the shop cooking up a big Pakistani fry up by the smell of it. I felt even hungrier with the smell of chapati frying. I selected my goods and heaped them up onto the cluttered counter. "That will be five pound thirty, thank you." I reluctantly parted with my treasured ten-pound note which I'd saved from my last trip to England and whipped out my mobile to make a note to find a bank ASAP. I noticed that the 'Notes' section of my phone was brimming over with notes about anything and everything, so I quickly made a note to delete all useless notes, next to the 'find a bank soon' note. All of them then!

It felt strange to be handing over actual cash, as globally, we are fast evolving as a cashless, virtual society. The next generation would probably not even handle real money – but rather use mobile phones for most transactions.

Back on the cliff top I noticed with uncalled for pleasure, that the crowd at the breakfast café were looking increasingly agitated, whereas I could now settle back in satisfaction on the low stone wall bordering the cliff top and munch on my crisps to the time of the swooshing ocean. It was blissful on the cliff-top munching and people watching. A person of interest to me was a slightly dishevelled, sixty-something woman on a quaint rusty red bike who peddled furiously past me, frizzy red hair flying around in all directions, and then disappeared into Razzi's corner shop at a cracking pace.

About five minutes later, she reappeared, over-laden with boxes of cornflakes, so the top (smaller) items kept falling out of the basket on her bike. I was close enough to sprint over and offer my assistance. "Oh, thank you so much. You are a real angel. If you'd just hand me the top box, I can manage then." She was even more English than the queen with her accent, and she shared pretty much the same sentiments towards immediate relatives as did good old Queen Elizabeth. "Much as I love them, my beastly relatives have descended on us – unannounced – for the Bank holiday weekend. They are eating us out of house and home. It was good for the first day, but it's become quite tedious by now. The children are whiney and the adults are still children. And they are all family, heavens to Betsy! We really can't possibly see them all again before Christmas!"

With those pearls of wisdom left hanging in the air, she was off with a sharp and prolonged tinkling of her bicycle bell. I ambled back to my bench, my crisps and my calming view, to ponder the complexities of families and stressful family bonding times. It seemed more likely than ever that Face-time Christmas sessions were just around the corner and that no one would ever need to see their immediate families ever again. Not in this lifetime anyway.

A stray drop of rain roused me from my ponderings. Only it wasn't a drop of rain but a large yellowish oozy dropping from a directionless seagull. The signs were coming thick and fast now. First the seagulls overhead when I was with Ian, now the lone seagull at my feet. Next? In Australian Aboriginal culture if a flock of white birds fly overhead it is a sign of much joy and rejoicing. If there was any validity in these cultural beliefs, I was in for a momentous holiday.

It was the eleventh hour for me and my bench. I could have stayed there all day watching the crowds build up, but I knew that Alice and Patrick would be up by now, and I wanted to shower them with the promised presents from Australia. There was a healthy supply of Crunchies, Twisties, and Vegemite amongst the loot I had lugged for twenty thousand miles. I also wanted to shower myself and shampoo my seagull soggy hair. I set off at a cracking pace this time, revitalised with my fatty flattened, oily English potatoes and a sense of achievement. I had done all of this by myself. Endured the plane trip, battled the jet lag and mingled with the locals. Not bad going for Day One.

"Oh Crunchies, goodie!" Although Alice had lived in England for thirty-five years, she was still a worthy carrier of Australian genes, which caused her to squeal and revel in the slightest of pleasures (especially where food was concerned.).

Patrick was typically English in his response. "Thank you for the gifts. Much appreciated." He was frowning as he added, "Don't know how good they will be for your diet Alice."

"Too late Patrick." Alice was halfway through her second crunchie bar. "Don't care Patrick. I get to taste glorious top-quality Australian sugar cane, mixed with honey and chocolate while you wallow in your soggy, sodden cornflakes."

I lowered my head and, ever the diplomat, balanced my own cornflakes bowl in my left hand and took a bite of my Aussie Crunchie from my right. Then I pointed out to both of them that I was not one to take sides. After our continental breakfast, we showered and readied ourselves for a day of rest. It is always important to be well dressed when in for a day of pure indulgent nothingness. Alice appeared in a floppy purple sunhat and an iPad, an iPhone and a cross stitch frame. She is passionate about her work and a committed social reformist in the area of deaf education. Such devotion to a job necessitated constant phone calls and emails (even though she was on holidays.)

I looked out the criss-crossed 'lattice glassed' dining room window and saw that she had settled herself under the wide yellow umbrella in the front garden, a jug of iced water and some green apples positioned neatly on the wrought iron table. It looked like a scene from Cezanne. Yep. That was Alice settled. Patrick had taken himself off to New Milton to do some grocery shopping, so that left me to re-acquaint myself with the rambling four-bedroom holiday house, and poke my head into unexplored nooks and crannies. I adored the house. It was so exquisitely English. Extensive French doors onto the terrace, large comfy lounge room (reception) and a steep narrow three bear's staircase leading up to three big bedrooms and the baby's room. There was a book-laden library and a powder room downstairs, and a big recently renovated bathroom upstairs. There was also a substantial ensuite off the master bedroom.

I fancied I would just rest my eyes before my anticipated exploration, but my eyelids were heavy, and my bed was beckoning. Maybe just five minutes. Which turned into five hours, and even then, I only regained consciousness because Alice was cruelly shaking me and repeating over and over, "Wake up Fil, dinner is on the table." I tried to wake up. I really did try, but it was never going to happen.

"Just give me a few more minutes Alice." (My mumblings.) "I just can't open my eyes quite yet." And with that, I was (again) out like a light.

Consciousness was drifting around somewhere in my befuddled brain, but it was misty and hazy and untenable. I was totally disoriented. It was a nightmarish awakening to day two of the seaside sojourn. Whereas yesterday morning I had awakened to the gentle breeze and the sound of twittering birds and the distant swish of the Atlantic Ocean, today was the complete antithesis. The room was stuffy and dark. The only sound was the strained gasping of the hot water boiler in the bathroom next door, struggling to kick in, and my panicked breathing as I desperately tried to orient myself. This was not good.

I tried to lift my head, but it felt like I had downed twenty shots of tequila the previous evening. I lay back, eyes closed, and waited for the universe to kindly return me to my rightful body state. We've all been there. Possibly for different reasons, and quite probably some stages of semi-consciousness were self-inflicted, but we've all been there. That morning after feeling. That coming-of-age ghastly state that every single human being must live through at least once in their adult lives. Mostly we keep these gruesome hours secret, and mostly we are ashamed or remorseful. I was neither. I just wanted to feel better. I remembered that I had emergency codeine stashed away in a shoe somewhere. With supreme effort I managed to heave the contents of my suitcase back onto the floor and retrieve the shoe and the tablet. Then, I slept again.

The second awakening of the morning went much more smoothly than had the dress rehearsal.

All hail double-shot codeine! I felt invigorated this time, and I was doubtful that the earlier events had ever happened. As I swung my legs over the side of the bed I stumbled and almost fell headfirst into the dressing table. I had tripped over the shoe which had harboured my codeine stash.

This meant that I had not dreamt the first awakening. But I moved on quickly. It was still very, very early and dawn was slowly breaking. The boiler (or whatever it liked to be called) was still churning and rumbling away in the bathroom next door, and I realised that no matter how much noise I made I would never really be any competition for that old institution in this house. So, I banged my suitcase and clapped open the old wooden cupboard doors. Only the dogs were roused by all the activity, so I assumed Alice and Patrick were still sleeping. I felt slightly indignant towards them not even waking to the sound of a stupendous battle (equivalent to the Battle of Hastings) in the next room, but I was quick to blame the boiler for over-riding me. At least I could select my outfit for the day in comfort and at leisure. I was going to look proper today. Right proper. No chance of anyone supposing that I was sneaking in early after a night on the town in New Milton. No fear. I selected a sedate comfy outfit of a light tracksuit and a short-sleeved t-shirt.

I stashed a sweater, mobile phone, the change from my ten-pound note, my credit card, tissues and a bottle of three-day old water I had carried with me from Australia into my backpack and made my way noisily downstairs. The dogs were yelping and jumping around at my feet. In a dare-devilled mood I encouraged them, but still the family slept on. As I stomped past the dining room table, I noticed the pile of postcards I had asked Patrick to pick up for me yesterday when he had been shopping. There was a book of stamps next to the postcards. I sat down and quickly scrawled a hello to my parents back in Australia. My mother lived for postcards and letters from her children when they were away. It was typical postcard speak, 'Hi from sunny Barton. Having a great time. Wish you were here. See you soon. Fil xx.' (Mum would no doubt equate that hurried scrawl with a Nobel prize winning essay.)

The pictures were supposed to do all the talking. I had selected one with a stunning photograph of the beach I was about to head off to again this morning, so at least there was some authenticity. I didn't intend to send many postcards this trip. I had trained myself up in using Facebook in the long Melbourne winter before this trip. Many a night had been spent clicking on friend requests and replying to random posts. I ended up with five hundred and twenty-nine friends, most of whom I had no clue about. The second cousin of the aunt of the best friend my sister had in Year Seven at school. Whomever she may have been. And that was a typical prototype. But I hadn't only been trained in 'friending' strangers. I had also learnt how to message economically and how to post pictures and superimpose scenes of places, people and things. I planned to Facebook and FaceTime big time this trip. I was moving with the times. No little black books with people's names and ticks in leaky rude red biro, for the number of postcards they had received in the month I had been away. No more. Finito! After my last trip of two months abroad, I worked out that I had wasted at least one and a half hours a day writing postcards and buying stamps.

I licked the stamp and shoved the card into my back pack. Next of kin only basis was to be my criteria for postcard sending (I was saving my saliva for a rainy day).

It was quite chilly outside. I had purposefully not looked at the time on my phone before I'd left, as I wanted to see if I could go by the position of the sun as it slowly crept over the horizon. I was over optimistic though, as there was no sun and I couldn't even see the horizon over the endless row of brooding black pine trees which lined the bumpy, uneven dirt road up towards the beach. There was no one else up either – at least not in this neck of the woods, so I pulled on my sweatshirt and began to walk briskly towards the beach.

# Chapter 6
## More of the Clifftop

About halfway up the road I slowed down for a swig of water and noticed two large red post boxes about ten metres apart. I remembered the postcard in my backpack. They were the old-fashioned type of red pillar boxes and they were positioned alongside the road in the midst of a pretty verge, with English cottage flowers in purples and pinks bordering both pillars. Someone really cared about the garden and the landscape. I was so busy admiring the neatness and 'spruced-upness' of it all, that the first pillar box was upon me before I had a chance to pluck the postcard from my backpack. That was really my downfall. Not paying attention. There is a well-respected branch of neuroscience totally concerned with paying attention. The slightest of diversions can cause chaos. It is a real field of science. Right up there with the Big Bang and String theories. The thing is, I am not usually as absent-minded about posting letters or postcards as I proved to be that morning, but I pretty much took the cake with my next action. To reiterate, there were two identical pillar boxes. One had 'All letters' etched into the paint above the posting slot. The other had 'Dog litter' etched into the paint above the posting spot. You can guess. Without my glasses, in my haste, and without paying any attention to the lettering, I quick as a flash posted the unfortunate postcard in the dog litter pillar box. Needless to say, none of my family in Australia ever got to read that carefully phrased script, nor the opportunity to ogle over the marvellous Barton coastline. That morning however, I was oblivious to my misdemeanour. It was only when later that day I was posting the picture of the identical pillar boxes on Facebook, that I realised my mistake. (I magnified the inscriptions on the pillar boxes). Judging by the sheer number of dogs I expected to be roaming around Barton, I feared the worst for the unfortunate postcard.

It wasn't even the first time that I had been foiled by a pillar box. Some years ago, in the rolling green hills of Southern Victoria – deep in the power line headquarters of coal mining territory, I needed to post an important letter. (In retrospect, an application for a job that I was never going to get.) We were driving up to the lookout and there wasn't a letterbox to be sighted. As we entered the deserted car park adjacent to the lookout, miraculously, I spied a solitary letterbox. There was nothing around it, and the vegetation was sparse. A social isolate, but it would do the job. I jumped out of the car (a friend was driving) and ran up to the box. Then, I stopped dead in my tracks. I just stood there, staring at the wording on the letterbox (really paying attention that time.) It read, 'Dangerous items must not be posted.'

I read: "Dangerous! Items must NOT be posted."

I was frozen to the spot. My friend was calling out impatiently. "Come on Fil. Hurry up. What on earth are you doing standing there staring at the mailbox?"

I couldn't answer her. I couldn't move. I just kept staring straight ahead. Irrational fears of mining explosions and implosions and booby-trapped earth flooded me. What would happen if I defied the glaring warning of danger and let the letter drop into the box? I was in flight or fight mode. I never did find out. I just stuffed the letter into my pocket and raced back to the car.

"What took you so long?" My friend was over me by then. "Nothing. I had a cramp in my hand."

"Oh, is that all?" She sped off down the hill immediately and we never did get to see the promised vista of the coal mines from the lookout.

I was almost at the top of the second hill and about to glimpse the early morning ocean once again. I relished the familiarity of this venture. I knew it wasn't going to last forever as I only had five more days in Barton on Sea, and I also knew that familiarity breeds contempt, but I was happy enough to take in the sea air and frolic a little. You see, we can do that as women. Men can't really go frolicking because it's just not a macho action. We may have taken eons to get to vote, but even Emily Pankhurst could frolic to her heart's content. So that's what I did. As a thank you and a tribute to Emily in England, and Enid in Australia, and the rest of the pioneering women all over the globe. In fact, I was so engrossed in my carefree emancipation that I did not notice a large metal sign positioned at the top of the road. I banged straight into it and my frolicking came to an abrupt end. I slumped into the gutter clutching my head, but I wasn't really hurt. It was just a comfortable position after the strenuous walk I'd just had.

Eventually I got fed up with sitting slumped against the cold bony sign post, and struggled to my feet, to try and read the offending sign. There were no words, just a weathered square metal icon of a walking stick and two old people attempting to cross a road. I'd never seen a sign like it in Australia, but it seemed an excellent idea. We have signs depicting kangaroos, wallabies, wombats and dangerous snakes. There are even signs outside nursing homes with old people stick figures, but none with actual walking. It would make for good dinner party 'convo'. I had almost reached the café where I intended to have a leisurely breakfast after my beach walk, when who should zoom past wolf whistling, but the boy in the red Maserati – Daniel. He slowed down when he saw me, backed up on the deserted road and offered me a lift. Well, what he actually said was "Wanna come for a spin wiv me?" Although flattered, I declined graciously and kept walking. Toy boys were not on the agenda for me today. Daniel had dematerialised in a gigantic puff of smoke, presumably intent on picking up a female passenger from the other end of the boulevard. Unlike me, he seemed not to be an ageist, and this was old lady territory. Up ahead I could see Ian and Lucy sitting companionably on the isolated cliff top bench. Lucy yelped excitedly when she saw me approaching, jumped off the bench and bounded towards me. Today I was happy to see her and took steps forwards and not backwards as I had done the previous morning. When Ian looked up to see what all the racket was about, he went all shy and lowered his cap. I insensitively ignored his obvious discomfort and called out cheerfully. "Good morning Ian. How are you today after your birthday celebrations?" He didn't answer me, just jumped up and beckoned me to follow him down the wide steep gravel path to the foreshore. The path was a precipice – steep and rocky. Once again, I was reminded of the pristine white sandy Australian beaches with mostly perfect beach access, and mostly perfect gigantic white tipped waves. This beach was defunct of both draw-cards. The access was horrendously difficult to navigate, and the supposed sand looked like age-old floor covering in a Bethlehem stable. A harness and sturdy climbing boots would have come in handy at this point.

Ian, in matching blue plastic sandals this morning, undeterred by the treacherous terrain, was surging on ahead of me. He was intent on reaching the shore line, and nothing was going to stop him – not even the unlikely spectacle of an unfit Australian woman in tow. Lucy was just your typical loyal dog.

Advantaged by four legs and bulk, she trail-blazed in front of Ian, obviously familiar with the almost lunar landscape. I wished I hadn't brought my backpack with me. I blamed it totally for slowing me down.

We had reached the water's edge. We'd passed a row of drab looking, paint peeling boat sheds and a few scrappy, seaweed-infested logs and piles of driftwood scattered randomly on the beach. Then nothing. It was a desolate and lifeless 'lunaresque' stretch of coast, and even the sun, struggling over the horizon, could do nothing at this early hour to add appeal. It was still so early though, and I knew that the en masse arrival of families and their beach gear and beach chaos, picnic baskets, deck chairs, cricket stumps and umbrellas would, later in the day, be a perfect accompaniment to the sun's efforts to enhance the potential glory of this beach. Besides which, Lucy and Ian loved it, and I was the gate crasher here.

"Did you know that this is called the Jurassic coast, and that some of the fossils found here are in the British Museum in London?"

No. I did not know that fact, but I did know that the whole place looked like it hadn't been touched for a hundred million years.

"Oh, that's really interesting Ian. You should do early morning beach tours, and then you could bring on the entertainment around mid-morning. Are you still in contact with Cilla Black?" Of course, I was humouring Ian, but he just stared back at me blankly as if he was trying to recall Cilla Black's actual telephone number. "Yes, I believe I do have the number somewhere, but I doubt she'd come all the way over here to Barton. Actually, I think she lives over there now." Ian was pointing his long, lanky left arm towards the horizon. "That's France over there!" Lucy barked in agreement. I smiled to myself. Ian was becoming more predictable by the hour. I liked him. He was a decent bloke, just a bit hard to crack at first. I even liked Lucy, but I wouldn't be going as far as Alice and Patrick who were besotted with their two 'girls'.

"Lucy, come here girl." I thought I'd get a bit of practise in, just in case I was asked to take Holly and Looby for 'walkies' tomorrow morning. I stroked and patted Lucy and then turned back to my conversation with Ian, not that he was very communicative this morning. He avoided my effusive look, probably fearing that I would start stroking and patting him next. Tease that I am, I was tempted, but I thought better of it, out there in the open. And, he'd left out the vital piece of information about it having been his birthday until he'd had his key in the lock yesterday. One could safely summarise that he was trying to avoid physical contact with me.

I could live with that. For something to do, I gazed hazily out to sea and the distant coastline, and I thought I could make out the White Cliffs of Dover. My geography concerning this part of the world was abysmal, but I knew we were somewhere near the English Channel, and there was a bulk of whiteness in the distance…

I thought I'd ask Alice when I got back later if the cliffs really were so close. We walked for about an hour. Up and down the same stretch of beach. We didn't walk to a lighthouse, or a sheltered cove, or even to a pier with pulsing lights, music and hot-dogs (and there was surely one up ahead). No. We walked up and down the same stretch of rubble and gravel probably fifteen times. (A clear sign of madness according to Albert Einstein-repeating the same thing over and over and expecting a different result.) I was finally saved from the sixteenth rotation by a jovial, buxom lady with a bedraggled looking dog, who had passed us on her way up the beach, and who was now on her return journey.

"Are you practising for a parade or something? Repetitive rhythmic walking?"

Ian just stared at her perplexed, but I was ready with my response. "No, not really, we are just waiting for the café to open. I'm going there for breakfast."

"Oh, the café is already open." She seemed delighted to be able to offer this gem of information. "It opens at 6:30 on weekdays. The late opening was only because it was a Bank holiday weekend and the staff can't abide the townies, so they open for as few hours as possible."

She looked at me and then at Ian. Then she turned her back on me and authoritatively addressed Ian. "Enid back yet Ian?" Ah, ah, so they knew each other.

Ian, the dark, dark horse, mumbled something back at her and then she mumbled something back at him. I had no idea what they were talking about. It sounded like Klingon to me. The tone was sort of lilting – half Welsh, half Cornish, half audible and definitely half-Klingon.

I left them to their indecipherable small talk and started ploughing back towards the steep rocky path up to the café. Surely the proprietors wouldn't think I was a townie? I was ravenous by now and drooling at the notion of a full English breakfast. This gave me added impetus and I practically ran the last fifty metres of the ascent. Sure enough, as I rounded the bend and glimpsed the café, the outside dining area was chock-a-block full. In the hour we'd been involved in our marching practise on the beach below, all hell had broken loose up here at the café. There were people everywhere. Dogs, children and screaming babies made up half of the crowd. How could all these people live here?

The beach themed double doors were wide-open so I sauntered in and found a tucked-away table. The décor inside was all retro and beachy. Blues, yellows, and Art Deco pinks. It was open and airy, and very homely. I didn't feel self-conscious about sitting down alone at the table set for four. I just dumped my backpack on the lacy tablecloth and began rummaging inside it for a prolonged diversion whilst I surveyed the lay of the land. Only four other people were inside. Most of the families were sitting outside at the rustic wooden picnic tables with the dogs and children securely fastened to the table legs. Just as well really, because although the main body of the café was affronting the road, the extensive outside grassed section extended back to the cliff-face. Alice had told me that in the last five years, parts of the cliff had fallen away, and I wasn't taking any chances by sitting outside with the locals. Maybe towards the end of the trip I would have built up my confidence, or even just had enough of being over cautious all the time. But I figured I had made it this far and I wasn't going to step on any potential minefields until at least next week.

The café had one of those open plan layouts, where the customers can see everything being cooked, as well as hear the frenzied shouting out of the orders and general stressfulness of everyone wanting bacon, sausages and two poached eggs at once. I noticed that there was a long line at the counter – people ordering and then returning to their tables. I thought it best to take up my place in the line, as I had promised Alice and Patrick that we'd go mid-morning shopping in New Milton, and that I'd take them out to lunch as a gesture of repaying them for their hospitality. The line was moving quickly so I only had to endure a wait of about five minutes. While I was in the line, I kept extending my neck every minute or so, to look through the small window behind me which offered the only view in the café of the path leading down to the beach. I was on the lookout for Ian, as I thought he might have consented to a cup of coffee with me before he disappeared for the day. Ian did not appear on the path, and I was almost at the counter, so I pulled my head in and looked straight ahead. Some people had come up behind me in the queue, and I heard the woman whispering (loudly) to the man, "Ronny, do you think that lady is being chased by someone? She keeps jerking her head to look out of that window, like she's looking for someone to come running up from the beach."

Ronny didn't care whether or not I was a battered wife. "Nah Sandra, she's just a tourist. Probably got sunburnt and she's stretching her neck. Look, it's all red." I felt my neck get redder. Luckily for me I had reached the top of the queue, and the bouncy little waitress in a frilly white cap and matching apron was asking what I'd have.

"I'll have scrambled eggs, mushrooms, grilled tomatoes and a cup of tea please."

"Purfek," was her response. Purfek pet!

I stared at her waiting for her to tell me the price of my purfek breakfast, but she just said, "Jason will bring it ova ter ya when it's ready. Next!"

Ronny and Sandra were next, and I didn't really want to see their faces, so I edged sideways and fled back to my table. They may have been staring at me as they dawdled past me, arm in arm, but I was pretending to be busily reading about the Jurassic coastline of Barton. I looked up to see the backs of their heads, and I thought I could see some red around the nape of Ronny's neck. People in glass houses and all that. I let it go though and felt better for it. Something to add to that ever-lengthening note to self on my iPhone: buy sunscreen.

# Chapter 7
## In the Café

"Vis is yer order lady." I looked up from my engrossing reading regarding the Jurassic coastline to be met by a pair of the bluest eyes imaginable. They were the deep blue of the ocean below, and the owner of the eyes was handsome as handsome could be. Except for one glaring flaw. His face was covered in pimples. It wasn't too glaringly ugly, but they packed enough of a punch to completely override the eyes. He was only a boy – about Daniel of the Maserati-age, but he was old enough to register acute embarrassment at his unfortunate pimpled visage. I assumed this boy to be Jason, as the frilly-aproned waitress had told me to expect a Jason to deliver my breakfast. Jason must have been used to customers fixating on his brilliant blue eyes and then his brilliant crop of adolescence in quick succession. I tried to look away and focus on the food, but Jason was too quick for me, and I could see his eyes clouding over as he realised what I was so intently focused on. Not that I could talk really. Me with the alleged bright red neck.

I finally managed a polite thank you to Jason, and his smiling response told me he was not one to bear grudges. "Your tea will be here shortly. Emma will bring your tea." They obviously had the division of labour down pat in this establishment. The men doing all the heavy work and the woman carrying the tea, coffee and milkshakes over to the tables. I hoped Emma would come soon as I was quite thirsty with all the drama of having had to avoid looking directly at people. I decided that when Emma showed up with the tea, I would look straight at her whole personage, and thank her for the drink.

Ten minutes later Emma traipsed over with the promised tea. It was in a cracked smallish pot, but I could see steam escaping the thinning spout, and that was always a good sign. There was also a pretty little jug of milk as well as a separate matching bowl with lumps of sugar. The patterns on all the breakfast crockery were flowered and reminiscent of bygone tea rooms. Just what I had expected, and I sat back smartly to indicate my pleasure at this iconic display.

"Would yer like me ta warm that milk for yar?" Emma was anxious to please as she could see that I had already polished off my breakfast and there had been no tea with which to wash it down. Not that I'd minded, as I still wasn't quite into the swing of the way they did things in England (drinking tea with everything they ate).

"OK, thank you that would be great." That's what we say all the time, we Aussies. "That would be great." I was aware that it was an overused phrase with me, but Emma seemed pleased enough with my response. "I'll be back soon," was all she said though, and she disappeared with the jug of milk. Emma was back with the warm milk in a flash. I thanked her profusely and poured a small amount into my cup with the English breakfast tea. It was very thirst quenching and a delightful additive to the strong English tea.

An English friend of mine used to constantly say, "There is nothing nicer than an NHCO!" (Nice Hot Cup Of.) I loved the phrase and said it wherever I went – for good measure. It caught on, and the acronym became a popular catchphrase in schools when I was a young teacher. One day one of the newer teachers at my school asked me what the letters NHCO stood for. (It had never come up before). My heavy Yorkshire retort to her was 'Nice Happy Children Only'. This euphemism stuck, and for years we would refer to our beginning of year classes as groups of NHCOs. (Some of us were unfortunately compelled by the end of the first week to add an extra N at the beginning of the acronym, that is, N for Not!)

After about ten minutes of enjoying my pot of warm milky tea, there was a commotion at the front double doors, and I looked up to see what was causing plates and cups and saucers to be flying off tables and crashing loudly to the floor. I couldn't really see the faces of the people who had brought the dog into the café, but I could see the faces of Jason, Emma and the two chefs behind the open-plan counter. They looked aghast and helpless really, confused and panicked. It was only one dog responsible for the instant pandemonium, but one was enough. I have not the slightest clue in the world why dogs always make a bee line for me. It could have been the African-plains deodorant and perfume I had been trying out for six months before the trip so that I could proudly say that I supported the tribeswomen and children of Northern Africa where the plantations harvesting the unique African flowers were flourishing. I cursed myself for my earlier fit of ethical highbrow, as I knew I was never going to be rid of the smell on my skin. It was a wonder Alice hadn't already commented on it. But then again, Alice was diplomatic to the core, and probably didn't like to ruffle my feathers this early into the trip. Or, it could have been the smell of another dog on my personage, because I had just spent the last couple of hours carrying Lucy up and down the stretch of beach below as she had seemed so tired. (Today may have been the first day she hadn't needed to walk alongside Ian – since I had turned up to take her place.)

Whatever the reason, another large white shaggy dog was now bounding towards me at an electric speed, and I didn't even have time to shield my cup, jug and teapot. The owners of the dog caught up with the hound just as my breakfast crockery (which I had so admired) crashed to the floor. Now I could see their faces. If anything, they looked proud of the dog's antics.

"Rufus. Heel. Rufus, sit! Rufus, stay!" The man was repeating the instructions to Rufus in a loud calm voice. At the end of every clipped phrase, he looked down at Rufus and patted him. Rufus had received fifteen patting before the wife or girlfriend intervened with. "That'll do Harry. Remember what they told us in the dog-training session the other day – no more than fifteen times or you will lose the effect you have on your dog." She then turned to Rufus and whispered in a purring voice, "Does Ruffie want some sausages now?"

Ruffie was no dumbie. He'd obviously played this same scene many times over, and he looked up at the hapless, love-struck conned couple expectantly, wagging his tail and yelping. Talk about over acting Rufus. They didn't notice.

I was still sitting at the table with my crockery in pieces at my feet, trying to decide how to get out without having to comment on how wonderful and clever Rufus was. I could probably go with the clever accolade if forced into praise for the dog. Then I would add…and cunning and sneaky and self-important and…

There were just too many ways to describe the clever Rufus.

Jason and Emma had snapped out of their flabbergasted state and were busily sweeping and piling up the broken crockery. One of the brasher customers was politely asking Emma if she might have some of the broken crockery for her mosaic business. She thought that the floral patterns would make a wonderful border for her latest project which was a beach scene mural. Emma scuttled off to find a plastic bag, and the mosaic lady turned and announced to the whole of the café that she had an important commission from the New Milton Council to create a mosaic depicting the Barton beach and cliff top. (I would have rushed over with a soap box for her to stand on and deliver her spiel, but there were none to be seen – no spare chairs either!)

"It will be ready this time next year, and if you get to see it, don't forget to look out for the border of floral porcelain." I was actually giggling to myself by this time. What a circus! And it still wasn't over in the café. The dog owners turned out to be a childless married couple who came in every Tuesday for breakfast before their weekly beach walk. They were well and truly 'Bold and Beautiful people' – Harry and Sue. He was so tanned and rippled and bursting at every seam that no one could really take their eyes off him for more than a second without feeling they were missing out, and she – well who could describe her? Long, leggy, tanned and beautiful would be a start, but justice would not be done. I will settle for terming them both 'stunning'. Rufus, on the other hand, was quite ordinary. Your typical dog – non-specific. But he had a mighty ace up his sleeve. He was 'their' dog! This honour was not to be sneezed at, and Rufus knew it.

I had turned away from them by now, but I could still hear her whispering to him that they hadn't brought enough change this morning, and that she'd left the credit cards at home. Harry was nonplussed.

"Dun madda Darl." He flexed his super tanned muscles. "I ain't ungrry vis mornin, you can share your grub wiv Ruffie." Darl seemed unsure, but Rufus had been listening keenly and his wagging tail meant that he was very sure. They scraped up a fistful of coins, and then Darl tiptoed up to the counter to place their order. I thought I would jump up and follow her, as I still hadn't paid – for the meal or the entertainment. I started gathering my phone and back pack when Harry bellowed over to me.

"Avin a oliday are we? Ya like our liddle town?" As he was shouting across to me Harry was bending down fidgeting and fussing with Rufus' collar. I heard most of the first sentence – about me being on holiday in Barton, but the second sentence was muffled, as Harry's head was halfway under the table. I thought he must have said, "Ya like our Lidl?" Meaning, did I like Lidl, the grocery food and merchandise German chain which I remembered from my Irish trip last year. I assumed that the chain must have come to Barton or New Milton in the time I had been away from here.

"Yes, I like Lidl. I went there a lot when we were in Ireland last year, and I bought oodles of souvenirs and tins of shortbread biscuits to take home to Australia." Harry just stared at me, probably thinking I had been let out for the day from a nearby asylum. I was clearly babbling on about something of no relevance to what I liked about his Liddle town.

Just then Sue reappeared, and Harry shot me a sympathetic glance as all three of them took leave of the café. As they moved away from me, I could hear the woman whispering (loud whispering) to Harry, "I got some take away sausages for Rufus' tea tonight. Look, it's down on the bill." When I was retelling my story of the beautiful people in the café to Alice and Patrick that evening, Alice piped up with: "That's true Patrick, Fil is telling the truth. They do itemise the dog sausages. It's what they do up there on the cliff." Patrick did not look convinced.

Once the beautiful people and their beautiful dog left the café, it went very quiet. There was still a lot of noise from outside, and the sun seemed to have climbed a bit, as it looked warm and inviting out there. I paid my bill by credit card and ventured out into the sunlight. Time to make my way back home.

# Chapter 8
## The Maurice Files

There was a low flat stone wall outside the café, and I took the opportunity of plonking my bulging backpack down and began rummaging in the side pockets for my sunglasses. I finally located them under a pile of tissues in the second pocket with the faulty zip. Buying the backpack had been an ordeal in itself, and there had been so many to choose from in the camping and outdoor shops in Melbourne we had visited before I'd left. In the end I got one online, and it looked nothing like it had in the catalogue. The good thing about it was that it was economical, and you could fit a lot into it. Also, it was waterproof, and as I knew it was always raining in England and Ireland, it seemed the perfect choice. The disadvantage was that there were so many nooks and crannies in the backpack. It was impossible to remember where certain items had been hidden. I am the queen of hiding things from myself. This morning it was the sunglasses which required a 'Sat Nav' to locate them.

Finally finding my sunglasses proved worthy of the hunt. It was very glary for 10 am, and the sun was starting to build up some real strength. It was an entirely different sun to the Australian one. In the heat of an Australian summer, it can reach fifty degrees in some places. My favourite holiday spot in Australia is Uluru – in the very centre of the country. I have been there at least a dozen times, and each time the landscape has changed. The big red rock remains a constant though, as do the elegant clumps of stately white ghost gums surrounding the National Park. Many an Australian artist has depicted this spectacular landscape. Many an Aboriginal artist has achieved great success – the most famous being Albert Namatjira who managed to expertly capture what he experienced on canvas.

A few years ago, we hosted a Polish couple, showing them the delights of the Australian outback, and wandering around the rock as well as visiting Kata-

Juta (formally known as the Olgas). The couple were the parents of friends of ours, and they had always wanted to see the Rock. The connection to my looking for my sunglasses outside the café was the fact that in the Australian outback you really need to wear sunglasses and a mosquito net over your head at all times. We had impressed this on my friend's parents, and consequently they took it to heart and kept the sunglasses and mosquito nets on 24/7. When they arrived in Melbourne after five days in the Red Centre, they were so used to wearing the sunglasses and mosquito nets that they didn't want to take them off at any stage of the day or night. That's what I call acclimatising. It was fitting as well, as they are lovely people and they told their Polish daughter who was engaged to an Australian and living in Melbourne, that they didn't really understand the coverings of the head and the face, but that they respected our culture and customs. Luckily, they did not meet any traditional Anangu people or they would have appeared sans clothes and shoeless at breakfast each morning.

 I was daydreaming again. My flashbacks to Australia were coming thick and fast, but I knew this was a typical withdrawal pattern, and that I would soon forget all about Australia as life in England became my heart's desire. Maybe.

 History was about to repeat itself, only this time the kerfuffle was outside the shop and across the road. As far as I could tell, there were no dogs involved. Yet. What I could see was an elderly lady trying to hold up an even more elderly man, yelling out as she did so to anyone who cared to heed her cries.

 "Come quickly, help, help!" No one came. The road was deserted, the customers outside the café were too preoccupied with their children and dogs to care, and there was I, sat on bench – staring.

 I came to quick smart, and raced over the road to help, grabbing my back pack as I raced. The woman was really quite panicky, and another elderly man was calling out to her, "Jean, shall I call an ambulance? Is Maurice Ok? What is the number for the ambulance? I've forgotten." Jean either couldn't hear him, or she was ignoring him and concentrating on rousing the slumped Maurice.

 I didn't really have the strength required to lift a man the size of Maurice, even with Jean's help, so I helped the man still standing (he turned out to be Jean's elderly husband) down the three steps from the veranda and guided him towards Jean and Maurice. The husband was marvellous. Although frail looking and seemingly quite doddery, he proved to be neither of these things. He was strong and capable. (He looked as though he might have ridden horses bareback in his younger days)

So strong, and so desperate to relieve his poor wife of the burdensome Maurice, that he singlehandedly yanked Maurice to his feet in a kind of reverse hymen lift. Jean clapped a little victory clap, knocking her palms together, and looked as proud as punch.

"Reg used to be in the army." She blushed. "He's ever so strong." I looked at Reg, trying to imagine which war he might have served in. Boer War maybe? Or earlier? Hard to tell. I was close with the horse-riding guess though. As soon as Reg had propelled Maurice into a standing position he let go immediately. Maurice fell for the second time – Jesus with his cross, except that Maurice was only carrying a satchel (not a two-metre-high wooden cross) which was still secure on his shoulder-ironic as it turned out, him being a sort of priest.

This time Reg was not so deft with his resurrection routine. He gasped and coughed and wheezed and genuinely struggled trying to get Maurice back on his feet. He'd half done it, with almighty pulling and pushing, when Maurice's trousers fell down and settled obstinately around his two splayed legs.

"Oh! My trewsers! My trewsers!"

Maurice was mortified. I stepped in and tried to pull them back up to his waist, and Jean just stood there, wobbling in fits of laughter. Maurice, who hadn't spoken a single word up until now, was still repeating over and over, "Metrewsers…metrewsers." It sounded like a Welsh phrase, and it was not unlike the conversation I had heard between Ian and his neighbour earlier this morning on the beach. Probably another peculiar local dialect.

I felt compelled to reassure Maurice. "It's OK Maurice, I was a nurse, and I've seen it all. It's OK, we'll get your trousers up quickly." Which we didn't, because Jean was useless, poor old Reg had been rendered useless, and as I couldn't move Maurice, I was also useless! No matter how hard I tugged and pulled, the thick well-made Sunday best trousers would not budge from around his legs. I stole a look at his legs, wondering if I should ask Jean and Reg for a blanket. I was not accustomed to meeting men in commando pose. I could see a brightly crocheted multi-squared rug sitting atop of Reg's wheelchair on the veranda, but I could not release my grasp on the one trouser leg I had, for fear of losing it. Maurice was getting more and more agitated by the minute.

"Maurice, it really is fine. Nothing to worry about. No one is looking at you. We are just trying to get you back on your feet, so we can see how badly you are hurt, and to stop the bleeding around your legs and elbows."

Maurice must have come down quite heavily. He wasn't a tall man, but he was stocky, and stout and he would have taken quite a tumble. I looked around helplessly for some aid, and then, just as it seemed like there was no reprieve, a funny little old Fiat car came choofing up the empty road and came to a shocked stop outside Jean and Reg's house. Out jumped a much younger looking man and he rushed over to our little group calling out, "What's happening?" He looked at Maurice with his trousers around his ankles and the blood everywhere and exclaimed, "Maurice are you hurt? Who will say mass this morning?" He then looked at the rest of us and called out in a panicked voice, "Do you think he'll be right by eleven?"

Mass was obviously the priority for this gentleman. He could not think beyond the fact that Maurice might not make it to mass, and that the congregation would be left without a priest. I felt sympathy for this much younger man with the mindset of a cornered mouse, but that didn't stop me blurting out to him.

"Can't you see he's hurt, and disoriented and embarrassed and cold?"

The man came alive then, as though I had slapped him on both cheeks. He hauled Maurice to his feet. I was still hanging on for dear life to the trousers, and I came very close to giving Maurice mouth to mouth in the middle of this series of swift manoeuvres.

Then Maurice was miraculously on his feet, and we managed to half carry/half drag him into Jean and Reg's living room. I looked around for the younger man, but he had disappeared.

"That was Jonathan Thompson," Jean informed me. "He's probably gone off to take Maurice's place at mass."

Jean was in her element trying to pacify and reassure Maurice that he did not need to worry, that no one was going to strap him into an ambulance or swap his trousers for a straightjacket, and that he would be able to go back to his wee little bed as soon as he could manage to conquer the three flights of stairs to his harbourside apartment. Every few seconds, Jean would urge Maurice to take his time, as she and Reg had no plans for the day. They may not have had any plans for the day, but I certainly did, and besides that, I doubted very much that Maurice would even be able to conquer one solitary stair, let alone three flights, but I said nothing. It was hard to interrupt Jean once she had made up her mind. I know I am persisting with the trouser analogy, but in the Jean and Reg household it wasn't difficult to work out who wore the trousers. All of a sudden, Maurice went deathly quiet and he seemed to sink back into the sofa where Jean and I had settled him. He looked as if he might be drifting off, and I seized the opportunity to suggest that I myself might drift off, as I had friends waiting for me at home, and that everything seemed to be under control in Jean's arthritic hands. Unfortunately, Jean had other plans for me.

"Won't you just stay for a nice cup of tea, and then when we're fortified, the two of us could help Maurice up to his apartment?" I hoped Jean's idea of fortification included alcohol of some description, but I very much doubted it. Had there been alcohol being dished out at this hour of the morning, it should surely go to Maurice before the able-bodied. Didn't Jean realise that my plans for today had not included this morning madness which seemed to be pursuing me at every corner? I looked at Reg to see how he was taking the news of my being invited to stay and drink tea as some sort of energy elixir and then have a nice wee chat with Jean before I would be required to support (drag) Maurice all the way up to his third-floor dwelling. Reg was no fool. He just winked at me and murmured in a resigned voice, "Jean likes you!"

And I liked Jean, but I also liked my carefully mapped out itinerary which had taken three months of fastidious planning before I had left Australia, and my plans definitely did not include Jean, or Reg or Maurice or Jonathan whatever his name was. Then Jean had an idea. "I'll just telephone Christine in vem flats upstairs and see if ve pet can pop down and give us an and with Maurice."

"Was the pet going to be involved in the removal as well?" I had watched many travelogues on England and Ireland in preparation for the trip, and I did recall that in country villages and hamlets throughout England and Wales, they kept donkeys as pets. Maybe Christine from upstairs had a donkey which might come in handy. Maurice **was** a lay minister after all, and a donkey would not look out of place to him with his religious affiliations.

Reg looked relieved at Jean's suggestion, and assured Jean that Christine's number was one he could remember – as it was on speed dial in his mobile. Mobile? Reg had a mobile? I thought quickly. If Reg had a mobile phone, then perhaps Maurice did too. I felt a tiny wave of guilt over the patronising fact that I had assumed their ages to have equated with antiquated telephones taking pride of place in their living rooms. Of course, they had mobile phones, and rightfully so! More rightfully so than the roaming packs of 12-year-olds I seemed to bump into in the big shopping centres, texting furiously, and with little care for where they were walking. My thinking was that if Maurice had a mobile phone in his bulging brown satchel, then there might have been the number for a next of kin, and that person would appear with the super-human strength and energy needed to haul Maurice back up to his bed on the third floor of the flats behind us. I thought it best to ask permission to look in Maurice's brown satchel before I began searching for the phone. "Maurice, I'm just going to open your satchel to see if your mobile phone is in here." I knew I was shouting at him, but I was beginning to realise that Maurice must also have been slightly deaf, and that the off-white shark's tooth-like mini horn was not a beach fashion accessory. Maurice was no ageing hippy, that was for sure. He was a gentleman and probably also a scholar. My nursing training was coming in handy. Before I had studied teaching, I had completed a year of nursing at a country hospital just outside of Canberra where I grew up. In those days you could only be a Nurses' Aid or a Sister on the ward. To study to be a Sister you needed to venture further afield to Sydney, and I wasn't really convinced that I wanted nursing as a career, so I opted for the Nurses' Aid Course. As there were really only two career options open to young girls in the early seventies' nursing or teaching, I tossed a coin and nursing came up heads.

I was a truly hopeless nurse, but all the patients loved me, as I could sing, dance and entertain them on a daily basis. My career as a nurse didn't last more than that first year, as in the eleventh month of my training a catastrophically unfortunate incident occurred which precipitated an abrupt end to my Florence Nightingale aspirations. On the day of my downfall, I was mid-flight in one of my mid-morning pop up concerts (not a phrase then, but now featuring in urban dictionaries everywhere.) This impromptu, high energy entertainment was taking place in the overcrowded geriatric ward, where there were about twenty steel framed single beds crammed into the large room. Devoid of the beds, the room would have been a stage to equal the Globe theatre in London. It was the beds which were causing the overcrowding and lack of performance space. All beds were allocated to patients so there would have been around twenty elderly patients making up the audience. I was hurtling along in my top hat (brought from home to replace my nurse's cap), singing and tap dancing to 'Burlington Bertie from Bow', when suddenly there was a tremendous piercing clapping sound. I stopped abruptly mid-phrase. (The line in the song was actually 'I just had a banana with Lady Diana') The seething source of the thunderous clapping was Matron, who had been passing the G ward and witnessed me in full flight. I guessed this was not applause. "What's happening here!" She'd bellowed and then hissed. "Everyone back to their beds at once!"

Matron was a formidable force at the hospital. Had been so for the past twenty years, and rumour had it that she would die in her office chair. Everyone was petrified of her, and if you stepped out of line you might not live to tell the tale. Nurses disappeared all the time and were never heard of again. She was particularly unkind to the Maori nurses, and she was constantly barking at them to "speak up and stop mumbling that gibberish!"

Most of them would just put their heads down and mumble, "Yes mertrn, I mean no mertn."

Their collective hope was that one day a sporty nurse in shining armour would come along and perform the Harka solo in front of Matron. This would hopefully frighten her to a crumbling blithering mass, and she really would die in her office chair. No one would be able to remember the resuscitation steps, even though we had all been made to practise on the blow-up dolls most mornings, as the Geriatric ward was a high-risk Code Red alert area of the hospital.

But it never happened.

Matron Bellow (nickname she had earned) was big bosomed and bulky to boot. Her meticulous uniform was always perfectly pressed, and her sensible enormous back shiny shoes were so loud and click-clacking that you could hear her approaching miles down the long beige linoleum corridors. Mostly people ran the other way when they heard that click clicking, but that morning I had been performing so arduously, and the audience had been singing along with such gusto and vigour that none of us had heard her roll in. Two frail old gentlemen had been propped up against the walls at separate ends of the ward. When I ceased performing mid-sentence, and Matron Bellow started her possessed clapping and foot stamping, they had been so traumatised and confused that they had both made a beeline for the same bed, positioned in the middle of the ward. They must have reached the bed at exactly the same time, as there was another loud bang-more like a crack – as they had bumped heads quite heavily. One of them appeared to be more worse for wear than his chum, as he collapsed in a pyjama – crushed heap on the punishing lino, whilst the other one jumped straight into the bed and covered his head with the flimsy green hospital blanket. Both ended up hospitalised (same hospital but in isolation wards), and I ended up in Matron's office with her booming out to me to, "Explain yourself at once nurse!" I couldn't.

I was so worried that the patient on the floor was not going to regain consciousness. Matron was not happy. "Give me one good reason why I should keep you here! This is a hospital. Not the Vaudeville Theatre!" I loved my uniform, I loved my faulty fob watch, I loved my lop-sided nurse's cap which kept falling off. But I knew that Matron was right. I was no nurse. Teaching it was!

Maurice was grabbing his bulky satchel and clasping it to his chest. "Please don't take my satchel. I don't own a mobile phone. This satchel is for when I say mass. It's full of 'mass things'."

Mass things all right! Masses of little white round cardboard circles, which spilled out of the satchel and scattered all over the flower-faded carpet. Maurice wasn't having one of his best days. "Oh no, they've all spilled. Everywhere. That is a month's supply of hosts and now they are all dirty. How can we use them now?" Jean didn't look too pleased with Maurice when he inadvertently inferred that her newly vacuumed carpet may have been dirty. Maybe Jean had just missed that dusty section under the sofa where Maurice was slumped. She held no concern at all for the contaminated hosts.

Reg, the long-time practised pacifist stepped in. "They'll be fine Maurice. Don't worry. We'll dust them down one by one in the kitchen later and give them a good polish. They'll be good as new. You can pick them up on your way to mass tomorrow morning when you feel better." Maurice looked gratefully at Reg, and then back toward Jean and finally at me. For some reason his look wasn't so grateful by the time he got to me. I realised that Maurice and I were not really hitting it off in the way that his neighbour Ian and I had, over the last couple of days.

"Do you think I could go home now?" Maurice was done with the deal in Jean's loungeroom.

Both Jean and I really tried our best to get Maurice back on his feet. But it was just too hard, and his trousers kept down falling again. "Perhaps if we try and tighten the belt the trousers will stay up?" Jean was full of bright ideas, but she was squeezing the life out of Maurice in the process. I offered to have a go, but Maurice wasn't having a bar of me anymore – probably thought I had seen too much already. Playing the nursing card obviously hadn't had any effect on this private gentleman. Jean had given up. "We need help. I'm going to try Christine. I just hope she wasn't on her early shift this morning." In the next few minutes Christine was contacted, and she appeared at the front door a few minutes later, all bustling and jolly and light hearted about what had happened to Maurice this morning. (Perhaps it was a weekly event?)

"Ya silly duffer Maurie. Fancy falling over when you had ta say mass. It's just aint right innit?" Maurice wore a no comment look and tried in vain to loosen his belt which Jean had fastened so tightly around his waist. His face had gone from white to a bright red. He looked like he was holding his breath until we all disappeared. "Come on ven Maurie, let's get you home." Christine and I positioned ourselves on either side of Maurice and we began our slow journey to the first hurdle-the front door. At that very moment it was flung open, and on the porch stood a smallish darting eyed gentleman with tanned, muscled skin peeping out from the most brilliant white tee-shirt ever. He wore faded pale blue shorts, no socks and casual red sneakers. His cropped ash-blonde curly hair was dripping wet, as though he had just jumped out of the shower, and he had a great big cheesy smile on his rotund tanned face. It was Jerry. Christine's husband. Jerry had been at work as a bouncer at the local disco until the early hours of this morning, and he had just woken up to the note which Christine had left, informing him that Maurice had fallen over in Jean and Reg's front garden. "Ere Maurie, yer alwight?" Maurice nodded weakly and Christine swiftly handed him over to Jerry. "Ver you go Jez, you can take it from ear wight?"

Jerry could and did. I tagged along with Christine just to see the view of the sea from the third floor, and also to have a squiz at Maurice's furnishings in his flat with the promised million-dollar view. Jean and Reg were left at the door and as Jean handed me my backpack, she made me promise that I would visit them again before I left Barton. I promised that I would.

Then there were four. Fortunately for Christine and myself, the two-person ancient lift (that nobody had bothered to mention before now) was working, and although it was a tight squeeze for the four of us, we managed to fit into the tiny space. (Poor Maurice just couldn't get away from me.) The front-door to the flat was directly opposite the lift, and although it took some fumbling around in Maurice's satchel, we finally located an enormous bunch of keys and Jerry began fitting each key in turn into the lock. None of them worked, and finally (after ten minutes of fumbling) he turned to Maurice in exasperation. "I can't open the door Maurice. Do you know which key it is?"

"It's not any of those keys Jerry. The front door key is under that big red polka dotted pot plant behind you." It was the longest sentence Maurice had spoken since the great fall. Jerry was not amused, even though Christine and I were trying to supress giggles. "Well, you could have told me that before I wasted the last five minutes Maurice." Jerry waltzed in through the door with all the arrogant neighbourly privilege in the world once the pot plant had surrendered the key, and both Christine and I had dragged Maurice inside. I told myself in no uncertain terms that next time I saw someone calling for help, I would instantly turn the other cheek, and the other arm and both legs and go straight home, regardless of the age, state of distress or fitness levels of the injured parties. This incident this morning had been worse than a full-blown mugging. I think I would rather have endured a full-blown mugging than this torture on the cliff top.

No sooner had we made Maurice comfortable on the oversized rich, red, ludicrously padded velvet armchair, and retrieved his reading glasses on-chain, the local paper and a jug of water, than he turned on all three of us. He looked like Ronnie Corbett in one of his lounge room skits. "Get out! Out I say! Leave me alone. You've all caused enough damage for one day!" I was shocked at this uncalled – for outburst from mild-mannered-but-proving-to-be-ungracious Maurice. The other two seemed unruffled. "It's alright Maurice, we're all going now. I will check in on you tomorrow morning before I go to work." But Christine may well have been talking to the wall, as Maurice had turned his back on us all, closed his eyes, and began snoring loudly. Poor Maurice must have been exhausted. On the way back down to the ground floor in the squashy, stuffy, smelly lift, Jerry thanked me for my help with Maurice, and wished me a happy holiday in Britain. "See you in Australia!" was his final comment, and Christine nodded enthusiastically. I realised that the English really have little clue about the sheer expanse of Australia, and the fact that most the country is uninhabited because it is too hot. "Yeah. See you. Nice to meet you."

Once I had left Jerry and Christine, I literally raced off down the hill back towards Barton cottage. Literally nothing, or no one, was going to stop me this time. Not Ian nor his neighbour, not the café crew nor the beautiful people, and not Jean, Reg, Christine or Gerry. Not even Maurice and definitely not even the elusive Jonathan Thompson, who had been neither use nor ornament in the entire morning's shenanigans. By the time I had named and shamed (out loud) the long list of Barton locals I was not going to stop for, I was halfway home. (Just past the pillar boxes if I was to cite my exact location.) I should have known it would be Alice, when my mobile rang. Everyone else I knew would have still been asleep in Australia, and I had not yet had the chance to contact any of my London friends to let them know that I had arrived in the country.

"Fil, where on earth are you? Where have you been all morning? Patrick and I were just about to send out a search party for you. How far away are you?" Alice didn't draw a single breath, so I kept half walking, half running home, holding the phone out from my ear as we all have no doubt done once in our lives, whilst she kept firing inane questions down the phone. She didn't stop until I was just near the now familiar bushy corner of our street, and then she paused abruptly, and asked me in a very serious tone, if I had gone shopping without them. (As if the idea had just popped into her head, and knowing me as she did, it would have been extremely likely.) "Of course not," I replied happily. "I'm right here!" And I was. Right at the back door peering through the bevelled glass. (Alice had locked the door two hours before, ready to go out shopping, so even though I began rattling the glass I couldn't get in.) Alice indicated to me through the glass that the door was double-locked and she pointed towards the French doors outside the lounge room. "Go through the lounge room, Fil," she shouted with irritation. "Patrick and the dogs are in there waiting too. And please hurry up. How long were you sitting on the beach for anyway? Five hours?"

How long is a piece of string?

The Department store we were shopping in, 'Bradbeers' was one of those glitzy, glossy, polished stores where everything is so perpetually new it shines, and all the shop attendants smiled at you at least ten times a minute because it was part of their contract to do so. A friend of mine who had worked in a similar Department store in Australia had confirmed this to be the case, and it made sense really, as their job was to make you feel at home in the store, and to spend, spend, spend! The friend worked on the perfume counter, and she had to be doubly careful that when she smiled, she did not break her concentration when spraying the customer's outstretched hand with perfume. She had told me she often missed their wrists, as it was difficult to concentrate on two things at once.

Alice, Patrick and I were in the Ladies section of the store, as both Alice and I were looking for jumpers. I also wanted to buy a reasonably priced cardigan for my mother, as she adored English clothes, and was always pointing cardigans out to me in her weekly 'English Woman' magazine. All the family chipped in for the subscription to this magazine every Christmas. Sometimes Mum would write a wish list for me when I was off on a trip to England, but this time she had specifically asked for a cardigan. Patrick was sitting studying his Latin verbs on the pink velvet-padded bench provided for bored husbands and partners, and Alice and I were in seventh heaven unfolding and messing up all the jumper and cardigan racks whilst we searched for our respective sizes and preferred colours. (This was not usual behaviour for Alice. She was normally folding and ironing and steaming jumpers so that they looked like that were just back from the dry cleaners.)

I have a few travelling traditions. One non-negotiable is that I treat myself with the purchase of a pale pink jumper whenever I am overseas. (Not always easy to lay one's hands on.) The last jumper I'd bought had been a Pringle from the Woollen mills in Scotland. This idea that I looked pretty in pink had originated in my childhood, when our kindly next-door neighbour, had insisted that Mum dress me in pink, as I looked very pretty in that colour. (She also told Mum that the next six girls, who were born in quick succession, looked equally perfect in pink.) Hence Mrs Sorrentino, the local dressmaker found herself with a solid week's work, stitching the matching pink dresses for the seven of us girls. I was twelve by then, and the pink was beginning to match my acne perfectly.

It would be hard to beat the institutional Scottish Woollen mills for a warm jumper in the south of England, but I was optimistic in this Department store. I remembered that both Jean and Christine had been wearing similar-styled cardigans this morning, and I toyed with the idea of buying one for my mother. Mum was probably closer in age to Jean than to Christine, but the cardigans did not strike me as age-specific once one had reached a certain age. There were obviously three types of fashion accessories in Barton on Sea. There were the Kardashian type runners and star-studded tight tracksuits favoured by the thirties – something set, the non-descript shirts, pants and sensible golf shoes of the middle-aged early retirees, and lastly, the lumpy cardigans, creased shirts, skirts, trousers, walking sticks, frames and motorised scooters of the octogenarians.

"What do you think of this one Alice?"

"For you or your mother?"

"Mum of course." I was holding up a Mrs Brownesque-type cardigan against my chest and looking at myself in the mirror trying to picture it on my mother.

"No! I don't like it. Too busy." I had to admit it was a little on the busy side. There were bunches of little English birds (robins I think) in reds and blues all over the front of the cardigan. The cardigan would have been a superb choice, had my mother been off to a meeting for the Gould League of Bird Lovers, but for every day wearing, it was probably a bit much. "May I be of any assistance to you two lovely ladies?" Up until now, the shop attendant had only been hovering and smiling. Stage one. Frequently smiling, and annoyingly hovering. It must have been time for stage two – move in for the kill. Alice, a local of sorts, knew just how to handle her. Scowl.

"No thank you, we are just looking."

"That's perfectly acceptable, keep browsing, I am just over here if you need me." She smiled again, and then moved over to the little counter in the corner, but still within hearing distance of our conversation, and began folding and refolding a pile of jumpers and cardigans. She was a dead ringer for Mrs Slocomb, the bossy saleswoman who starred in the British sitcom 'Are You Being Served', although I think dear old Mrs Slocomb may have had the edge in looks on this unfortunate woman. Cruel people would have described her as having the face of a robber's dog – but I couldn't bring myself to even think like that before I had my pink jumper in my hot little hands. Alice and I finally selected a jumper each, and I found a lumpy plain large buttoned brown cardigan for my mother. Alice bought hers first, and I lined up behind her. There were no other customers on this floor level, so we had the shop assistant's full attention. "Would you like me to gift wrap the cardigan for you?" I warmed immediately to this astute woman who had the sense to realise that a plain lumpy cardigan such as this must surely have been a gift for an elderly person back home. "Or is it for yourself madame?" I lost the warming feeling just as immediately as it had come upon me.

"No. Wrapping it would be really good. Thank you very much." I noticed that her name tag was super-sized, but I didn't have my glasses on, so I could make out some letters, but her name was still quite blurry. She saw me squinting at her name tag.

"We deliberately make our name tags big so that the elderly customers can read them and address us by name." I really did try to read her name, as I could see she was itching for me to address her on a first name basis, but the dim shop lighting and my poor vision were both against me. I had a stab anyway.

"It's very nice of you to go to so much trouble wrapping the cardigan Dolly."

The woman gave me a concerned look.

"Oh no dear!" she exclaimed. "I'm not Dolly. My name is Polly. Did you forget to put your glasses on?" Alice was standing to the side near Patrick, and she burst out laughing.

"That's just Fil for you. She's too vain to wear her glasses."

I wasn't too vain. I was just too lazy most of the time to go rummaging through my enormous handbag to find my reading-glasses. Just recently, at an airport in Australia, a frenzied gentleman seated beside me in the waiting lounge, had implored me to lend him a pen. He was very jumpy, and it seemed it was a matter of life or death for him to copy down a very long series of digits. (He kept repeating the digits over and over) I had my expensive silver Parker pen (with my name engraved on it of course) in my bag at the time but was reluctant to hand the pen over to him, in case my plane was called, and I would have to rush off. I knew that I had a few hotel-souvenir pens buried somewhere in the bottom of my bag. To save time looking, I tipped the entire contents of my bag onto the floor in front of us and began rummaging around for one of the cheap pens. The look on the man's face was priceless. As was the retort he came back at me with. "I remember now. Never, never, never look inside a woman's handbag!" Too late Mr A, whole eight kilos of 'stuff' had begun coagulating in front of him. He couldn't cope, and was off like shot, repeating the numbers being called out to him from the other end of his mobile, and attempting to commit them to memory.

The effect of the frantic rummaging in my over-sized bag was that I now had three pairs of glasses to contend with – reading, driving and sunglasses. Sometimes I even resorted to using a magnifying glass if I was looking for a miniscule location on a map, or when trying to thread a needle. (Not that I had thread many needles since primary school sewing classes) Polly was smiling again, but this time she had a purpose. My potential vision impairment. It wasn't really that drastic, but I resolved to wear my reading glasses when in shops, or if I encountered plentiful signage anywhere. We located the lift down to the ground floor, and Patrick mumbled that he would like to wander off and have a poke around in the second-hand shop on the corner, before we had lunch. It was already 3 o'clock and we hadn't eaten, so Alice suggested that we eat first, and then we could split up and venture solo into our favourite shops. I relished that idea, because I knew Alice would go to the health food shop, and that Patrick would go to a second, second-hand book shop, and I would go to Lidl. I really love shops like Lidl because you can get whatever your heart desires there. I wanted lots of small items like toothpaste and hair shampoo and chocolates. Lots of chocolates.

We decided on a candid little café which served food all day, and since potatoes-in-their-jackets was the house speciality, we all partook of the potatoes. Patrick had bacon added onto his filling, but we girls opted for the vegetarian version. They were scrumptious. Extra cheesy and piping hot. It was almost 4 o'clock when we finished licking our lips. I was really enjoying the slow-paced afternoon after the excitement of the morning.

"I think I'll walk up to Lidl and then make my own way home if that's OK?"

Alice agreed that it would be good form for me to get to know the back streets of Barton by walking up to Liddle and back to the house. (When had she become so English with her phrasing?)

"Could you get some fresh cream when you are there please?"

I find it amusing that people emphatically request 'fresh cream' – as if they expect the cream to be curdled or something worse if you didn't bother to check the use by date.

"Yes. I'll get some cream. See you later."

It was much, much later when I saw them again. I spent at least two hours in Lidl, roaming up and down the aisles and examining the labels and nutritional contents of foods I was never going to sample in this lifetime. I love to imagine cooking up all these exotic dishes. I am no cook though, as I find it challenging to stringently follow a recipe. I tend to just throw in all the stated ingredients and hope for the best. Jamie Oliver is possibly the only chef I have a great amount of time for, and that's only because I love his cockney accent, and the way he throws handfuls of incongruent ingredients together with panache and style. Alice is the complete opposite to me. She diligently pours and measures and stirs and pounds in exactly the recommended rhythmic motion and amounts. I wouldn't even know where to start with measuring one hundred grams of anything. Securing the cream was causing me some angst, as I wasn't sure what size bottle or brand to purchase. In Australia we are spared this agony in front of the supermarket fridges, as we just don't have the choices they have in England. There is cream sitting in the fridge in front of you, and you pick it up. End of. So, I tried the Australian way-I just closed my eyes and picked. Most of the staff in Lidl were very young and were nearly all Polish. I have some Polish friends in Australia, as well as in Poland, and I know a couple of polish words and some polish delicacies. One of the delicacies is the pierogi, and I wanted to ascertain if Lidl sold pre-cooked pierogi, and if so, where might I find a tray of them?

The girls on the front tills were in fits of laughter at my polish words with the Australian accent. They crowded around me, abandoning their registers and irate queues of customers waiting to buy their frozen meals for tea, just so as they could hear my accent. "Keep talking, tell us more, tell us about the dumplings and the pierogi." It was probably the best entertainment they had experienced in months, and no one was about to miss out on hearing my pigeon polish. I was finally saved from the Polish paparazzi by the manager, who appeared at my side pleading with me to stop talking, as his workers were very distracted by me. How could this be? I seemed to invite curiosity and chaos wherever I went in Barton. Maybe it would be better to stop talking and just complete my purchases and leave. The workers seemed sad to see me heading for the door, but the manager had a big smile on his face as he rushed over to open it for me, and hand me a free chocolate bar because I had been a 'good customer'. (I was no fool – the chocolate bar was just bait, to get rid of me for good.) I would have preferred a tray of frozen pierogi.

It was much cooler and clouding over when I eventually emerged from Lidl. I had two quite full bags to carry (cream included) but it was fine because they equalled each other out. I knew that Lidl was about half an hour's walk from home – I just didn't know whether to turn left or right. I stood there for about two minutes deliberating, and then again remembered my pledge to always turn left. So, I tuned left. And it was right. I was on the road to Barton, and I had my bearings back. When I finally made it home, I bolted up to my room for a lie down. Alice was busy preparing the evening meal, and Patrick was still reciting Latin verbs. The dogs were fast asleep in their day-beds. Although I could feel the powerful dark-side of the dreaded jet lag, I forced myself to stay awake, and after about half an hour in the twilight zone, dragged myself back downstairs to offer to help Alice with the preparation of the evening meal. She looked at me doubtfully and issued me with the sous-chef job of chopping up the salad vegetables. I was more than happy with that. I categorically did not want to be responsible for the main meal, as it was to be chicken snitzel – which I always manage to burn to a frazzle.

From my point of view, we had a splendid evening, with me telling Alice and Patrick all about my adventures on the beach, at the café and in Jean and Reg's front garden. I'm not sure if Alice would have used the word splendid to describe the evening. She just kept shaking her head in disbelief most of the time, but Patrick seemed to be thoroughly enjoying my stories. His voice was as dry as the chardonnay he was sipping when he retorted, "I've been roaming up that same path for the past ten years, and nothing like that has ever happened to me." Patrick seemed quite chaffed that it was only my second day in Barton, and all those exciting escapades had come my way. After the storytelling session the five of us settled down comfortably in the lounge room. Pointless was on television. It was one of Patrick's favourite shows, so we all joined in enthusiastically (even the dogs) with the pointless answers to the pointless questions. Post Pointless, Alice turned the television off and we all relaxed in our own idiosyncratic way. Alice in her largish floral recliner with the intense fluorescent lamp for her intricate needlework, and Patrick on the comfy corduroy-cushioned sofa with a dog either side of him. I was already bedded down in the only other armchair in the room and I promptly fell asleep. When I awoke sometime later, it was to Alice urging me to go up to bed, as I would get too cold sleeping in the chair. Patrick had already retired, having settled the dogs in their night cages, and Alice had locked all the doors and turned out most of the lights in readiness for the night. "Goodnight Fil. Remember, we're leaving early for our shopping expedition into Limington. If you do end up going up to the beach again tomorrow morning, don't forget to be back here by nine thirty. No excuses! We want to leave early, and then we can have the afternoon to relax around the house."

I decided that I would skip the beach in the morning, as we would probably be doing a lot of walking around Limington and who knows what sorts of distractions may have been lying in wait for me up on the cliff top. It was safer to stay home and wait until Patrick had backed out his pride and joy Jag in readiness for the early morning take off. Yes. That's what I'd do. With this important decision made, I dragged myself slowly up the stairs one by one. Tomorrow would be my third day in Barton. I wondered what was in store for me. I was asleep before I could answer myself.

# Chapter 9
## Out-of-Town

In Australia we tend to call Wednesday 'Hump Day'. Not all of us, just the workers of the world. Since I was on a British seaside holiday, I didn't need to take any notice of the days, but it still rang a bell with me when I remembered it was Hump day, the minute I opened my eyes. (Thankfully, it was not a dreaded school bell, the bane of all teachers' lives.) The other difference this morning was that I did not have to get up until at least 9 o'clock. It was still very, very early. I could tell by the thin slither of pale lemon and pink light peeping in through the gently flapping floral-print curtain. Not yet fully developed, the shaft of light was so slim and so ethereal that it might have disappeared if I turned my back on it. I lay perfectly still, and kept watching and waiting, willing it to the fullness of life. I allowed my mind its usual morning wanderings and began to think of how and why we are all here. Even though we don't like to admit it, many of us live in fear, which is by far the ruling emotion of our world. Love, the opposite of fear, is what most of us strive for. Time is on our side in the throws-of-childhood and as children, we drift off to sleep with thoughts of love, warmth, comfort and play. That's us in the Western world though. In the East, the Middle East, and in many of the war torn Eastern European countries, the very young are the most vulnerable. They are exploited, exposed, hungry and already exhausted from life. I started to feel guilty about the children of the world. When I was teaching, I could justify myself with the naive notion that I was doing all I could to help make the world a better place for children. Now that I was here, in these snug surrounds, I wasn't so sure of myself. A few years back, the humanitarian 23-year-old son of a good friend of mine, decided to quit his comfortable high-flying job, and band together with three mates to raise money to put a stop to child trafficking. They had made up their minds to cycle from London back to Melbourne to raise money for this appalling situation in

Burma. The lads raised over a quarter of a million British pounds, and it took them over a year to complete the journey. But they survived. Not only did they raise the money, but more importantly, they raised awareness and consciousness with their endeavours. They actually woke us all up. I wished, at the time, that I could have joined them, but they were on bikes. Pushbikes – not motor bikes. And the Himalayas were in the way. We all donated instead.

I was still lying there silently, thinking up ingenious (not too taxing) ways to better the world, when I heard a tap-tap-tapping on the lounge room window, which was directly below my bedroom. I jumped up and poked my head out of my bedroom window. It was fully light by now, and the breeze had dissipated. Directly below me stood Ian, patiently attending to his syncopated tapping. Lucy lay curled up at his feet.

"Ian! Ian!!"

I didn't want to wake up Alice and Patrick with any loud shouting, so I tried a sort of 'loud whisper'. Ian finally stopped tapping and looked up at me, squinting in the newly born sunlight.

"Oh, there you are Fil. Rapunzel, Rapunzel, let down your golden hair!" Ian was chuckling to himself over his early morning joke, and Lucy, sensing her surrogate master's pleasure, joined in by barking loudly. Lucy's barking was so loud that it must have woken Holly and Looby, who had presumably been asleep in their dog cages in the loungeroom. Much scuffling and banging and scratching at the French doors followed. Ian had gone quiet. I quickly slipped on my kimono-style robe and started for the stairs. Alice must have also woken up with all the barking and banging, and we both arrived at the top of the stairs at the same time.

"What's happening? Are the girls alright?"

"I think so. I presume so. Actually, I don't really know. I was asleep."

"Fil, you must know something, you are never asleep at this time of the morning. Hang on, who is that outside calling your name?"

I side-stepped Alice without bothering to answer her and raced-two-at-a-time down the stairs. I stumbled on the last stair as I was being closely followed by Alice, and she was doing her best to overtake me. And she did!

"Holly, Looby, Mummy is here now, what's the matter diddums?" Both diddums were still in their cages, and Lucy outside the doors, continued barking and scratching. Act one was still not over. With Alice fussing over the cages trying to unfasten each one in turn, I seized on the opportunity to unlock the loungeroom French doors. Ian was not there. Only the barking, scratching Lucy.

I heard a rustle and gasping in the bushes, and I thought it would probably be Ian, unaccustomed to people and causing a fuss, hiding in the bushes. But it wasn't Ian. It was Patrick!

"Pat! What are you doing here?" Useless rhetorical question I know, but I wasn't expecting to see all six feet of him curled up in a ball and a red checked dressing gown in the holly bush outside the kitchen window. "Patrick are you hurt?" It was a legitimate question as it turned out, because Patrick was not so much hurt, as in pain. In his haste to glimpse the burglar he thought to be lurking near the loungeroom doors, Patrick had jumped into the holly bush about an arm's length away from the imagined burglar. Except that he had forgotten to put on his slippers as he had raced down stairs and out the back door. He had stood on a rather large thorn and was now whimpering in pain. For two mornings in a row my skills as a nurse were required. "Here Patrick, balance on my shoulder and lift up your right leg. I am a whiz at getting out thorns, wasp and bee stings."

Whenever any students were stung by a wasp, I was summoned, scooped out of whatever class I was taking at the time, and urged to pull out the sting from the wasps or bees which plague the Australian school yards in lunchtimes in Spring. Once my reputation as a wasp de-stinger was established, it became a seasonal occupation for me most lunch times. It meant exemption from yard duties as well, because one had to be on call throughout the lunch hour should the wasps (or bees) decide to punish some unfortunate child or duty teacher. No yard duty was hard to take, but I suffered it in silence.

"Patrick, stand still!" Patrick was a bit woozy from just having woken up, and he kept over balancing and almost toppling to the ground. "How about if you just sit down on the ground and stretch out your leg, and I'll pull the thorn out from there?" With no alternative, pale-face Patrick was forced to agree with me that a horizontal position was called for, and as soon as he was settled on the ground, I reached over and skilfully (my word) whipped out the sting. Patrick yelled in pain, and that yell actually brought a sudden silence to the garden. Lucy stopped barking, and the girls, who were still locked in their cages because Alice was having difficulty with the latches, also ceased their descant symphony of barking and yelping. Patrick was grappling to stand up, and I gave him a hand. He looked even paler than usual, and I suggested that he go back into the kitchen, and that I would make him a nice hot sweet cup of tea. All the time I was talking to him, I was on the lookout for Ian, but he had well and truly disappeared. We made our way around the side path of the garden en-route to the back door. As we passed the next-door neighbour's house, a rotund balding head popped up from the cabbage patch and a sing song welsh voice called out. "Lotta action occurring at number nine this morning. Bit early for gentlemen callers innit?" He was looking directly at Patrick as he see-sawed out his lines, but I didn't really think he was implying that it was Patrick who was entertaining the early morning gentlemen callers. He surely meant me. Must have been slightly cross eyed. "I have no idea what you are talking about Bert." Patrick had serious indignation, mixed with slight guilt in his voice at being caught with one bare foot, a strange woman and in a red-checked dressing gown.

"If you must know, I was chasing a burglar and I had a thorn in my foot. Fil here is a nurse visiting us from Australia, and she just happened to be out in the garden at the same time as me, and she pulled a thorn out of my foot." Patrick's tone had changed from victim to victor by the end of his laboured explanation to Bert. But Bert wasn't born yesterday, and he wasn't buying Patrick's story. "That what happened?" Bert had turned to me hoping for a juicier rendition of the early morning events.

"Yes."

My early morning mood of joy to the world was souring. This balding, nosey neighbour was just fishing around for a way to malign my Patrick. I felt so protective of Patrick that I actually took him by the arm and helped him to hobble towards the back door. At the door I turned around to Mr nosey neighbour and added. "The gentleman caller was not for Patrick. He was there for me!" Patrick looked shocked and even paler, but I was proud of my fighting words. Bert looked at me in awe and went back to weeding his underdeveloped cabbage patch.

It was fate again. Fate that positioned Patrick in the holly bush, fate that had compelled Bert to do some dawn gardening right along the border to number nine, and fate that was now solely responsible for Alice standing at the backdoor cradling both Looby and Holly and glaring at Patrick as though he had committed a cardinal sin. Naturally I thought it was going to be me who got the entire blame for the chaotic events of the 'sleep in' morning, but I was suddenly willing to sacrifice Patrick to the clutches of his disbelieving wife. I had saved Patrick from the thorns, and from Bert's suspicion and now it was Patrick's turn to save me.

He was a good sport, was old Patrick, and since he had reached the sanctity of the back door, he seemed to brighten up enormously. He didn't even flinch at the scornful woman in front of him.

"Oh darling, you're up." Patrick was a clever conversationalist when he wanted to be. "Are you just about to feed the girls?"

Alice was a big softie when it came to Holly and Looby, but she was also hard enough to add a touch of sarcasm to her voice when she ping-ponged back at him. "Well, somebody had to let them out of their confinement. You'll have to buy two more bolts when we go shopping this morning." Patrick fidgeted with his glasses, ensuring they were on straight, and then looked at me. Coward and peacemaker that I was, I said nothing. So, Patrick answered for both of us.

"Could do."

Patrick was well-versed in Latin and history, and he often came up with short sharp succinct phrases often overused by politicians and great orators. 'Could do' was one such example. From memory, it was none other than the great Winston Churchill who must have given Patrick the idea for that phrase. Churchill had been questioned over whether or not the enemy was likely to bomb Waterloo Bridge in London. 'Could do' was Churchill's brief (prophetic) reply. Alice was over-accustomed to this non-committal response, and she knew that meant 'probably not'. This realisation did nothing to improve her mood. She inevitably turned to me. "Who was that man's voice I could hear this morning calling out Rapunzel?"

"It was Ian. You know Ian from the cruise ships and the house up on the cliff with the great view."

"Ian, you mean Ian from the beach came here this morning, to our house?" Alice sounded incredulous.

"Yes. That Ian, but he's gone now. Lucy is still here though, she's around the front."

Holly and Looby seemed to recognise the name of one of their canine clan, and at the mention of Lucy's name they jumped excitedly out of Alice's protective, somewhat suffocating eternal hug, and trotted off around the side of the house. Profuse barking and happy howling followed. Patrick seized on the chance to disappear, whispering something about the gents calling him. He may have had the gents calling him, but I could trump that. I had a gentleman caller calling me, and he had unwittingly woken the whole household. Probably the whole neighbourhood by now if Bert was a fast talker. "I can explain Ali." I reverted to the shortened form of her name, hoping it would remind her that she was my best friend in the world (Northern Hemisphere).

"I have no idea how Ian found me this morning. I forgot to tell him that I wasn't going up to the beach today, and he just came looking for me."

"Why does he call you Rapunzel?"

"I have no idea."

"What did you tell him about where we lived?"

"Well, nothing really specific. Just that it was at the end of the beach road, and that you turn right then, and that Patrick had a green Jag which he parked in the lane outside the house because you had a new car that needed garaging. No more than that. Quite scant information. Not much to go by really." Alice just looked at me and held her breath for so long I thought she was going to explode, but she finally released all the pent-up air and cried out to me in a fed-up voice,

"Fil, you just don't think! What if Ian is a peeping Tom and he was waiting for us all to wake up and get dressed? You shouldn't have told him where you lived." She had a point. A good point. This called for an apology from me to both Alice and Patrick. Not that I believed Ian to have been a peeping Tom. Ian was so black and white in his thinking that if I'd called him a peeping Tom to his face, he would probably have denied it on the grounds that his name was 'Ian' and not Tom. Alice was like a dog with a bone. "And what about that Lucy dog? What are we going to do with her? Has she had breakfast? How am I going to feed Holly and Looby in front of her? We haven't got enough sausages to feed three dogs, and it wouldn't be fair to Lucy to just watch."

See, that was Alice for you! All huffed and puffed one minute, and then so kind and thoughtful the next. Where dogs were concerned that is. But to be fair it wasn't only dogs Alice showed concern for. In her work as a deaf teacher (teacher of the deaf) she came into daily contact with babies and young children who were either partially or fully deaf. Alice worked so hard to improve the quality of life for these children. She really was a miracle worker for many desperate children and their parents. "We could cut up the sausages and share them amongst all three dogs." Now that was a brilliant suggestion on my part, because Alice was smiling at me and asking me to go around the front and fetch all three dogs whilst she did the breakfasts. Did that include my breakfast, I wondered. Knowing Alice's obsession with healthy eating for the dogs, I guessed not.

We fed the dogs and then ourselves without fuss. I think we all had our minds on separate things. Patrick seemed preoccupied with making a list of everything he needed to do this morning in Lymington. Alice was also preoccupied, fussing over Lucy (who had been allowed inside the house) and making phone calls to a friend of hers who lived on the cliff top road. Could she possibly come down to fetch Lucy and take her home to Ian and Enid? And me? I was churning out the postcards in record time. "I thought you were going to put everything on face book and then people could see the pictures?" Alice picked up three of the postcards I had written, and scoffed. "Fil, these are all the same. Same pictures and same lines. Even your signature is the same."

"Well, it would be wouldn't it? I can't very well change my signature for every postcard."

"No. but you could change what you were describing, and you could have bought three different postcards."

"No, I couldn't have. It was three postcards for a pound at the airport, and I only had a pound on me." (No technically true. I had the saved up the ten pound note I had handed over to the Pakistani shopkeeper on Monday.)

We were arguing like an old married couple, so I stopped and gave in.

"You're right Alice. This is rubbish." With that, I tore up the postcards and concerned myself instead with writing dates and the names of people I'd met on my holiday so far. I was up to sixteen already, and that was not counting Bert next door. Alice didn't even notice that I had vehemently torn up the postcards. She was on the phone again, this time to the Lost Dogs Home in New Milton. Yes. The dog did have a collar. Yes. We did know where the dog lived. No. We did not have time today to take her home. I knew that Alice would never leave Lucy in the cottage whilst we went shopping, just as she was never going to leave Looby and Holly at home either. All three dogs couldn't come with us, as that would be dog-napping in the case of Lucy. (And probably also in the case of the girls, as they spent most of their time napping anyway.) That left us with only one option which might work, and that was for one of us to take Lucy back home to Ian.

"Patrick, can you please drop Lucy off at Ian's when you take the girls for a walk this morning?"

Patrick is so affable, and so obliging. He is the perfect host, and he wasn't going to disagree with Alice in front of me and the girls.

"Could do." This time it meant yes.

Patrick and the three dogs left straight after he had showered, and that left Alice and I to deal with the breakfast dishes. There were quite a few dishes and bowls this morning, what with the extra guest. After we had finished the dishes, we both went upstairs to have our showers and groom ourselves for the promised shopping expedition to Lymington.

I was in no hurry, as I knew that Patrick liked to let the dogs run wild on the cliff for a good twenty minutes. And it was a forty-minute round trip to the cliff top. I had at least an hour. I chose my outfit for the day wisely. Rain was forecast, so I included a light jacket, walking shoes and an umbrella. It took me less than half an hour to get ready. Alice was still singing in the shower as I waltzed past her bedroom, and I was tempted to knock on the shower door with the password Rapunzel and inform her that Ian was back was waiting in the kitchen. I didn't though, as I valued my life, and I wanted to see the promised market town.

Downstairs was very still and quiet without Patrick and the dogs. The house was so big that you couldn't really hear what was going on upstairs unless you were standing on the stairs. I was in the dining room flicking through the local paper. There seemed to be a plethora of articles and pictures on the precarious Barton cliffs, and I was glad I had avoided getting too close to them. Soon enough Alice came galloping down the stairs, wet curly hair flying, and a large white resort style bath towel wrapped around her body.

"Fil, disaster! Have you seen my pale blue dress? I thought I'd left it on the back of one of these chairs."

"Uhuh, sorry. I haven't seen it. I haven't even been into your room since I arrived. I've only stood at the door a few times and listened."

This made Alice laugh, and as she did so she wobbled and the towel that she had wrapped loosely around her body fell abruptly to the ground. That made us both laugh, and Alice was trying to re-position the towel around herself when Patrick walked in through the loungeroom doors with only two of the dogs.

"Where is Lucy?"

"Back where she belongs."

"You mean with Ian?"

"No. Enid. She's back from the bank holiday weekend away. Apparently, she got back last night." Patrick was fussing around the paper strewn dining room table, collecting lists and vouchers, pamphlets and keys, his wallet and his enormous water bottle. "I'm going to start the car. The doors in here need locking, and maybe pull some of these blinds down? I'll wait for you both in the car." Alice scuttled off to get dressed in whatever she could find to wear, and I waited on the sofa, flicking through magazines like I was in a waiting room. When Alice returned, dressed in a smart red outfit, we both dutifully skulked around the downstairs rooms, shutting curtains and pulling down blinds. It looked like the inside of a funeral parlour by the time we had finished. Then we gathered our bags, coats and umbrellas. The dogs had followed Patrick out, so we only had to lock the back door after ourselves. We were off to Lymington at last!

Although the road was quite windy and bumpy the scenery was very picturesque. Sometimes we were crossing quaint little stone bridges on dirt-roads, and other times we met up with the motorway at a T junction and were forced to stay on the motorway for a few miles. For the most part we took to the open county, and it was just like the England of old. Narrow lanes, hedgerows scraping the car, little pubs and farm shops tucked away in the copses and glades, and generally so like Robin Hood country that I expected Robin and his band of merry men to jump out of the bushes and burst into song with "Robin Hood, Robin Hood riding through the glen". (Except that we were in the wrong part of the country.)

The dogs loved the jaunt. Alice had pushed them into the back of the Jag where I was ensconced, and they kept jumping all over me and throwing their faces out the window so that the wind could ruffle their fur. I am normally quite reserved when it comes to dogs sitting on me, but these two were very cute, and I knew that if Alice could see me in the revision mirror nursing and clasping the dogs to my chest in wedded bliss, that I would be in her good books for at least the next twenty-four hours.

She could see me. I could see her smiling back at me. We kept up our cone of silence all the way to Lymington. The first stop was a large electrical store on the outskirts of the town. Alice and Patrick's vacuum-cleaner was on the blink, and since we would be leaving Barton on Sunday, they needed to purchase a new one for the big clean up scheduled for Sunday morning. I was secretly thrilled that we were stopping at an electrical shop, as I wanted to have a look for a compact travel keyboard which I could plug into my mobile phone. It would just make things so much easier for me taking notes and jotting down my ideas on life. Once inside the shop, Alice and Patrick wandered off to peruse the vacuum cleaners, and I turned left at the entrance – which was my custom now. I rolled that six straight away. Smack bang in front of me was the computer section, and there appeared to be an abundance of computers, laptops and keyboards. It would just be a matter of which ones were designed for travelling. I thought about all the travel technological items I had brought with me to this fair country in my travels over the years. Electric travel kettles, electric travel toasters, travel hairdryers, travel hair curling wands, travel shavers, travel irons even travel digital alarm clocks. The list went on and on, but I noticed that the technology sections looked overstocked compared to when those same shelves would have housed the required travelling items of some years back.

Realistically, who still needed to pack travel irons and travel toasters and kettles? The competition for hotels, B and B's and hostels has become so fierce, that you could expect to find any of these items you required in the cupboards of your hotel room. (Yes, even three-star hotels). Or you could dial a wake-up call, or you could order room-service, or you could send your dry cleaning and washing down to reception for them to deal with. These items, although all necessary, have mostly become redundant for the hip post-modern traveller. I was the perfect example of the technologically savvy traveller. I had my iPad, my Smart phone, my head phones and my chargers. I had a stylus pen, and I was now on the hunt for a folding, portable keyboard so that I could complete my technological glory box. I was the sort of person advertising agents were constantly on the lookout for, as I would know all the right things to say about travel technology when making advertisements.

Either that or the glory box could come in handy in its own right.

"What sort of keyboard are you after?"

The tall, skinny, gum-chewing boy who was calling out to me from behind the shelf in the next aisle, bobbing his head up and down like a swimmer practising the butterfly stroke, was quite pushy I thought. His shaven head and large hooped earring through his nose would possibly have increased his pace if he actually were a swimmer. I was still in the browsing phase, and I had not asked anyone for help in my selection of a keyboard. I was keeping a very low profile and moving along the aisles as quietly as I could.

"No. It's OK. Thank you, but I'm just browsing." The boy pushed on. "If it's a keyboard that you're after, we have quite a selection of them in the next aisle. If you like I can hook them up to a port and you can try out your typing."

"Thanks, but I'm fine. I will know what I'm looking for when I see it." The boy looked away, disappointed that there would be no sale, and I just stood there examining every single keyboard, but not really liking any of them. After a few more minutes, Alice and Patrick reappeared, and proudly informed me that they had purchased a 'state-of-the-art' vacuum at a very reasonable price, and that they were ready to leave. Was I ready? Yes. I was ready. I hadn't found anything I'd liked, and I figured there would be many more stores and malls in London, where I would be sure to get exactly what I was looking for. In the course of those five minutes, the disappointed gum chewing boy had been moved to a lowlier shift on the front entrance. "Thank you for your custom and please call again." His entire rehearsed phrase was directed to Alice and Patrick. He completely ignored me. I turned to him and whispered. "Later." His puzzled expression mixed with a hint of fear was revenge enough for me.

"What was that all about?" Alice was curious about my relationship with the boy. "Nothing."

"What did you mean later? Do you want to call in here our way back to Barton? It's a bit out of the way Fil."

"It was nothing. It was between me and him."

Alice could tell she would get nothing out of me about the boy, so she tried another tact. "Do you want to go shopping first, or eat first?"

"Eat first." Patrick, the silent partner, came to life at the mention of food.

"If that suits you two," he added hastily.

"Sounds good," I spoke for us both. All we needed was to drive a little further into town, find a park and eat. I was surprised at how busy and how big this market town actually was. There were people and cars and tractors everywhere. At every corner there was a tractor, and on every tractor, there was an old farmer (male) in dungarees and a regulation farmer's hat. There were also children and babies everywhere. There seemed to be a population explosion of babies and toddlers in this neck of the woods. That was probably a good sign for the economy, as young families meant jobs, services and schools as well as a healthy tourist industry courtesy of all the shops which inevitably become part of the infra structure. Eventually we found somewhere to park the car, and we all traipsed across a stone bridge which spanned the river which seemed to split the town in half. I kept lagging behind, because I was so intrigued by the age and colour of the stone which had been used to construct the bridge. A guide book would have come in handy. The longer I dallied, the further I got behind the other two. If you lived in England, bridges such as this were common place, but in Australia this bridge would have been worthy of a day excursion and perhaps even a Visitor's Centre status, with tea rooms and a children's playground attached.

There were two fishermen in a dinghy directly under the bridge, and I called out to them, asking if I might take their photograph. I didn't really want a photo of the two men, or even their dinghy, but of the river itself. Unfortunately, they were obstructing my view and my potentially perfect picture.

"Why would you want our picture?"

"I don't really, it is just the river, and maybe your dinghy that I'd like to capture."

"Oh well then that's different. Bernie, bob down now."

Both men threw down their nets and lay flat in the dinghy. I felt bad about that, but I snapped away like a professional paparazzi, hoping for one decent shot amongst the twenty or so I was taking.

"Thanks guys. Looks like you are having a peaceful time fishing. Hope you catch some fish!" Back home, if you came across fishermen or women, you would just saunter up to them and casually whisper in their ear, "Yagettinany?"

The English way seemed much more civilised, and easier to learn how to pronounce. I was so far behind Alice and Patrick that I decided not to hurry. There was only one main street in this town, and I figured that they would wait for me at the next T (no traffic lights to be seen).

As I descended the cobblestone-bridge I waved over the side to the two fishermen. They were hauling in a net full of some sort of shiny black and brown fish, but I didn't have time to go back and take a photo of the catch. No doubt it would be the fish of the day on some nearby restaurant's menu tonight. I could see Alice and Patrick up ahead, and I waved to them as well. But their backs were turned so they couldn't see me. Other people could see me though, and they were looking at me strangely. I was the epitome of a tourist, with my walking boots and backpack, I knew that, but they didn't have to stare! Then I realised that may have been staring at me because I was waving at everyone. They probably thought I was a television personality, or someone well known, because I was waving, and calling out to perfect strangers. I didn't really care what they thought, because I knew that I wouldn't ever see them again. When I reached the corner of the main road which was lined with shops and cafes, I spotted Alice and Patrick sitting on the bench outside a shop adorned along its doorway and gables with rows and rows of pretty flower baskets. From where I was standing, I thought it might be a florist, but as I got closer, I saw that the shop was a café, and the flowers in the baskets were part of the colourful shopfront. The door and the window frames were painted bright yellow.

"What do you think of this place for lunch?" Alice stood up when I reached the bench where they were sitting, but Patrick remained seated.

"Looks lovely. Very cottagey and very pretty. Do you think the flowers are real?" Alice had reached over and touched a few of the flowers.

"Petunias alright."

I was impressed with the display and her knowledge of flowers, and I wondered if the floral theme would be continued once we got inside. Patrick didn't look like he was going anywhere. "What's wrong Patrick? Aren't you coming in with us?"

Patrick shook his head, pointing towards his foot and replied, "I'll be in shortly. I'm just resting my foot which is still quite sore from this morning."

Alice called him wimpy, and marched into the shop, just missing a low-lying hanging basket brimming with cornflowers. She pretended that she didn't see the hanging basket. I gave Patrick a sympathetic smile, and assured him that we wouldn't order until he came in. He smiled gratefully back at me. The meal was more than hearty, and I didn't think we would be wanting much for tea, judging by how much we all ate. Patrick soon forgot his ailment and tucked in enthusiastically. After lunch, we wandered the streets of Lymington and ended up with two bags of food shopping and seven bags of souvenirs and presents for me to send back to Australia. I wanted to get all my 'present-shopping' out of the way in my time at Barton, so that I could concentrate on museums and the tourist traps when I got back to London. Usually I end up spending days looking for requested presents when I travel overseas. The situation is improving though with online shopping and low shipping fees for goods. Over the years I have been asked to bring back glass plates from Merano in Italy, Claddagh rings and jewellery from Ireland, and thick warm winter coats from England. In addition to this there have literally been hundreds of other small requests for goods and clothing, watches and video cameras from Singapore, scarves from Scotland, 'Osh Gosh' clothing from USA, even casino chips from the Nice Casino. It actually got to the point where I just had to say no to people, when they asked me to bring them back heaven knows what. No. No. No! I didn't not have room in my suitcase. I did not have time to post them back. I would not be doing it.

Do you have any idea how difficult it is to say no? Well, I did it. Hardly anyone talks to me when I return from my travels, sulky lot that they are, but they soon snap out of it when they see all the presents I've brought back for them. The difference being that I had chosen a gift specifically for them, and it had been me who had decided what I would buy and where. This trip, I would be buying everything in Barton and surrounds. And maybe a few gifts in Ireland, if I managed to make it there this trip. My plans were not yet finalised, and I still had to purchase my ticket to go home. I really liked the Irish Lidl stores and the Irish book shops. The airports would be my last resort. Way too expensive, and too little choice.

I was pleased that I had managed to get seven shopping bags worth of presents on the first full day of shopping. I don't think Alice and Patrick really understood how many people back home were counting on a present.

"Do you really think people deserve these presents?" (It was her way of saying that she couldn't be bothered lugging all the bags back to the car, especially when she was acquainted with some of the recipients back home in Australia and knew them to be ungrateful wretches at the best of times)

"No idea." This was my new overused phrase of the week to rival Patrick's 'Could do'.

We had reached the car and Patrick set about neatly loading the parcels in the boot of the Jag. Alice soon forgot about her grievances with me regarding the presents, and she began telling me a story about a deaf student she visits, and how the little girl got up to all manner of mischief. Alice was at her happiest when she was talking about her job and her students, and Patrick and I were happy because Alice was happy. We had a happy, windy trip home.

That evening we again dined in, and the evening, though pleasant and comfortable, was not nearly as eventful as the morning had been. My jet lag was officially over, and I conformed by waiting till it seemed like a suitable hour to retire. By nine thirty I was done in. "I'm off to bed. Goodnight all."

The dogs barked, and Alice and Patrick both nodded. It had been an action-packed day.

# Chapter 10
## New Forest (or Is It the Old Forest?)

We were all up early the next morning. Alice and Patrick because they had someone coming to look at the blinds in the loungeroom, and me – because I was off on a bus tour of the New Forest, and according to Alice, the bus left from the cliff top at 9 am. I dressed in much the same fashion as yesterday, only this morning I included a colourful scarf, as Alice had mentioned it was an open roofed bus, and that the views were best from the top of the bus. I was very excited this morning, as I thought the New Forest was just beautiful, and I wanted to get some eye-catching pictures to post on my face book page. When I had been researching the New Forest, Hampshire England, I was pleased to find out the most frequently asked question on Trip Advisor had been. "Will I see animals and water?" The very same question which had been plaguing me, and the answer I was about to uncover in the next few hours. I double-checked that I had everything I might possibly need for the day. My instructions from Alice were to buy myself a sandwich at the lunchtime stop, and not to drink too much, as the designated rest stops were few and far between. I was cashed up, courtesy of the auto-bank in Lymington yesterday, and I was taking a twenty-pound note with me, which I had hidden in my money pouch around my waist – just in case. I knew I wasn't in a high-risk mugging country, but I was venturing off the beaten track, and one never could tell these days.

I left the house in high spirits.

Someone was waving at me from the top of the cliff road. I thought it might be either Daniel or Ian, but it was neither of those two. It wasn't anyone I knew, and when I reached the cliff top road, the person just looked at me, and then beyond me. It was a young boy – younger than either Ian or even Daniel and as I got closer and closer to him, he shrieked out in a high G, "Holly, Holly!" I turned around and realised that Holly was not prickly coastal vegetation he had stumbled upon, nor a person, but a dog, a tiny black curly haired poodle, who was waddling along about ten steps behind me. I hadn't even realised that she had been there all the time. Or maybe she had just started following me? Some people say that when you have a little dog following you around, it is the soul of a lost spirit on its way to heaven, but still within the stratosphere of the earth. I say it was just a dog following me.

I walked quickly past the young boy and looked around for the bus stop which Alice had impressed upon me, would be on the Cliff Road. No bus stop to be seen, and the bus was due in ten minutes.

"Excuse me, but are you a local?"

I had doubled back to ask the boy, who had been gratefully reunited with Holly, and was rocking her backwards and forwards and repeating her name. What was it with England and dogs?

"No. I'm not a local, but I've been here for three weeks on holidays. Does that count?"

I wasn't sure if that counted or not. That would depend on his knowledge of geography and the positioning of the bus stop.

"I am looking for the bus stop. I want to catch the bus that does the day tour of the New Forest, and my friends told me that the bus stop was up on this road."

"Yes. It is. But it's at the other end of this road. Are you a fast walker?"

I was fast enough, if I had all day to run and rest alternatively. As I was more of a tortoise than a hare, I knew that I was not going to be fast enough to sprint to the end of this long flat road to the intended bus stop. Where was Daniel and his red Maserati in your hour of need? Where was Jonathan Thompson in his rusted-up Fiat? Where was Ian with his lanky gait? My chances of wearing my colourful scarf today were starting to fade.

I made it to the bus stop just as a big red open-top bus pulled up. I was panting so much that a smartly attired lady, complete with black leather driving gloves, offered to help me up the inside stairs to the driver's window. I managed to gasp and wheeze back at her that I was OK, that it was just that I was so unfit. She looked at me in a concerned way.

"Are you in training for anything, my dear?"

"Not really. Could be." That little phrase was coming in darn handy these days. I wasn't entirely satisfied with the phrase though, as it tended to sound dismissive when I said it, whereas when Patrick said spoke, it just meant 'end of story'. It was another thing for me to practise before I went to bed tonight – that 'could be' phrase. The gloved woman had moved forwards into the body of the bus, hot on the heels of another woman. (Hopefully the gloves were not going to be used for an ulterior motive.) My presumption, mainly from their body language was that they knew each other. When I poked my head around the corner of the newly polished (and still wet) spiral steel stairs which had led up to the top deck, they were the only two people up there, and they were sitting next to each other squashed up in the smallish yellow and blue vinyl seats. Everything in Barton was blue and yellow! I smiled at both of them.

"Made it! I didn't think I would!" The helpful well-heeled lady smiled back, but the companion just scowled and turned her face to the side of the bus. Being thick skinned, I dismissed her rebuff, and plonked myself down opposite the smiler, eager to talk about where the bus was headed for today, and to gain her opinion on the sort of a day we could expect-weather-wise. She was a skilled conversationalist, and we chatted on about the intriguing Barton coastline for the first ten minutes or so of the bumpy journey up and down unmade country roads. The woman informed me that she'd come down from London to buy a cottage with a veggie patch and retire by the sea, after a lengthy career as a head teacher in East London. She had always wanted to go back to the seaside, having been farmed out as a child to stay with a country family during the dark days of the Second World War.

"What do you do most days, now that you've retired?" I wanted to build up a picture of retirement living, and how I would occupy my days when the time came for me. (I was planning on the time to just 'come over me' when I returned from my trip, not that I had let anyone else in on my little secret.)

"Oh, bits of this and that. Long walks, swimming in the summer, gardening, and more gardening."

Her alluding to gardening was the perfect segway for me to prattle on about my own association with gardening as a passionate past time. In Melbourne, we have a holiday home by the sea, which has the most amazing garden. Our seaside abode is not all that far from the big smoke of Melbourne (by Australian standards of distance), so it is possible to drive down most weekends in summer on a Friday evening for the weekend. The back garden is terraced and designed to supply house guests (and ourselves) with seasonal organic produce when in residence. It was a great deal of work, and required relentless commitment to watering in the long, harsh Australian summer, but so worth it, that it was easily the best feature of the beach house. Joanna (the smiling lady) was very interested in our Australian beach garden and our punishing climate. She enlightened me that England was entirely different in climate and soil, and that it was so much easier to grow cold climate veggies than to grow vegetables which thrived on warmer conditions. I thought this to be stating the bleedin' obvious, but I kept silent. The friend had no such tact.

"That's not always true though Joanna, is it?" She must have been listening to our conversation all the time, even though her head had been turned in the opposite direction.

"I find it to be pot luck when and where the vegetables will grow, not so much seasonal, but more providential." She turned away from both of us again as she delivered this uppity pontification, and just as she did so, the scarf that she had twirled so sophisticatedly around her head was whipped off by a low-lying passing tree-branch. The bus continued on its bumpy merry way, and the multi coloured silk scarf was abruptly left behind, flapping in the breeze-free at last. Joanna's friend was aghast, as her hair was suddenly so wind-blown that it would not stay down, no matter how much smoothing and patting she did.

"Not to worry, Elizabeth," Joanna pacified. "You will be able to pick it up again on the way back, we will just have to be ready for it."

Elizabeth did not look convinced, and promptly turned her head away from both of us again. She was a bundle of misery for the rest of the trip, and no matter how much Joanna tried to include her in our conversation, she refused to open her mouth. She just kept muttering to herself, "I loved that scarf!"

There was a bit of commotion going on outside the bus, and we seemed to have been stationary for quite a few minutes. Maybe someone else had lost an item of clothing or headgear, and the driver was deliberating whether or not to turn back and retrieve the lost items? No, such luck, as it would have cheered Elizabeth up no end. We had only stopped to pick up some new passengers, and they were being very slow about getting on the bus. A fifties-something lady in hot pink shorts, a white lacey low-cut ruffled shirt, over tanned to the point of leathery skin, and open Roman sandals was pacing the pavement between the bus and the motorway in an effort to relocate her lost husband. (At least she was calling out some man's name at the top of her lungs. "Where the bleedin ell r ya," to quote her verbatim.) When a scruffy looking gentleman around the same age as her finally appeared, she dragged him by the scruff of his neck onto the bus, with him protesting loudly that he: "Dinna wanna see va New Forest, he hadn't even seen ve old forest, and did she av anee 'paracetermoel' for his fumpin head?"

"No, I avent." Hot pink pants hissed back loudly at him, "Now get on ve bus yer git and belt up. Everyone's looking at ya."

I will admit that I did sneak a look at him when he finally stumbled up the winding stairs leading to the top of the bus where the three of us were seated. But it was only a cursory glance, and I didn't like what I saw in that momentary second sighting. The wife had been entirely correct. He was a prize git! Unshaven, dishevelled, and badly dressed, he looked as though he had spent the past week in a crammed lift party. I was relieved when they settled themselves on the last seat of the bus. They were four rows behind me, and I relished the space and distance between us. Apart from the occasional exclamation from the excited wife, when we hurtled through a particularly pretty village, they were mostly silent. (He was probably asleep) The poor woman must not have got out much, if trees and houses in a village excited her.

Brochures can be totally misleading. The glossy pamphlet I had picked up in Lidl the other day had promised a leisurely sightseeing tour in an open aired bus, and a leisurely amble around the New Forest. There was to be a scheduled ablutions and lunch stop at an old seventeenth century pub, and the guarantee to be back at the Tourist bureau pick up spot by 5 o'clock. The brochure might well have been penned by Nostradamus himself, as not even one of these prophesies came true. What did eventuate was a hair-raising hurtling through village after village with the bus driver/guide blurting out joke after joke about the countryside, punctuated by lengthy intervals of silence, whilst he waited for a collective laughter response from the hostage passengers. He did not give up with the jokes until we were all laughing. We had to feign copious amounts of laughter in the end because some of us, myself included, managed to work out that he wasn't going to stop until we did.

Although the pub had been old and authentically English, it had not been a great stop-over, as it suddenly started pouring rain, and when we got to the bathrooms, there was no flowing water as there was something amiss with the plumbing. Those of us who wanted to use the ablutions were forced to resort to the pre-automatic flushing days of filling up buckets from the little well around the corner from the block and hurling the murky water into the toilet bowl from a great height. One lady was exceptionally tall and thin, so she was allocated the job of throwing the water into the bowls. She was exceptional in her field and might well have been an Olympic shot-put champion. Unfortunately, she spoke not a word of English, and another lady who kept telling us she was fluent in French offered to translate for the shot-put champion.

"Dans l'eau. Dans l'eua," was all she kept repeating to the tall French woman, and the woman just stared back at her as if she had not a clue in the world what the woman was talking about. To me it sounded like the woman was saying 'down low', meaning to throw the water down low. I also thought that the woman wasn't speaking French at all, but English with a Devon accent. At that point, Joanna-the retired head teacher well experienced in a number of English dialects chipped in with the best possible solution.

"She's telling her to actually get in the water, and the French lady thinks she's telling her to jump in the well to fetch the water." I should have been able to help more, as I had studied French at school, and I was racking my brain to try and remember the French phrase for 'just keep throwing the water into the bowl at regular intervals'. The problem was I just couldn't remember the words for throw, bowl, just, or keep. To be frank, I couldn't remember any of the words in the phrase at all. Everyone had a go at miming the required action, and finally it was the scarf-less Elizabeth who got through to the French woman that it was not really necessary to throw the water from such a great height, and that we were all grateful to her for helping out. Elizabeth conveyed the gist of the message by whispering in the French lady's ear. This worked a trick, because the French woman worked twice as hard and twice as fast at throwing the water from the more economical waist height, once Elizabeth had finished her long whisperings. I decided that I would now think of Elizabeth as the 'well whisperer' instead of the scarf-less grouch. For our part, we all chipped in, by forming a Congo line from the well to the toilets and passing the one bucket we had been allocated backwards and forwards up and down the line. I tried to see what the men were doing, but there were none of them to be seen, so I supposed they must have come up with a different idea for flushing. (I wasn't going there.) The publican must also have had trouble with the electricity, as our quiches were stone-cold. All in all, not a pub for which you would be likely to write a favourable review without a great wad of notes being involved.

But it was quaint, cute and flower filled, and they could have just been having a bad day. The rain wasn't helping, as everyone was complaining of the damp and the cold, and the dining room was freezing. The publican could not have been more apologetic. "Never 'appened before like vis. No water and no electricity. I wonder if Julia forgot to pay the bills before she took 'erself off to er muvers last week?" He looked puzzled and slightly embarrassed by the predicament which was unfolding. Husband of hot-pink-shorts saved face at last by coming up with the most sensible, logical suggestion of the day.

"Ow about we all get back onta ve bus end ead ome?" Bravo sonny Jim. Best idea yet. We were a motley crew by now. Wet, hungry and tired. The bus driver had stayed on the bus with his own packed lunch whilst all the drama had been unfolding, so he was the only one amongst us in fine spirits on the journey back to Barton.

On the way home, it poured cats and dogs, and we were all forced to squash up in the slightly drier downstairs section of the bus. Sensing the collective mood of doom and disappointment, the driver had given up on his jokes and had turned his microphone off. Because he wasn't commenting on the landscape or the flora or fauna, I had no idea what I was photographing with my minuscule iPhone. The unusual flat, low, forested landscape cheered me up almost as soon as we left the pub. I forgot about my dampness and hunger pangs and concentrated instead on capturing great pictures of this terrain. I really missed my old Leica camera, big and cumbersome and heavy to lug around yes, but at least I could count on crystal clarity from the pictures. I just didn't have the same degree of confidence in this tiny appendage. I could not, therefore be blamed for securing a shot of some amorphous looking animals of the New Forest drinking at the distant smallish lake and tagging the pic with the comment. 'Cattle and bison of the New Forest drinking at their lake.' Alice, however, could be blamed for her shaming and exposing of my ignorance by replying to my comment, "Fil, they are ponies! There are no cattle and bison in the New Forest."

Oh yes. And double demerit points for Alice as well, because she might well have just come into the next room and told me in a quiet, helpful, sympathetic voice that there were only ponies in the New Forest. She did not need to announce my misunderstandings to the whole world. The only other photograph of extreme interest to me was the one I took of a deserted treeless field, with only an old battered paint-peeled caravan left half-falling down, smack bang in the middle of it. I had with me, a guide book which had a short reference to the New Forest, and although I had missed the bit about the ponies, I had read an interesting snippet about how the Romani gypsies had populated these very fields since the early Sixteenth Century, but that in the last twenty years the local councils were permanently moving them on. They would often just leave a solitary caravan in the middle of a field as a legacy. These nomadic people earned the name travellers, because they would travel around the country leading a very nomadic existence. In Australia we have a similar situation with the aboriginal people (also historically nomadic.) Outside Parliament House in Canberra – the Capital city (yes, my birthplace) a colourful (if not faded) aboriginal tent city has been standing proudly for the last forty years. Less than five hundred years to go for the Ngunnawal people if the English travellers were a valid benchmark. Considering the Australian aboriginal people have inhabited Australia for the past sixty-five thousand years; that paltry amount of time should fly for them.

The rest of the afternoon flew by in a whirlwind of muddy ditches and lanes and tiny thatched-roofed cottage hamlets with only a few scattered houses, more even muddier ditches, more open fields and many more hedgerows. We finally pulled into the Tourist Bureau designated set down spot, at around ten minutes ahead of schedule. The driver didn't bother to turn his microphone back on. He just let himself out of his little encaged driving area, and waded into the wet aisle, thanking us all for having taken the tour today, and that on behalf of the company, he hoped that we had all enjoyed ourselves, and that he would see us all again soon. He then added that he would be driving the bus back to the depot via the Cliff road, and that if anyone wanted a lift back closer to their home to save them getting soaked, he would be happy to do so-just to raise their hand. No one except me did so. I think they must have mostly been tourist staying in hotels, and that they were going to take in the shops which were still open. The two women who had been sitting with me on the first part of the journey waved me goodbye, as I hadn't been able to position myself near them on the rainy return journey. Elizabeth (well-whisperer) still wasn't wearing her silk scarf, so she must have missed the chance to whip upstairs to retrieve it when we had passed the spot some twenty minutes before hand. I wondered if they were off to buy her a new scarf in 'Bradbeers'. Probably.

Once everybody was safely off the slippery bus, I made my way up to the driver to slip him a one-pound tip (my usual tipping note), and then I stayed standing there chatting whilst he backed the bus out of the Tourist Bureau. 'Don't bite off the hand that will feed you' was an old Irish saying that my grandmother had repeated on numerous occasions to my mother, and my mother had impressed this upon us as we were growing up. It was a good thing to know, because it got you to a lot of places you might have had to walk to, had you not buttered up a bus driver here and there.

"Where da ya wanna be dropped off?" Either he still had his earplugs in, or he was choosing to ignore my conversation of the last few minutes. I had just told him where!

"Oh, anywhere half way up the road will do, thanks." He winked at me. Now that he was in no hurry to complete the tour circuit, the driver manoeuvred the bus slowly along the muddy road and embraced the opportunity to prattle on endlessly about his twin passions – Archaeology and Palaeontology.

"I was born in Barton and I'll die in Barton. I'm happy here with me ma. She packs me a cracking lunch every day, and every weekend I take her for a drive in me battered old Hillman. Loves it she does. Can't get enough of it. We got a good arrangement. She leaves me alone, and I leave her alone. We live just up there." He indicated up a side street which ran erratically towards the beach. It was an expensive Barton side-street, so I could only assume that 'ma' had money.

"Me ma used to know a lady called 'Mary Anning' when I was a young un, and me, ma and Mary used to go beach roaming looking for dinosaur bones and other stuff." I was fascinated with the depth of his knowledge and passion for the place where he had been born and raised. I suggested that he might try and weave some of his archaeological experiences into his planned microphone talk. I didn't wish to offend him by suggesting that his jokes were somewhat tired and lame, and that tourists would probably be far happier with a dinosaur hunt from the windows of the bus, before turning inland to the New Forest.

"I would do that if I could afford to work for meself. What I'd really like to do would be to start up me own mini bus tour of this coastline, and then I could entertain the tourists with both me jokes and the history of the area. Do you think people would pay money to listen to my guided talks?" I wanted to remind him that I had just paid twenty-five pounds to listen to him cracking jokes without much mention at all about the history of the places around Barton, but it would just have hurt his feelings.

"Here's my corner. Anywhere here will be good." True to his word, he brought the bus to an abrupt halt, and hastily activated the heavy doors so that I could alight safely. Not that there were any cars or any other living souls in sight in the sodden, deserted lane. It had gone six by now, and most people were either cooking tea or tucked up in bed for the night-depending on their age and state of health.

As he closed the doors the driver called out to me, "Maybe I'll see you next time you come to Barton, and by then I might have my archaeological tours up and running." I was close enough to read his name, Perry. "Thanks Perry, I'll look out for you next time."

When I arrived back at the house, Alice was out in the garden in the drizzle and an old plastic green raincoat, doing some paperwork for a new five months old baby, who would be starting in the deaf unit in September. It must have rained heavily in Barton as well that afternoon, as the grass was soaking wet and I could see that the garden umbrella was still dripping slowly. In England and in Ireland, the school term began in Autumn at the beginning of September. Next month, it would be a lot quieter in Barton, as the children would have all gone back to school and the shop-keepers in the newsagents, toy shops and lolly shops could all breathe a huge sigh of relief. Their profits would probably go down, but so to would their blood pressure.

Alice looked up when I closed the gate behind me, and she called out encouragingly. "Did you enjoy yourself Fil?"

"It was beautiful. I had the best time." It was true, I had enjoyed the day immensely. Tomorrow would be fine and warm according to the weather forecast, and I decided that I would get up early again and do the beach before anyone else stirred.

"I think I'll just get myself something to eat and head upstairs for an early night."

"Good idea. Sleep well. I'll check in on you later."

As I passed Patrick he looked up and uttered in a low deadpan voice. "You had a gentleman caller. A different one this time."

"Who was it?"

I was racking my brain trying to think of whom it might be, other than Ian.

"He said his name was Maurice, and he was on a bicycle. Said he got the address from Ian, and that you had left your sunglasses at his place the other morning. How many of these old gentlemen do you actually know?"

I couldn't tell from his voice if he was humouring me or if he was being serious – implying that I was bringing questionable doubt to the community as to why there would be so many gentleman callers at number nine.

"I think I know about six by now, but one of them is quite young. That's Daniel, but he has a sports car, not a bike."

"No, it was defiantly Maurice, because he said that he was the one who had the fall the other day, and that it hurt to peddle up hill."

"Oh, OK, thanks Patrick." I was just going to dismiss the whole thing. It was good of Maurice to bring back my sunglasses. (which I had decided that I'd lost on the beach somewhere)

"I'm glad Maurice is OK and that he's back on his bike. Did you say to him, 'On yer' bike now' when he was going back home?" (I had been practising saying that before I left Australia, in case I met someone on a bike when I was travelling.)

"No." Patrick had turned back to his weeding. "He was going to push it up the hill, so I couldn't very well say that, could I?"

"I guess not. Thanks Pat, I'll be up in my room if you need me. I have some important business to attend to." Patrick just nodded. He was well used to the secret women's business that needed attending to.

I had it in my mind to do a search of the Barton coastline, as both Ian and Perry had confirmed that there had been much fossilisation going on for centuries around these parts. I tried to remember the name of the lady that Perry and his mother had been fossil hunting with in his younger days. It probably would have been at least sixty years ago, judging by the look of Perry's well-worn face, and his totally grey hair. I remembered it was 'Mary' someone, but when I finally found a reference to a Mary who may have been hunting fossils, I was very surprised to discover that there really was a famous fossil hunter, and that her discoveries were now safely ensconced in the British museum in London. Her name was Mary Anning, and she was born in 1799. If she was the same lady that Perry and his mother had partnered, that would have made her around one hundred and fifty when they were fossil hunting. She must have been well fit. Dreaming of longevity, crumbling cliffs and dinosaurs, I fell asleep.

# Chapter 11
## Fish 'n' Chips Night

"Do you have fish and chips back home in Australia on a Friday night?" Ian wanted to know all about what we did back home. He had been to Australia only the once, and that was just for one night when one of the cruise ships on which he was working had docked in Sydney Harbour.

"We do, most of the time, as there are more Greeks in Australia than in Greece itself, but customs have changed over the last few years. Now people tend to vary their Friday night indulgences, as there is such a variety of cuisines from other countries to choose from. Sometimes we just order online, but no one has yet cottoned on to the fact that there is a market for fish and chips online."

"We have them either Friday or Saturday nights over here, and the fish and chip shops are packed from 6.30 pm."

I heard him, but it wasn't really registering, and tonight seemed a long way away. Besides which, Patrick had already volunteered to go and collect the fish and chips, and Alice and I had already placed our orders. (and those of the dogs.) Once we had finished discussing our dietary requirements for the evening, Ian and I continued our early morning walk in silence, interrupted only by a distant symphony of squawking gulls and squealing children. It seemed very early for children, but I knew the drill from back home. One parent returned to work in the big smoke to earn enough to pay for the week's holiday at the seaside. The remaining parent would therefore be responsible for child-minding from Monday to Friday. Today being Friday, would be the last day of hard labour for some exhausted parents. Ian was quite a fast walker and I was slipping behind. I decided that I needed a rest and flopped down on the sand. Ian and Lucy ploughed on, as if they were daily competitors in the hundred-mile beach walk to be completed mid-morning. Whilst I was sitting on the sand, I noticed a biggish clump of shells a bit further along in the sand, partially hidden by driftwood. I was reminded of my younger days when I would comb the beaches for shells, and triumphantly lug them home, clean them thoroughly with soapy water, and then paint them in beach colours. To finish off, I would thread them onto a piece of string and parade around the house with my newly painted necklace. I wondered if there were any shells worth collecting and taking back to Australia as a memento of Barton beach-fossils and shells. I quickly googled Barton beach to see if it would be possible and ethical for me to take shells and fossils back to Australia. Although google informed me in a dead-pan voice that the sea-beds at Barton on Sea were highly fossiliferous, there was no mention of whether or not shells and fragments of fossil could be taken out of the country. I decided to wait and ask Ian, as I had once brought a basket of fruit into customs at Singapore airport, and had almost ended up in Changi Prison for my trouble. I always brought plastic fruit home to Australia after that incident. (for the adults as well as the children)

After our walk, Ian invited me back to have a look at his home, as he knew from my conversations that I was very interested in architecture and houses. We arrived at his cottage around eight thirty, but Ian's wife had already left for work, and I doubted that Ian would want to show me around the house by himself. I was wrong.

"Hilary's already left for work, but we can still have a tour of the house if you like."

You know when you really want something one minute, and the next minute you don't want it anymore? That was me that morning. I think I had just been carried away with the notion of a house directly opposite the sea with a pretty garden and a million-dollar view. It wasn't really Ian's house that I wanted to see, but any house on any beach that had so much to offer. Ian had ushered me into the sunny porch before I had time to say that I would come another time when Hilary would be home.

"Does she work Saturdays?"

"Who?"

"Hilary, does she work on Saturday – tomorrow?"

"No, she doesn't work on Saturdays, but she will be busy tomorrow mowing the lawn, so you might as well come in now and I'll show you around." I was a rat in a trap, so I followed Ian into the living room. It certainly was a spectacular view, and we were at street level. I could only imagine what sorts of views the apartments behind Ian and Jean and Maurice's homes enjoyed.

Ian was bustling around from room to room, pointing out little artefacts which he had picked up over the years when the cruise ships had docked, and adding a little anecdote to each treasured item. I realised that at the rate he was talking, and the amount of buried treasure in the rooms, we would be there for some time, so I lured him into the back sunroom, where he had told me Hilary had set up her little hobby business of scrapbooking and card marking. Unaware of my ploy, Ian was happy to be lured, as that gave him the opportunity to embark on a long and technical monologue about the state-of-the art card making press they had set up in the room, and how it was very expensive and very unique.

"Cost us over five 'undred quid that did! It'll take at least ten years to recoup the money in the cards Hilary sells."

Both walls in the room were lined with brightly painted bookshelves, and the colourful shelves were crammed full of cards. There looked to be well over a thousand cards (If my estimation skills were up to scratch.) I doubted that that the recuperation would be as soon as a decade (more like a century), but I said nothing to Ian. I just nodded and smiled back at him. The whole guided house-tour took well over an hour, and I was tired by the time I left Ian. I promised to get back up to the beach early on Sunday morning, which was the day of our leaving Barton and heading back to London. Ian was placated with the intended arrangement, and I went on my merry way back to the cottage where Alice and Patrick had led me to believe they would be 'pottering around'.

They were almost pottering. Patrick was in the garden with a wide brimmed sunhat weeding, and Alice was on the terrace also weeding, except she was 'reading' and pretending to be weeding. She had a row of little cottage pots in front of her on the outside table, and she also had a cookbook next to the pots, which she was intently studying. So, she was actually weeding and reading simultaneously. Patrick looked up as I arrived. He asked me how Ian had been.

"Good. He was good. He gave me a tour of his home." Patrick smiled, shook his head and kept on weeding. Alice just called out. "Lunch is cold meats and salad. Would you like me to do you a boiled egg?"

I said that I'd organise lunch, which I did, and the rest of the day passed quite quickly after lunch, with Alice doing paper work, Patrick reading and me rearranging my suitcase. That was one of my favourite pastimes when I was on holidays. Arranging and re arranging my suitcase. I could spend hours engrossed in the task. Three hours later I emerged from my bedroom and I asked Patrick if he was going to get the fish and chips soon, and if so, might I accompany him, as I'd like to see a real English seaside fish and chip shop.

"They are just the same as Australian fish and chip shops, Fil. What do you think will be different in the shop?" Alice couldn't really understand why I wanted to go and line up in a fish and chip shop for an hour when I could have been curled up on my bed with the sunshine and a good book.

"I dunno. I just like to see the differences in the shops. No real reason."

Alice had turned back to her paperwork and texting as soon as she'd chastised me, so Patrick and I made our getaway. We left the dogs to keep Alice company. I was probably in their bad books as Patrick told me they usually went with him on a Friday evening to pick up the fish and chips. I made sure I fussed over both of them before we left, assuring them that we would be back soon with their din-dins.

The Fish and Chip shop was about ten minutes by car. When we got inside, it was still early enough for us to be the only people in the shop. While we were waiting for our order, a group of young girls, about 16 years old, tottered in, tumbling over themselves, giggling, laughing and whistling at the two young lads in blue and white striped aprons and funny little white hats behind the counter who were serving the fish and chips.

"Cor blimey, go won en order Susan, you know what ta ask fer." The other three girls were giggling away and urging Susan to put in their order to one of the boys behind the counter. Susan stopped tittering and lunged forwards. As she did so, she accidently fell into Patrick, and he stepped backwards to get out of her way. Susan quickly regained her balance, but this unexpected disturbance sent the pack of girls into new fits of laughter. Susan wasn't laughing. She looked embarrassed, and she looked away from Patrick straight at me.

"I'm sorry missus. I didn't mean to trip im. We wasn't laufun at you n'all. Just laufun cause weez 'appy ta be out like."

I couldn't really understand what she was saying, and the other girls' shrieking and squealing didn't help. I considered whether they might have been drinking but it was still only six in the evening, and they were all dressed up to the hilt in what looked like readiness for a night on the town. They were probably going to the night club where that Mr Essex was the bouncer. (I couldn't remember his name-lived above Jean and Ronald) The skirts were short and colourful and the platform cork shoes were so high that even tottering looked to be a challenge. They were all identically dressed, and only the hairstyles gave them a sense of individuality. What I noticed most though, was the amount of caked-on makeup and mascara. That made me smile, and I felt a certain warmth and fondness towards the girls as I remembered going out on the town in my youth, thinking I looked gorgeous, but really looking like an expanded rainbow fish with too much makeup. The brashness and abandonment of the youth was certainly alive and well in Barton on Sea.

    Susan finally summoned up the courage to ask one of the aproned boys for five pounds of chips, and he was gracious (or used to it) enough not to question her order, nor ask if they wanted some fish with the chips. They probably could have done with some fish as the pack of them were so skinny you could see xylophones of bones, but they also probably couldn't afford fish – which I noticed was much more expensive here than in Australia. There were the typically sea themed yellow and blue booths in the shop, and as the girls had only ordered chips, their order was ready before ours, so they all squashed into a booth and Susan spread the bundle of chips out on the table. I was astonished at how many chips you could get for five pounds. They were steaming hot and very yellow and fat. They looked like really good chips! The girls tucked in ravenously, stuffing their mouths with chips and more chips. The aftermath squealing and shrieking seemed to be twice as loud as it had been before the skinny-minnies had been fuelled with the fat. It may have been duck fat that they used in the seaside fish and chip shops, because they girls were totally hyped up! Patrick looked relieved when the smaller aproned boy handed us our order. I was quite OK with all this silly behaviour, but it seemed to embarrass Patrick. Or maybe it was just because he was so reserved, and they were so female, and so loud. Still, it was a bit of entertainment in the quiet Friday night shop. That was one difference I could report back to Alice when we got home. The fish and chip shops in Australia on a Friday evening are chockers with people. Noisy and squashy. You can wait one hour in the city, and up to two hours at the beach in the height of summer. There is the opportunity to phone in your order, but you still might have to wait. The other difference was the price of the fish and chips. Way more expensive in England, and it was the smaller island. It didn't make sense.

    Alice had set the trays out for us when we arrived home, and the dogs were settled in front of their own separate trays and dog-bowls. We took up our designated positions on the sofa for the English quiz show Alice and Patrick were in the habit of watching on a Friday evening. I was beginning to feel more and more like a resident of the 'Sunny Vale Retirement home'. The giggling girls this evening had made me feel my age, and I wondered if by now, they would be at the nightclub bopping away and throwing down the shots. This way of spending one's evening, often in a drunken stupor, was referred to as clubbing, but I find this word to be ambiguous. Clubbing to me was more likely to mean going out to a club for a session of bingo, or chess, painting or flower pressing. Taken to the extreme, it could have meant boxing or fencing or extreme physical activity which may have involved contact. (clubbing in the sense of clobbering.) Life changes!

After we'd stacked the dishwasher, I made my excuses and crawled up to bed. I had no idea why, but I was again, totally devoid of energy. I lay in my bed above the lounge room and listened to the muffled voices of Alice and Patrick and the television. Then I abruptly fell asleep.

# Chapter 12
## "Walkies"

Today was the day we were off on an adventure – the three amigos on safari. We had decided over the fish and chips the previous evening, and in between my retelling and embellishing of the 'Fish and Chip shop chronicles', that we would go for an energetic walk in the New Forest, and then for a farewell lunch at one of the New Forest Pubs. We had originally planned to venture out for dinner in the evening, but we decided that we would get more out of a lunch, as none of us really relished the thought of being out late on a Saturday night. When I stumbled downstairs, bleary-eyed to make my usual liquid breakfast – elixir of a cup of strong black coffee, Alice was already in the kitchen, and Patrick called out good morning as I passed him in his library beneath the stairs. He had his head buried deep in a history book, and it was becoming a very natural look with him. I have a Pinterest board which I add to most days. By far my most popular board, with the greatest number of followers, is the one I've entitled "Reading poses young and old". Patrick's pose this morning was one I had pinned many a time, but none of them were exactly the same, and none of them were Patrick. I raced back upstairs to retrieve my phone.

"Patrick, may I please snap you in your reading pose for my Pinterest board?"
"I've heard of a Pinterest board. Is it similar to a 'Most Wanted' poster?"

I chuckled a little at his joke and coaxed him into posing again. That night, I received fifty likes for the pin. Patrick may have been on the right track with his 'Most Wanted' joke. I was thinking about the people I'd seen reading whist I'd been up at the beach café, and how authentically beachy their natural poses would be for my boards, when Alice interrupted my thoughts.

"10 o'clock take off suit you Fil?"
"Yes. Fine. Can't wait."

I'm not very vocal at all in the mornings. Still half asleep most of the time, and it takes me a while to warm up. After my second cup of coffee, I was ready for a long, hot shower and an opportunity to assemble my backpack. Not that we were going on a long trek, but the old Boy Scouts motto 'Be prepared' kept popping into my head. I just had this feeling that we might need bandages at some stage today.

"Do you think we should bring our raincoats?"

Alice peered out the kitchen window and agreed that it might be a good thought to bring our rain jackets and umbrellas with us, just in case. There was some leftover fruitcake from Lidl in the fridge, so I got it out and popped it onto the table so that I'd remember to put it into my backpack when I carried it downstairs later. Then I filled up my water bottle and took to the stairs two at a time. That is something I have noticed a lot of people doing when they think that no one is around. That, and dancing around their houses and singing their favourite songs at the top of their voices. (Sometimes scantily dressed) I thought I'd make a list when I had time, of all the things people do when they think they are alone.

We were all ready by 10 o'clock, and when I got back downstairs, the others were both at the front door talking to a lady I didn't know. As I tried to sneak past, Alice spotted me and spun around in a perfect pirouette. "Oh Fil, this is Isla from next door. We were just organising for her and Jack to come in this afternoon for 'afternoon tea'. Will you be around?"

I smiled at Isla and wondered if Jack was a husband or a dog. Everyone around Barton seemed to have dogs, and I had seen a few roaming the court where our holiday cottage was situated.

"Lovely to meet you Isla. Yes, great. I would love to be part of the afternoon tea. Thankyou. I'll look forward to seeing you this afternoon." Patrick took the opportunity whilst I was speaking to slip away unnoticed, and Alice and Isla chatted on for another minute or so. It was then that we heard a bellowing voice which seemed to be coming from next door. (We were all huddled around the open front door) "Isla! Isla! Where the devil have you got to woman?" Immediate confirmation. Jack was a husband. Isla mooched off and Alice locked the front door, bolting it down like we were all off to war and wouldn't be back any time in the near future. I moved off too, in order to retrieve my water bottle and the cake from the kitchen. I could hear a horn honking impatiently outside, which probably meant that Patrick was already in the car waiting with the dogs. We were now fifteen minutes behind schedule, and Patrick would not be pleased.

"I love these windy dirt roads with the trees hanging overhead. Looks like we are back in the sixteenth century, don't you think?" She was right. It did look ancient and deserted. I was expecting there to be loads of cars and tractors on the roads and loads of tourists walking along the tracks near the roads and back-lanes on this bright sunny August morning, but we saw no one. Only ponies. (They were up close now, and quite obviously ponies)

"Do you want to try the two kilometre walk from this car park up ahead?"

Patrick was already turning into the Carpark as he asked the question so yes, we did want to try the walk.

"Is it the hill walk?"

Alice was not very fond of hills or even slight inclines when she was walking.

"I'm sure you'll be able to cope dear." Patrick was a practised walker, up hills and down dales, as he took the dogs for their morning and sometimes afternoon constitutional, rain hail or shine. I noticed with pleasure that the car park was flat, and the tracks off to the left and right were also both flat.

"Which way?"

Patrick said he didn't mind which track we took, and Alice was non-committal. I piped in quickly with "Left. Let's do the track here on the left." They both agreed. So far turning left at every possible opportunity had proved to be fortuitous. I feared for the repercussions when the time came to travel around Ireland, should I decide to go, but that was still three weeks away. I knew from past experiences that Irish street and road signs were always pointing in the wrong direction, and that it didn't really matter if you chose to turn left or you chose to turn right. You would still be hopelessly lost! (and there would be cows or sheep blocking your path)

Our path had a slight incline, but none of us were hindered by it. We trotted along in companionable silence for about five hundred metres, and the dogs were happy with the pace. I discovered that if I walked directly alongside of Patrick, I would never lag behind, as I was consciously using his personage and the length of his stride as the perfect yardstick. The dogs were also synchronised in their step. Alice sometimes lapsed in her step, but she managed to regain her position alongside of the rest of us without too much fuss. We were a regular little brigade. The walk took us past quaint tucked-away cottages with flower-filled gardens, fields stuffed with ponies and sometimes grass munching goats. The air was fresh and bracing despite the sunshine and we were all content and lost in our own thoughts. I was doing my mental appraisal of the week and trying to add up all the people I had encountered since last Sunday. It was no good though. I just couldn't get past the hectic morning when Maurice fell over. There were so many people involved in getting him back to his flat.

There was something going on up ahead. We could hear children's voices, and then a man's voice calling out for them to stop. As we came up over the incline, we could see the source of the racket. A young girl with a bright pink bicycle helmet was on the ground, and a man and woman were trying to help her up. There were two other older children a little further ahead still on their bikes. And of course, there was a dog. The dog was yapping loudly and fussing over the little girl even more than the adults. Looby and Holly immediately raced ahead to support the dog in his/her yapping and yelping. The little girl started screaming as our two dogs came bounding towards her, and Alice called out in her most reassuring teacher voice, "It's fine sweetie, they won't hurt you. They just want to help." David Essex had it so right when he huskily sang "Oh what a circus" in Evita on the London stage every night in the late seventies. This was some circus in the middle of the New Forest. We just needed a smattering of musicians with lutes and fifes and Puck himself to jump in from off stage left and exclaim loudly, "But you have just slumbered here whilst these visions do appear."

I was daydreaming again. Alice was tugging at my sleeve. "Fil, you're a nurse. Aren't you going to do anything?"

"It's alright, I'm her father and I'm also a doctor. I can handle it thanks." The doctor was polite but firm, and he was flexing the little girl's leg gently whilst he tried to coax her to stand up with his spare arm. The wife did nothing. Utterly useless. Patrick had manoeuvred the dogs away from the scene and called out to us that he would keep on walking. Being Patrick, he would have had the beloved dogs in mind – not wanting them to be in the way in the little clearing where we were all congregated. Alice and I hung around for a few minutes, and in that time the little girl managed to stand up. Her bike looked a bit worse for wear, but we could see that she was OK. Probably just shocked. The stunned silent mother had gone on ahead to look for the wayward brothers. The doctor turned to us. "Thanks for stopping. Enjoy the rest of your walk." A man of few words yet again! We left the doctor and his daughter there and kept walking straight ahead.

Patrick was waiting up near the next clearing, and we all collapsed on a rickety old thatch bench which just happened to be there.

"Well, that was exciting. How about some cake?" I knew that exciting was not the entirely correct word to use for what had just happened, but I was struggling to find the right word. Things changed a bit after the incident in the clearing. We kept walking, but it was starting to rain, and our moods were now more sombre. After about ten minutes of walking in the rain, Patrick suggested that we turn around, pack it in, and head back to the car.

"The rain is so pesky, and it looks like we are in for an afternoon of it."

It was still a little early for lunch, but we could sit outside in the courtyard (he assumed there would be a courtyard) if it stopped raining and have a drink. Alice and I both agreed enthusiastically. Back at the car Patrick and Alice changed from their walking boots into more casual shoes. I was still wearing my versatile sketchers, and Alice remarked on their shape and design. "They are so comfortable Alice, you should get some for when you go for those long walks on the beach."

She was in agreement, and we decided that when we got back to London we would go 'Sketchers hunting' in Kingston upon Thames – near where they lived in London. I was glad that Alice had praised my shoes. I had purchased them especially for the trip, and I intended to get as much wear out of them as possible in my time away. I didn't bring any other shoes with me, unless you counted the jiffies I wore on the plane. I just supposed that I would buy some going-out shoes when the time came to go out. So far it hadn't mattered, as we hadn't really gone out anywhere fancy. As a tourist you could get away with far more blatant disregard for clothing and footwear than you could do in your native country. Unless there was a dress code or footwear rules in certain places, you could dress how you liked or in whatever attire was most comfortable. I loved that part of travelling. Before I left Australia, I googled packing tips on what constituted optimum clothing for an overseas trip. Wise people had earnestly informed me that Google and Wikipedia are not always to be trusted, and that the truth is often stretched to extremities. But, in the case of the packing tips, the advice was sound. The professional packers were those individuals who were able to 'smartly and efficiently gather up everything that needs to fit into your bag and organise it into categories'. Basically, there were tips on how to store everyday items, and how to roll your clothes up in tight balls to make more room in your suitcase. Consequently, I spent ages arranging my case and making sure my clothes were washed, clean and ready for the day's outings. I was pleased to discover that there was an app for listing and modifying clothing and travel paraphernalia. I was moving with the times. I downloaded 'Pack Point' to help 'customise pre-prepared packing lists based on weather and activity and not only that, it legitimated my inexplicable fascination for packing. It wasn't only what went inside the suitcase which enthralled me. It was the case itself, and all the various compartments as well as the different materials, sizes and weights of the cases. I also loved trunks, hat boxes, rucksacks, backpacks and duffle bags. Psychologists would have had a field day with my obsession for containers of any sort. The only two containers I was not so keen on were wooden boxes and bronze urns. But then, who was? That would have been dead boring!

When we found the car park of the pub Patrick had recommended, it was already full, which we took as a sign that the food and drinks would be good. Also, it had stopped raining, and the barely visible sun was outdoing itself to showcase the grape-laden courtyard, which I had glimpsed just beyond the carpark. Things were starting to look up for us.

"Err, I don't think so."

Patrick was frowning as he said this, and Alice echoed exactly what I was thinking.

"You don't think 'WHAT' Patrick?"

"I don't like our chances of getting a park in here."

"Well, no Patrick It's full, but there is supposed to be another unmade carpark for patrons of the pub a bit further on. I saw the sign, just keep driving slowly."

The dogs and I were all sitting up on our haunches in the back of the car, so it was easy for me to guide Patrick through the narrow farm gate and over the deep muddy puddles into the adjacent carpark. It was the complete opposite to the first one. It was completely devoid of any cars, and only an old rundown caravan stood sedately in the corner of the muddy field.

"This would have been a travellers' field not so many years ago."

I announced this fact as if I knew everything about travellers and gypsies of all sorts. In fact, that was about all I knew, and that had been courtesy of Perry, the bus driver. It was enough information to impress my friends.

"Fil," Alice seldom employed admiration in her voice. "How do you know?"

"Intuition." I replied smugly. "Pure intuition."

I was enjoying the kudos knowledge can so swiftly deliver, when I inadvertently took my eyes away from the huge ditch which only I could see, from the back seat.

Kerplunk! We all lurched forwards as the Jag settled awkwardly into a gaping hole in the muddy field.

"Patrick, what are you doing?" Alice had no idea there had been a huge ditch in the field, or that Patrick could not possibly have seen it. As I say, short-lived glory for me, when Alice realised that I should have been guiding Patrick and that I certainly should have warned him of any impending danger. (either me or the dogs, and they were hiding by now)

We all jumped out to examine the damage, but there was none-only the two front wheels wedged into the water-logged ditch. Patrick wasn't worried at all. He was smiling and happy, and ready for lunch. (Loved his food and glasses of vino did Patrick) He just shrugged his shoulders and uttered in a matter-of-fact tone, "Well get it out after lunch. Let's go and have a drink now."

The courtyard was a happy affair. Groups of people were settled jovially into their benches and deckchairs in various states of eating or drinking, and it was finally, fully sunny, with just the slightest breeze. The rain had completely disappeared, and people were laughing and talking animatedly in their family or friendship groups. The dogs were in their seventh heaven, because Patrick had tied them to the foot of our table with the thick longish rope, he kept in the car should an occasion such as today eventuate. We enjoyed a ploughman's lunch and a jug of cider to share between all three of us. (We had our own glasses – we did not pass the jug around for a greedy gulp.) The dogs had water and our meagre scraps.

After the meal, I left Alice and Patrick chatting at the table, and ventured around the front of the pub to take some photos. It was so pretty and typically country. Whilst I was there snapping away, a bulky man in a shirt and waistcoat approached me and asked me what I was doing. I should have thought it was obvious that I was taking photos of the pub, but I told him anyway.

"Did you know that this establishment is over 500 years old?"

"No. I didn't know. How do you know that?"

"I'm the publican. Have been so for ten years now. See that bedroom up there?" He was pointed up to a tiny dormer window nestled into the thatched roof of the pub. "Yes."

"That's my bedroom. I'm up there alone every night. Sometimes the wind howls and the rain thunders down, but I'm there alright!"

He was a big man, red headed and big. I didn't really know what to say when he pointed out his bedroom to me. I didn't really think it appropriate, but I just didn't know what to say. At least he hadn't asked me up there to look at his etchings. I wanted to run back to Alice and Patrick, but he really was harmless. Just too big.

"I think you have a lovely pub, and I'm sure the rooms are just as lovely."

With that said, I fled. Back around the side of the pub, to the safety of the courtyard. I looked for Alice and Patrick, but they weren't there. They must have wandered back to the car already. When I got to the car Patrick was in the driver's seat revving up the engine, and Alice was standing to the side of the ditch urging him to swing hard to the left. "Harder Patrick, harder."

There were two young lads leaning against the fence watching the goings-on, in fits of laughter with Alice's comments, and when they realised the difficulty Patrick was having in getting the car out of the ditch, they came over to us and offered their assistance. They were both strong farm lads and they soon had Patrick and the Jag out of the ditch. I was very impressed with their good manners and willingness to lend us a hand. We probably looked like old fuddy-duddies to them, but they ignored our impediments and helped us quite willingly. I was reminded again of how accommodating the English are. These lads were living proof of that.

Once we were back on the road, Patrick suggested that we do a second, less taxing walk around the small lake in the middle of the New Forest.

"That sounds good Patrick. Did you notice the name of the pub, 'Slough Inn'?"

Yes, Patrick loved anything to do with history, so he was keen to pursue the conversation. Alice was cat-napping with the dogs.

"Slough is a very old English name. Means muddy ground that is very soft. Quite appropriate for the car park when you come to think of it."

I was fascinated by the name – 'Slough Inn'. When I posted a picture of the pub on Facebook later that evening, one of my friends in Australia posted back that she really would like to come to England one day and visit the 'Ough Inn' (pronounced 'ugg') as it sounded intriguing. My bad photography! I had cut out the 'S' at the beginning of Slough. In my head, I blamed the publican. He had rattled me and caused me to falter in my photography.

We were pulling into our third car park of the day. This time it was very neat and gravelled, and there were plenty of places in which to park. Despite the automobile depletion, there were loads of people down at the lake, which was only about twenty steps away. It looked like a scene from a Brueghel painting. There were families and children and old people and dogs and more dogs everywhere. Some were picnicking at the tables, others were lounging on rugs and many more were just sauntering and strolling around the lake. Alice was all perky after her cat nap, as were the dogs, and she suggested that we all walk around the lake. I was feeling quite lazy, and I remembered that I had brought my sketching pencils with me in case I saw something I would like to sketch. I liked what I saw immensely, so I opted for sitting beside the peaceful lake sketching, whilst Alice and Patrick went for an hour's stroll. That should have given us all enough time to do what we wanted to do. We had been walking as we were talking, and we were now almost in the water. Alice and Patrick went off on their merry way up the hill, and I turned to go back to the car to retrieve my sketch pad and pencils from my backpack. A battered old camper van had pulled up beside Patrick's car, and I had to smile and wave at the people sitting there in the car, because it was difficult for me to get my back pack without coming perilously close to their van. They were a very friendly and very elderly couple, all propped up in the front seats with back cushions, a thermos flask on the dash board and a bundle of fish and chips each. I could see the fish and chips because they were propped up so high, but I could also smell them. (Not the elderly couple, the fish and chips) I was starting to feel a little peckish, even though we had not long finished lunch.

The old couple didn't talk at all, just smiled at me and nodded and waved. Then they went back to their comfortable silence with each other and the peaceful serene view of the lake. I gave them one last smile and made my way back down to the water's edge with my sketching bits and pieces, and my fold-up picnic rug to sit on. I always carry a rug and a scarf with me in my backpack when I'm travelling as you never know when you might need either or both of them. When I found the perfect spot to sketch, I spread the rug out on the ground, and carefully placed my pencils and pad alongside it.

The vista I had chosen was lovely, and I couldn't have wished for better. The light was all Constable and Turner. The waters of the lake were lapping gently towards the shoreline, and there was a grassy island directly in front of me with a carefree group of birds floating in the water below the island. The water was a little greyer near where the birds were floating, but I was only sketching in grey lead, so it didn't really matter what colour the water was. Directly to the side of the lake I noticed a cluster of model boats, and I looked around to see who was controlling these boats. I saw a group of young lads a bit further up, and to the side of me, up the hill slightly, there were two older men in deckchairs deep in conversation. I wasn't that far away from them, and I could hear their conversation quite clearly. "Ya think Alec will turn up?"

"Dunno. Suppose so."

"Ya think we should just start without him?"

"Dunno, up ter you."

"Let's just start without him."

I wondered what they were about to start doing, so I edged my rug and materials closer towards the pair. The older one noticed me moving, and called over to me,

"Trying for a better view are ya?"

"Yes." I wasn't giving anything away. "Yes, it's a bit sunnier up here, and I like to try and create the shadows in my drawings."

The man seemed to accept this weak explanation, and started chatting to me about the New Forest, and how he and his mate Eric came down most afternoons to race their model boats and get some peace from all the women in their households. Both of them were keen to start up their boats as it was obvious that Alec was not going to turn up today. The man's name was John, and he told me that he knew all about Australia, as he had worked on the construction of the Sydney Harbour Bridge. He wore well, and he certainly didn't look his age, which would have been around one hundred and five if he were to be believed. John also had a dreadful chronic cough, and he kept coughing all the way throughout our conversation. In between the coughing, he would light up a cigarette and puff away with not a care in the world for the two of us drowning in the smoke.

"Can't understand why I have this persistent cough!"

Eric and I could have told him why there and then, without too much insight!

When he finally finished an incredibly long coughing fit, John jumped up out of his deckchair and made his way back up the hill behind us to his car. Eric looked like he was about to give up on whatever it was he hadn't yet started, and he said to me in a resigned voice, "Looks like it's just you and me. Know anything about model boat racing?"

I realised that he and John and the absent Alec were down there to race their boats. I certainly had never attempted that pastime before, and I knew that it wouldn't have been something I would choose to do on a Saturday afternoon.

"I don't really know anything about model boats. Sorry."

As I was talking, I saw John half running back down the hill carrying a box. I felt instant relief. "Here comes your friend. You can still race the boats."

John apologised to us for racing off to the car so unexpectedly.

"Needed to get a few things from the car. Ready old chum?"

They started fiddling around with the controls and getting themselves into the correct starting position in their deck chairs, leaning backwards and forwards, all earnest and serious, until they were settled.

I turned back to my sketchpad and began to draw the island in the middle of the lake. I was so engrossed in my sketching that I did not notice the two men were packing up their deckchairs and moving closer to the lake, a little further around the corner. Eric called out to me as they edged away.

"See you later. We need to move up a bit closer to the lake. Enjoy your holiday in the New Forest." I assured them that I would, and they moved off. About ten minutes later Alice and Patrick appeared and we decided that we needed to get back to Barton, as we had the neighbours coming in for afternoon tea, and we still needed to pick up some cakes and fruit.

It didn't really take that long to pick up the cakes. Patrick raced into the cake shop, and Alice and I waited in the car. When we got home, we still had about an hour until the guests were due to arrive, so we all chipped in and tidied up the house and readied the table for the afternoon delights.

Then we sat in the lounge room and waited.

Isla and Jack were first to arrive. They lived directly next door to Alice and Patrick and the four of them had been friends for over a decade. Isla and Jack lived permanently in Barton and were both retired. She had worked in retail, and he was ex-army. She wore a red and white floral skirt and a twinset in pale purple. And pearls. Jack was more casual. He wore a flimsy white cheesecloth shirt and safari pants and casual tan slip-on-shoes. They both looked dressed for the occasion, and Jack's hair was still wet. His-Eau-de cologne was very strong, and I think he might have spilt most of it over himself on purpose. It was hard not to wrinkle up my nose when I accidently stood too close to him. Isla must have been immune to it, as she was hugging him towards her-and yet still breathing normally. The other guests, Babs and Camilla, were two retired head teachers who lived in the house opposite. All the houses in the court were arranged in a semi-circle, and everyone could always see who was at home, and what they were doing in their gardens. Bert, the early morning gardener from the other morning had not been invited. So, there were seven of us, all sitting up expectantly in the spruced-up lounge room waiting for Alice and Patrick to bustle back to the kitchen and carry in their best teacups and the promised cakes.

It was a pleasant afternoon. Jack was gracious enough to listen to my stories about Australia, and Isla had a good sense of humour, and laughed at most of my jokes. The other two were more reserved, and it was harder to drag much conversation out of them. They were happy enough to just listen and nod from time to time. They both brightened up enormously when the cakes arrived, and they dug in with gusto. I thought that this pair of epicureans must have had a few too many bland school dinners in their days as head teachers, and that the afternoon tea cakes were a real treat. The English cakes are really, really, good. Whenever we have afternoon teas in Australia, we drool over the memory of English cakes and cream buns. I can recite the litany of Poundcake, scones with jam and cream, Buttercake, Angelfood cake, Spongecake and my all-time favourite, Red-Velvet cake – without the slightest of provocation. We can never even come close to the taste of an English cake. Alice had gone all out with presentation. The cakes were neatly arranged on a flowery tiered platter, with the creamiest cakes on the bottom tier. This pleased the two teachers immensely, as this put their favourite cakes in close proximity to where they were wedged in together on the sofa. While Alice fussed, and Patrick and I entertained Isla and Jack, the two head teachers silently devoured the cakes. I was watching them as I was talking, and it reminded me of the midnight feasts Enid Blyton had so aptly depicted in her school stories. The difference here being that it was the young girls not the teachers who had tucked into the cakes and lashings of Ginger Beer. They say we revert back to our childhood so easily.

Jack was engaged in an extended monologue about how he spent his days now that he had retired, and the rest of us were so squashed on the sofas that we were obliged to sit there and listen. I found it to be quite interesting, but the others seemed just plain bored. Probably heard the same story every time the afternoon teas were held for the last ten years. There were still a few cakes and bowls of nibbles left when the bloated head teachers decided to make a move. I was impressed with their etiquette. They had wisely left a discreet number of cakes on the cake-stand. I considered whether this may have been a pre-planned ploy, but I decided that they were probably just full up to pussy's bow with their sugar overload, and that what appeared to be good manners was simply a happy coincidence. Jack began to struggle to his feet when Babs and Camilla moved. He made a big fuss of looking at the mantlepiece clock and exclaiming loudly, "Good gracious, is that the time? I should be in bed." Gammy leg in tow, he shuffled over to Isla, who was wedged between the hosts on the other sofa and pulled her to her feet.

"Come on Illy, it's late and we haven't had our tea yet." Jack was one of those individuals who just cannot seem to shake off any previous existence they may have lived through. For Jack, it was the army. Isla had told Alice, who had told me, that Jack was a very regimented person. He spent his days living out his army routines of meals and drills, and if it was 6 o'clock, it was time for the evening meal in the mess.

After they had all left with promises of a catchup in the next holidays and hugs, kisses and fond farewells for me, the three of us attended to our own mess. It didn't really take that long, as the dogs had licked up all the crumbs and stray pieces of cake from the carpet, and Patrick was a whiz at stacking the dishwasher. Alice scurried around the room fluffing up the cushions and dusting down the dustless coffee table. There was really nothing for me to do, so I collapsed in a heap on the sofa Alice had just fluffed up, and mimicked Jack in my sternest army voice. "Attention! It's 6 o'clock, and we haven't had our tea yet!" Even Patrick, who was busy with assigned kitchen duties had a loud chuckle.

# Chapter 13
## Towards Hampton

Sunday dawned bright and hot. That was probably because I had slept in way beyond the acceptable sleeping in time, and it was already after 10 o'clock when I looked guiltily at my mobile. Murphy's law. If you want something to happen, do not bother. The complete opposite will always happen. I had wanted to be up early to help with the cleaning and be all ready for the planned midday take off. My first thought after realising my tardiness, was that there was not going to be time to go up to the beach to farewell to Ian. He would be disappointed, and so would Lucy, who would now miss out on being carried on the morning walk along the beach. I thought I'd scribble Ian a quick note and persuade Alice to make a slight detour up to the beach on our way back to London. It was not a planned tactic but sleeping-in had been a good move. I had unwittingly moved the king two spaces forward. (1.e4 in chess-speak.)

When I pottered downstairs after my shower, the rooms had all been vacuumed, papers tidied, books returned to their shelves, vases emptied, kitchen cleaned, and Alice and Patrick's cases were lined up at the door ready to be carried out to the cars. Patrick and the dogs had gone 'AWAK', and Alice was on her mobile in the front garden.

It was a miracle.

I grabbed an apple from the basket of food which was on the kitchen bench, also packed and ready for the journey. As I passed the dining room window I waved to Alice, but she turned her back at that very second. I wasn't sure if this meant that I was in the dog-house for sleeping in, or whether she was so engrossed in her conversation that she kept unconsciously swirling and twirling like a whirling dervish. I waited a few seconds, and sure enough, she was pirouetting again. As for being in the doghouse with her for not setting my alarm or pulling my weight with the chores, she would have been right. I was in the dog-house. This very room in fact was where the dogs slept, so it was literally a dog-house. (I noticed then that the dog's cages had disappeared, most probably one was already in the boot of each car.)

Back upstairs, I managed to throw everything higgledy-piggledy into my treasured over-sized suitcase, completely disregarding all the packing tips I had so carefully rehearsed and practised nightly back home in Australia before the trip. I did try to locate my packing list on the mobile app, but I had forgotten to charge my phone last night, and the battery was now dead. There was no time for organising the clothes and paraphernalia into categories. I just scooped everything up and threw the bundles into the suitcase. Then, I did the typical tourist thing. I sat on my case. Unfortunately for me, the case cracked loudly, and clothes started spilling out as I tried to stand it upright. There was a huge crack right along the top of the case to equal the San Andreas fault line. (obviously not all 1200 kilometres of the fault line but getting close with the potential ramifications of this disaster.) I was more annoyed than upset or alarmed. That the case had broken, clearly meant one thing. The material must have been exceedingly flimsy and/or the case faulty. It did not occur to me that my excessive weight and impatience may have caused the case to crack. It served me right for buying this polycarbonate purple suitcase which looked glossy and smart, but which was obviously rubbish. The tag was still attached to the inside of the case, and it read, 'Polycarbonate luggage is scratch resistant and lighter than plastic. It is revolutionary.' Revolutionary alright! There would be an even fiercer enactment of the French revolution than Les Misérables if Alice found out that I had broken my case by sitting on it. Jean Valjean may have been on the run in France, but I was going to have to leave the country. And possibly in the next half hour. Waiting until nightfall would not be an option. "Fil. What on earth are you doing up there? Hurry up. It's time to go. Do you want help with your suitcase? I'll come up and help you." The last four words were louder and more echoey than the first four, and I sensed that she was already half way up the stairs. I panicked, but with fear-infused adrenalin, managed to stuff the suitcase back into the cupboard where it had been seething all week, obviously wanting to punish me for thoughtlessly banishing it to a dark cupboard in an unfamiliar country. Great! A kamikaze case! Then I stood in front of the cupboard and pretended I was tying up my shoelaces. (Those shoelaces were featuring in too many of my awkward moments.) This was defiantly an awkward moment.

Cue Alice: "Fil, what's happening up here. Have you packed? Where's your suitcase? Has Patrick already taken it downstairs?" I hesitated. If I said yes – that Patrick had already taken my case – then she would be pacified and flit off to do her hair or answer her mobile which seemed to ring 24/7. On the other hand, that would be a lie, and little lies lead to big lies, and I could end up in London with none of my clothes or possessions. I would just have to face the music.

"No!"

"No? What does that mean? No, what?"

"No. The suitcase is not downstairs."

"Well, if it it's not downstairs, then where is it? Is it in the hall? I didn't see it!"

"It's in the cupboard. This cupboard."

I moved to the side and flung open the cupboard door. I just wanted to confess and get it over with.

"It's broken. Cracked all along the top. I'll have to get a new suitcase."

"Oh, stop exaggerating, Fil, let me have a loo…what have you done?"

"Nothing. I just sat on it. It was so full of Lidl presents and clothes and tiny koalas that it broke."

"No, Fil, it broke because you sat on it. Don't you know how heavy you are?" I thought that was a bit rich. I wasn't that heavy! Just tall and big boned.

I started to lug the suitcase all the way out of the cupboard and managed to lift it up onto the bed. Alice had stopped chastising me, as she could see that the mishap really had been an accident, and that my heart had been in the right place buying all the presents and wanting to inundate England with Australian fauna replicas.

"OK. Not to worry. Here's what we'll do. I'll go down to the kitchen and find a couple of big garbage bags, and you can shove all your things into them. When we get back to London, I'll take you into Kingston upon Thames, and you can buy yourself a new suitcase. OK?"

I was so relieved that it was going to end well, that I agreed overenthusiastically to the plan. "Now hurry up Fil, Patrick will be back very soon, and we need to get on the motorway before the traffic starts to build up."

Five minutes later, Alice brought the garbage bags in to me, and I filled them up and stuffed them into the suitcase. This time it was easier to shut, as the bags stuck out the side with the crack. Once Alice had checked that I was following the plan correctly, she had left me to finish tidying up the room, whilst she went downstairs to check that all the windows were shut, curtains drawn, and that there were no dripping taps or wet towels left behind.

It was sad to say goodbye to the bedroom. It was a beautiful room, with great energy and a consistent warm breeze through the generous windows. Still, it was time to move on. I had to make two trips downstairs there was so much luggage. My travel bag from the plane was even heavier than I remembered. I also had some of the presents and five hardcover books I had picked up in New Milton when we'd been shopping there.

I left the suitcase until the second trip, and by the time I had dragged it to the top of the stairs, I was out of breath. I quickly checked to see if either Patrick or Alice were hovering near the foot of the stairs, but it was very quiet, and I couldn't see anyone.

Quick as a flash I sent the suitcase hurtling down the stairs head first. I thought it would just slide down the stairs one or two at a time, but I didn't know my own strength. Instead of dribbling sedately down the stairs, the suitcase was instantly airborne, and it managed to crash into the banister and then woozily right itself on its pathway towards the bottom. It was all over in a few seconds, but Alice has the ears of a dog. She hears everything. Everywhere!

"Fil, what was that almighty thud? What on earth are you doing now?"

"Nothing." My reply was shouted in a sing song voice, as I wasn't sure which room she was in.

"Didn't sound like nothing. Are you hurt?"

"Only my feelings, from before when you said I was too heavy to have sat on the case."

Alice appeared in the doorway of the kitchen. She looked perplexed.

"I'm sorry Fil. I just meant that you should have thought about it a bit more before you sat on the case."

"I know. Sorry for making everyone late."

"We're not late. Here's Patrick now, and you can get him to carry out you case, and we'll be on our way. Everything is done." Alice was saying all this in a very cheery voice. I wanted to ask her if we might go past Ian's and drop in the note I had hastily scrawled. But I didn't want to push my luck with that one. I had his email address, so I would email him from London and explain my no-show. As we drove out of the gravelled Barton driveway for the last time, I looked back at the house and the pretty garden and wound down my window. Bye-bye beautiful Barton on Sea! Until next time. We were on the motorway in no time, and Alice did not pussyfoot around when she was driving. More like lead-footed it around. We had zipped in and out of at least ten little villages before we hit the motor way, and it was all a whirlwind of houses, flowers and a main street in most of the villages. At this rate we'd be back in London in under two hours. I just wasn't sure if we'd be alive to tell the tale.

It had only taken us an hour and a half to get to Hampton, which was where Alice and Patrick had lived for the past five years. Hampton is a leafy outer suburb which most Londoners know well, because of the imposing Hampton Court Palace, home to Henry the Eighth and his cronies. I was eagerly anticipating visiting the palace on this trip and spending at least a day exploring the apartments. The last time I had been there, two years beforehand, I had run out of time, and only managed to see the gardens (which boasted the largest grapevine in the world, planted in 1768 by Capability Brown) and of course, the Tourist shop attached to the palace. If I hadn't spent so many hours, and so many pounds, on memorabilia and presents in the shop, then I would probably have been able to have joined my friends in the palace. I hadn't been in anybody's good books that day, as a group of us were going to do the tour of the palace, and because we were a party of ten, a hefty discount was involved. Unfortunately for me, I was in the middle of purchasing a handful of Hampton Court palace snow globes containing the shrunken, shrivelled plastic head of Anne Boleyn, when my friends reached the front of the ticket queue in the ticket office across the lawn from the Tourist shop. One of them (reputedly the fastest runner, although none of them were very fast in my opinion) anyway, this friend was the youngest, the fastest and the one least likely to cause a scene and force me to abandon my piled-up snow globes, tee shirts and a bargain bust of Henry the eighth, follow her, and make up the tenth person – and ipso-facto qualifying for the discount.

"What are you still doing in here? We are just about to buy the tickets, and we need you to make up the tenth person, they are doing a head count." This made me laugh, as I was about to purchase a head myself-a severed head of a queen in a snow-globe.

"I don't want to be the tenth person. I am fed up with being the tenth person wherever we go."

"OK. Il just sprint back to them and tell everyone they are going to have to pay five pounds extra because of you, shall I?"

"If you like. I can't come now, I'm waiting to be served."

"OK. Fine."

She looked at the pile of snow globes, each containing the bleary miniature head of Ann Boleyn which I had dumped down on the counter, and exclaimed with irritation at my stubbornness. "It'll be your head in one of those fishbowls when I tell the others you aren't coming!"

With that she was off across the beautiful green, flat, freshly mowed lawn outside the shop. Off to deliver the bad news. Off to seal my fate. I didn't really care though. It just meant that I missed the tour of the palace, and that they'd need to get a friend of a friend to take my place next time they went as a group.

Suited me really. I never did like crowds.

That incident had happened almost two years to the very day. I would see if Alice wanted to come with me to the Palace on Saturday. Maybe not Patrick though. Two's company, three's a crowd and all that.

"Fil, wake up, were almost home, I just need to call into Little Sainsburys to get something for tea tonight." Alice loved Little Sainsburys almost as much as I loved Lidl. All the time we had been in Barton, she had been moaning on about the lack of variety and freshness you could expect if you shopped at Lidl.

"Do you want to come in, or wait in the car?"

"I'll come in with you. And I'll pay for the groceries. I can't remember what a Little Sainsburys aisle looks like, and I love seeing all those unusual products on the shelves."

It was true. I loved looking at the groceries and the fresh salads. Most of all though, I couldn't resist staring at the mouth-watering pre-packaged foods which extended for row after row in the frozen food section. We don't have the variety in Australia. Nearly everyone I know, who has been to London, has confessed to spending hours ogling at the British food, and agonising over what to buy for tea. The food halls in Harrods really take the cake though, and friends of mine (myself included), have been known to have spent entire shopping afternoons in the food halls in Harrods.

'Little Sainsbury's' was opposite the station, and it was little, and it was full of little people serving. (Not leprechauns, or dwarfs, just cashiers who appeared to be vertically challenged.) The supermarket was quite busy for a Sunday evening (Alice informed me,) and we weren't in there for very long. Organised Alice knew exactly what she wanted, and she whipped up down the aisles like a whirlwind with me in tow. I realised that I was not going to be able to focus on the shelves with any degree of intensity – which was my usual practice in London food stores. I knew that my time would come during the week when Alice returned to work, and I was left to roam the streets of London at my will.

I kept quiet and offered to pay for the groceries. Alice was pleased with my proactiveness.

When we arrived at the house, Patrick's car was already in the driveway, and the boot was open.

Patrick appeared almost immediately.

"The fun and games have begun again with Joan." His voice was low, and his words enunciated.

I had not the slightest clue what he was mumbling about, but Alice seemed to be in the know.

"Why? What's happened now?"

"She's inside, in the lounge, because she can't get into her house. She's put the keys somewhere, and she can't remember where."

I was slowly beginning to remember who Joan was. The last time I had stayed here, there had been a daily visit from the next-door neighbour-Joan. Joan was at least eighty-nine, maybe older, and she lived alone in the rambling brick house next door with her two sausage dogs. I wondered if the dogs were also locked out of the house, and if so, would they be inside with Joan in the lounge room. I distinctly remembered those two dogs as being the smelliest, ugliest, snappiest dogs I had encountered in my travels abroad.

As if reading my mind, Alice piped up with. "Don't worry Fil, Winston and Prunella will be next door in their baskets." They have a doggy door. Thank heavens for that. I secretly praised the inventor of the doggy doors.

Patrick was getting agitated. "What shall we do? I can't find the spare keys we have to Joan's house."

"Oh Patrick, stop panicking!" The ever-efficient Alice was taking over. "I have her spare keys here in my handbag. Let's all just go in and see Joan."

Joan was half sitting on the couch dressed in a red velvet pinafore and thick black stockings. One of her stockinged feet was curled up under her legs. She looked very much at home in her next-door neighbour's lounge room, squinting at some faded old photographs. (She was squinting because she only had one good eye, the other looked very glassy) The photographs may have belonged to Alice and Patrick, but I couldn't see any open photo albums nearby, and they did look very old and yellowy.

"Oh Alice. You're back. Did you go yesterday? I was looking for you everywhere."

Joan jumped up to give Alice a hug, and I was surprised at how petite she was. She must have shrunk inches since I had last seen her, or maybe she had always been sitting down? I couldn't remember.

Joan was looking expectantly at me, as if trying to remember who I was.

"Who is this Alice?"

Nothing like being forthright.

"Oh Joan, you remember Fil. She was here two years ago. She is visiting from Australia."

"Don't like Australia. Full of dirty convicts and all the filth from England. We can't even beat them at cricket. Are you sure you aren't South African?"

What was it with the South African thing? I hadn't even opened my mouth, so it couldn't have been my accent. Perhaps it was just that I was tall. Tall might have equated with South African heritage in Joan's mind. She may have had an aversion to the Boer war as well as to the entire Australian population.

"So, do you have a name Australian girl? Come on lass, out with it! Cough up!"

Alice and Patrick were trying not to laugh, and I decided to humour Joan, and beat her at her own game.

"Yes, I do have a name, but I quite like being called 'Australian Girl' – so 'Australian Girl' it is!"

"Spiffing. Just spiffing. I do like a girl with a bit of fight in her—" Joan had raised her fists in a mock boxing motion and seemed to be thoroughly enjoying the banter.

Alice suddenly intervened.

"Joan, it's getting late, I've got your spare keys here. You can take them to open up and bring them back tomorrow. Shall I get Patrick to help you open up?"

"No, I'm tickety-boo, Alice. I'll just take this here Australian girl with me, to make sure I get inside, and then she can come back into the bosom of your home."

"Oh, that's a shame dear. The only people the British detest more than the Irish are the Irish themselves." With that slung at me, she slammed the door in my face. I made sure I could hear the dogs barking at Joan's arrival, and raced back next door before she could hurl and more insults my way. At that moment, I remembered a saying one of my friends in Australia loved to throw into conversations. "You wonder why you leave your native shores." She could have been right today. Of course, Alice wanted to know if Joan was safe inside the house, and if the dogs had been there. I answered yes to both questions, and then I turned to go outside to the car to bring in the luggage and my broken suitcase.

"Not to worry, Fil. Patrick has already brought everything inside. Your room is ready, and tea will be ready in half an hour."

I started to relax a little. Maybe Joan had a point. Maybe it was better not to cross the English with the Irish. It created a predicament for me though, because I loved both countries, and if I were forced to choose between them it would be impossible.

We had a leisurely meal and then an early night. My bedroom window looked out onto the enormous flat backyard with very few trees or plantings. Although Alice and Patrick had been in Hampton for five years, they had concentrated on renovating the house itself, and they were going to tackle the garden as their next big project. The house was very state-of-the-art. Polished floors of honey coloured oak, huge white skylights across the lounge and dining rooms, beautiful thick honey-coloured wooden doors to all bedrooms, and a gorgeous main bathroom and equally gorgeous ensuite in aquamarine blues with a massive showerhead and a free-standing claw bath. I could go on and on. I fell asleep counting features of the home instead of counting sheep.

# Chapter 14
## More of Hampton

The planes woke me. Not one plane, but at least twenty planes flew overhead in quick succession. It was as if I was an unnotified, surprise judge, in the Hampton air show. Except that there was no air show. It was just normal Heathrow air traffic. I had little recollection of the early morning planes the last time I'd stayed in Hampton, possibly because I was in the smaller bedroom on the other side of the house. Or maybe I had just been oblivious to this thunderous noise. After lying there for the better part of an hour, ticking off the frequency of the planes, I decided to get up and go for a walk. It was becoming a pattern for me, these early morning walks, but I just felt like some exercise. Alice and Patrick had not stirred, but I inadvertently woke Looby and Holly, who came racing up to me as I tried to open the double locked front door as quietly as possible. I toyed with the idea of taking the dogs with me, but I wasn't sure where Patrick kept their leads, and knowing my luck, they would run away, never to be seen again. I couldn't take that chance, so I left them yelping, and slipped out the door.

It was a beautiful, sunny, blue-skied September morning, and up ahead, I could see red double decker London buses rattling past. It made me smile to think I was in London. Well, quite a way out from the centre of London, but the postcode should still have been London. I would check that later. I had my wallet and backpack with me, and in a split-second decision, decided to hop onto the next bus, and stay on that bus until I recognised a familiar landmark. Then I would jump off and find a trendy little coffee shop, where I would partake of my first London breakfast.

Alice had work today, and Patrick always had his morning coffee when he took the dogs for their morning walk, so I would not be disappointing anyone by breakfasting alone.

The first bus to rattle along had 'Hampton Court' displayed prominently on the front, and I jumped on excitedly.

I had a prepaid Oyster card, and apart from not really being sure whether to insert the card or swipe it, I was quite familiar with how to use the card to get around London. The only thing I needed to remember was to keep topping it up, as public transport in London can be expensive. I intended to do a lot of walking this trip, as part of my new health regime, but I wasn't going to start today. All in good time.

The coffee shop I found was just beside the Hampton train station, and there were brightly coloured chairs and tables outside the café even at this early hour. The bus had been so crowded, I'd had to stand. I'd forgotten that this was a working day, and people were on their way to work and maybe even school. Looking at their gloomy, downcast faces had jolted my memory. I think I must have stood out like a sore thumb, because I wore a tourist smile, my heavy backpack and casual travelling clothes. People did seem to be looking at me, and it must have been my smile and my attire which caused them to stare. It couldn't have been because I was Australian. The dead giveaway with me is always my voice, but I hadn't spoken, except to ask the driver if I needed to swipe the oyster card. I was relieved when I spotted a tiny café when the bus stopped at the station, and half of the passengers jostled their way down the steps and raced off to catch the train into Kingston or Richmond or Twickenham or even central London. I waited until the commuters had all toppled off, and then I followed suite, except that I did not follow them up the steel mesh stairs onto the overpass which the signs indicated, led to the city bound platforms. Instead, I made a beeline for the café I could see across the road.

Coffee shops in big cities all over the world have one thing in common. Everyone is always in a rush to pick up their take away coffees, and then race off to wherever they need to be.
This tiny little coffee shop was wedged between a hairdresser and an Indian restaurant. I doubted very much that I would be gorging myself on the full English breakfast, when I finally found the end of the queue at the doorway to the neighbouring Indian restaurant. The length of the queue, and the fact that no one was actually eating or drinking at the brightly painted tables with the vases of fresh flowers, convinced me that big breakfasts were not their signature dish, and that I would do better to just grab a coffee and jump back onto the next bus home. As I took up my position in the queue, an Indian gentleman dressed in full

Gherka regalia appeared in the doorway to the Indian restaurant where I was standing. I thought he must have been wanting a coffee like the rest of us, and that he was going to take up his place behind me, but he just nodded and stood beside me still nodding. Then he cleared his throat and stamped his feet in some sort of ritualistic calling to the Gods, and began chanting out loudly, "Come to Salah's Indian restaurant tonight. Come one and all, bring your families, you'll all have a ball." He was so loud I had to lower my head and put my hands over my ears. All the other customers in the line in front of me did the same. He even startled the children. A little girl of about three who was clutching her mother's hand screamed and let go of the mother, putting both hand up to her ears. I was glad she was five places in front of me. The whole scenario was typical me. Wrong place, wrong time. Had I been at the front of the queue, and not at the back, taking up the Indian restaurant's entire doorway, then I might have been spared the antics of this eccentric ethnic town crier. The little jingle was repeated at least five times, and I hadn't really moved up much in the queue.

This was all just getting too hard. In Australia there are queues at coffee shops, of course there are queues, but this was ridiculous. This little coffee shop could not rest forever on the laurels if its cuteness and English heritage. There would just need to be more staff employed, and they might have to relocate. Tomorrow! I poked my head out of the queue in a fruitless effort to count exactly how many people were in front of me. The Indian chanter took this as a sign that I wanted to strike up a conversation with him whilst I was waiting in the line.

"You are a tourist, yes?"

"Could be."

"That is the most unusual name for a woman, Coobee? Where are you from?"

"Australia. Look. I can't really talk this morning. My throat is very sore, and I just need a hot drink." This information excited him.

"We have hot Lassi drinks in the restaurant. We aren't open yet, but would you like me to obtain one for you?" I've had the Lassi drinks before, and they are not my favourite. Too milky, too white, too thick and too sweet.

"No. That's OK thanks. I'll just wait here patiently in the queue. I'm on holidays. I have all day to wait." Gotta love that retort! It felt like it took all morning to reach the head of the queue. By the time I had ordered, it was half past 9 and I'd been missing in action for two and a half hours. I cursed myself for not having left a note saying that I was going for a coffee. I could have mentioned any coffee shop anywhere in Greater London, and Patrick would have known straight away that meant I would be gone for hours. I was remembering now, that he had mentioned to me that it was hard to find a good coffee shop anywhere in London. I'd probably missed both Alice and Patrick by now.

Alice would have already left for work, and Patrick would be taking the dogs for a walk.

On the upside, the coffee was really strong and flavoursome, and I managed to grab the last slice of banana bread that had been sitting in the glass bowl on the counter. (I didn't just grab it, I did pay for it.) On the bus on the way home, I digressed from my usual day dreaming of counting houses I wished to own, switching instead to composing a review of the coffee shop in my head. It would go something along the lines of: "Visit the tiny coffee shop opposite Hampton train station, and you can expect to get 'barista style', expertly brewed coffee, with the freshest of banana bread. But the buck stops here! The unsightly location sandwiched between a hairdresser's effusing chemicals, and an Indian restaurant effusing curries, does nothing to entice the potential coffee connoisseur. If you can manage to ignore the long queues and suffer the smells, you're in with a chance." I knew I was wasting my time even contemplating the fate of the coffee shop, but it was something to occupy my mind as the red bus rattled me back home.

The day was peaceful enough. I returned home, Patrick, Looby, and Holly returned home, and finally Alice returned home. She came bearing gifts of take away Pizza, and it saved us all thinking about tea. I had done nothing except daydream all day, while Patrick had attended to his emails, and Alice had visited homes and schools with hearing impaired students. I was planning to go to Hampton Court Palace the next day, so I had an early night, after having checked which bus to get on for Hampton Court.

"It's the '111' Fil, you must remember that. It's easy."

"Easy for some, but I have never been good at remembering numbers."

I am suitably challenged when directed to choose a password with a certain amount of numbers and letters. Then they add the bit about the requirement of a mix of upper and lowercase letters, and they have well and truly lost me. Everything I do nowadays seems to require a password. I try to keep it as 'One, two three, Open Sesame', which is a password I can easily remember, but it gets a trifle confusing when there are twenty or more portals where I have that same password. I was glad that I had brought my little red address and passwords book with me as a back up to the mobile. It would come in very handy.

# Chapter 15
## Hampton Court Palace

When morning finally arrived, I was extremely relieved. It had been a full moon, and I'd tossed and turned all night. It was also unseasonably warm, and not having been able to pry open the window in my bedroom meant the room was a virtual hothouse all night. On my last visit to Hampton, Patrick had gone to great lengths to explain to me every painstaking detail of how one had to twist and turn the knob at the same time, and then push lightly against the pane. I had tried then with no success, and two years of weathering had done nothing to make the windows easier to open. Consequently, I sweltered in my mini hothouse. I made up my mind to treat myself to an unusually long hot shower. By the time I emerged from the bathroom, smothered in Gucci body lotion, I felt marginally better. Some food would help. Alice was already up, busying herself with concocting a healthy protein drink which she had for breakfast on work mornings.

"Ughh, Fil, what's that sweet sickly smell?"

"Uh, that's just the last of the Gucci body lotion I brought with me. I thought I'd use it all up to save carrying it around in the plastic bags. If I had a case it'd be better."

I hoped this subtle reference to my damaged suitcase might jolt Alice's memory, and that she would offer to take me to John Lewis in Kingston to buy my new suitcase. Negative. Not happening. Alice must not have heard me, as she was engrossed in ladling carefully measured quantities of powders and liquids and chopped up fruit into the blender. The noise was so loud, when she switched on the blender, that the dogs and I made a hasty retreat to the lounge room. Patrick was already in there, reading one of his history books, and smiling as the three of us rushed in. "I knew we should have left that wretched machine at the beach," was all Patrick had to say. I wondered why Alice had even carted the blender to the beach if she only swallowed the potions on work days. Probably as a backup, in case she had been summoned to go back to work whilst still holidaying in Barton, and she needed the sustenance. The wretched machine, as Patrick had so aptly described it, had suddenly died in action, and we could hear frantic whisking and clanking of utensils. Then Alice was calling out to both of us. "I'm off. Remember to let Magnus in if I'm still not home." I hadn't heard of Magnus before, and again, I wondered if Magnus might be a pet of some sort. "Magnus is the Physio."

Patrick wasn't giving much away.

"He comes to the house once a month. For Alice. Not me."

"Oh."

I was sure Magnus would be further explained by Alice at some stage. I wasn't going to get much out of Patrick. He had already turned back to his history book. It only took me half an hour to get ready for the big outing to Hampton Court Palace. I remembered the strict instructions I'd had impressed on me by Alice to only catch the 111 bus, as the other buses did not stop at Hampton Court Palace, and I would be stuck on the buses for ages. I included one of the miniature koalas when I was packing all the odds-and-ends I would need for the day out. I'd been very slack about handing them out, and I wanted to think that I'd left a little bit of Australia in as many places as possible. Hampton Court Palace seemed like a good place to stand and deliver.

The bus was empty compared to yesterday. I sat down and spread out my belongings so that I could rummage around in my backpack on my way to the Palace. Just some last-minute checking that I had all the provisions I needed, and that my passport was safely secured in the pouch around my waist. I probably hadn't needed to bring my passport with me, but I decided it would be better to have, but not need, than to need and not have.

The 500-year-old palace was looming up in front of me. It was magnificent and majestic and took up nearly two entire blocks. The infamous Henry the Eighth certainly knew how to make 'em so that they lasted. If you disregarded the four-lane mini highway which encircled the palace like a great grey bitumen moat, this positioning could be described as idyllic – across from the river, and surrounded by the King's paddock, which was where English Kings rode their prized horses with commitment to rival Gandalf's charge in the 'Lord of the Rings'.

I was the only person left on the bus by now, so instead of pressing the buzzer alerting the driver that that I wished to alight from the bus at the next stop, I made my wobbly way from the back where I had been sitting, towards to the driver at the front. Unfortunately for me, he did not look at me, but just kept staring straight ahead, all the while bopping up and down to some background music. We were coming up to a fairly substantial roundabout, and I knew from Alice that the Hampton Court Palace stop was categorically before the big roundabout. I fumbled for the buzzer closest to me, but I couldn't reach, so I had to put down my backpack and sketching bag and race over to another large buzzer I could clearly see, which was closest to the door in the middle of the bus. I reached the buzzer just as we sailed past my stop and had begun hurtling headlong into the roundabout of all roundabouts. It was bigger than any of the Canberra roundabouts I had grown up with, and that was saying something, as Canberra is the unofficial roundabout capital of the world. Non-locals have been known to have spent entire days circling the roundabouts of Canberra looking for their exit. (any exit would have sufficed) That didn't happen with the bus though. The driver knew exactly where he was headed, and it was off at the first exit, then full speed ahead, probably into Central London or beyond. I realised with a sinking heart, that I would not be getting off the bus until the next stop, and that I would have a very long, lonely walk back to the Palace. There was no choice for me. This was a rock and a hard place and very long field with a road in the middle. Totally deflated, I pushed the button and waited until the next stop.

The stop was adjacent to the King's field, and virtually in the middle of nowhere. I had tried to memorise the route the bus had taken after my missed stop, but it really wasn't the direction that was my problem, it was more the distance I would have to walk. Once I had alighted, I set off to retrace the bus route with a heavy heart and an even heavier load. I thought about hiding my back pack in the bushes and seeing if Alice would drive me back there later tonight, but then I remembered that Magnus was coming, and it would be too dark by the time he left. I would just have to grin and bear it. Served me right for not pressing the bell from the back of the bus when the Palace stop was coming up. I knew one thing though, and that was that Mr Bus music man driver was not going to be the lucky recipient of today's koala. He would just have to wait until the cows came home, as mother used to say.

My feet and back were aching by the time I shuffled into the gates Hampton Court Palace some hours later. I did stop halfway along my journey for some water and biscuits, and I did dawdle a little as I rounded the corner and was greeted with the glorious sight of the Palace gardens, but it still took a long time to get there. I came up with a brilliant idea whilst I was trudging along, that I would give the koala of the day to the first person I met. That turned out to be the security guard on the far left-hand side of the gates to the palace, which was the entrance for the direction from which I had approached. There were guards on all four compass points of the huge red gates, but this man was closest to me, and he would be awarded the lucky spot prize. "Hello. Good morning. Is this the entrance to Hampton Court Palace?"

It sounded like a ridiculous question, even to me, but the roundabouts and the fields and the roads had confused me, and I felt slightly disorientated.

The security guard didn't answer. He smiled warmly at me, then he nodded, but he didn't speak. A woman of my word to myself, I ploughed on.

"I am going on the tour of the palace today, and I wanted to give you this."

I began fossicking about in my backpack for the solitary koala I had brought with me. The guard must have thought that I was offering him money as some sort of bribe, arguably to gain access to some of the secret palace rooms I had read about.

He was well trained in dealing with potential trouble makers. "No thank you, I am Russian. I do not take any bribes."

"Of any sort," he added.

"No. it's not a bribe. It's a koala from Australia." The man didn't look like he knew anything about either Australia or koalas. He had looked much more confident when he had been talking about bribes. Quite animated in fact. I kept feeling around in my backpack as I was talking to him, and he was looking back at me suspiciously. Then he started feeling around in his pocket and pulled out a walkie-talkie at the same moment as I triumphantly located the errant koala. As soon as he saw the koala, his whole demeanour changed, and he spoke excitedly into the walkie-talkie. "Rhys, Rhys, come in Rhys, Come and see what a tourist lady has given me. It's a koala bear."

I could hear the incredulity in the other guard's voice as he shouted back to the Russian. "Blimey Rusko, what yer going to do with a polar bear? Whatz occurring up your end?" I assumed that Rhys was Welsh, the clues being his name, his loud singsong voice and his turn of phrase, 'What's occurring?'

He must also have been a little hard of hearing as he had heard 'polar bear' when Rusko had definitely shouted out 'koala bear'. They were both incorrect.

The little furry ball I was handing over was not a bear of any sort. It was a koala from Australia. A marsupial which many people took as an emblem of Australia. The koala went way back with the British. It was first sighted ten years after the First Fleet arrived in Sydney cove. The scientific name for the koala means 'an ash grey pouched bear' – but who goes by their scientific name these days?

"It is categorically not a polar bear Rhys, it's a koala bear."

I had to intervene. It was time to set the Russians and the Brits straight for once and for all.

"No, no, no! The koala is a koala. Just a koala. It is not a bear!"

Rusko seemed to get it, and Rhys had gone all crackly and dropped out, so I just pressed the koala into the palm of Rusko's hand and called back to him. "Give the koala to one of your children, or save it for one of their Christmas stockings."

I realised that the Russians probably didn't have room for stockings at Christmas time, but Rusko would surely find some use for the little fellow. I lowered my head as I passed the tourist shop on my left and headed straight for the ticket office which I knew to be directly ahead. The ticket booths were inside a small tin clad, free-standing building, and when I stepped inside there were posters everywhere urging customers to pay with a card. This suited me well, as I would then have coins for food or drinks inside the palace. I remembered from my previous visit, that there was a second tourist shop near the back entrance to the palace, and I thought that I might complete my tour at the back entrance.

There was also a well-stocked needlework shop near the back section, and I wanted to find a present for Alice. Anything from the shop would send her into a tailspin. Some years ago, Alice had attended a term of evening needlework classes at the Palace, where she had made some lifelong friends. I knew she would appreciate a gift from the shop, and it wouldn't hurt for me to get some reserve brownie points in. I averted my eyes from the posters and tried to focus on the attendants. There were three of them, all sitting up like Jackie. (Australian idiom). There were no other customers lined up. I assumed that was because it was almost midday, and the early birds would have been halfway around the palace by now. I looked at all three of them sitting perched up on their stools like stuffed bored birds on a wire, and immediately turned my back on them in a grand pretence of quietly shutting the door behind me. There wasn't any real necessity to do so, but I just wanted to stall for time before I decided which one of the three to approach for my ticket. The three wise monkeys all acknowledged me in the typical English way of nodding and smiling, so I couldn't rule any of them out on the grounds of unfriendliness. Fair play to all of them. It was just going to have to be a gender call. There were two women and one man. Two against one, I would have to go with the man. I knew that whilst I was busy with the male attendant and my credit card, the two girls would have the opportunity for a girly natter without the male attendant feeling left out. Another deciding factor for me was that the male was in the booth to the far left, and I could turn left without too much deliberation. It was the universe again, turning me left at all possible opportunities.

The male ticket attendant wiped the smile off his face as soon as I faced him. Not the best work ethic I suspected. Maybe the universe got it wrong? I ignored his sourpuss face and requested a day-ticket to the palace and the gardens. "Do you have a London pass?"

"No. But I have a passport. Right here!" I cradled my bulky passport which was sitting on my stomach like a load of lard.

The male attendant was not amused. The two female attendants were giggling and taking the opportunity no doubt, to poke fun at their co-worker with the poker face.

"Sorry. I was just joking. I just want to buy a ticket for today. Thanks."

"That's 20 pounds forty p. On card?"

I swiped my card and beamed at him. "Thank you very much and have a nice day." He looked at me with a puzzled expression, and then at the two girls. They were busy attending to an onslaught of customers who had just arrived at the ticket office. The customers looked like one big extended family from some eastern European country, and there were at least twenty of them. I thought that they must be getting a premium discount by declaring the pensioners, kids under five, babies and wheelchair disability members of their group. Not to mention the more than ten people-discount. It would have been quicker to have let them all in for free, the angst it was creating for the two girls struggling with percentages. I wanted to take back my "have a nice day" to my attendant, as he was doing nothing to help out. He seemed to be delighting in the confusion. He was being, what Patrick would have called, a prat.

I left the prat and the mathematically challenged attendants cooped up inside the stuffy little boxed office to fight it out and made my way up the red-scoria gravelled pristine path towards the grand entrance to the palace. It was all very regal. There were six or more hefty well-fed Henry the eighth lookalike ticket collectors at the top of the path, just before the tunnelled entrance to the palace quadrangle. They were all bellowing out, "Hear ye, hear ye, hear ye!" Hear what? There was nothing to hear except some feint piped madrigal music coming from the elaborately rigged gigantic speakers in the corners of the entrance. The pipers sounded like they were on their last breaths. If there had been a dearth of people in the ticket office, there was a plethora of people out here all waving their tickets in the beefy faces of the Beefeaters. It was a motley crew, of mainly tourists from all corners of the world, but there were also some squealing school children up ahead of me, buzzing and skipping around in glee and anticipation of gore and pillage. One of the children proudly waved their banner, which identified the group as holiday program participants. I remembered that school had not yet commenced for the year. I could have told them that there was to be none of that to be seen inside the walls of the palace. They would have been better to have stayed in school and watched a U tube clip of beheadings. Some historical places were for children, and some were not. I couldn't see what they would find enticing in the apartment rooms. Maybe the Tudor kitchen, for free food samples was where they were headed. Kids were always hungry, so that could have been a winner.

One of the Beefeaters had snatched my ticket and stamped it approvingly, and then swiftly propelled me into the tunnel. As soon as I was in the grey stoned vortex, I got my bearings. Not much had changed in the stark bare tunnel in the last few centuries.

The time passed very quickly. I 'oohed' and 'ahhed' with the best of them and moved in inimitable iambic pentameter from room to room. No one seemed to realise that I was tagging along with a group of elderly Japanese tourists with some serious movie camera moves, and it was easier to follow than to have to decide where to go.

If anyone looked at me in the group, I would just bow at them, and it seemed to placate them. I wished that I had brought my kimono dressing gown with me. They might have concluded that I was a Japanese elder, trying to relocate my Japanese ancestors. It was three thirty before I stopped for a breath and something to eat. I had brought some chocolate and water with me, and as I couldn't seem to find a kiosk, I just sat in the sunny courtyard and wolfed down the chocolate. I saved the water for later. For the rest of the afternoon, I took leave of the Japanese, and wandered off by myself. They were pleased that I was able to converse in their native tongue. One of the schools in which I had recently taught, had Japanese as the second language. The Japanese teacher had been kind enough to have given me lunchtime Japanese lessons. Except, I wasn't very good, and at the end of the ten-week training, I emerged with only one word I felt really comfortable using, and the ability to count up to ten. I remembered the word Konichiwa, and it came in real handy. The Japanese women in the group seemed particularly proud of me when I suddenly remembered the word for goodbye, sianara. I was a winner with the Japanese!

There was still so much to see, but again time, the arch enemy of the tourist, got the better of me. It was 5 o'clock when I fell upon my sword at the back exit. The needlework shop, and the back-entrance tourist shops were both long closed, so Alice would not be getting any presents tonight. I trudged back up the red gravel park towards the roundabout which would give the 'Place-De-La-Concord' a run for its money and squashed myself into the tiny bus stop bench next to a large Caribbean woman with bags to rival a third world food drop. She was the only person on the seat, but the copious number of bags in her possession took up the rest of the space, so there was not much room for me. As I was almost in her lap, she was forced to look at me.

"You come along from that big palace over there?"

"Yes. You look like you had a good afternoon shopping."

"No. I just popped out to get some bread and milk from the corner shop."

Even though she looked like she was from another country far away, I got it that she was as English. As English as Captain James Cook had been, and that she was probably more likely to be cooking up an enormous flat fry pan of bread-and-butter pudding, than one filled with fried rice and curries like the ones I had seen at the Kingston and Camden markets, the last time I had travelled. She must also have been a private person, and as soon as I made the inadvertent mistake of commenting on the quantity of groceries she had bought, she stood up haughtily and began collecting the shopping bags from the bench. I was dismissed. The 111 bus came bounding along a few minutes later, but the woman didn't get on. She just sat back down as soon as I had vacated the seat. The last I saw of her, she was sitting there rummaging through her shopping bags. The bus trip home seemed to be shorter than the initial journey, and the bus was very crowded. A young boy with masses of dark curly hair, and olive skin stood up and chivalrously offered me his seat. I accepted his gesture gratefully and closed one eye for most of the journey home. I kept the other one open in case I missed my stop and ended up somewhere I would have to walk home from. When I finally clasped my hand on the front door knob around six thirty, I noticed a compact little blue van with "Magnus the massage man" scribed across the doors, parked next to Alice's car. We had company. One clue was that Patrick's Jag had disappeared.

Once inside, I was aware of quiet moaning and loud heaving coming from the lounge room. I thought it might be Joan from next door, as we hadn't seen her all day, but when I tentatively peeked into the lounge room, it wasn't Joan, but Alice, flat down on a massage table, and a big blonde Viking of a man bending over her. Neither of them noticed me. I guessed the Viking must have been Magnus of the massage van. It was a sight for sore eyes in that lounge room. Magnus was kneading Alice's neck, and she was moaning in pain. (I hoped it was pain and not pleasure.) Magnus was the one responsible for the heaving. Every time he lifted his enormous hands, and squeezed the neck of the unfortunate Alice, he would let out a heave of almighty proportions. It was a sound akin to a walrus in pain, or that made frequently by certain (unnamed) tennis players as they thumped back the ball to their opponent. Magnus hadn't seen me, and I didn't like the look of what was going on. I feared that I might be next if I approached them, so I quietly tiptoed back the way I'd come. I really thought I might keep tiptoeing all the way back to the 111 and ride the buses for the evening. That was the storyline in one of the English T.V sitcoms I remembered vividly from my childhood. 'On the Buses', a classic English comedy, which had been very popular in Australia, and believed to have been a true depiction of what happened on the English buses. I almost found out first-hand what really happened on those evening buses, but just as I was turning the knob on the front door, Alice's voice came through loud and clear. "Fil, is that you? Come in here and meet Magnus, he's dying to meet someone from Australia." I wanted to keep tiptoeing, but I knew that Alice wouldn't let up until she found out if it was me at the front door.

"Yes. It's me Alice, but I've been walking a lot today, and I'm all muddy. I think I'll just have a quick bath. I won't traipse all the mud through the house. Hello and goodbye Magnus the massage man."

Alice didn't reply, but Magnus shouted back. "Hello. See you after your bath."

Uh, I don't think so Magnus. I needed to take a very long soak in the gleaming bespoke claw bath. I had never been in a claw bath before, and it was something Alice had told me I could do any time I was staying with them. What she didn't tell me was that it took ages to fill up. I had raced into the bathroom straight from the front door, and now I was just killing time waiting for the bath to fill up. I hoped Magnus did not need to wash his hands in between torturing Alice.

The bath finally filled up, and I poured in some bath oils for good measure, disrobed, and jumped in, but I had overfilled it, and as soon as I sat down, it was overflow code red. I squealed out, "Oh no!" but luckily the lounge room was far enough away that I couldn't be heard. Then I had to jump back out of the bath – desperately seeking towels to soak up the water. I flung open the only cupboard in the bathroom, and the top-shelf was full of neatly folded and ironed blue towels (matching the tiles.)

I didn't really want to use more than one of the towels, but I ended up using the entire pile and they ended up in a heap on the floor beside me. I was glad I had locked the door. No one would suspect that disaster had occurred in the bathroom – that the floor had been flooded and a month's supply of towels soiled in under five minutes. While I was in the bath, I was trying to think of a plan of attack to prevent Alice finding out what had happened to her towels. I knew Patrick would just laugh, but Alice was a different kettle of fish. I would probably end up washing and ironing and dying towels all day tomorrow instead of roaming the streets of Kingston upon Thames at my leisure. it was a dismal thought.

When I finally felt it was safe to emerge from the bathroom, all was quiet on the western front. Magnus must have left, and Alice was lying down in her room. Patrick had an evening class and the dogs were in the laundry until Patrick returned. This information was all conveyed in the note Alice had left me in the dining room. I had a solitary meal of bread and cheese, tiptoed past Alice's silent room, and took myself off to bed. I would not be having another bath in the near future. It would be showers for me, or maybe even the old-fashioned sponge-down. It would remind me of my nursing days, and it was a much safer option.

# Chapter 16
## Kingston upon Thames

The early bird was about to catch the worm. Not me. But a real little English bird. A robin I thought, but I hadn't really taken much notice of the English birds when I had been a girl guide, and we had joined up with the Gould League of Bird Lovers. I was semi-satisfactory at recognising and classifying Australian birds (especially if I heard their distinctive cries) but English birds, well, they were just too prolific. The humble, distasteful worm was easier to categorise. It was a wiggly reddish worm, squirming around in the bird's beak. Nature, the cycle of life and the tide of time, just kept on turning. Impatiently, the still to be named bird flew off with the worm in its mouth.

It was still very early, and I was venturing out to Kingston upon Thames for a 'squiz' and a shop around. I loved Kingston, with the murky grey river and the green surrounds, and it was so exciting to be going back to a place you love. The settlement of Kingston is, of course right on the mighty, dirty Thames, and there are scores of affluent residents who are lucky enough to live on the river itself in handsome houseboats, or to have their very English manors mirror the bluey-grey waters. There is a very large shopping precinct in Kingston, and I was looking forward to traipsing around in search of promised presents and unique English antiques. (which I collected) The red double decker bus was customarily crowded despite the early hour, and I was the last person to clamber onto the bus at my stop. I had dallied too long with the bird and the worm.

Thankfully, the quartet of gaggling high-school girls in front of me pushed and prodded each other up the stairs to the top of the bus. Fearing that there might be a prolific colony of them up there, I flopped into a tiny segment of the closest vacant seat, next to an elderly lady with a grey woollen hat pulled down over her eyes. I could tell she was old by her hands and the wrinkles around her neck. (not that I am wrinkleless.) Her face was pressed up against the window, and she didn't move a muscle when I tried to wedge myself and my cumbersome backpack into the crammed slither of a seat. After about two stops, when no one got off, but plenty more people got on, the old lady roused herself and turned full circle to face me.

Guess who it was? Joan!

"Joan. Hello. What are you doing on the bus so early? Where are you off to?" I fired the questions at her in rapid succession, hoping that she would manage to come up with a plausible answer to at least one of them, but she just stared at me with a dazed blank look.

"Do I know you?"

"Yes, Joan, you know me. I'm the Australian girl from next door. I'm a friend of Alice and Patrick's."

"Who are they?"

"Your next-door neighbours Joan. You must remember." I felt a little ashamed, semi-bullying the poor woman to remember people, of whom she obviously had no recollection. If she couldn't remember Alice and Patrick, then there was little chance of her remembering me. "Not to worry Joan, how are the dogs today?" I thought that a direct mention of the canine creatures so dear to her heart would be worth remembering, but Joan was going the 'Full Monty' with the memory lapsing today.

"Don't know anything about any dogs. Are you going to Kingston lass? Can you help me get off this bus when we get there? I can't seem to ever find the doors, only the windows, and they are quite small. I should get proper stuck if I tried to scramble out of one of them."

Our conversation abruptly ceased, as Joan had turned her face back to the small, familiar window, and she was singing a sort of hybrid English folk song softly to herself. Alice had told me that Joan had spent her childhood travelling around in gypsy wagons and that she came from a family of some importance in the travelling fair industry. No wonder Joan, at eighty something was able to skilfully tuck her legs up, under her posterior with perfect poise. She may well have been the star attraction riding the show ponies at the fairs. I'd check with Alice tonight.

We had arrived in Kingston. The entrance into the town was grand and ceremonious. Typical English village. There was a time when kings of England had also ridden show ponies over the very bridge we were traversing. We had just flown past the King's field, where I had plodded along yesterday. The bridge was a proud monument to the pageantry of days gone by. It was just so quintessentially old England. Joan was oblivious to my rapture.

"Here we are girl. Can you help me down and take me to the bank? I don't really know why I am going there. Despicable places with despicable fees. Still, I must have a reason, and it will no doubt come to me very soon."

No please or thank you, but there was gratitude in her eyes. (Well, the one good eye showed a wide-eyed grateful pupil, while the other eye just squinted at me.) It was definitely only the eyes doing the extended monologues today. Joan clutched my arm with the tenacity of a sixth-sensed titanic passenger, and we both stumbled down the steps to the red cobblestone pavement of Kingston upon Thames.

"The bank. I need the bank! Which way to the bank?" As soon as we had both tumbled out onto the pavement, Joan had forcefully abandoned my arm, and rushed headlong into the mall, calling out to anyone who would listen as if she were on the Speakers' Box in central London. I felt embarrassed for her, as the looks she was procuring from staring shoppers and tourists were defiantly not embracing. Rather, the crowds looked uneasy, as if a mad old woman and her unwilling sidekick (me) had suddenly appeared centre-stage in an outdoor theatre.

A distinguished looking gentleman with a shock of silver hair peeping out from underneath an almost bowler hat, a walking stick and even older in appearance than Joan, stepped forward into the arena and grabbed Joan by her coat.

"Calm down old woman. You are making a scene. The bank is at the end of the mall. I'll take you there if you promise to belt up!" Charming turn of phrase, but it seemed to work on Joan, who was, herself, not adverse to slipping the odd swear word or two into her every other sentence. They went off up the street together, arm in arm, as if they'd been married for a lifetime. I was left at the bus stop, splayed in disbelief at what had just happened, watching their bent-over backs as they made for the bank. I was probably sending poor old Joan off to the wolves by giving her my blessings to elope with the stranger on the shore (river bank) but it was too late to do anything about it. Another rap on the knuckles from Alice was looming up for me in the not-too-distant future. For the time being though, I was going to use my get-out-of-jail-free card and paint the town red. Something was wrong. There were just too many children everywhere! Children laughing, children racing, children squealing, I was inundated with them. I suppose, that being a teacher, I was wired to attract them. This morning though, my temper was short, and my head was thumping with the echoing squawking. Then it hit me. Today was the last day before the summer break ended, and the excitement was fever pitched. The mothers seemed more excited than the children, as they could finally see the light at the end of the tunnel after six long, enduring weeks with their darling children. All the children must have excelled at public speaking, as at every rack of stationary, I could quite clearly hear the plaintive wails of "Oh please, please Mummy! I simply must have that penguin notebook. Everyone will have that one, and I don't want to look uncool tomorrow at school." Or, "Can I get this Mummy? Please Mummy. I've been proper good all holidays."

I'll bet they had! I had a list, and the first category on my list was fine tipped black pens, drawing paper and more sketching grey leads. Unfortunately for me, half the population of school children in greater Kingston had the very same list, and they had all left their 'back-to-school' shopping to the very last minute. I edged my way into three different stationary shops, and they were all packed with acres of children. I was totally astounded at how much merchandise was being purchased. The shops were buzzing, and so crowded that I decided to swallow my list and seek solace in the church where Alice had directed me to visit, to view the local art show which was running all week. The church was peacefully quiet compared to the pandemonium of the mall, and I sank gratefully into one of the pews for a spot of meditation. I am practised in the art of meditation and have been attending a weekly meditation session for the past decade. No sooner had I settled into the pew and began silently repeating my mantra than there was an extremely loud thump, and I was forced to open my eyes. A frumpy, short old woman with a masses and masses of white frizzy hair, and a long fawn trench coat fastened too tightly around her buxom body, was attempting to squeeze into the same pew as me. She had capsized her shopping trolley, and the bundle of fresh vegetables she had stowed in the weathered and worn wooden contraption all scattered over the polished floor-some of them rolling down the slight incline to the double church doors. The old lady didn't talk, but just twitched and nodded at me, but I had lost my mantra moment, and it was hard to get it back. I settled for helping her retrieve the rolling vegetables, and escorted her back to the double doors, which I held open for her. I couldn't think why she had wanted to sit next to me in the church. Probably just lonely, and I looked like a kind soul. So kind was I that I had ushered her to the nearest exit. I managed to slip a koala into her shopping trolley when she was blessing herself in the font near the exit doors. It would be a nice surprise for her to discover later in the day when she unpacked her trolley. I was going to tell her that I had put it there, but there wasn't time, and that would have spoilt the surprise. Once she had gone, the silence was acute, but I was done with meditating. I was hungry, and it was lunchtime. I set off to find the John Lewis Department store cafeteria, having been told by two independent sources (Alice and Trip Advisor) that the food there was very palatable.

The John Lewis Department store would have given Harrods a good run for its money in terms of a glossy exterior, an expertly designed series of large shiny windows, and clever positioning of merchandise in the windows and within the store itself. The first person I sighted when I pushed open the heavy wooden revolving doors was a middle-aged lady-attendant on the floor with a well-endowed multi-coloured feather-duster clasped in her left hand. Her expression was intense, and she was madly dusting the rows of notebooks and packaged envelopes with expensive gold trimmings.

"Excuse me, but I am looking for the Cafeteria. Could you please point me in the right direction?" She could point alright, could Gladys. That was the name she bore which was staring me in the face as she beamed back at me. Memories of squat, grubby Michael on the beach in Ryan's Daughter, with his toothy grin and inane wide-eyed look came flooding in. I shuddered and tried to focus on the positive. This person, Gladys-had a perfectly acceptable smile, and she was doing a great job dusting out the shelves and the stationary with her over plumed implement. She used the implement to point towards the far side of the shop, but apparently, she had no clue of where she worked.

"No, sorry. I 'avn't a clue. I bring me own lunch from om, me mum packs ett." Great! A female Perry from the bus in Barton days.

"Oh O.K. Not to worry, Il just find the information board." I was talking to Glady's apron-clad back as she had moved on from me in a fuss of self-importance. I had to admit that it was an important cog in the wheel of the Department store-that dusting job.

I found the store directory quite smartly and easily as it turned out, and the Cafeteria was predictably located on the fourth floor. It gets me why overzealous architects who design massive Department stores always position the Cafeterias adjacent to the Children's clothing and Toy sections. Ingenious really, when you think of the enormous market of screaming grizzly children when it comes to food and toys. Not so smart upon close examination of their greasy fingers in tug-of-wars with the merchandise. I made a smug mental note to self that I gratefully did not have any children in tow.

The sign said restaurant, but everyone knew it was a glorified Cafeteria. I looked around casually for the queue, but there didn't appear to be one. There were a few people in the casual line ahead of me, but you wouldn't really call it a queue. I tried the nonchalant look as I did not want to seem over eager to stuff my face full of pre-cooked Cafeteria food at the top of this prestigious Department store.

I know what Trip Advisor and Alice said, but one look at the food lingering in the Bay-Marie told me that they had both blatantly lied! Directly in front of me, was an old bent-over Indian woman in a colourful orange and blue Sari. Her face would have been a perfect road map to the Taj Mahal and back, except for the piercing grey steely eyes, which were really quite beautiful. My third octogenarian for the day. I had a clear view of her as the two people who were actually in front of me were bending over-one to attend to a grizzling baby in a pram, and the other to scrutinize the array of cream cakes in front of her. Half of the Indian woman's scrawny body was perpendicular to the counter, and she appeared to be engaged in an animated, heated conversation with the two serving girls. I also had a clear view of the girls from my vantage position. The girls were young and well fed, with rosy cheeks, netted hair and regulation striped cafeteria aprons tied tightly around their plentiful personages, in a matronly fashion which belied their youth. The Indian woman causing all the disturbance was practically ancient, and in at least her fifth incarnation, but my goodness, could she talk! She had a high squeaky sing-song voice, normally associated with outback Lyre birds in Australia, and she did not stop to take a breath. I was fed up with her from my non-existent distance. Her voice was so piercing, the whole food line could not help but collectively listen in and follow the heated banter. The old Indian woman was insisting that the cheese on her potato-in-a jacket needed to be melted more.

"I want you to tip off the cheese and then cook the potatoes more, and then put the cheese back on. Can you please oblige me?" One of the serving girls, with a distinctive Devon accent kept repeating to the old woman, "I aint gunna be able to get all vat cheese offa vu potatoe."

To which the agitated woman was responding, "No, well I can oblige you." With that she scooped up the plate, and with Bollywood style pizazz tipped all the cheese onto the counter (carefully securing the potato to the plate with her spare hand). The devilish smile on her squashed-up face clearly screaming out, "Don't mess with me girlie."

As fast and agile as Peter Rabbit in Mr McGregor's garden, the taller girl scurried off with the potato still on the plate, leaving the counter full of bright yellow English cheese, sloppy sour cream and a solitary, perfectly rotund pickled onion, which inevitably rolled all the way down the counter, and was out for a six by a small excited boy at the end of the queue.

"Look Mummy, a juicy white ball. I gotted it. Eeww! It's all slimy and cold, what is it?" The little red headed boy immediately scooped up the pickled onion and popped it into his wide opened toothless mouth. He just as quickly spat it out on the full. This little ginger was clearly not going to be planning a ploughman's lunch for his wedding banquet in years to come. Meanwhile, the shorter girl had started trying to clean up the mess on the counter, but she seemed to be making an even bigger mess with every stroke of the dishcloth as the cheesy mixture got bigger and bigger. She gave up in frustration, literally threw in the towel, and raced off to join her partner in crime. That left the counter unmanned entirely, except for the girl at the end of the snaking silver runway that was the slender tarmac for the laden trays. She was apparently unable to serve customers, as she did not move from her perch, but instead picked up a glossy magazine, and began flicking through the pages with a bored look on her face. The other few customers who were in the line had just drifted off with all the commotion, and that left only me and the old woman. I gave her a sympathetic look, as I did genuinely feel sorry for her, but not sorry enough to stick around and wait for the aproned girls to return. There would be no hot dinner for me today, but I didn't mind, as it gave me an excuse to purchase my favourite lunch-crisps! I grabbed two packets and made my way to the magazine-flicking girl behind the cash register. She looked at me as though I was either very poor or very mean with my money. I was neither, just not willing to spend the rest of my day waiting in a going nowhere line.

I had waited for a whole day once in Florence, in a supreme effort to get inside the Uffizi gallery. Despite the heat, and my dedicated resolve to enter the hallowed halls of the gallery, it closed at 5 pm, even before I had reached the half way mark in the queue. I had resolved then that I did not do queues. I would prefer to miss out and find something even bigger and better to do. After I had wolfed down my two packs of very English, very stale Walker crisps, I washed them down with a pink plastic mug of over-warm water from the water fountain at the end of the counter (had to line up behind the kids). I was exasperated to boiling point. The whole lunch incident had been a disaster from the minute I had spied the Indian woman. It wasn't her exactly. It could have been anyone causing the fuss and bother. It was just the age-old trials and tribulations of the human quest for food and shelter. The primeval instinct which forces one into an unnatural state of hostility whilst furiously hunting and gathering. I am convinced that women are more prone to be accommodating and less scene-making, and therefore tend to find themselves in the backseat. But I also hold to the tenant of "beware the back-seat driver", coupled with that great Shakespearian observation, 'hell hath no fury like a woman scorned.'

The two girls' reactions to the Indian woman had proved that categorically. And then there is the cultural variable. Statistically, the five happiest countries in the world are the Nordic lands, with Finland coming in a clear winner in the Happiness Stakes. Coincidentally, Finland is also up there with the crème-de-la-cream of education systems, and they (who are they you ask?) the powers that be, attribute the continued Finish success with education, to the fact that happiness and well-being prevails in the schools and in the workplace. People notice each other. The Principal greets the students every morning as they enter the school gates, and the public boldly look the homeless in the eyes, probably because there are no homeless, and the Finnish word for homelessness has become defunct).

I needed to do something drastic to calm myself down. As I stepped out of the massive wooden entrance doors of John Lewis, and into the now struggling murky grey September sunshine that was typically, unpredictable England, I had my head in the clouds as usual. I hadn't noticed that there was a vast stretch of pavement looming up in front of me, devoted to packs of pedestrians overladen with their purchases, and the odd red bus or two. Ironically, it wasn't a London double-decker bus which nearly turned my daydreaming into a permanent and irreversible state of sleep. No. Not the red bus, which would have been a spectacular way to have gone and would have been rich fodder for the biographer of my eulogy. It was a humble bicycle. A state of the art, faster than a speeding bullet humble bike which almost sealed my fate that afternoon in Kingston. It all happened so fast, I could barely realise that I had, in a split second, wasted one of my nine lives. My head was down, so I had no way of seeing the sleek racing-bike which came flying around the corner from the top of the hill and straight through the cobblestoned square. (I found out later that this was a common shortcut to the M8, but that it was mostly taken early morning and late evening when the square was all but deserted.)

In the wink of an eye, a sturdy arm pushed me to the pavement whilst at the same time jumping out of the way of the hurtling bike. Not only that, the guardian angel (woman) had a baby strapped to her chest, and she must also have been carrying bags of shopping, as they ended up on top of me as I fell heavily. And the flash of a rider was gone. In retrospect, I wondered if the cyclist might have been one of those pickpockets on wheels (normally motor bikes) who zoomed past tourists in shopping centres and whipped passports and money belts from totally surprised and shocked travellers. But when it happened, that thought didn't even cross my mind. I just knew that I was on the ground, with spilled John Lewis bags at my feet and on my stomach, that my head was thumping my neck was contorted, and my knees were grazed. On the upside, the woman and the baby were still upright, and she was hopping up and down trying to assure me that I was not badly injured and that it had been a despicably reckless thing to do – shortcut to the motorway through the square at this time of day, as there were bound to be pedestrians crossing and going about their business and their daydreaming. Feeling my age (a daily sentiment these days), I struggled to my feet, woozy and more than a little dazed. We both started bending down to pick up the spilled groceries. A few other shoppers who had been walking behind us had shown initial concern, and rushed over to help, but once they could see that all three of us were unhurt, they disappeared into the nearest arcade to continue their important shopping. The mysterious would-be assassin had vanished a millisecond after I fell, and since neither of us had managed to get any sort of description on him or her, other than that he or she was clad in a dark blue lycra body suit and a black gladiator shaped helmet, it would be safe to assume them to be halfway to London by now. I thanked the woman who had saved my life effusively and assured her that I would be on constant guard from now on for cyclists of any description. Not that I wanted to lump all cyclists into the hell-bent on destruction category, as I have many friends who are respectful and courteous cyclists. There was always one or two in every profession willing to stain the reputation of the whole group. The little girl with the masses of Shirly Temple curls had started wailing.

"I wamm icequem."

"Yes, sweet pea, we'll get you a chocolate ice-cream-cone as soon as we put all our packages in the car." The little girl was old enough to know that meant much later, and she continued wailing. It was time for me to move on. I suddenly felt an urgent need for a neck massage. I could see an old-fashioned street sign with a lamp above it indicating that there was a Beauty Parlour in one of the little arcades across the road. I gave the little lisping child a pat, the lady (Sonya) a quick hug, and we parted ways. The two of them to the car park, and me to the converted alley-ways the old-fashioned sign had been pointing towards. The cloistered corridors with the half-moon ceilings I had entered reminded me of Oxford, and I hoped that I would be able to make it back to that wonderful city of academia on this trip. I hadn't made any real plans for the London and surrounds, but the Irish leg of the trip in two weeks' time was all booked and paid for. Oxford was in with a chance. The Beautician's was easier to locate than I thought it would be. Before opening the door to the shop, I peered in through the front huge lead-light bay window and observed that it was quite crowded for a mid-week morning. My grazed knees were causing me some serious discomfort, and I looked longingly at the massage tables all lined up like huge crayons behind individual purple chiffon curtains. Each table had a different coloured cloth draped over it. The tables were long, and looked inviting, but they were also all occupied. Quite an enterprising service industry by the look of it. I pushed open the door, and an old-fashioned bell tingled. I was beginning to slowly appreciate the charm of these little anachronisms in Kingston upon Thames.

A thirties-something girl with her head in a magazine, rainbow coloured hair, silver hooped earrings and a flowing orange caftan looked up immediately.

"Help ya?"

I put on my most polished Australian accent. "I was wondering about the possibility of a massage. I had a tumble, and my neck is very stiff." There were two other girls in crisp white jackets sitting on flower-power beanbags with huge sunflower prints, directly behind the receptionist. They burst out laughing when they heard my accent. In addition to their outbursts, I could hear what they were whispering to each other, and it wasn't very complimentary. I ignored them on the grounds that they were very young, very immature and very insensitive. If they had to live with these less than admirable qualities for the next sixty years, it was not my place to be teaching them basic manners. The hippy receptionist was smiling, but she had the decency not to acknowledge the girls, nor comment on my accent. I felt relieved when the two white-coats sashayed over towards a back counter and began mixing potions of wax and what looked like hair colours.

The receptionist was addressing me. "We can fit you for a massage tomorrow about this time, madame, would that be suitable?" I was impressed with her eloquent phrasing, and engaging smile. I was less than impressed with the fact that I would have to come back into Kingston tomorrow to receive my neck massage. I decided that if my neck was still hurting tonight, I would beg Alice to ring Magnus, and see if he could fit me in any sooner than tomorrow afternoon.

"No, that's fine, I'm busy tomorrow. I'll just leave it thanks."

"We could fit you in now for a facial. Would you like to wait five minutes for that?"

I didn't really fancy a full facial makeover, but I had been meaning to get my eyebrows fashioned and waxed whilst in England. Maybe today was as good a time as any. I would strike while the iron and the wax were both hot.

"Oh OK. But I'll just get the eyebrow treatment please. I'll leave the facial for another time."

"Certainly!" The girl was excited now. "We can do you right now. Savishna is free, and she specialises in eyebrows. If you could just make your way over to the couch, we'll get you started."

Savishna, of a similar age to the rainbow-haired girl was extremely pretty, and with crowning glory jet black hair. After about five minutes of my being settled on the comfy yellow couch, Savishna sidled over towards me. She was petite, of Indian appearance, and dressed in casual sportswear. She looked as if she had just returned from the gym after a lunchtime workout. Despite the deodorant and strong perfume, I think I was one hundred percent correct in my assumption of how she had just spent her lunch hour. She bent over me to examine my eyebrows, like a plastic surgeon surveying the scope of a highly technical operation. She was very intense and very strong smelling. Memories of the musky perfumed monk from the airport came flooding back to me. I smiled up at her and decided that I would answer any questions that came my way in monosyllables as it would be difficult to talk with her hands all over my face, and there was still the ever-present challenge to my olfactory glands with which to contend.

"Just lay back now and close your eyes. This brow will be first."

It's times like these when you wish you had a mono brow, and the pain would be all over with in one swift rip. Except that there never really was any grief for me in the capable hands of Savishna. I closed my eyes as directed, and the next thing I felt was a kind of soft stitching happening above my brows. No hot wax, no ripping sensation, no tweezers plucking savagely through the forest of tiny hairs. Nothing, only a slight tickling as what felt like cotton or dental floss was being threaded through my brows. Threading! That was it. I'd heard of eyebrow threading, but I'd never actually seen or felt it being done. This was my kind of eyebrow makeover. The only downside was my ego being ever so slightly bruised when Savishna remarked half way through the treatment that my brows were quite hirsute. Didn't she know that brow bulk was highly fashionable? Some of the top models looked as if they had spent days colouring in and rubbing out their brows, to achieve that sexy brow look.

"We come from Italian stock-on my dad's side." I wanted Savishna to know that I was well aware of the density of my brows, but that it was definably a cultural throwback, and not an intentional fashion statement. Savishna couldn't have cared less about my heritage. She was engrossed in some sort of finger-dance with the cotton cord, pushing it one way, and pulling it the other. It reminded me of a lumberjack sawing wood with a half-moon saw. Backwards and forwards in sync with the background mood music. Whatever the method, the result was a vast improvement on what I had looked like before I had sought out this seesawing craftswoman.

"All done."

Savishna hip-hopped up and down to the pulsing background music, and I followed her lead and bopped off the table, nearly twisting my ankle in the process. It was getting harder and harder to be hip these days. I thanked Savishna and commented on her creative technique.

"Yeah right. Tar rah then. Been fun. Catch ya!"

The real fun part was handing over my credit card, and coping with the immediate phone alert which read: "Sixty-nine pounds."

I jumped for joy though (in my head) when my quick calculations had come up with a figure of at least three hundred pounds for a full massage and facial. I had saved myself over two hundred quid, which I would have been forced to fork out, had there been an appointment time for me today. Thank you, face-Gods! As an added bonus, I would now be safe to sail through the passport check out booths when I queued up to go to Ireland in a couple of weeks. I had read an article recently which had emphasised the importance of facial recognition at airports. It probably wouldn't have affected me as the concern was at the extreme end of quandary. Basically, if one started having copious amounts of plastic surgery, it could be an issue for recording facial data at airports. Especially if you entered a country with one face and exited with another. Just to be on the safe side (and the frugal side) I would wait until I was in Ireland to have the full facial and massage. Losing too much weight might also pose a problem if most of the weight drained from the face. I also resolved to eat as many cream buns and Chelsea buns as I liked whilst in England-just to be on the safe side. I would starve myself in Ireland.

I had been ambling along cobblestoned Kingston alley-ways whist I had been making my grooming and eating plans, and I'd ended up outside the entrance to a large modern looking mall, with glass and glitz and graffiti to rival any similar mall in downtown America. I could see a shop just inside the doorway advertising teas and tea products. I thought that a tin of tea might make a thoughtful present for an old lady friend of mine in Australia. So, I entered the mall with a purpose. Mostly I just window-shop or pick thing up and then leave them on the counter-chickening out at the last minute, but today I had my list, and there were three people to buy for. Pat, another octogenarian lady who enjoyed English tea, was the first person on the list for today. The young girl in the shop was predictably Polish, but she was in a class above the Lidl shop assistants. I could tell from her flawless, makeup caked skin, silky hair with the modern cut, kohl black defined eyes and the expensive silk shirt and woollen plaid skirt she wore. Her accent was also eloquent. It was a wonderful shop with a wafting smell of meditation oil and sweet smelling-candles, full of rows and rows of little wooden drawers containing teas of all sorts. It was just like stepping into one of the medieval Apothecary stores which had been prominent in medieval England. I thought it very clever of the owners to design their shops in the tradition of the old apothecaries in a town like Kingston upon Thames, which reeked of the medieval world.

"We have any sort of tea you could wish for, madame. What is your pleasure?"

My pleasure was to just pick up the nearest tin of tea which had a 'Made in England' stamping, and to pay for it and move on. I was getting very hungry and associated with this hunger was the beginnings of another headache and lots of yawning. I changed my mind whilst I was pondering which flavour would be best, deciding instead to go into London tomorrow, and visit a larger store. The girl was still prattling on. "Do you prefer tea leaves or tea powder?"

My ears pricked up when I heard about the powder option. Since the recipient of the tea was quite elderly, and lived alone, I thought it might be a good idea to buy her two tins of the powdered tea. "What is the best-selling tea flavour?"

I hoped she would inform me that it was peppermint, or even black current tea, but she surprised me with the retort "Strawberry". I knew that strawberries and cream was the favoured afternoon tea at the tennis during Wimbledon, but I hadn't really ever associated England with strawberries.

"Do you have any maple tea?"

The girl looked at me in surprise. "I haven't heard of maple tea before. Are you Canadian?"

She was not only extremely well-groomed; she was also very intelligent.

"No Australian but we had visitors from Canada last year, and they brought some maple tea with them. It was so sweet and thirst quenching; but I can't find anywhere in Australia that sells it." The girl looked doubtfully at me, but she was good at her job, and she knew how to humour the customers. She disappeared behind a thick orange and pink Laura Ashley printed curtain and was gone for about ten minutes. When she reappeared, all she said was,

"Apologies for the delay, no Maple tea, I've just been checking on the computer out the back of the shop." I felt a trifle let down that I had just spent ten minutes of my life waiting for someone to tell me something they could have done in ten seconds on the computer right there in front of me, but I hid my disappointment well I thought. The girl – Rita, didn't notice. I put it down to character building for me. Impatience was one of my biggest faults. Being impatient often led to recklessness on my part, and I needed to learn how to take the tests graciously when I was unsuspectingly confronted with them. One thing was for sure though. Rita would not be receiving the koala of the day. I may have slightly averted my impatience, but my stubbornness was still alive and kicking. I gave Rita a sickly-sweet response to the news which should defiantly have earned me customer of the week status.

"That's fine. No problem. I'll just take two tins of the strawberry. One can't ignore the opinion polls." Lugging the enormous fancy brown bag Rita had handed over to me, I made my way out into the enclosed body of the mall. It was very light, with a huge glass dome to rival Notre Dame in the centre, and masses of tangled escalators going up and down connecting the four levels of the shops. The floors shone like polish had just been applied. (It was still a bit slippery too.) We've all been there once or twice in our lives. Most of us under sufferance because the hustle and bustle, the glaring white light and the blasting hip hop music can be quite hard to take. I was reminded of Caesar's palace in Las Vegas as I stepped into the main arena of the mall. The walk-ways snake off in all directions, revealing a relentless progression of shops with uniform glass sheets for windows at the front, and tables and steel frames inside piled high with sparkling merchandise. This place is in stark contrast to the noisy trading happening not more than two hundred metres away.

The ancient market of Kingston-on Thames looks like something out of My Fair lady, and yet here was this sheer juxta positioning of worlds. It was all about serving a purpose. We live in an instant gratification world. I wanted to buy toys and tea and clothes – I came to the mall. Had I wanted fruit and vegetables and grains, I would have scuttled off to the ancient outdoor market across the cobblestoned square close to where my fate had almost been sealed some hours before. A toy shop was next on the list on my I phone. I really do want to move with the times and stop humming *Blowing in the Wind* and writing lists for everything I need to buy. Hence, I have taken to streaming music and talking to Siri on my phone whenever I want to note something down. Siri is good at her job for the most part, but my accent is sometimes a source of confusion for her, and I often end up with responses like "I can't find anyone in your address book called 'Spag-Hettie' when I clearly asked Siri to add spaghetti to my list".

Siri is also challenged by place and street names, as I found out last year in Ireland, and would probably do so again on this trip. Something to look forward to. A glossy stationary shop was directly in front of me, and the number of children clogging up the front entrance where the bargain half priced items had been placed was phenomenal. It looked like the Kingston headquarters of the Pied Piper of Hamlin Society. Again, good marketing strategy, because the children would force the parents to enter the shop to pay for the goods. Snap! The doting parents, uncles and aunts fell unwittingly into the trap, and would no doubt sheepishly emerge some hours later, laden to nonrecognition with books and stationery for their bubble-wrapped children. What was wrong with writing on slate? I desperately wanted to go into the stationary shop, but in anticipation of total pandemonium inside, I gave it a wide berth. The toy shop would be a safer bet, as all the children would be in the stationary shop. Priorities.

I was one hundred and one percent correct! The toy shop was deserted, and I waltzed in with a big Cheshire grin on my face. It was so peaceful, and there was so much room in which to move. I also had my choice of shop assistants.

There were three of them – all young girls. They left me alone to browse for a few minutes, but then one of them approached me with a sunbeam smile which put mine to shame. She was in the wrong shop. She should have been in the chemist next door, selling toothpaste all day. They would have made a killing. Not only did she wear a big smile, she also wore a glitzy cocktail outfit and high heeled patent shiny red shoes. I kept staring at her outfit, and her smile widened to the size of a small river. I was pretty certain she was Polish.

"You are surprised by my costume yes?" Well, I wouldn't have called a cocktail outfit a costume, but yes, I was surprised. Surprised that she had come to work in such an audacious outfit, and equally surprised that she seemed proud to be parading about in the outfit.

"I am Magda, a little mermaid, and the other two – Eva and Irena are also mermaids."

She indicated to the other two girls behind the counter, and I could see then that all three sported the same attire.

"Oh yes, I knew that." As I spoke, I realised that the song playing in the background was *Under the Sea* one of the more popular songs from the soundtrack of *The Little Mermaid.*

"Do you have any fidget spinners?" I was trying to say the words fidget spinners with some sense of authority, as if I knew what they were, or that I would have been able to locate them by myself, and that I was just politely allowing her to do her job by inquiring. In truth, I didn't have the faintest idea what they might be, their colour, their actual size or function. All the information I had was that they were on the smallish side, and they would fit easily into my suitcase when I was returning to Australia.

"It is the pleasure I have to demonstrate to you the fidget spinner. This is a wonderful gadget. This model will always give to you the satisfactory spin."

Great!

Just what I had yearned for my entire life. Such a lot to look forward to at night in this country. A satisfactory spin which truly gave me a deep sense of satisfaction. It made me smile to think of what a satisfactory spin would be like, and where and with whom it would be likely to take place. The little mermaid serving assistant took my twitching cheeks and inward chuckle to mean that I could identify wholeheartedly with the satisfactory spin, and that I had really known what was entailed, but that I had been too shy to approach the attendants outright and ask for the toy that gave to me the satisfactory spin.

"This one, she was reaching over and selecting a bright green flying saucer type object about the size of my palm, this one is the 'most satisfactory' and the longest lasting."

She was earnest and honest in her approach and seemed totally unaware of the associations she was conjuring up in my mind. And there was the reddening tell-tale face again, that I just could seem to shake in times of acute discomfort such as this. I decided to end it there and then. "Fine. Great. I'll take ten of them and then everyone will be well and truly satisfied. Any colours will do. Thankyou."

The girl was over the moon with my bulk purchase. She quickly gathered ten of the spinners and skipped over the counter with them. The other two mermaids were still leaning on the counter talking quietly to themselves, having a wonderfully lazy time of it. There did not appear to be any supervisors in the shop, and they were content to just loll about and wait for customers. There were rows and rows of German and Swiss wooden puzzles and building blocks, train sets and tea sets-toys of all descriptions and sizes. Of particular interest to me (apart from the fidget spinners) were the rows of golliwogs positioned on a very high shelf overlooking the counter. I wondered if these dolls were as popular as the fidget spinners which provided one with the satisfactory spin. I didn't dare ask to buy a couple of golliwogs as well as the spinners. I had to be content with gazing at them from afar.

The girl was handing me my bag with the fidget spinners, urging me to come back again very soon, and that she would be happy to show me how any of the toys in the shop worked.

"You seem to be the person who appreciates the satisfactory spins in life." I was. I was proudly that person! I assured her that I would return very soon. All three of them waved me off and then resumed their nattering in Polish. (Probably wondering what on earth I was going to do with ten fidget spinners.) The mind boggles!

I figured that I was probably their only, best, and most unusual customer for the day. Sailing through Customs was going to be fun!

It was getting on for mid-afternoon by the time I finally emerged from my window shopping in the mall. I was bereft of bags and this state was very conducive to window shopping and browsing, since I did not have to dump my bags on the shiny linoleum floors outside the shops each time I wanted to look in windows, or comb through racks in clothes shops, desperately searching for my size. It didn't make a whole lot of sense that the sizes were all small and smaller. But, on reflection, I supposed that the clientele who visited the mall had an average age of twelve and that the clothes for the more mature and well-rounded women would be found in either the big department stores or the little boutique shops which dotted the main street outside the mall. I thought about looking for one of them, but it was really getting later and later, and the buses would be too crowded if I dilly dallied any longer.

Outside in the town square, there was another commotion going on. It wasn't really intended as a commotion, but there was a great deal of noise and bustle, and people gathered around a gentleman with an accordion, yodelling and jumping around singing at the top of his voice. He was dressed in the classic accordion player's costume of white shirt, a pointy hat, braces, shorts and knee-high white socks. He also wore clogs on his feet, just to complete the authentic German look. Some of the onlookers were clapping to the music and dancing around in circles, but mostly people were just rushing past the commotion on their way to the trains and the buses. The accordion player was ignoring the crowds, just entertaining himself and his band of dancers. As I tried to inconspicuously slip past with my laden backpack, one of the dancers grabbed my arm and started hurling me forwards and propelling me onto the next person waiting to catch and encircle me. I was suddenly in the impromptu dance.

The man who had initially grabbed and included me had probably thought that I was part of some rehearsed street theatre, as I suppose I looked the part with my back pack, thick laced walking shoes, jeans and my blue checked shirt. Whatever his reason, he was at least ten people in front of me in the dance, and I was in for the long haul by the sound of the music which seemed only to be repeating the same polka dance bars over and over. I could see the buses up ahead of me when I finally reached the undefined boundary of the stage. Quick as a flash, I leant backwards as far as I could and contorted my body forwards away from the lady who had her hands on my waist spinning me around. She looked surprised and then offended, but she let me go abruptly, and I fell forwards. For the second time in as many hours, I fell heavily on the pavement and hurt my left arm as I fell. It wasn't hurt enough though, to stop me hot-footing it away from the mad folly and down towards the bus depot. Surely no one would follow me down there. No one did, as they were still dancing around in circles, and the polka was nowhere near ending.

I found my bus almost at once, and it was empty apart from some school children who weren't at school because it was still holidays. Maybe they just enjoyed riding the buses. They didn't really bother me as they made their way up the winding stairs and disappeared from my sight. We waited about ten minutes before taking off, and the bus took the very same route I had just hobbled on foot. The first stop was the square where the accordion player was still hard at it. I slid down in my seat and only resurfaced when we were almost in Hampton. What a day! I was again exhausted and literally dying of thirst.

When I cautiously unlocked the front door, and dumped my backpack in the foyer, I realised that the house was deathly quiet, and not even the dogs had appeared. Where was everyone? Then I remembered that Patrick had taken the dogs off overnight to his friend's place in the country, so that the two of them and their respective dogs could go for a long walk tomorrow and talk politics about the state of affairs in England. Alice had a late meeting, and that left me. I had a bit of a rest, and then let myself back out of the house, making sure to deadlock the front door. Alice had impressed on me that even though they lived in an affluent respectable neighbourhood, they were not immune to break-ins, and that crime was rife everywhere around London. The corner shop was only five minutes away, and I had the idea to buy some really sweet, really fizzy drink to quench my thirst, and maybe some of the delicious homemade samosas they sold for Alice and myself so that we didn't have to cook tonight. (I wasn't sure whether she would have eaten during the meeting.)

I located the soft drink fridge easily enough, but the samosas I picked up were frozen, and I wasn't sure if they were the particular homemade variety of which Alice had sung the praises on many an occasion. I would just have to ask the shopkeeper. I found him at the front of the shop standing resignedly behind the counter. He was Pakistani, youngish, dark, incredibly good looking and quite charismatic. He informed me that he had frozen samosas, but that they would take too long to thaw, and it would be better to buy ready heated samosas. We conversed for a while as the samosas in the pie warmer behind the counter needed more heating. In the course of our conversation, he explained to me that he lived above the shop and that he owned the whole premises with his brother. He also slipped into the conversation that his brother was married with three children, but that he wasn't married and that he was available, and would I like to come for dinner to his parents' house tomorrow evening? They lived about twenty minutes away, and the whole family would be summoned there to meet me.

I didn't know how to react to that totally unexpected lengthy, left field request. But I ready with my response.

"Um, I think we are going to my friend's grandmother's house tomorrow night for tea, and she would be devastated if we didn't show up, but thank you anyway. I'll just pay for the drinks and the samosas." The Pakistani man was not fazed by this swift rejection; in fact he appeared quite indifferent to my response.

"Not to make a worry. Another time perhaps?"

Yes. Another time perhaps. Another lifetime perhaps. I was just not well enough prepared to become a Pakistani wife for many, many reasons-the main one being that I still had my whole trip in front of me. I was past child – bearing age and I couldn't speak Urdu to save myself, even though I had many Pakistani friends in Australia. I loved the food though, and that was swaying me slightly towards this shop-keeper. Most of my Pakistani friends were nuns or relatives of the nuns, so it wasn't as if I knew what to expect of life in an extended Pakistani family. No. The more I mused, the more I realised it wasn't what the universe had in mind for me.

When I rounded the corner to Alice and Patrick's court, I could see that Alice's Mercedes was parked in the driveway, and that the lights were blaring from every room visible from the street. Alice liked to let onlookers know that there were a lot of people home when she was home alone. I couldn't blame her, what with all the talk and newspaper reports of break-ins and the increasing crime rates, but I had to smile at the way the house was lit up. It looked very inviting and beckoning, quite the opposite to what Alice had intended when she had switched on all the lights. She wanted to keep the criminals out, but she was unsuspectingly inviting them in. I rang the doorbell twice and knocked loudly before I put my key in the lock. That was just to let Alice know that it was me, and not a stranger entering the premises. I then made a bet with myself that the first thing Alice would say to me when she saw me would be, "Oh, it's you Fil. Why are you making all that noise?" As sure as eggs, those were the exact words to escape her lips, the only difference being the inflection in her voice when she said the word, you. The way she said you, to me, made me feel very welcome and very needed. I knew that I was only the flavour of the evening because Patrick and the dogs were away, but I just shrugged off any tiny bits of jealousy which were threatening to land between us, and informed Alice that I had her dinner in my backpack and that there was still steam coming from them, so we had better eat pronto. Alice hadn't eaten at her meeting, and she was very pleased with my decision to buy the samosas and soft drink. We locked the doors and settled in for the night with my samosas and my stories of the day. Alice loved the threading of my eyebrows story best, but I just couldn't get past the Pakistani shopkeeper on the corner asking me on a date to meet his whole entire family. Who really needed Arabic sheiks when there were eligible Pakistani merchants available just around the corner, not more than one hundred metres away? Maybe that trip to the suburbs with Mr Pakistan to have dinner and meet his family might be worth considering after all?

## Chapter 17
### Bombs Away!

A muffled dripping sound was forcing me out of my haphazard dream and into the real world of the beautiful bedroom, with the soft morning light, in which I was sleeping. I couldn't focus but I could recognise the sound. Rain. Rain on the roof and window panes to be precise. I managed to finally regain my sight, and I realised that today was the day I had ear-marked for a visit to Buckingham Palace and the Changing of the Guard in the Parade ground. I had witnessed the spectacle before on previous trips, but never alone, and I was little trepidatious of how I might fare as a sole tourist. I did feel nervous, but I couldn't work out whether that was because I would have no one to 'goo and gah' with at the Palace, or whether I was just nervous of horses in general. The last time I had been at Buckingham Palace, one of the Queen's Guard riders had fallen off his horse, as a trio of riders crossed the road. Although the crowd were alarmed, and many onlookers started running in the other direction, the culprit horse seemed unfazed, and trotted off for a leisurely stroll up the street near the back entrances to the palace. I was quite near the scene of the fall, and even though we did not run away, my irrational fear of horses came straight back to me. We went home after that. Today I would be alone, that was true, but I would make sure that I latched onto a tourist family or two and stayed close to them at all times. I wasn't fearing a kidnapping. No one would want me – as I had no one to pay the ransom, and also, I wouldn't fit in the boot of a car. Too much work to kidnap a heifer like me. I think I'd be pretty safe to proceed with my plans for the day. Even though it was only seven thirty by the time I was ready, I decided to leave the house and head for the station. Alice had set off at the crack of dawn for an early meeting, and I knew that if I hung around much longer, Joan from next door would appear and probably ask me to make porridge or kippers or something for her breakfast. Funnily enough, as I stepped out onto the footpath of the court, I was engulfed by a strong fishy smell coming from Joan's loungeroom which was at the front of her house. The front door was wide open, and the two dogs were madly chasing each other's tails in the overgrown to jungle proportions front garden.

If I showed the slightest interest in what was happening at number 11, or even turned my head slightly to the left to see if Joan was somewhere in the jungled-garden, I would have been sucked into the vortex that was Joan for the entire day. I knew this instinctively. So, what did I do? I ran. And ran. And ran. All the way to the bus stop. When I got there, I pulled my scarf savagely around my face to a state of incognito and leant against the wooden frame of the bus shed. I had too much on my agenda today to be distracted by needy neighbours.

The bus came along just before I suffocated trying to hide inside my scarf. It was full as usual, and I was all prepared to stand for the next fifteen minutes when a scruffy teenager who had been huddled into his seat with headphones and an ear ring through his mouth, jumped up and offered me his place. I tried to thank him, but he had put his headphones back on, and was rolling his eyes and head back to the music. I kept smiling at him whenever he looked my way, but he was not playing the game. After about five minutes of smiling, I turned my head the other way, and when I looked up again, he was gone. We had pulled up at the station, where most people got off, including me. I was to have the chance this morning to see for myself what the Bermuda triangle-up and over the overpass was really like. People had disappeared over the horizon of the overpass a few days before when I had been lined up at the café across the road. Spurred on by a desperate desire to see what was up there, I raced up the steps without stopping. Once I reached the top of the overpass, I was out of breath, so leant against the railing whilst the seasoned commuters who had been sensible about the steps, sailed passed me and disappeared down the other side It was the hare and the tortoise for real, but I was no hare-just the silly bunny who wanted to be the first and the best, but who ended up being the last and the worse for wear. From then on, I took to the steps one by one, shuffling down the other side of the overpass like a hundred-year-old grandmother tackling the Great Wall of China with one hundred days in which to do it. When I finally reached the bottom step, I could see with pristine clarity, that the tortoise commuters who had overtaken me, were already boarding the train, and the conductor was already blowing his whistle and waving the driver off. "Looks like you missed that one then." I turned to see a dapper old man with a spotted red bow tie chuckling to himself and leaning against his walking stick. His voice was a trifle muffled, as his face was buried in an enormous handkerchief, and he started blowing his nose loudly as soon as he finished his astute observation of my predicament.

"No, that probably wasn't my train, and anyway, I can catch the next one. I've got plenty of time."

"Where are yaofta?"

"Buckingham Palace to see the Changing of the Guard."

"Hard cheese about missing the train, you could've been early n'all n seen the horses parading around a bit."

Now that was what I called inside information. Here was a gentleman with his ear to the ground. Admittedly, he was wearing a rather large ear piece in his left ear, but the right one looked to be working normally. He could hear me at least.

"Well thanks for that piece of information. I actually wanted to avoid the horses as I'm scared of them a little, so it suits me fine to be a little late."

"That's the spirit lassie. You go and be late, and don't go near them horses. Off ya trot now!"

He chuckled loudly at his equine joke, and with the chuckle came a great splattering of a sneeze. I took my leave of him quick smart, and then emptied my bottle of water all over my hands and arms to ensure there was not a scrap of the spray left on me. I suddenly felt another spraying, but this time it was on my face, and this time it was quite heavy and quite consistent. Rain. Again. Well, this was England. I scuttled towards the waiting room of the station, and found a seat squashed in between an elderly couple who had plonked their suitcase down between. Both had huge crumpled maps pressed to their faces, and neither of them even looked up at me as I swivelled down. (The man had moved the suitcase off the seat, but he maintained his scrutiny of his map as if he were planning the battle of Waterloo.) I wished I was a big, bald, tattooed hairy bikie with a bandana wrapped around my baldness. Instead, I was probably quite inconspicuous looking in my jeans, sketchers and blue wind sheeter. I waited three minutes and they still hadn't even noticed me, so I hopped off and moved towards the booth, deciding that I would ask the stationmaster when the next train into central London was expected. The stationmaster was also busy consulting a timetable, but as soon as he saw my face pressed against the small booth, he slid the window along and beamed at me.

"Would you like to purchase an oyster card? Where are you travelling to?"

"I'm trying to get into Victoria station so that I can walk to Buckingham palace, although I'm not sure about how I'll go walking in the rain without an umbrella." I was kicking myself now that I hadn't had the foresight to bring an umbrella or a raincoat with me. I had both items in my broken suitcase back at Alice's, but I just hadn't given enough thought to the expected weather.

"Best train is the Hampton to Waterloo. You can get a bus from there, which will get you very close."

"Will it take long to get there?"

"Depends on what happens along the way, but it should be no more than forty minutes. Be careful when you get there, the pace is right fast n'all in London."

He was then on for a chat, and began telling me his life story, including his dreams to appear on West end in a long running musical. He told me that he spent nearly every night cooped up in his bedsit above a fish and chip shop, practising the lyrics to Les Misérables and Phantom of the Opera in the hope that he would one day be plucked from the sooty damp waiting room at the Station and miraculously transported to the barricades of the French Revolution. I just prayed that he was rehearsing "I dreamed a dream" and not "Castle on a cloud" or it would be 'Cosette' (aged ten and a girl) that he might end up playing. A novel twist to the longest running musical on the West End!

With our love of the theatre in common, Dean and I got on like a house on fire, and neither of us noticed, or heard the train approaching. Fortunately for Dean, everything at the station was automated, and he did not really have to do much at all. When he did finally notice the train had reached the platform, he panicked, and went into a tailspin. I was immediately abandoned. I had been searching around in my backpack whilst we had been chattering, and I came up with one of the koalas which was buried right down at the bottom. I reached inside the window and placed the tiny koala on the ledge, which already housed little vases full of plastic flowers and mugs and spoons with engravings. Perhaps there had been other tourists with a similar benevolent streak. I was glad that a fellow thespian with his head in the clouds was getting a koala.

Then I raced off to catch my train.

I found a semi-empty carriage towards the rear of the train and settled myself down in a back corner. No sooner had I relaxed than a tall stately woman with a striking crop of purple hair complete with bright pink highlights plonked herself down beside me. Her entire demeanour was quirky upon quirky.

"I hope you don't mind me sitting here, but I like to talk to people on trains. They are so interesting."

"No, its fine really. Please sit down."

I had really wanted to take the opportunity to organise my backpack and money belt so that everything was in order for the big day at Buckingham palace.

"Off to somewhere exciting pet?"

"Not really. Just Buckingham Palace."

I was being facetious in my underplaying response, but the quirkiness was deep seated, and the purple-people-eater woman missed my innuendo.

"Yes pet, I suppose that with all the places you have seen in your travels it will be just another grand home to you. Have you been to Hampton Court Palace yet? By the way, my name is Lucinda. I live in a council flat by myself. I have four grandchildren and they keep me on my toes. I'm always warm, even in winter, and it's not the menopause and it's not too much sex. I was a lighting assistant in the theatres in London all my life. I could tell you some stories about actors. Do you like the theatre?" I shook her outstretched hand. "Hello Lucinda. Yes, I have been to the local Palace, just a few days ago actually. But today I'm not going into the palace rooms, I'm going to see the Changing of the Guard. I needed to get there early as I'm not sure of how far I will have to walk." I then added the most important slither of information, "Yes, I love the theatre. I've been involved with the theatre all my life in some way or another."

Was that enough for Lucinda to sit and mull over? Might I now commence my backseat, incognito rummaging? I was trying to do what I should have done last night, which was ready myself for the big day ahead, and lighten my load. But the added weight of my water bottle and fruit snacks was already causing me anxiety. Since I had not eaten any breakfast, I fished out my browning banana and started peeling back the skin. Australians eat a great deal of bananas, being such a hot country, and my peeling was expert and deft, thanks to years of banana snacks in my childhood. Now Lucinda was impressed.

"You certainly have a way with bananas, don't ya petal? Us poms wouldn't even know what to do with a banana." I could have retorted with the fact that Benny Hill, Dick Emery or any of their fellow comedians had known full well how to entertain audiences for years with banana related skits. But I didn't. I just fished deeper into my backpack and came up with a mandarin, which I offered to her in good faith. She thanked me, but refused, informing me with birth-right authority that I might need to ration out my mandarin to myself during the day –

what with the toffs and crowds in central London. First Dean, and now Lucinda telling me to prepare myself for the pace of Central London.

Could it have changed so much?

We ended up nattering on for the next ten minutes whilst the stations flashed by. We were on the express train to Kingston, and after the Kingston stop the train would resume the regular morning's snail-pace stopping at all stations. Lucinda stood up briskly, as soon as the announcement echoed through the carriage that the train was approaching Kingston upon Thames station. "Cheerio oh love, I'm off to do some Christmas shopping for my grandchildren. See you in the theatre." She winked and was gone. Now to my backpack culling.

To ensure that not another living soul would dare to enquire if the seat next to me was taken, I moved forward three places and slid across to the window, carefully arranging my backpack and spare jumper on the seat next to me. I would clean out the backpack in the privacy of my bedroom tonight. For now, it would serve as a buffer to the hordes of seat-seekers who might board the train from now on. The little mound I had fashioned with my bulging backpack and the bulky jumper somehow reminded me of the 'lump to my left' from the plane on the way over to England. Even though there had been no life in the lump, I still felt a slight pang of remorse that I was never going to see it again – whatever it was. My plan worked a trick, as when we stopped at the next station and about ten people boarded, no one even attempted to sit next to me. A well-heeled gentleman clutching a newspaper and a brown briefcase positioned himself directly behind me, and a young, hyped-up schoolgirl sat down opposite me. Up ahead there were quite a few bobbing heads taking up at least four rows, but they were quite a way from the three of us. They appeared to be a group of hardened commuters, intent on reaching their destination and not in the least inclined to languish around in convivial chit-chat. That suited me fine. I would just close my eyes and have a little rest. I was just dozing off when my mobile rang. I assumed it would be Alice, as it would have been after midnight in Australia, and too late for a social call from anyone there. It wasn't Alice. It was Carmel, one of my sisters ringing from Australia with heightened loud panic in her voice. "Fil, Fil, are you alright? Where are you? Have you heard the news?"

"No. What news? Is everything OK in Australia?"

"Yes, it's not us, it's you. There has been a terrorist bombing on a train going into London. You're not on a train, are you? Please say you are still in bed!"

"Yes. I'm on a train, which train is the bomb on? Which line, there are hundreds of them." The mobile then went dead, and I looked down to see that glaring phrase, 'Call failed'. I tried calling back, but to no avail. That was the end of my connection with the outside world. Consequently, I went into a state of immediate shock. Australians have minimal historical precedents for terrorist attacks. There have been a few serious incidents in the past, but not on the scale of England or France. I had shouted back my response to her startling news, and this caused all the commuters in front of me to turn their heads and stare at me in surprise and disbelief. The schoolgirl opposite me jumped up and down in her seat and started calling out in a panicked voice, "A bomb! A bomb! There's a bomb on the train!"

Once the shock settled for me, I reached over to try and assure her that there were literally hundreds of trains en-route to London at this very moment. Just as I was pushing her back down to her seat, and urging her to try and stay calm, the train lurched forwards, and stopped dead in its tracks. I looked out of the window and could see that we were perched on a precipice of a bridge. Everything went quiet, and then there was a crackling sound of the microphone being tapped wildly, and then came the high-pitched squeaking voice of the conductor, letting all commuters know that here had been an incident on a train not far from us, and that we were just waiting for the all clear to continue on our journey.

The school girl I was holding down in a suspect brace wriggled out of my grip and flew down the carriage screaming out, "A BOMB! There's a bomb on this train. It's on this carriage!"

The girl was becoming hysterical, or perhaps she just enjoyed scaring herself and others. She stated running up and down the aisles, and I felt helpless to stop her. Since none of us really knew which trains had been targeted and implanted with bombs – all we could do was sit back and try not to panic until we were told to do anything different. I picked up my backpack and jumper and stuffed them down on the floor under my seat. If we were going to jump from the train, I would not be needing my backpack, and like a true tourist, I had my passport and some spare cash firmly fastened around my waist. If there was a bomb on the train, it was not looking good for us, as we were probably about two hundred metres off the ground on a land bridge over a quarry.

With sweat pouring off my face in the increasingly stuffy carriage, I slunk back in my seat and closed my eyes. I could still hear the commuters ahead of me whispering their concerns to each other – or maybe they were whispering to family on their mobiles. Mine was dead so that was not an option for me. I had to smile (weakly) when I imagined what Alice would say when I told her about this morning's adventures. I felt a sudden tapping on my shoulder and turned to see the amused face of the business man in the suit. His lap was covered in newspaper, and he was chuckling to himself. He promptly delivered his witty one-liner with a deadpan expression and genuine incredulity, "It's sad that we are forced to rely on news from the Antipodes to find out what is happening in our own country." With his pseudo-pompous pontification completed, he turned back to his more comfortable and credible newsfeed. I just stared at him and wondered about the poor woman who had married him. She would probably have to put up with his pertinent life quotes every evening for the rest of her life.

The young girl opposite me had finally returned to her seat, her job of inciting the masses completed. I didn't think she truly realised the severity of our situation – perched on this land-bridge – ten metres or so high and kept in the dark as to whether or not we had a bomb on our train. As far as we knew, only our carriage was aware of the train bombings. It was extremely unnerving – this uncertainty of fate. The microphone was being switched on, and there was much tapping and heavy breathing coming from the speakers.

"Attention passengers. We have a situation! There has been an explosion on a nearby train, and London transport has been accelerated to critical code, which means we will be required to remain stationary until further notification. Please do not panic! As far as we know this train is not yet affected by the incident."
Yet? What did he mean not yet? It was becoming more and more difficult to remain calmly seated. A mobile rang loudly, disturbing the silence which had descended upon the carriage. It was the young girl's phone, and we could all hear what she was saying, as the train was stationary and silent. "Nah Mum. I'm good. Ain't on our train."

"Yeah… Yeah… Yeah. Oh kayyy! I'll get off at the next station. I think we are on the big bridge near Teddington." As soon as she put her phone down, the girl leaned over to me with a delighted expression on her very pale face.

"Guess what? I don't have to go to school today, and my mum's picking me up to take me out to the mall. Howz that? My lucky day. Bring on the bombs!"

The man behind me piped up with his next one-liner, "Out of the mouths of babes!" even before I could think of an appropriate reply which would somehow get across to this sassy, shallow-minded girl the seriousness of our situation. Mr Antipodes had his fair share of British humour, and little Miss Sunshine with the satchel had not a clue about the precariousness of life and death. At twelve or thirteen, life is sometimes little more than one big shopping spree. I fell somewhere in the middle, being inclined towards both shopping and humour.

So much had happened this morning, and I worked out that it was probably still only about 9 o'clock, or just after. The train showed no signs of stirring, and we seemed settled on the bridge.

Everyone went quiet again, and I wondered if the same thing was happening in the other carriages.

We would never know, as there was no further word from the train driver or the conductor. Just as I was about to retrieve my backpack and take out my jotting book to make some notes on the incident, in case they also needed to be included in my eulogy, the train gave a loud groan and lurched forwards. It sounded like the Loch Ness monster heaving its way out of the depths of the Scottish waters.

The girl opposite started jumping up again.

"We're moving. We're moving!" She began gathering her worldly goods together, and overladen with her heavy school bag, hockey stick and a violin case, made her way shakily towards the carriage door. No one was going to beat her out of the train at the next station. I still wasn't sure whether to jump up and race down to occupy the position directly behind her. Mr Antipodes saved me from this agonising decision.

"Up to you, but I don't think you need to get off just yet. If there was a bomb on the train, we would have heard about it by now. This is probably the safest place to be right now. Outside of 10 Downing street that is."

I smiled back at him and realised that he was a man of the world who knew his stuff. (10 Downing street had fortress-like gates at either end of the block on which it stood.) I would just stay in my seat until we reached London Waterloo. Then I would reassess my movements. I had forgotten all about Buckingham Palace with all the drama. I'd just have to wait and see what was actually happening in the outside world this morning. I'd stay put in my seat till London and then I would assess the lay of the land.

The train was drawing to a halt. I could see the girl jumping off as if she was going to a 'One Direction' concert. She was so excited. Her parting words to all of us. "Later everyone. Hope you make it." This girl may have been naïve, but she certainly knew how to work the crowd. About three of the commuters must have been scared off by her parting words, as all three of them jumped ship at the last second. One left it so long to make the decision to leave that he managed to catch his tie in the doors as they closed. He looked like he was about to asphyxiate himself, but luckily someone pressed the button and the doors re opened. He then disappeared for good.

That left about four of us on the carriage as the train wove its way over the myriad of intertwined tracks into London. Except for me, everyone looked as if they were on their way to work. I was so obviously a tourist. We tourists are very, very recognisable. No incognito for us. Backpacks and bulging stomachs hiding money and passports are the dead giveaways. I didn't really care that I was the only tourist on the train. As soon as we got into Waterloo there would be hundreds of thousands of us. I could sense that my tribe was waiting for me just around the corner, and if they weren't there in their hundreds, there was always Australia House in Earl's Court.

Waterloo was straight ahead of us, I could clearly see the large-print map on the carriage wall. We were still on the above ground tracks, so it wasn't as frightening as it would have been in the underground, imagining that every briefcase held a bomb. The microphone was crackling through the loud speaker again, and the frustrated and 'slightly peeved' sounding conductor was trying to ensure everyone's attention with his tapping. He began with his usual prelude, "Attention passengers," and continued on with, "this train will shortly arrive at Waterloo station. Please ensure that you have collected all your luggage and personal belongings, as this is the end of the line. You will need to change for the underground to travel into central London. Thank you for travelling. British Rail and good morning."

Everyone was moving at once toward the doors. Only Mr Antipodes stayed where he was. "No sense in hurrying." (He was still humouring me.)

"It's not like we are going anywhere."

I had to agree with him, so I sat back down and began searching for my oyster card in readiness for the manic rush I knew from experience, would be taking place at the turnstiles. I slipped the card (which was in a little silver and white pocket-wallet) into my own pocket without much thought and stood up. I was distracted by a scuffle on the platform outside the train involving a guide-dog and an elderly woman. The dog was leaping up and yelping and the woman was trying to calm the dog down. It wouldn't be calmed. Dogs and children have that sixth sense nailed, and this guide-dog could definitely sense that all was not well with the world of trains this morning.

I had alighted from the train and was body-surfing up the platform with the seemingly hundreds of other commuters who must have been crammed into the other carriages, when the next major incident occurred. They were a fierce lot, hell bent on making it to work only two or so hours late. It had been unavoidable, and as yet, we still did not know the severity of the morning's happenings. I was allowing myself to be surged along with the crowd, when I remembered that I needed to present my oyster card for tapping. I had pre-loaded the card on my last trip to London, and I knew I had at least fifty pounds credit left on the card. I started patting around in my pocket for the card, but it wasn't there. I then tried the other pocket – to no avail. I scanned the ground close by, hoping that the card had fallen out of my pocket, but it wasn't anywhere to be seen. I then remembered that I had been in an enormous hurry when I'd supposedly stuffed it into my pocket, and I began to doubt whether I had even done so at all. Possibly, I had been so anxious to flee the train that I had dropped it or left it on my seat. I was suddenly desperate to get back onto the train and look for my card. I didn't stop to think it through rationally. I just wanted my card back. As I tried to jump back onto the carriage I thought to be the one I had just left, a heavy hand yanked me backwards, and at the same time blew into a shrill whistle which simultaneously pierced the air and my ear drums. Two other guards came running up towards us, and one of them flanked himself across the carriage doorway, barring me from jumping onto the train. The third guard started patting me down and calling for back up. This morning was turning into a nightmare.

"I haven't done anything. Why are you patting me down and squeezing my arm? Let me go!"

The first guard let go as soon as he heard my accent, and the second one relaxed a little with his patting, but he did not stop entirely. I thought that he must have practised this fleecing of suspected terrorists and espionage agents many times on dummies, and now that he had a potentially real suspect in front of him, he wasn't going to give up that easily. The third man just shrugged and sauntered off, realising that although I may have been a forgetful time waster, I was no lone terrorist.

"I left my Oyster card on the train. I just wanted to hop back on to look for it. I'm going to Buckingham Palace this morning – or maybe tomorrow morning at his rate." The whistler seemed to think my excuse plausible. He took a chance on me, and I was very grateful. No one likes to lose their lifeline Oyster card in London.

"Wait here and I'll go and take a look. You picked an awkward morning to lose your card." He didn't know that I knew the morning to be more than a touch awkward for a great many people, but I wasn't going to let onto him that I knew about the bomb. Even I could see that would make me very questionable. I played my part well. I lowered my head and whispered back to him. "Thank you very much. I was three seats from the back on the right-hand side. The card-wallet is silver and white. I have a spare ten pounds in it, so you'll know it's mine. I just hope that this is the right carriage. It was. The station guard emerged five minutes later proudly holding the Oyster card wallet high above his head, yelling out, I've found it."

Thankfully for me, it wasn't a bomb that he'd found, or that would have been two of my lives used up in as many days.

Once the guard handed over the card to me, I found added strength, and sprinted down the platform towards the exit. It was almost deserted, and a familiar wave of uneasiness overcame me once more. I didn't like the fact that the platform which had been seething with commuters, shoppers and tourists less than fifteen minutes ago – was now a ghost platform. Not a soul to be seen, and something was not quite right. I tapped my card and found the escalator out towards the street. On the way, I noticed that a large makeshift barricade with bright red witches' hats had been positioned in front of the entrance to the tube, and that there were about two or three guards stationed at behind the barricade. The guards looked very official in their helmets and some sort of glass protective shield. Something serious must have been going on, but maybe it was just the bombing incident. It was hard to know what to do and who to talk to. I began to wish that I had told the whistling guard that I knew about the bomb on train. He might then have shown pity towards me, and spilled the beans as to what was really happening with London transport today. But I'd cooked my chook and made my bed, as we say in Australia when we cause our own downfall. I'd just have to try and make my way to Buckingham Palace alone. I'd missed the Changing of the Guard, but I could still take photos. There were bound to be other tourists with the same idea.

Once outside, in the drizzly London streets, I began to feel better. I took some deep breaths and concentrated on getting my bearings. Directly in front of me was a bustling Mc Donald's restaurant, and I wandered in and found a semi-quiet corner in which to sit and compose myself. There was still the nagging thought in the back of my mind that my family and friends couldn't know if I was safe from the bombing, or even if there had been any more bombs. I retrieved my mobile, and joy of joys, there was a strong signal. It was miraculously working! I didn't want to tempt fate by delaying things any further, so I texted my sister straight away, with the good news that I was still alive and kicking, and that the bomb had not been on my train. I felt quite weak and woozy, so I once I'd sent the text, I lined up and ordered a muffin with jam and a coffee. The gum-chewing girl on the counter asked me if I had been on any of the trains today, and when I admitted that I had been on an early train from Hampton, she pricked up her ears.

"Ja know that ver was a bomb on a train? It's on all the news and the telly."

"Whatcha know about it? Was it on yer train?"

"Nothing. Sorry. I know nothing. I was asleep on my train, and when I woke up, we were here." The girl seemed disappointed that I had no blood and gore to report, but I wasn't in the mood to relive the scene. After my snack, I sat back on the red vinyl bench, re-arranging my backpack and sorting out my passport and cash. I wanted to make my way to Buckingham Palace on the buses, as I didn't really feel confident enough to get back on the trains. The buses would have to suffice. When I found the bus stop (which was back outside the train station), there were two middle-aged women jumping up and down in front of a tall pole displaying the buses timetables. The women were both quite short in stature, dressed in sensible clothing, safari-style plastic rainhats, and carrying umbrellas. Their conversation was hilarious. I wasn't eavesdropping, just standing too close. It went something like this:

"Do you think the bus will be long?"

"Which bus?"

"The bus to Bethnal Green – that's where we are going isn't it?"

"Yes, but I can't see the times. The numbers are too small. Can you give me a leg up, I might be able to see better if I'm closer to the timetable."

"What, here? Out in the open with everyone having a gander at us?"

"Yes, here Helena. There's no one around, only this traveller girl."

She was indicating to me, and I tried to look away, but I was desperate to find a bus that would take me to Buckingham Palace. I hoped they didn't think I was a traveller of the gypsy variety, standing too close so that I could purloin from them. The gypsies were not popular in London, I knew that from experience.

"Don't mind me. I'm just a tourist. I won't look, I'll turn away, but while you're up there, could you see if there is a bus going to Buckingham Palace?"

They both laughed, and then, hey presto, Helena bent over, and her friend hitched up her skirt and jumped onto her arched back, as agile as a cat. I was very impressed with the way they worked so deftly together as a team. They would have made a great cat burglar duo in their heyday. The friend was calling down to Helena, "You couldn't pass up the magnifying glass could you, I can't really read this timetable properly, but I think there is a bus at eleven fifty-five heading for Bethnal Green. I can't see Buckingham Palace written anywhere."

Helena tried to reach her handbag which she had placed on the ground next to her when she'd bent over, but it was zipped up, and she couldn't reach the zip. I was not supposed to be looking, but I could see everything that was going on quite clearly from my sideways position.

"I'll pass you the handbag if you like."

"NO!" The hissed response was from both of them, and quite vehemently delivered. I wondered what was in the handbag that caused them both to react so strongly. They were off to Bethnal Green, and I knew that to be an area of London well known to crime and robberies. Something about these two cat-woman was decidedly fishy, but I just couldn't put my finger on what it was. I was best off rid of them, and I knew just what to say. "That's fine, I'll wait here anyway. My bus must come along soon." But my plan backfired on me, and all three of us were still waiting at 1 o'clock. No other potential passengers were to be seen. Finally, a tired looking red bus came creeping along. 'Victoria Station' was displayed on the front window, and I delightedly sprang to attention. The two women did not look pleased that my bus had come before theirs, but one of them came good and politely informed me that this was my bus. I thanked them, waved, and climbed aboard. I fully expected to hear about their afternoon on the 6 o'clock news crime watch segment, so convinced was I that they were London's answer to Bonnie and Clyde.

What was happening around Waterloo today? The bus was almost deserted, and I had my choice of a seat. Since I wasn't sure how long I'd be on the bus for, I ignored the stairs, and made my way to the back of the bus which was also elevated, but to a much lesser degree than the double decker section on top. I just got myself settled, when the bus stopped again. We couldn't have gone more than one hundred metres. We had rounded a corner, and then stopped. I looked out the window and saw that unlike the previous stop where there had only been the three of us, this stop was overcrowded, and they all seemed to be pushing their way onto the bus. Many of them had piles and piles of bags, and nearly all of them carried umbrellas. They were all mostly woman. I could see a couple of grubby boys amongst them, but the women dominated. The front of the bus filled up quite quickly, with the back of the bus (where I was seated in solitary silence) suffering the same fate. In a matter of minutes, we were chockers. I had a woman the size of Mrs Claus sitting on top of me, and she had about five friends who all congregated around her. They were full of talk about the bombing, so at last I was to receive some real facts. These women looked worldly! (other-worldly?)

"So, I said to Esther, what do you think has happened, why aren't the buses and the trains running?"

"And what did Esther say?"

"She said that there'd been a bomb on a train at Parson's Green, and that all the London Transport System has been shut down for who knows how long. They're only letting a few buses continue to operate. I suppose this bus must be one of them."

"Esther'ed know if anyone does. Do you think we should still go and see Buckingham Palace today?"

I was surprised to hear them say that they were headed for Buckingham Palace, as they had quite an accumulation of parcels between them, but maybe they'd been early morning shopping?

"Well, we could still go, but I'm a bit lost now, as this isn't our usual bus."

I couldn't hear the other women's responses to this, as there was a great deal of shouting coming from the front of the bus. We had made another stop while the women were talking, and I had been so engrossed in their accents that I hadn't bothered to look up and assess the new passengers. The yelling continued. It sounded like the lady who was arguing with the bus driver wanted a different bus, but that she'd been waiting so long for a bus that she'd hopped on this one. Join the club. We were all in the same boat. The argy-bargying stopped, and the woman came tottering up the aisle toward us. I was ensconced in the women's' club by now. A full-fledged member after three minutes and a common cause. The woman kept slipping and sliding her way towards us, and I knew why she was tottering like a baby first finding his or her feet. The shoes she wore were totally ridiculous. At least five inches high, and pointy stilettoes. Didn't the woman know it was to be a wet day? I don't think this woman knew or cared about the weather or making a spectacle of herself. She was also spectacular for another reason. She was brashly dressed as if her place of employment was an after dark establishment with a red light outside the doorway. Which no one would have batted an eyelid at, had she been twenty, but this woman was pushing eighty, and it was not a good look. Her hair was dishevelled, and she had that sort of mad look in her eyes which indicated her acute discomfort at not having been able to locate the right bus.

"I wanted to go to Pimlico!" The woman was calling this out to all in captivity as she tottered up the middle of the bus. No one made eye contact. By the time she had reached us, she must have realised that no one cared where she was headed-or why. One of the women standing up in front of me was a kind soul, and she called out to the totterer, "There's a little bit of room for you up here, but we aren't going to Pimlico."

The tottering woman hastened toward us, leaning on seats and railings as she tried to maintain her balance. When she reached us, she was gasping, as she really was quite old when you observed her close up.

I tried to push Mrs Claus off my side of the seat and my lap, so that the woman could sit down.

"Take my seat, I'm getting off soon, I'm going to Buckingham Palace." It felt good to be the reclaiming my youth. With me, it was usually the other way around. However, I wasn't going to Buckingham Palace at all. I just felt claustrophobic and I needed air. I decided that it would be better to hop off the bus and walk. I had my map, and if I made it to Victoria station, I would find the next train home and go and sit on the back porch with my book. London just didn't seem to be the place to be today. Of course, that never happened. As soon as the gang heard that I was getting off at the next stop, they all started making signals to each other to do the same. The newcomer (who was still standing) copied them in their nodding and back patting affirmations. If we were all going, she would need to be in on the act. The bus had stopped, and we hadn't reached the next stop, as we were in a side street with no bus-stop. There was a familiar tap-tap-tapping of the microphone, and the driver's voice came through loud and clear. "The bus will stop here. There will be no more buses travelling this route today. London transport has been required to shut down whilst the authorities deal with a suspected bombing on the trains. Please collect all your goods and leave the bus. Thankyou."

The gaggle of women stopped their patting and smiling and jumped up from their seats. One of them was trying to organise the group, but there were so many of them that panic set in quickly. "Quickly, everyone off! Grab your bags and hurry. We don't know what's really happening."

I could have told them that I knew a little bit about what was happening, but she was right, we didn't really know whether bombs had been planted all over London, or just on a train this morning. It seemed unlikely that we would be anywhere near any bombs, but a decision had been made to stop transport, and we needed to respect that decision. It would be a pleasant walk to Victoria station, and by the time I reached there, the trains would surely be back up and running. I pushed my way towards the front of the bus and started to cross the road directly on my left. Apart from our bus, there were no other vehicles on the road, and the only pedestrians were the people who had just alighted from the bus. Most of them scurried away, and I thought that they must have been locals. That left me with the befuddled totterer and the gaggle of women. I waved to them and kept walking. They waved back and started following me. All ten of them. I ignored them for the first two or so minutes, but then I felt guilty that they were in the dark about the bombs and were probably all scared stiff. I turned to face them.

"Did you want to follow me to Victoria station?"

Mrs Clause spoke for them all. "Are you going that way?"

"Yes, I think it's up this very uninhabited road."

"Well, it couldn't hurt. Yes. We'd love to walk with you, wouldn't we everyone?" They all nodded, even the woman dressed up to the nines, so we set off towards Victoria. All eleven of us!

Being the only one of the eleven with a semblance of map, accelerated me to leader status. I led, and my disciples followed. It didn't seem to bother them that the streets were all but deserted, and that apart from our group and a few helmet and orange clad bored road-workers leaning on their shovels drinking coffee, not a living soul was to be seen. It looked like it would have been a quiet area at the best of times, but this was plain eerie. The workmen nodded and smiled as we processed past them, and one called out brazenly, "I could take my pick from you lot, I could."

His fellow workers jostled and egged him on, and he was encouraged by their reactions. He went further with, "How about you, stiletto shoes?"

The women who had been last to join our group didn't seem to cotton on straight away that he was addressing her. It was only when he stood smack-bang in front of her and wolf-whistled, that she seemed to understand his absurd implication. She looked affronted at first, but then she must have changed her mind, because she smiled coquettishly at him and asked if he might take her to

Pimlico as she needed to get home to change her shoes. The cheeky little sod and his co-workers just burst out laughing and went back to drinking their coffees and dunking biscuits. I kept up my newly assigned position of squadron leader until the next big intersection, where thankfully, there was a bit more action. People were striding along, and there were black taxi cabs and cars, and even the odd red bus. The women of my tribe were elated with all the movement. It was a perfect oasis. There was even a fairly large, very green open park opposite. Mrs Clause was, again, the most vocal,

"I know where we are. I recognise that park over there!" Her friends and the stiletto woman all started jumping up and down and hugging each other. You would think they had been found alive and safe after a nuclear blasting or having been buried in underground caves for weeks on end, so intense was their relief.

I took the opportunity to take leave of them at that corner. They were all orientated and happy, and the first lot, led by Mrs Clause, had made a new friend in the "desperately seeking Pimlico woman".

"So, I'll be on my way now. Nice to meet you all." I wished that I had brought more koalas with me this morning, but I couldn't have known the day would turn out as it had so far. We went our separate ways, and I just kept walking in the direction of Victoria – according to my map. I had been trudging along quite happily, relishing the freedom and sucking on my half-squashed mandarin, when I passed a hairdressing salon. The salon was sandwiched between tall terraces and appeared to be the lower ground floor of a beautifully preserved Georgian town-house. I stood there for a few seconds peering in the window. Only one person was inside the funky salon A pretty young woman of possibly thirty, with masses of dark curly hair. She was propped up on an elevated purple and orange stool at the counter, reading a magazine. I could see the magazine quite clearly through the wide glass window at the front of the shop. I thought that a snap of her reading in the empty salon might be an interesting addition to my Pinterest Board. I was just about to dispose of my mandarin peels and enter the shop, when the girl flew off her raised seat and came catapulting out of the shop, almost colliding with me at the entrance.

"I saw you peering through the window. I'm trying to find the news channel on this little old transistor. Normally we only have mellow mood music playing, and I can only get static on the other channels. Do you know what has happened here this morning? There are road blocks everywhere and there is hardly any traffic on the main street up there. Well, not compared to a normal day. And also, two regular customers haven't turned up for their appointments."

She seemed like a lovely person, and quite genuine, but I really didn't know any more than I'd heard from Australia this morning.

"Can't you turn on another radio, or use your phone to get the news?"

The girl looked doubtfully at me.

"We don't have any more radios in the shop, and my phone isn't charged. The other girl usually has all the gossip, but she's ill today – at least, she hasn't turned up either, so I assume she is ill."

I didn't want to alarm this girl, but I was struggling with subtlety.

"Can't you ask one of the other shop assistants why it is so quiet this morning?"

"No. There are no more shops up here. Only rich houses and apartments. See."

I could see for myself that there were no other shops, only this bespoke hairdressing salon with the funky furniture. It did not seem the right day to offer to get my hair cut, even though she probably did have the time to do it today, since the customers were dropping off like flies.

"I should keep walking, I've a long way to go."

I really had no idea how far it was. The map I had wasn't to scale, and I was hopeless at reading maps at the best of times. Not my department when travelling with friends, as I tended to get everyone hopelessly lost and heatedly angry with me. I would just keep walking this English desert. Thinking of the Australian deserts made me hungry and thirsty, and I hoped there would be a 'Prete a Costa' on the horizon sometime soon. The street I had come upon was wider than the one where I had met the hairdressing girl. That was a good thing, because I could see shops on the other side, and one of the shops was a 'PretE'. I positively skipped across the road to the shop, as I had sampled 'PretE' sandwiches on many an occasion, and I knew them to be delicious. I waltzed into the shop, happy to be back in the thick of civilisation. There were cabinets upon cabinets of refrigerated sandwiches and rolls, and I made my way like a blind person to the sandwich bar. I didn't need to look. I just knew instinctively where to go. There were plenty of people in the shop, and the trendily dressed young boys and girls behind the counters were run off their feet. I was in seventh-heaven and felt very peaceful and lethargic standing there transfixed in front of the refrigerated sandwiches. It was the perfect de-stressing zone for anyone who had been through the ordeals I had endured in the hours since I had opened my eyes at 6 o'clock.

"Ya need any 'elp deciding what yer gunna av?"

One of the girls from behind the counter was standing beside me, offering me assistance in my agonising decision making. She was not privy to the fact that I have been known to stand for hours staring at sandwiches in food cabinets. She seemed intrigued that I was so mesmerised by the food.

"It's all fresh vis mornin, iv vats what's worrying you." No. that wasn't worrying me in the least. I was totally au fait with the freshness of the food, I just couldn't make a decision to save myself. Perhaps this was delayed shock. I reached out, and with closed eyes grasped at the first sandwich I touched.

"Good choice. My fav!" The young girl in the skimpy yellow shorts, tights and a polka-dot vest was nodding her approval at my random choice. I opened my eyes and discovered that I had fortuitously selected my very favourite 'sanga'-egg and lettuce. The girl, Hayley (on her name tag), bounced off back to her post. I followed but lumbered more than bounced. My bones were starting to ache, and I was still a long, long way from Hampton. I intended to eat my sandwich whilst I was walking to save time. It was going to be chaotic enough getting home from the city without being late, and in the thick of the commuters.

As I was munching, I slowed my pace, and I could see an official looking sign looming up indicating that the next building would be the Education Departments of London. There was a guard (they were everywhere in London) stationed outside the building, and he acknowledged me and my egg sandwich as I approached him.

"Wouldn't mind onea vose meself. Cant ever resist ve smell." He was a hyped-up little pavement-hopping mite, and he seemed to be enjoying just witnessing someone walking sedately up the street.

"Is this the London Education Department?" I had not even considered that there might be an Education Department in London, and yet here I was, fated to be eating an egg sandwich right outside the entrance. The mite nodded. "Is it possible for the public go inside for a look around at the library and the common areas?" I had been inside the Education Department buildings in Melbourne many times, and I didn't stop to think that this building might have had stricter rules and protocols than we do in Australia.

Nevertheless, I fully expected him to shake his head, but he was nodding in affirmation of my request. "Yes. Anyone can go in. As long as they don't bring food in with them." I hastily stuffed the other half of my egg sandwich into my backpack, and into the Tardis I hesitatingly stepped. There were heavy double glass doors leading into the vast foyer of the Department. I summoned up my strength and pushed as hard as I could. I must have replenished my energy levels with the half of the egg sandwich I'd scoffed down, as the heavy doors swung forwards and then immediately back onto me. I lost my balance but managed to catch myself and my breath just in time. I t wouldn't have looked too good, me bursting through the doors and collapsing on the other side. Inside the foyer it was all very contemporary, and there was a very large and very long polished-oak desk in a half moon design. About five people of assorted ages and genders were propped up behind the elongated desk. They all had their heads down as if in prayer, in apparent concentration on their tasks, and no one appeared to even notice me, despite my grand entrance. It was very quiet in there as well, almost as quiet as it had been outside, but I was used to the silence by now, and I marched up to the nearest receptionist and announced myself. A very bad move as it turned out.

"Excuse me, but I was wondering about the possibility of joining a tour of your Education Department this afternoon? The helpful guard outside told me that it would be possible to come in and look around. I am involved in Education in Australia, and I was just interested in a different country's perspective."

The woman was big, and black, and extremely sleep deprived by the look of her. She was born-again angry and very dismissive of me. It wasn't going well, even before she opened her mouth. When she deigned to speak, it was to inform me in no uncertain terms that the Education Department was under strict security, and that serious consequences were imminent for whomever had allowed me access to the building. Furthermore, I was to leave immediately, or she would be calling the real guards! I backed out of there as fast as I could. Once outside, I scanned the street for the guard who would soon wish he had never set eyes on me, but he had vaporised. Just as well, as the loud, snarly lady on the desk was livid. (Yes, I did glimpse her name, but it had too many syllables and not enough vowels to interpret in the few short seconds I had shared with her.) The brief encounter inside, which could have been the highlight of my day, had left me disheartened and disappointed in London. It would be best to move on and forget about the interlude. It really was a drop in the ocean compared to the events of today. I needed to forget about being a teacher and concentrate instead on being a tourist. So, what would a genuine tourist do next? I still had a couple of hours of sightseeing, and I was almost at Victoria station.

From memory, there was a big cathedral around the corner from Victoria, and I felt perturbed enough to want to go and sit in the church and do some praying and meditating. When I found the cathedral about half an hour later, I first explored the foyer area, and then approached the woman on the desk at the back of the cathedral. Although they had desks in common, this woman was the complete antithesis to the woman in the Education Department. She was around seventy, and very sprightly, very animated, and very happy that I was going to be attending the mass.

"We don't get that many tourists wanting to sit through the whole mass nowadays. They are too busy going on tours and buses around the city."

"Not me." I assured her. "I am happy to rest on a pew and pray." She looked at me as if I were one of the Fatima children, all grown up and miraculously English-speaking. Impatiently, she thrust some religious pamphlets towards me.

"Read these tonight before you say your evening prayers."

Steady on lovie (I was dying to say), I'm not that holy. Just exhausted!

The mass was long. Very long, and people kept shuffling over me, settling themselves in my pew (when there were so many empty ones) and then jumping up and vanishing. I noticed that there was a 'Toilet' sign above the doorway into which they were all disappearing. And they were all old!

After the mass I was trying to make a quick getaway, but the priest had made an even quicker getaway than me, and there he stood, pontificating on the steps of the Cathedral in all his frocked glory, shaking the hand of everyone who had demonstrated the strength of character and endurance skills to sit through his excruciatingly long homily. The marathon homily had started off focusing on the train bombing this morning and how extra prayers for the injured or traumatised were badly needed. He then shifted gear and egotistically turned the rest of the homily around to himself, and how he had recently lost his mother who had nambi-pambied and spoilt him all his life. He had detectable pride in his voice when he mentioned his mother's name, 'Mildred'. I wasn't really listening to that part of his homily, as I had heard these puffed-up ravings about intense mother and son relationships too many times back home. D.H Lawrence was spot on with 'Sons and Lovers' sixty years ago. Nothing much changes on that frontier. I hung around in the foyer, racking my brains as to whether there had been a secret back exit which might take me out into the street without having to shake the priest's hand and listen for the second time to his life story. If I did meet him, I wouldn't be opening my mouth, as once he knew I was Australian, that would be the next hour gone. I found a side door which was possibly a fire exit, but I didn't care, I just needed air again, there was far too much incense in the church. (The priest had nearly wiped out half the congregation with his frequent incense splattering routine.) I followed a little windy overgrown path down past a Childcare centre which was packed with kids. It was funny to think that these children were all happily frolicking in the centre of London, blissfully unaware that they were occupying premium land, and that their Centre was situated directly across the road from scores and scores of famous brand name shops. The mouth of the winding path spilled out onto the front steps of the cathedral. Sure enough, the priest was still out there, shaking hands and earnestly conversing as if he were the father of the bride.

It's that thing about thinking of something and then it actually happens. I was just thinking about a bride, and then, lo and behold, a bride materialised in front of me. A bonafide bride with a gorgeous white wedding gown and a lacey veil and a train and a bouquet. There was a groom as well, in a jet-black tuxedo, and bow tie. He had a camera dangling from his shoulder. They were standing smack bang in the middle of the quadrangle which led up to the steps of the spectacular cathedral. If the priest had seen the couple, he was ignoring them, as he still had quite a line of well-wishers to greet. I gave them a great big smile and a wave as I scurried past, and the petite beaming bride, awash in whiteness, beckoned to me. "Could you please take a photo of us?" I scoured our surrounds to see if there were any other members of the wedding party who might take the photo, as I had my doubts as to whether I could assure them of a photo in which both their heads were intact. I was notorious for chopping off heads when taking photos of people. I couldn't see anyone even remotely resembling a member of a Chinese wedding party, or even a guest. "Sure, I can do that for you." They looked so young, and so happy, and so in love that I could hardly refuse her plea, even though my head was a-buzz with alarm-bells louder than Westminster.

Smile! And again! I clicked away in varied frenzied poses I had witnessed the paparazzi performing on television. This couple had created a monster. I bent my knees, squatted (with difficulty) and swayed from side to side, juggling the camera the groom had handed me like a pro. I gestured to the couple to move closer, and then further apart. I was really getting into the swing of it when the groom, fearing that my next command would be for him to throw the bride up into the air and catch her, whilst I captured her airborne and still smiling, signalled me to stop. Regrettably I thought, as I imagined that a shot like that, on the day of the bombing, outside the Catholic Cathedral in Westminster would have done wonders for England's multi-ethnic policies.

"We must go now. We have only two hours in London, and we want to go across the road to the Top-Shop." I knew about Top-Shop from the multitude of modern clothing shops in Australia. The one time I lost my senses and was dragged into a Top Shop which had just opened in a glitzy arcade in Melbourne, I had sat on the husbands' bench and buried my face in my hands, fearing that someone I knew might be in the shop buying a present with their great granddaughter. Full of skimpy size six tops and high cut shorts, overalls and trendy attire in general. Mostly for the young and the very, very young.

The bride and groom were now thanking me effusively, and we exchanged emails, so that I might keep in touch with them. They slipped into the conversation that they'd already been married for a year, and that they were in London on a second honeymoon. They wanted to parade themselves in their wedding splendour, and just see what happened. Unfortunately for them, it was the day of the bombing, and the crowds just weren't around. So, nothing happened at all. The priest had mentioned in the mass said earlier, that thousands of commuters who normally descended upon central London every morning, had stayed home instead, when they'd heard about the skeletal transport system which would be operating today in the capital.

"We didn't really have excitement here till you came along and noticed us. Now you have brought the crowds." I looked around to assess the fullness of the crowds, but there were only a dozen or so people scurrying across the stark, wide square, and the priest on the steps was about to hi-five his last adoring fan. Hardly Wemberly, or Wimbledon capacity! The bride and groom were itching to skip off. "Thank you and please keep in touch." With that, they raced off hand in hand, the abundant train of the bride's dress netting almost half of the road as they disappeared into the pleasurable perimeters of Top Shop territory. I looked down at the scrunched-up email and postal address in my hand, thinking I would see an Oxford or Cambridge address. Instead, it read Carlton, Melbourne, Australia. You just never knew whom you were going to meet next when you were a tourist in the largest city in Europe!

I probably stood there in the middle of the square, staring across the road at the Top shop façade, for about five minutes. Once again, indecision had engulfed me. Should I hop on the next bus and venture into the heart of London for a heavy dose of West End window-shopping, or should I turn back towards Victoria station and head home to Hampton before the crowds? Even though many of the commuters had stayed in their homes once they'd heard of the train disruptions, thousands more had already been at work in the city when the incident had occurred. One thing was for sure about London. There would be wall-to-wall people whatever the hour. I knew it to be a fact (from my Guide Book) that the population of London city swells by three hundred thousand every day of the week, with all the commuters. I had planned to purchase some half price tickets in Leicester Square for some musicals later in the week, but it had started to rain whilst I was pondering, and my wet face and dampening sweater clinched it for me. Home James!

There was a trendy little squashed-in card shop on my left, with racks of postcards lining the outside perimeter of the shop, along with trestle-tables full of bargain cards and London memorabilia. I flicked through the racks and ended up with about a dozen postcards with different scenes of London. Then I made my way inside. It was quite crowded in there, but I was content to browse whilst I was waiting to be served. There were racks and racks of raunchy cards which would have made even Hugh Heffner and his bunny girls blush. I couldn't resist reading some of them, and I had to laugh at a few of the innuendos and British puns in the wording of some of the cards. It was my turn to be served, and the girl serving (there was only one girl serving in this tiny shop,) was waiting patiently for me to remove my head from the card I'd been chuckling over and present my postcards for payment.

"Some of vem give you a larf n all, don't vey.' The dark eyed girl spoke with a delicious, smoky cockney brogue, even though she looked like she should be picking apples on the family farm in Sicily."

"We sell most of vem cards to ve punters oo come in ere avta work and a few drinks on Friday nights. Vos cards are a big deal in London. Most of 'em oo come in ere are so far gone they don't even know what ver buying. It's just a sorta fing 'round ere. Vey go out and drink vemselves stupid of a Friday night and ven spend ve rest of ve weekend recovering. Most of em do vat. I've done it meself and had ta live on crisps n coke n pizza for the rest of ve week, cause I spent mi 'ole pay on booze."

It seemed a ridiculous waste of money to me, but as long as it wasn't affecting me, I really couldn't have cared less about the Friday night antics of the Londoners. The Sicilian cockney was finalising my purchase, and she smiled at me and gushed, "Av a good oliday n'all."

I admired her spunk and friendly customer service, so I handed her one of the tiny koalas. She looked very happy to receive a gift from a perfect stranger. I'm not sure if she knew why I was handing her the koala, but she just smiled gratefully at me and mouthed "fankyou".

It really was an Aladdin's cave of a shop, with many of the little souvenirs related to royalty. There was a curious little battery-operated bright pink figurine of Queen Elizabeth waving. It caught my eye as I was edging out of the cramped shop, and on impulse I selected one which was already boxed, making sure the colour on the side of the box was hot pink. I then battled my way past shelves packed with merchandise, back to the girl. I felt quite cheered up in this shop, away from the doom and gloom and rain outside. All the other customers had drifted off, and that left only me and the shop assistant.

"Think I'll also get one of these queens please." The girl giggled at the way I put on a posh upper-crust accent and mimicked the waving queen, and we chatted amicably for a few more minutes until another customer appeared and needed to be served. I left the shop for the second time in high spirits, ready to face the tube.

It turned out I needed that stamina, as I was rushed headlong with the surge of passengers down the almost perpendicular set of steely steps into the bowels of earth which was the underground. If I'd thought of Dubai airport as otherworldly, the London underground is in a world of its own. There is an entire network of trains and shops and food outlets scattered for miles and miles underneath the metropolis. If you were a Londoner, you would have grown up with the tubes, but for the tourist, it can be a very daunting and hostile environment. Especially if you are travelling solo, as it is difficult to get your bearings down there, and many a tourist has been known to have hopped on trains going in the complete opposite direction to where they intended to go. That was nearly me! I had been surging along with the best of them when I saw a train to Waterloo. I just wanted to escape the underground as soon as possible on today of all days. The last time I had been in the underground two years ago, I had been with a friend travelling across town from Camden to the Kew Gardens. We had to change somewhere underground, and for this particular route, you needed to make your way to the next platform via a lift. Unfortunately for the two of us, and the other thousand or so passengers, neither the lift nor the escalators were working. While we tried to scramble up the fire-exit stairs to the next level, an announcement came over the loud speaker that there was a fire on the platform below, and that everyone in the underground would need to use the fire-stairs to reach the streets above. It had been chaotic and very frightening, and neither myself nor my friend had coped very well. At least the trains were running today, and I wouldn't have to stay down here that long, if I could just find the right train to board. The Waterloo destination looked promising. Luckily for me, there were seasoned travellers and native Londoners willing to help – apart from one lady, who was galloping along the platforms dragging her small daughter along with her and screaming that she couldn't find a train to board, and that there were potential bombs on all the trains. All in all, it was pretty ordinary, for an extraordinary day. I had to change trains at Clapham Junction, and that took some negotiating, including a strenuous workout on the steep steel-mesh steps connecting the platforms. The station guards kept changing the platforms for Hampton, and I couldn't help but compare this shuffling of platforms to the changing of street signs in Ireland when the Irish wanted to confuse the British about their exact locations. It was slightly disconcerting but compared to the grand scale ramifications of my sister's early morning phone call, it wasn't even a pinch. We all coped, and two hours after I had bought the cards in the Westminster shop, I put my key in the door at number nine – safe in the suburbs, and decidedly going nowhere that evening!

# Chapter 18
## Les Mis Et Al

The minute I opened my eyes I could smell something very foul. It wasn't trapped everywhere in the air but coming from the far corner of the bedroom where I had dumped all my bags and rain gear the night before when I had fallen into bed, exhausted beyond exhaustion from the day. At first, I'd thought it might be the damp sweater or even the still wet rain coat neither of which I had bothered to hang out to dry in the bathroom, but it was a stronger smell than just dampness. My next assumption was that it might have been my boots, which I hadn't yet got around to cleaning since the beginning of the trip. But again, after some deep sniffs from the safety of my bed, I dismissed the boots as the source of the smell. It just wasn't a damp earthy smell. It was more like sulphur. Then I remembered that smell. It was egg! Defiantly an eggy smell. Very strong and very unpleasant. I jumped up out of bed and wound the widow out as far as I could, in the hope that the smell might dissipate. But it lingered on. I approached the corner of the room where I hoped I would find the source of the smell, and as I did so, it got stronger and stronger. I half expected a wet smelly dog to be buried underneath the pile of clothes and bags. At least that would be a plausible explanation. Looby or Holly could have nuzzled their way into my room in the early hours of the morning when Patrick had let them out for their twinkling. (as he called it) But there were no dogs. Nothing alive at all. Just the horrid pungent smell! And then it dawned on me. The egg 'half-sandwich' I had stuffed into my backpack yesterday afternoon. I'd forgotten to throw it out last night. I had felt sick with fatigue and gone straight to bed.

    I tipped everything out of the backpack in one swift manoeuvre, and the culprit sandwich toppled out with the rest of the contents. It really was bad. No wonder I'd felt sick last night. The bedroom would have been a mini gas chamber. I'd have to get rid of it as soon as possible. I checked my mobile. Still only 6 o'clock. Perhaps a little early to disturb the whole household. Alice would not be pleased with me when she found out that I had woken the dogs on my trip to the outside bin.

I would just have to think of a Plan B.

I was perched on the end of my bed racking my brains for a solution to this self-inflicted problem when I came up with a brilliant idea. I would wrap the sandwich up in a plastic zip-lock bag and tie an old scarf around the package. I would then lower the scarf package out of the window and onto the grass outside my window. That way I could zip back into bed and read my London Guide book, and I would be able to breathe normally again.

That is exactly what I did. I then closed the window and sprayed half a can of deodorant around the room for good measure, and in case Alice came into the room with an early morning cup of tea for me. I was sitting up in bed some two hours later when Alice knocked on the door, and then entered straight away.

"Fil, I just wanted to let you know that I will be working from home today, so you can keep sleeping in, and just get your breakfast at your leisure. Patrick's already left with the dogs, and he won't be back till lunch time, or even early afternoon. Are you getting up soon?" I was quite cosy and comfortable in my room, and as I had packets of chocolate biscuits and crisps stashed away in the drawers. I was never going to starve.

"I think I'll just have a lazy morning Alice. No sense in rushing if it's just us – and you'll be in your study anyway."

Alice accepted this decision with a nod and turned her back to go. She was just closing the door when she turned back to me and asked in a curious voice. "Fil, what is that funny smell in here?" She then added, "You need to open the window, it's quite stuffy in here."

(And now I was really praying.) Please don't let her go over to the window. Please don't let her go over to the window.

I jumped up out of bed, sending my glasses and I pad flying, and rushed headlong into Alice, pushing her towards the door. "Hurry Alice, I think I can hear your mobile ringing, it could be work." The mere mention of work was an elixir to Alice and sent her scuttling at top speed towards her study. I heard the study-door slam as she hurtled into work-mode. Sometimes work is the best distraction. I breathed a huge sigh of relief and picked up my glasses and I pad. I would just lie low for a while. Just until I could think of how to dispose of the egg sandwich. From now on I would abstain from eggs in general. Too much trouble entirely! I was thinking about travelling, and eggs in general, and I remembered a story from quite a few years ago, which one of my friends had recounted one evening at a dinner party. She and her sister, and another friend were travelling to London from Melbourne in nineteen seventy-three. They travelled mostly by bus, and this involved stopping in many different countries along the way. My friend is allergic to eggs, and her sister went out in sympathy, and also avoided eggs the entire trip. The third person, Prue, loved eggs, and consequently ended up with three eggs every morning for breakfast, courtesy of the two sisters. One time, about halfway through the six-month overland trip, the three of them went to a tailor to get some cool cotton dresses made. The tailor quickly and smartly measured the two sisters, noting down their measurements and promising them sensational dresses. He then turned to Prue, took one look at her, and dug his heels in, refusing to loop the tape measure around her waist. When she pressured him as to why he would not measure her, he surveyed her purposefully, and slowly exclaimed,

"I sink you eat too many of ze eggs!" Prue has been off eggs since nineteen seventy-three. It was a good story!

I lay there in the twilight zone for about another hour, recalling television shows and books I'd read over the years with a reference to disposing of something you didn't ever want anyone to find out about. Not guns or drugs or bodies or anything – just something harmless like an egg sandwich – which was causing me all this distress. In the end, hunger and thirst got the better of me. (I'd already drunk all the water I had in the room with me, and absentmindedly eaten half a packet of chocolate biscuits.) I felt a little sick from all the chocolate on an empty stomach, and I needed to keep my strength up for the day ahead. Poking my head out of the beautiful stately oak door to my bedroom I checked across the hallway to see if the coast was clear. All was quiet on the western front, so I quietly closed the door and crept over towards the window. I craned my neck to see if the sandwich was still attached to its makeshift extra-large umbilical cord. Roger that! It was still there. I figured I had two choices. I favoured the first, which would have involved getting dressed quickly and racing out to retrieve the sandwich, wrapping it in newspaper and throwing it in the bottom of the bin. The second solution would be to just throw the whole offending conglomeration, 'scarf and all' into the nearest bush in the garden. If I threw it into the middle of a bush, it would be very unlikely that anyone would find it, and it would have decomposed before Alice and Patrick were ready to landscape the garden. Even though I wanted to go with the rubbish bin solution, I thought it would be easier all round to simply throw the sandwich into the bushes. With a bit of luck, the foxes would forage it before too long.

So that's what I did. Unbeknownst to Alice, who had not stirred from her Ikea work station, I stole into the garden with a pair of scissors from her needlework basket, and a pair of plastic gloves from under the kitchen sink and applied my midwifery skills to the sandwich at the end of the scarf. One swift chop and the deed was done! Next, I threw the scarf back in through the window which I had left ajar. Finally, I hurled the sandwich into the nearest bush – and then raced back into my bedroom and slammed the door.

The force of the slamming must have disturbed Alice, because the next thing I knew there was a sharp rapping on my door, and Alice was calling out, "Fil, what was that loud banging noise?"

"Oh, nothing Alice, just the wind blowing my door shut. I'll be out in a jiffy, I'm just finishing getting dressed."

I heard Alice moving away from my door, followed immediately by a loud exclamation of: "Ohhhh!"

I was almost dressed, so I opened my door and moved quickly towards Alice who was still standing in the corridor staring up at the clock on the wall. She looked at me in alarm, and then continued. "Is that the time? I'll have to fly. I have an important home visit in Teddington this afternoon."

I offered to make her a cup of tea before she left, and she was delighted that I was being so helpful. She rewarded me with a gracious smile and disappeared back into Ikea-land for a final check of her paperwork. I had almost reached the kitchen door when the front door bell rang. And rang, and rang, and rang. Someone was in a hurry to be let in by the sound of it. I hesitated, not knowing whether Alice would come bursting out of her study and play lady of the house, or whether I should step smartly into that role and answer the door. Of course, it could have been 'Jehovah's Witnesses', and in that case, I would wait for Alice to deal with them. Either way, I would wait. Finally, the chiming stopped, and there was dead silence. Alice appeared straight away.

"Who was that at the door Fil?"

"I'm not sure."

"What do you mean you're not sure? Was it anyone we know?"

"I mean I'm not sure because I didn't open the door, and now the doorbell has stopped ringing."

Alice looked at me in exasperation. The gracious face had completely disappeared, replaced by the more common, fed up one.

"Fil, it could have been something important. Have a look outside and see if there is anyone walking up the road."

I dutifully unlocked the door and stepped down the three steps to the grass. I looked up towards the head of the court, but there was no one in sight. All I could see was a red bus rattling by. I wished I was on it. I turned and was just about to go back inside and report that it must have been a phantom bell ringer, when I glimpsed a bright red flash of material from behind the privet bush outside the lounge room window. Then it moved, and a head popped out. It was Joan – the neighbour, and she was crouched in behind the bush, clutching what appeared to be a photograph album. She looked as if she was being pursued by a gang of hitmen, intent on stealing incriminating photographs contained in her album.

"Joan. Joan. It's me, Fil. The Australian girl. Are you alright?"

Joan just stared at me and then called out, "Who on earth are you?" I surmised that this must have been her usual way of greeting people, as it seemed to be the repetitious phrase Joan used on everyone – even her niece who shopped for her – according to Alice. I persisted, knowing that Alice would soon appear at the door, and this would make her even later than she already was for her afternoon meeting in Teddington.

"Joan, why were you ringing the bell? Do you want to come inside and have a little chat?" I realised that I was throwing away any chance I might have had at writing some poetry or even painting in this, my first free morning, but Joan looked so needy and so helpless that I felt compelled to show some compassion. As soon as I mentioned the word chat, she sprang to life, and all three-feet of her beat me to the steps, and beat me to the front door, and finally, beat me to the most comfortable chair in the lounge room. Patrick's reading chair – but Patrick was out, and the chair had been vacant.

After she had settled herself into her preferred foetal position on the couch, Joan decided that she could do with a nice hot cup of tea. She was looking at me expectantly. I ignored the look and was just getting myself comfortable on the three-seater coach opposite Patrick's chair, when Alice called out from her bedroom, "Fil, who was at the door?"

Joan answered for me. "It's me, Joan." Joan may have had a bung eye, but there was nothing amiss with her hearing. Alice suddenly appeared, like a genie from a bottle. "Joan, how nice to see you. Did you want Patrick?" Alice was very skilled at fobbing off Joan – especially when she was late, as was fast becoming the case.

In Patrick's absence, I stepped in to save Alice. "I'll just pop the kettle on for Joan. Do you still want a cuppa Alice?"

She didn't, and within two minutes she was off like the wind. That left Joan sitting in the lounge room waiting for her cup of tea, and me – looking for the teapot. When I returned to the lounge room with a laden tray, Joan was still clutching the photo album as if her life depended on keeping it intact. She kept looking out the window, and then intermittently ducking, so that her head was well below the Plimsoll line of the bay window. I had no precedent for this strange ritual, but I supposed it to be associated with old age – so I said nothing. Consequently, there was quite a long period of silence between us – interrupted only by Joan's over loud chewing of my chocolate biscuits. (I had raced off to my room and piled the last of my secret stash onto a large floral plate which I'd discovered hidden at the back of a top cupboard in the kitchen.)

I unintentionally broke the silence with an impromptu sneeze, and Joan looked at me with concern.

"Not coming down with a cold are you, Australian girl?" I wanted to beg her to please stop calling me Australian girl, but I supposed it was only me getting annoyed by the quirky term of endearment. At least it branded me. As soon as she saw me, that was the association for her – except that she detested Australians. I didn't bother to answer the well-being question. Instead, I changed the subject, bringing it full circle back to Joan.

"What's in the photo album Joan? Was there anything you wanted to show us?" I said 'us' but the other two would not be back for ages, so I was going to have to fly solo with her secret, whatever it turned out to be.

"I can't remember why I've brought it in with me, but I did have a good reason when I started out." Joan made it sound like she had crossed two deserts and an ocean to get to our house, when it was only no more than twenty steps to her front door. Her memory lapse only lasted five minutes, and then she suddenly rocketed to her feet. "I've remembered, I've remembered why I have the album. It's that man! That painter man I met in Kingston who wants three hundred pounds. He's waiting in my house now."

I had no idea what she was talking about, so I pushed on with the gruelling grilling. "Joan, what man in Kingston, what did he paint? Do you mean he is going to paint the outside of your house?"

Joan looked at me as though I had two heads. "No! No! Not my house. Me! He painted me!" She was banging her torso as she shouted this out to me, and I immediately thought of a tattooist, and then Joan's age. It just didn't make sense. It was incredible that she would even know about body painting. And what motifs would she have chosen? No. She couldn't have promised a tattooist three hundred pounds to cover her with aqua and pink ink.

"What do you mean, paint you, Joan? Why would you want tattoos all over you?" Even as I said it, I was thinking of the many tattoo parlours I had seen in Kingston, and added to that, Joan had been brought up in the fairground environs, and many of the travellers were resplendent in colourful, exaggerated tattoos. Perhaps, as a throwback to the past, she just needed some more paint and ink applied.

"Joan, did you mean to say that you have already been recently painted? Is that why you were hiding in the bushes before?" Joan was looking quite baffled by now. She obviously couldn't make me understand what she meant. She tried again. "No, Australian girl, I wasn't really painted. Not really me. It was the photograph I gave him a while ago, and he painted me in the fairground. I was eight and very pretty if don't say so myself. I had golden ringlets and I could ride a horse bareback in the circus ring in my knickers."

The light finally dawned for me. Joan must have met some travelling portrait painter – somewhere in Kingston and had commissioned him to paint her picture from a photograph she had given him – presumably a photo from the album she was still clutching territorially. She must have promised him three hundred pounds for the commission, and now he was sitting up in her living room, waiting for his money. Where the painting was, remained a mystery. Finally, we were making progress.

"Joan, do you have the three hundred pounds to pay the painter?"

"No. I do not. I only have five pounds, and I'm saving that to give to Patrick for our Friday night Fish and Chips. I remember now, I came in here to ask Patrick if he would take me down to the bank. I want to take out three hundred and fifty pounds." Meanwhile Mr Painter Man was still sitting on the sofa next door waiting for his payment. I thought quickly. "OK, Joan. Here's what we are going to have to do. You sit pretty and wait, and I'll go over to your house and get rid of the painter. He can't just sit there all day and wait for his money. I'll ask him to come back this evening when everyone is home, and that will also give us plenty of time to organise the money side of things for you. Does that sound like a plan?"

Joan didn't answer me, as her mouth was stuffed full of the last of the chocolate biscuits. I left her scoffing there and raced next door. Sure enough, there was an anxious Baltic looking gentleman, bearded and around fifty or sixty, sitting perched on the edge of the sofa, with Joan's two dogs either side of him. Winston and Prunella seemed to have already adopted him, and even when I burst in on the cosy scene, neither dog stirred. Maybe they just craved male company. They loved Patrick, and now this gentleman. I extended my hand to him, and he took it, and shook it. He then told me his name was Sergei, and that he was waiting for his payment for the painting he had been commissioned to paint by the old lady Jean, who lived in this house. I wanted to remind him that yes, it was her house, and since she was nowhere to be seen, he should not be there alone. It was called trespassing!

"I go. I come back when it comes dark for my money, understand?"

Yes. I understood with crystal clear clarity. He had taken two weeks to paint what looked to be a near perfect depiction of a little eight-year-old Joan, with masses of oily curls. Joan would love it, if he was still willing to part with it tonight.

"Yes. That will be fine. Come back around eight this evening, and we'll seal the deal." He looked like he had no idea what 'seal the deal' meant, but the mention of 8 o'clock this evening seemed to satisfy Sergei, and he was off like a shot, dragging the fairly large oil painting behind him. He wasn't taking any chances with not getting paid the full three hundred quid.

As soon as I could see him disappearing up towards the bus stop, I locked up Joan's house and raced back to Number 9. Joan was asleep when I entered the loungeroom, and I tiptoed past her soft snoring and into the kitchen, where I made myself tea and toast with marmalade, even though it was already past lunchtime. Patrick still hadn't re appeared, and Alice was out for the afternoon. Although Joan was snoring loudly by now in the lounge room – it was peace at last. I settled down on the big couch opposite Joan, scoffed down my tea and toast, and promptly fell asleep myself. I was never going to be able to go back to work when I returned to Australia at this rate of inertia!

A loud clanking of keys in a lock woke me, and I was trying to uncramp my feet, when Holly and Looby came bounding into the lounge room where Joan and I had been asleep moments before.

"Holly, Looby, come back her. Back here at once!" Patrick was assuming his authoritative voice, and I suspected that he didn't realise that Joan and I were in the lounge room, as the house was so quiet.

I called out to him straight away. "Patrick. We're in here. Two strangers in your house, and not a wife in sight!" Joan was fully awake by now, and she sat up expectantly when she heard the word wife. She had never married, and it would have suited her very well to have Patrick as a husband. Someone to tend to the overgrown garden, to tinker with the car, walk the dogs, and chop the wood for the fire. That, and the fact that Joan adored Patrick, and in her eyes, he couldn't do a thing wrong. A pity really that Patrick was not equally smitten. Not that he didn't like and respect Joan. He did. He just did not worship her to the same degree as she did him. Joan was going to need more than her gypsy heritage to snare Patrick. Patrick, for his part was always there for Joan. He told me in confidence that he thought of her in the same way as he thought of his own dear mother, even thought she had passed away some years ago. When Patrick entered the lounge room, he did not seem in the least surprised to see Joan on his chair. He just nodded, and threw himself down next to me on the couch, beckoning the two dogs to jump up on his lap and snuggle in.

"Alice get off, OK then?"

And just like that, Joan was on the bench again. In Patrick's eyes, there would never be anyone ever who would even come close to Alice in his affections. He lived and breathed for three things only. Alice, food and his beloved books. I'm not able to offer a confident fourth place to the dogs, as some serious rivalry could no doubt be expected from the likes of his Latin verbs and the good old vino veritas. That was Patrick for you. A kinder, softer soul you could not hope to meet. This morning he was really being tested by Joan as to the depth of his kindness.

I was explaining to Patrick the events of the morning, and how I had found Joan camouflaged in the privet bush. Patrick, as dry as ever, retorted with. "At least she wasn't in a mulberry bush dressed only in a light dressing gown."

I chuckled to myself, but Joan misunderstood, and she assumed that Patrick was talking about her and not himself.

"I don't call this tunic a dressing gown, Patrick. It's my best outfit. Now are you going to take me to the bank or not?" Patrick must have been well used to random demands from Joan, as he just looked solemnly at her, shrugged, and mumbled, "Could do!"

Joan of the bionic ear sprang to her feet tout-suite.

"I'll just fly back home and get my bank book. Are you coming too Australian girl?"

I declined the outing, riveting though it would no doubt be, with the excuse that I wanted to do some washing and get myself organised for this afternoon, when I would be going to see the matinee performance of Les Misérables. When Joan had left, I briefed Patrick on the reason for Joan wanting him to take her to the bank in such a hurry. Patrick was a banker in a previous life, often travelling to Capital cities all over the world on business. He was well regarded amongst international bankers, and the complete antithesis to the acronym 'FILTH' (failed in London tried Hong Kong.) Patrick listened to me and then stood up abruptly.

"I'd best go and see to Joan." With that he was off. The dogs trotted behind him with their tails between their legs. They realised from Patrick's tone and retreating back that they were not to be included in the next outing. This realisation didn't stop them from following Patrick, but the door closing in their faces was a bit of a clincher. As soon as they stopped scratching at the front door, they bounded back into the lounge room, where I was still seated on the sofa trying to decide my next move. Time was of the essence now. I wanted to do a load of washing, but I couldn't see how I would have time to squeeze it in. With a decision made, I quickly readied myself for the next big happening of the day – an afternoon at the theatre. I was really, really excited about going to see Les Misérables for the twelfth time. For about a year, a week would not pass when I did not have the soundtrack to 'Les Mis' blaring through the speakers in my car on my way to work. It was a year of my life when I needed to travel one and a half hours each day. Ample time to play the double-disc. That was some time ago. These days I just play my favourite tracks from random musicals through the port in my car – connected to my iPhone.

It was a simple dressing process that morning. Black upon black. A perfect theatre going outfit. Another of my traditions – superstitions – misapprehensions were rearing their ugly heads. I always dress in black for the theatre, and then jazz it up with colour. This penchant for black came from my old auditioning days in Sydney and Melbourne, when I employed the fanciful, and utterly untenable idea that I would be an actress in the musical theatre. I was twice rejected by the National Institute of Dramatic Art in Sydney, even though I made it to the last ten performers in the auditions on both occasions. Feedback from the selection panel had me as too young at sixteen, and too old at twenty-five. From then on, I abandoned my grandiose ideas of performing for Australia in iconic films and Eurovision, and opted instead for local theatre, where I was always ensured a part, as I had been so close to attending NIDA. My greatest claim to fame was as understudy to the female lead in a performance of 'The Princess and the Pea' with a fairly noteworthy Melbourne theatre company. Excitedly I memorised all the lines and songs which were to be performed by the female lead. At the same time, I deviously searched for ways to trip her up, or cause her to lose her voice on opening night, so that I might score the lead. It never happened, and I was forced to take up my lowly position as one of the twelve princesses in the chorus. I had no lines to speak, and no solos to perform. I was in the back row because some of the steps to the 'Can-Can' tended to allude me on more than one occasion in rehearsals. The musical director informed me that I had been positioned in the back row because I was so tall, but I speedily and sadly cottoned on to the real reason for my banishment to the backbench. I had two left feet! Although I knew this to be a valid point, I was still resentful of the fact that the girl who had won the lead role had at least four left feet – but there was no dancing involved in the lead role. The most she had to do was to extend her chiffon covered arms to the prince and fall blindly into his outstretched arms. Hardly a Ginger Roger's move. To top it all off, the very worst thing to happen in the Princess and the Pea chronicles, was that I had overexaggerated my role as a chorus princess to many of my family and friends, and they were all eager to come along on opening night and fill the theatre. Well, they almost filled the theatre, as when I danced my way onto the stage and took up my position in the third row of the chorus line (with the three other can-caning underachieving princesses,) I had a clear view of them all pertly and proudly positioned there, like neatly arranged skittles in a bowling alley, taking up the first ten rows of the local theatre. I rose to the occasion though and can-canned my way through Act One with moves to equal a Moulin Rouge professional dancer. In the chorus songs I bellowed, and when there was dialogue between the leading actors, I stood centre left erect, almost to the point of rigor mortis – smiling like my life depended on it. My jaw ached, and I could feel the pancake make-up drizzling in mighty rivers down my face. I could feel myself reeling from the savage intensity of the blinding stage lights, but my smile never wavered. After the show, there was a "meet the cast" supper in the foyer. My friends and family all loyally congregated there, and although the foyer was quite large and grand, we were still squashed, and forced to brush shoulders. It was an impromptu bonding time for some of my relatives who had not spoken to each other in years, so I guess I did the right thing for once in precipitating this reunion. I was praised on my singing, congratulated on my appearance and glitzy costume, and slapped on the back for my skilful dancing. One of my more astute friends summed it up clearly for me, and inadvertently sealed my fate with that company. Her exact words were, "Fil, you did very well, but really, all you did was smile. I've never seen anyone smiling so much without even a crumb of a line to speak."

I feared she spoke for all of them, and from that moment on, my career in the theatre came to a grinding halt. The only remaining vestige of the crumbling empire of Show Business for me was the insistence to myself to always dress in black for the theatre.

Once I was ready to leave, it was a brief walk to the bus stop, a lightning trip into Kingston, and then a longer train trip into Victoria Station. I liked to go from Victoria into the heart of the city, as I was familiar with the tube stations and I knew which line to take. I did not know however, which line to take at the half price tix counter in Leister Square, when I lined up an hour and a half later. Both lines were as long as three shopfronts, and they were not moving more than half an inch every five minutes. I kept fishing into my pocket to check the time on my mobile, as I was aware that the matinee began at three, and it was already nearly two. For some unbeknown reason, at least ten of the people lined up in front of me decided to give up the ghost, and they disappeared from the line. Maybe they were too hungry to keep waiting. I'd sampled a train station treat when I had changed trains at Clapham station. Defiantly not gourmet, but edible, and I had nibbled it all the way to Victoria.

It was close to two thirty when I reached the front of the queue. The dark young boy serving was very friendly, and really knowledgeable about the musicals and the shows he was promoting. He was surprised that I hadn't booked my ticket for 'Les Mis' in Australia, but I assured him that I would be happy with whatever seat he was able to rustle up for me.

Humility mixed with flexibility pays off in some ways, and bounces right back to bite you in the face in others. The payoff for me was a seat in the stalls with an elevated view, and no pole in front of me. (Concrete pole that is.) The biting back bit was the man to my left (almost on top of me) who alternatively munched peanuts and popcorn and sang his way through both Acts. His munching was loud, and his singing was even louder. I shuffled away from him as far as I could on the narrow seats, but there was only so far that I could wriggle, without ending up on the floor. At intermission, I decided I would take leave of the nut-munching singer and stretch my legs. Once up on my feet I trail-blazed my way to the ladies. A mountain goat would have struggled! The stairs were old, wooden, rickety and extremely steep. The bathrooms were even older. Not the theatre experience for the feint hearted. Everything was in hobbit dimensions, and I could barely squeeze into the bathroom, which only had two toilets cubicles. Luckily there were only four people congregated around the sink section, and one of the toilets was available. As I tried to exit the cubicle, disaster struck. The door remained locked, no matter how hard I tried to jiggle it open. It was a 'No Go.' The centuries-old latch/lock simply wouldn't budge. I tried poking and prodding the lock for about two minutes with little success, and since I wasn't sure if there were still people in the bathroom, I started calling out loudly to anyone who might be passing by. It was to no avail though, as the thick doors would have been tightly closed, and if anyone was outside, it would be highly unlikely for them to be lingering on the stairs, or even on the small landing, as there just wasn't any room. I had no alternative but to stand there and call for help, hoping that someone would be racing into the bathroom at the last minute. The bell had already sounded to signify the end of intermission, which meant the lights would soon be dimmed, and the cast would be hurtling headlong into their first song of Act two. If I didn't think fast, I would be trapped for the duration of Act Two. In the end I did the only thing I could do. I stood on the toilet seat and hoisted my leg over the top of the cubicle. (I had checked for feet underneath the cubicle next door, even though there was not a sound in the entire bathroom.) I was grateful for my long black boots, as I took them both off (a balancing act on the toilet seat) and threw them down at the upright toilet seat of the next cubicle. (Being goal-shooter in my netball team for twenty odd years paid off-as my aim was straight, despite my shaking hands) The force of my throw caused the upright-lid to the toilet seat to fall forwards. Next, I rolled up the purple shawl I had tied around my shoulders (in case it had been chilly in the century old theatre) into a tight ball and threw it down on the toilet seat to give the seat some bulk, and to act as a cushion for me when I jumped. Finally, I bent down, and grabbing my handbag, jumped up onto the ledge between the two toilets swinging my legs over to the other side. I was poised up there, willing myself to jump down onto the seat on the count of three, when the main door to the bathrooms was flung open and the door to the cubicle I was just about to parachute into, was pushed forward. A petite, immaculately coiffured Asian woman, dressed to the hilt and dripping with jewels stood there, staring up at me, and calling excitedly to her companion, whom I could not see, because the petite woman was blocking her. That didn't really matter, because I could hear the companion quite clearly, jabbering away in mother tongue, and clearly distressed. I wondered whom they thought I was and what I was doing, splayed on the top of the cubicles now dressed entirely in black with black stockinged feet. The famed Manchester Big Cat – down for a spot of culture in the capital? The woman below me was calling up to me, "What you are do? You are stunk?" I realised how it must have looked to her and the companion, but I knew I didn't have time or the inclination for a full account of myself.

"My door is stuck, and I had to climb over into this toilet. Can you and your friend give me a hand please?" Even though it hadn't sounded like English was a first language for the Asian duo, they cottoned on quickly enough, and both women put their hands up towards me, and eased me gently onto the seat. I landed softly and safely on the purple shawl, and the two ladies got the giggles as soon as we had wedged and squeezed ourselves out of the cubicle. I picked up my shoes and shawl and bundled them into my large bag. I could hear the first song still being performed, and I tried unsuccessfully to get the two ladies to stop tittering as opened the door to the theatre. It was no use, they were beyond reason. This was a great source of entertainment for them, and it had tickled their tummies to see me on the top of the cubicle like a big black cat in sheer black stockings about to pounce.

I left them on the first landing in the semi darkness, pretending that I'd never seen them before, and made my way stealthily, stair by stair, and on all fours with my head bent, back to the peanut singer. To my enormous delight, he wasn't in his seat, and I could stretch my legs and bend my arms for as far as I liked. I kept waiting for him to reappear with a fresh bag of peanuts and large print lyrics to the songs to hand out to our row, but he never did. I was in heaven. The finale of 'Les Mis' is my favourite part of the musical, and this production did not disappoint. It nearly brought the house down, and most of the crowd were on their feet demanding encores – which ensued. I was really fired up by the time I left the theatre, and wished that I'd attended the production with Alice, as she too was very musical, and she loved the songs. We wouldn't have to wait too long to find ourselves in theatre land though, as I had bought her surprise tickets to Kinky Boots the musical, and we would be there on Saturday.

Not that I knew the Kinky Boot's score, but then neither would anyone else, so we could be assured of not being landed with another singing peanut-eater for a next-door seat neighbour. It was almost 6 o'clock when I left the theatre, and the streets were teeming with commuters and late-night shoppers. An old pro at the trains by now, I was home in Hampton in no time, and sleep that night was never easier. I just kept humming *Castle on a Cloud*, and was off like the wind. I dreamt of 'ladies in white'. (No, not the *White Ladies* funeral company we have in Australia.)

# Chapter 19
## Friday in the Suburbs

Some mornings are so uneventful they do not even register. The morning after 'Les Mis' was one such morning. If something different to the ordinary routine of the daily grind happens, then it is easy to remember events. But if all is as it should be on your particular planet in the universe, then nothing is amiss, and nothing is memorable. What cements memories is the triggering of the memory, and the impact of an occasion. Nothing to report means leave well enough alone. The best way for me to dodge any potential morning mishaps and misdemeanours seemed to be to remain snuggled up in bed, listening to the morning melodies of the orange sky. The birds and the jets, both early risers were in full-flight early morning warm ups, with their respective twittering and swooshing. Not that I minded. The birds were sweet and enticing me to smile at their high-pitched antics, whereas the jets were just a force with which to be reckoned. In alternate renditions, they managed to keep me open-eyed. When I am awake early on holidays, I either draw, paint, or write. I decided to experiment with my pastels, as I had an idea for a busy, colourful depiction of Victoria station in London, and it seemed as good a time as any to start sketching again. I had brought the pastels with me in the hope of reigniting my passion for drawing, which had lain dormant within me for the past five years. The last time I had sketched with pastels had been probably been around five years ago at Uluru (Ayers Rock) in Central Australia. The implements I was using were very thick stubby pastels, in an attempt to sketch and colour a famous natural watering hole (Mutitjulu) at the base of the rock-popular with tourists as a resting spot. The pastels were at least six centimetres thick, and my pride and joy. There were only five of them, and an even thicker black one. I had purchased them at great expense in London some years prior. The resting spot had only one bench, constructed in natural gnarled local wood. The bench was positioned facing the magnificent deep pool of water. The watering hole, situated below the steep red face of the Western side of the rock, almost made it to billabong classification. (In case you make it there one day.) Uluru itself is twenty-six kilometres in circumference.) A magical place. Spiritually satisfying and a landscape to make you want to cut off an ear as a humble offering to the sheer beauty of the terrain. (Not that I was tempted, because I needed both my ears to listen out for packs of wild dingoes – they'd reputedly taken a tiny baby and munched away, so I knew I would have no hope.) It was still early morning, and the watering hole was deserted. No tourists and thankfully no wild dingoes. I was engrossed in my taxing task of sketching the rock face (one short, straight, black line after another, but I needed to concentrate) when from the corner of my eye, I noticed something moving and rustling. I leant over to get a clearer view, and in that split second, dropped the thick black pastel I was clasping. In exquisite slow motion, the pastel fluttered down into the grate, and settled comfortably in the red parched sand beneath. Gone! Probably for the next thousand years, until some over-keen archaeologist from the Time Team dug it up and examined its properties – marvelling at the primitive twenty-first century technology. The dropped pastel wasn't just any old paltry pastel. Far from it. She was the queen bee of my pastel pack. The black, the matriarch, the highest of the high and three times the price of the individual-coloured pastels. At least twenty pounds worth of powdered pigment if I recalled correctly, and it had taken three days of scouring London art suppliers to source exactly what I had required. When I had finally struck gold in a tiny, tucked away, musty art shop in Soho, I had reacted as though it was something to be treasured – rare and revered. For the past five or so years since the demise of the thick black pastel, I have travelled to Uluru every alternate September, and my first port of call early on the very first morning of my holiday, is always the watering hole. Akin to the pre-dawn Stonehenge Druids, I bend over on the mesh floor-covering and revisit my old friend the thick, black, pastel. Last year, when I was alone at the watering hole, bent over paying homage to the pastel Gods, a tour-group of around twenty tourists descended upon me, and there was I, humped over on all fours, knee-deep in conversation with my old friend. The amazed German tourists (I recognised the word 'snell') all fell into a respectful silence. Sizing up the situation, I lumbered awkwardly to my feet, and announced to the group, "Well, that was cleansing! You guys should try it sometime. It's a very ancient aboriginal ritual." I then turned and fled. After a minute or so of fleeing, curiosity got the better of me, and I spun around to see what they were doing. Sure enough, many of them had their heads bent to the wire mesh. Either they were summonsing the Dreamtime, or they had also lost their pastels. Or both!

I was propped up in bed busily sketching to my heart's content when there was a soft knocking at my door. It was Alice. "Fil. Are you awake?"

"Yes. Come in Ali."

Alice came in quietly and closed the door softly behind her, carefully lifting it from the handle as she did so. That way there was no abrupt sound of shutting.

"What are you up to today, Fil?"

Alice liked to know what was on the agenda for the day. Super organised and all that.

"Remember, I'm riding the buses today, Kingston and then Richmond?"

Alice must have forgotten my plans, as she just looked blankly at me.

"Remember we talked about my plans last night?"

She was still looking dazed, so I jumped up out of my bed, upsetting the apple-cart of crayons as I did so, and gave her a quick hug. Very uncharacteristic for me, but she'd looked a little lost, and I was unsure of the source of her perplexity. If hugging was not my usual style, then this uncertainty was definitely not Alice. The hug instantly reinstated her.

"Will you please be home by six, Fil, because Patrick is picking up the Friday night Fish and Chips, and he will be back by then. Joan is coming for tea as well."

I assured Alice that I would be back in time, and that seemed to pacify her.

"I'm off then. Have a good day and please don't invite any strangers for tea."

She grinned, lifted the door gently again, and disappeared. I assumed Patrick and the dogs to be still asleep, or Alice would no doubt have banged the door, so forgetful was her morning mood. Abandoning my sketching, I quickly showered, dressed and was outside within twenty minutes. Alice's car had gone. Patrick had not appeared, and the dogs were presumably still snoozing. I checked my phone for the weather, and it was to be twenty degrees and sunny. Perfect touring weather. I was at the bus-stop in record time, and only had to wait around ten minutes, before the bus came bouncing along. Since I had planned to do a self-organised tour of both Kingston and Richmond today, I was free to decide which township to visit first. I flipped a coin and it came up heads. Richmond it was!

The bus was winding along towards the river, and I had great view of the posh triple-storey houses from my look-out on the top deck. It was a real estate enthusiast's dream ride. To top it all off, it was a beautiful balmy London morning, and everyone on the bus seemed in good spirits. There was a woman deep in conversation, in the seat behind me. Her voice was very loud, and I thought she might be talking on her mobile, or into a Dictaphone, as she was barely drawing a breath. I had observed two women huddled in that seat when I'd scanned the bus for a vacant seat myself, but I wasn't sure whether they were travelling together. I stole a quick glance, and noticed that they were both still there, and identically dressed in knee-length, camel-haired English overcoats. Both also sported little silk scarves, fastened tightly under their chins and covering their heads entirely. It seemed the standard uniform for the older, more mature English woman – overcoat and scarf – and they looked comfortable in their dress code. Both had their feet obscured from my scrutiny, but I guessed their shoes would have been just as sensible and equally as comfortable. My thought drifted to my own experience with dress codes, in schools. Most Educational institutions have a dress code, which is nearly always a call for 'neat and casual attire with no unnecessary displaying of flesh'. One school in which I worked for a number of years had a five-page manifesto on appropriate and acceptable dress code, and this was updated monthly along with other policy documents. It hadn't affected me, as I had earned the status of jaded dinosaur teacher by then, but the young teachers were traumatised by the dress code committee, and subject to scrutiny on a daily basis. The policy stated, 'Categorically, no cleavage, no open arms or legs and definitely no open-shoes such as sandals or thongs.'

Of course, the men were exempt from this anachronistic policy, so they would appear in beach wear most days, and be praised for their efforts. The women teachers took to layering and sweltered through the summers in the process. I was glad that I had been no spring chicken when the strict dress codes came in.

I didn't turn around again, as that would have been inappropriate, even though my curiosity was compelling me to take a closer look at the two women seated behind me. The one-sided conversation was intriguing. The one in the green silk scarf was the spokeswoman, and the other just kept repeating, 'ng yeah' in response. I didn't think she could have been listening to her companion at all, as she never wavered in her utterances. The friend could have informed her she was going to a red-light district in Richmond for some afternoon delight, and the reaction would still have been: 'ngy yeah!'

Green-scarf was relating her outing into London last week.

"It was chaos! I was on the train to Piccadilly Circus and when we got there, the cars kept going around and around like little dodgem cars at the fairground." She then switched subjects almost mid-sentence and continued on with a happy tirade about how her son had taken her away last weekend, but that he hadn't bothered to inform her of the intended location.

"We had a wonderful time together. We ended up in Oxford. Some of those little villages along the way were delightful. They were so quaint and like a breath of fresh air. It was quite warm, and the daffodils were just coming into bloom, but it was such a long way." I thought, *Well, I shan't be going back to Oxford in a hurry.* "And what a lovely lunch we had before the rain came down like stinging nettles. I was soaked to my bones and so cold! The rain came down so unexpectedly, I got a real shock. I didn't have a raincoat because I didn't even think to bring one with me. I came back on the first-class train we were so wet. I should have taken all my life possessions with me.

"My shoes were totally ruined!

"My pearls were soaked to the string, and all I could find to put over my head was a newspaper. Then I had newsprint all over my face. I was mortified, and Johnny just laughed. He said, 'Ah ma, we'll survive Muriel my mother dearest!'

"I'm telling you Pearl, I had not the faintest idea where I was going, and it was raining so hard and that did not help."

I sat there, spell-bound throughout the entire monologue. I couldn't help but listen. Her east end accent was compelling. All the while she'd been prattling on, Pearl had been interjecting with her favoured phrase. I counted up seventeen 'ngyeahs!'. It was cheap entertainment for me on the bus to Richmond-on-Thames.

I was quite disappointed when we pulled up outside the Richmond station and the two women stood up to alight. The conversation had been far better than an audio-book. Neither woman even glanced at me, so I was safe with my serious eavesdropping habit. Had the bus trip been longer, it would have been fair to assume that Muriel would have talked her way to Land's End.

I stood at the wide, sloping front of the entrance to Richmond station, committing the landmark to memory in case I decided later in the day to train it back to Hampton. My stomach was sending me hunger nudges, just little pings, so I sauntered into the nearest cafe (happened to be a 'Prete').

I didn't bother with my usual sandwich gazing, but arbitrarily selected an orange juice and salad roll, which I nibbled on as I trickled my way down the hill towards the shops. (I saved the juice for later)

Richmond's main Street is a road – boarded quadrant, and I was a little confused at first as to which way to turn. I kept to my mantra and turned left initially, but eventually had to turn on my heels and walk up the shoulder of the quadrant, as I was hopelessly lost. Dozens of red buses grand-prixed their way past me as I plodded on – reckless driving in my opinion, as there were shoppers (including children and babies in prams) galore. We just don't have the population in Australia to be this overcrowded. The shops were an eclectic mismatched mix between the big, bland Department stores, and the older, smaller bespoke shops with their 200-year-old facades of wood and shingle cladding still beautifully preserved. I was on the hunt for a light raincoat, as the bright blue sky of an hour before had turned a sulky grey and was threatening rain. I was noticing other people's rain coats and jackets as I traipsed up and down the shop-filled quadrant. There appeared to be an oversupply of puffy black knee length jackets in Richmond. Every man and his dog was dressed in these jackets. The puffy jackets did a super job of androgenising the wearer, so I never really knew for certain if there were men or women walking towards me, until they got up close and I could see make up on the women. Not that wearing makeup defined gender. Whilst waiting at the lights to cross over the bridge heading towards the river, I could clearly hear an elderly woman, dressed in a black puffy coat parroting on to her friend. "I wore this coat to a night barbecue, and I should have been freezing, but I was quite warm in my puffy jacket. I think I'm joining the coffee shop brigade."

I winced at her description of the coat and the tenuous association with coffee, and I fancied I might buy one for myself if I chanced upon a style I liked. It would complement my black theatre outfits and make me feel like one of the initiated here in affluent Richmond.

I had reached the end of the architecturally stunning arch-stoned bridge, and was making my way down to the riverside, with the intention of spreading out my swag and attempting some preliminary sketches of the mighty Thames. It was a relief to be flying solo. I have come to the decision that if there are two of us sketching the same scene, one person is inevitably better, but if one is alone, there is no comparison, and hence no hierarchy. My mind took me back to Uluru for the second time that day to the occasion when I had been landscape-painting with a good friend and fellow amateur artist. We had erected our easels side by side, in order to paint the impressive Rock from the same angle. We had set up in the car park viewing section, about two kilometres (as the crow flies) from the Rock itself. Over the years, the large red gravelled car park had earned five-star rating amongst the camera-clad tourists, especially in the crepuscular hours, as one can clearly watch the colours of the rock changing dramatically. Both my friend and I painted as we envisaged, but of course our paintings bore not the slightest resemblance to one another. Ninety-nine percent of the time Jenna is a perfectionist with an eye for colour and fine detail. For my part, likening me to a short-sighted cyclops would be an overgenerous accolade. I have no eye at all for detail, and I tackle bold strokes and mix my colours with carefree abandon. I lack convention and ipso-facto, any real talent in the eyes of the art world critics. As I was painting that evening, a tall tourist draped in an bagwan-type shawl approached our makeshift camp and peered silently at both our paintings. Then she turned to Jenna and whispered, "You have a real talent my dear. The strokes are so defined, and the colours are so authentic to the Rock." Jenna was delighted with the compliment and I nodded encouragingly at her. I had been telling her for years, with utmost sincerity, that her paintings were really good, so it was fortuitous for her to receive this positive feedback from a perfect stranger. Then it was my turn. The woman was contorting herself over my painting, in my face, and in my personal space. I was feeling extremely uncomfortable, and defensive. I really thought that she was going to sensitively suggest that I may have been colour blind, because I had painted the Rock in my own bohemian choice of colours and depicted it as twice as big and blobby than it really was. But she didn't. She discontorted herself, stood up straight, patted me on the shoulder and announced to the world (there was quite a pack of international tourists in the immediate vicinity).

"We have here a painter who defies convention and disregards hundreds of years of tradition. Come and look." Within seconds I was swamped by the public. Most of them just took a peak, giggled and moved on, but I did have that moment of fame. We laughed about it later, especially the bit when the woman proclaimed my genius with colour to the people. The incident made for an entertaining dinner-party story for years to come. Given that the woman had a Dutch accent, some loyal friends even tried to convince me that she may have been a descendant of one of the Dutch masters, and she had innately recognised genius style when she'd seen it. I believed that to be true at the time. Now, I'm not quite so sure of my talent.

It was with the past glories of beautiful Uluru in mind, and a second shot at fame in the art world, that I positioned myself at a painter's distance from the river bank and began erecting my portable easel (a wooden clipboard), accompanied by six little thick plastic cups for my colours. No wonder the backpack had been so heavy this morning. I'd forgotten about the sketchbook, mini easel and assorted brushes and oils I'd included at the last minute. After a couple of hours alternating between painting and resting, I'd had enough. No one had come and squinted at my work and announced to Richmond-on-Thames that Monet's illegitimate granddaughter was in town. No one even came near me. They were all too busy poking their noses in and out of the eclectic Richmond shops to bother with some tiresome tourist painting their beloved river in purple and oranges. Persistent light showers of rain had left me damp and irritated, and I was really quite parched. I'd guzzled down my orange juice earlier and sacrificed all the water in my water bottle to my paint-streaked hands, so I was on the hunt for a mini market with water bottles, and a warm dry cafe with hot tea and cakes. I did resolve one thing in Richmond, and that was that I would never even make it to the preliminaries of the "Great landscapes of Britain" painting competition on this trip. No stamina, and definitely no undiscovered talent.

I found a warm, dry cafe on the corner as I exited the bridge, and although they didn't stock water bottles, the girl was kind enough to fill mine up. She was fussing over me, asking if I required a towel to pat down my glistening, dripping-wet hair, as well as explaining the ingredients of the displayed cakes and slices in great detail. It could have been because I was the only customer in the shop. But I think it was more that she was just generally hospitable and eager to please. A refreshing trait. Her name was displayed in large print on her badge – 'Stacey'.

Most people like to be referred to by their name, so I made sure I uttered 'Stacey' at least ten times whilst languishing in the cafe. Stacey was pleased with my good manners, and I rewarded her with one of the tiny koalas. She was thrilled, and quickly stuffed it into her apron. She was a sweet girl, but she just would not stop talking. My friends and I often retell the story of a mutual colleague who could talk his way off the Titanic and simultaneously sell both his maternal and paternal grandmothers. He worked part time in a jewellery shop in an enclosed mall, and one day a group of us were outside the shop chatting to him. His job that particular morning involved bellowing out on a megaphone, enticing customers into the store to buy expensive jewellery. A mutual colleague was approaching, and quick as a flash Matt whispered to me, "What's this guy's name again?"

We all chorused out, "Jim! His name is Jim."

Matt stepped forward authoritatively, and extended his hand to Jim, shaking Jim's hand profusely and shouting out to him. "Jim, Jim nice to see you, old buddy!"

Less than ten seconds before, Matt hadn't had a clue about his name, but Jim was none the wiser, and he felt important because he had been remembered. That day Jim bought two hundred dollars' worth of jewellery, and Matt earned himself a hefty commission for the sale. We nick-named Matt the prime minister after that incident, because he could talk his way out of anything.

After my tea and cream cakes, I kept walking back towards the station. En-route I was struck by the number of Charity shops selling second hand goods. The English appeared to have a long-standing love affair with them. I recalled Patrick spending many an afternoon browsing the opportunity shops in Barton, so I thought I'd wander into a couple of them on my quest for a cheap rain jacket. I unearthed a plastic poncho-style rain coat in the third shop I visited. Long and glaringly green. It was love at first sight. I would have paid top dollar for the quality thick plastic covering, but it was only one pound, and a little closer to my price range. I paid this king's ransom price, immediately slipped it over my head, and paraded gallantly out of the shop into the pouring rain – so confident was I that the raincoat would do its job.

People were staring at me, I knew that, but my thick skin protected me from their scrutiny. It was only when I passed a Department store with a front window display involving mirrors, that I realised why people were staring. I had forgotten to take off my backpack when I'd put on the green rain-poncho, so I looked like a gremlin hunchback of Notre Dame on tour in the rainy English countryside. The hump was enormous, and I hurriedly took off the poncho and removed my backpack. The heavy rain had abruptly ceased, and the drizzle was so fine that it was really quite pleasurable, feeling it spraying against my face and on the back of my neck. It pays to have short hair sometimes. The poncho was soon quite wet, so I teased out a plastic bag from the backpack and rolled it up into a tight ball. I would have to remember to take it out and spread it over the drying rack in the laundry tonight, or it would smell, and I would be in the same position that

I had been in with the egg sandwich. Who ever said travelling was easy? Too many decisions to make, and too many bags to carry!

It was almost midday, and I thought it best to start making tracks to Kingston, as I'd enjoyed enough of the delights of Richmond. It had been quite a hectic morning, and I felt a little apprehensive at catching the train to Kingston, in case I missed my stop. 'Busing it' would be a much smarter choice, as I was familiar with the streets, and from the vantage point of the enclosed top deck I would be able to pin-point exactly where to hop off. As soon as I found a bus stop with a 111 sign amidst the other signs, I hung back in front of the shops imitating the rest of the commuters, leaning against the glass shop-fronts and trying to look as if I knew exactly where I was headed. It didn't take long for my bus to rear its frantic head. As it was already quite full, I didn't even bother with the downstairs section, but made my way directly towards the winding spiral stairs which led up to the top deck.

The sun was quite high by the time we reached Kingston, and there was an abundance of warm sunshine filtering onto the shops and into the alley ways. With no rain in sight, I was all ready for an afternoon of escapades in Kingston upon Thames.

I was getting used to this peripatetic way of life. It felt good to be back in the sunshine and warmth of Kingston and I adored the little cobblestone arcades and windy paths and alleys. The last time I had been in Kingston there had been fun and games in the John Lewis Cafeteria. I decided to give John Lewis the wide berth, and wander into the shopping arcade where I had met the girl who'd promised me that if I purchased a certain toy, I would soon be experiencing the satisfactory spin. It hadn't happened that night, and I was still waiting. It could be just what I had in mind for today.

I didn't however make it to first base, because along the way, I spotted a Japanese restaurant which had a long line of customers standing guard outside the doors. Hungry crowds waiting was a healthy indication of a top-notch eatery, and I loved Japanese food. It was almost my birthday, so I talked myself into a birthday treat, and lined up behind the last person in the queue.

The woman in front of me was also alone, but there was a family of about six before her. I couldn't see much beyond that, excessive bobbing heads but at least we were moving. The maître-D was also moving, heading towards me with a wide grin, and a very boyish English rotund face. Although he was dressed in traditional Japanese costume, he definitely wasn't Japanese!

"You are alone?"

He was directing his question to both myself and the woman in front of me, and we both nodded, confirming that we were indeed alone.

"Good. And now you are together. Follow me please."

He strode off towards the head of the queue, nodding to the tired-of-waiting starving masses on the way, assuring them that there would soon be room for the larger groups, but at the moment it was just the couples who could be accommodated. It didn't bother me that I was to be coupled with the perfect stranger to my right, but it seemed to slightly upset her.

"Err, excuse me young man." She began to protest vehemently, "I won't be paying good money to sit next to a tourist. I'm London born and bred I am."

I ignored her insult, forgiving her on the grounds of confusing me for someone who cared about sitting with strangers, but the maître-D was having none of that talk.

He was diplomatic but firm with her. "Madame, as you can see, there is only a large carousel in our restaurant, and no one is sitting at tables. You will be seated on a stool which has just been vacated, and it is highly unlikely that you will be sitting next to this beautiful lady." He meant me. I was the beautiful lady, and the Londoner was the wicked witch of the west because she had complained even before we had entered the restaurant. The Samurai's no-nonsense tone worked a trick as the woman put her head down and didn't utter another word.

Presumably because she'd been in front of me, she was seated first, and mercifully it was at the other end of the conveyor belt, so there would be no need for small-chat on my part. The cuisine was excellent, lots of small dishes, and I thoroughly enjoyed my birthday treat to myself. The food kept travelling around and around the corner on its polar express, and all customers needed to do was to reach out and select whichever dish their heart desired. The downside was the hefty bill when it came, but I had feasted like a Queen, sampling many appetisers I'd never even heard of before. I tipped the English boy who had done his best to accommodate me and left-slowly. There were still hordes of people lining up even though it was around two thirty, and well past lunchtime.

Outside the restaurant was crowded with shoppers and gaggles of bored teenagers hanging around the fronts of the shops, but not actually venturing inside. That wouldn't have been cool. I wanted to walk off my enormous lunch, and a saunter along the river seemed like the ideal option.

Outside the mall was a hive of activity. The buskers and the resident accordion player were in full flight. I braved myself against the noise and frolic and rushed across the square towards the river.

It was much quieter and more peaceful riverside, and I parking myself on one of the brightly painted benches and studied a flock of carefree water birds gliding along upstream. I then closed my eyes and began to meditate.

I must have fallen asleep because when I opened them again, it was to a much greyer sky and I felt quite chilly. I snapped some photos of the river from different angles and ambled off to find somewhere warm to have a cup of tea. I ended up in the John Lewis cafeteria again-my old stamping ground, as It was close by and easy to find. Although it was late afternoon, people were still eating hot meals – all day lunches were apparently the norm in the big cafeterias. I had only planned on having a cup of tea, but not wanting to appear a cheapskate, I also selected a slice of teacake and a green apple. With skills honed from countless childhood cafeteria visits, I managed to manoeuvre my laden tray along the track towards the young girl sitting on a high stool at the end of the track. She was extremely pretty and manicured to perfection. Dressed in the standard uniform of the eateries in the big Department stores, she looked expectantly at each new customer as if they were the first person she'd seen for years. It was a blank look, like the guards at Buckingham Palace, and a little disconcerting for the customer, as one did not know where to look. I called her bluff and gazed at her full on. Immediately she looked away. I tried conversation.

"You've got a great little job carved out for yourself here. Do you enjoy meeting customers and having little chats?"

It was a vain attempt at humour on my part, as the cafeteria was famous for its carvery – serving all types of hot meats. The girl just smiled at me, and finally replied, "Ngyeah!"

I smiled back at her. I was beginning to get used to these 'Klingon' derived languages which were favoured in the south of England. I stood there, clutching my wooden tray full of my afternoon tea, and weighed up my chances of getting a table to myself. It was very busy and crowded for this late hour, and I realised that I might need to share. Just as I was about to ask a lady who appeared to also be alone if I might share her table, a family of four stood up and started collecting their belongings and shopping bags. I quickly employed the universal three-step rule of solo table pouncing. Number one hover in the vicinity of the table as soon as you detect movement. Number two-stake your claim. Number three-make yourself comfortable and try to decide how to reserve the table whilst you line up and load up your tray. Group-table-'pouncing etiquette' is a different story. If you have a party of four, and you split up to scout, you have four times the opportunity of the solo scouter.

The table I had claimed was directly opposite a group of Turkish scarf-clad women. There were six of them in rows of three at a long table, all laughing and having a great camaraderie time. There was a large metal steaming teapot ceremoniously centred in the middle of the table, and the women were all happily devouring a heaped platter of pumpkin-coloured scones. They were eating them sans jam or cream, even though the cafeteria was also famous for its Devonshire teas. The clan were all wearing grey and black covered scarves. Maybe all of their husbands had died, or maybe they were the cast of 'Seven brides for Seven brothers' on an afternoon tea break? Or maybe they were celebrating someone's birthday, or just out for a monthly morning tea? There were stacks of brimming-over shopping bags at their feet. They were obviously not tourists. The tourists are very, very recognisable. No incognito for them. Back packs and bulging stomachs which hide their passports is the clue. They always appear flustered – looking at their phones for directions or seeking out ablution locations. In the department stores they are mostly found to be congregating around the mobile phone accessories departments – or the food courts as hunger is the constant companion of the tourist. I could see quite a few of them tucking into their afternoon teas and taking 'selfies' or group photographs with the beautiful, scenic Thames in the background. The cafeteria was situated on the third floor of the department store, and the view of the river from the full-length windows was spectacular. I turned my attention away from the Turkish contingency and focused instead on the two people seated directly behind me – a man around thirty-five and a cheeky three-year-old. The man was dressed in a blue pin striped suit, but he also had a back pack chained to his back. He was giving the child lunch. It was all organic and the little boy was begging for sweets.

"Oh dah, pl…ease? I just want to get me some jelly."

The young father wouldn't give up on the organic veggies he was shoving into the child's mouth.

"No Declan. This is lunch. It's all organic now, and you know what it'll do for your hair."

I secretly thought the organic veggies had already done more than enough for Declan's hair, which was a spectacular white shoulder length curly shiny mane. Wise beyond his years, Declan must have had the same thought, as he continued to protest. "Oh, but sure da me hair is already groweed. I need jelly now."

I'm not sure who won the argument because an announcement suddenly drowned them both out. It was to inform customers that the cafeteria would be closing at 5 pm. When I looked back, they had disappeared.

After lunch I spotted them again in the audio technology part of the store. Da was looking at the most expensive CD players and Declan of the tangled white curls and very trendy John Lewis clothing, was climbing all over the furniture. His father was oblivious. He was focussed on sourcing an expensive Wi-Fi system to rig up in his study. I could hear the conversation between Da and the salesman. The salesman was valiantly attempting to explain to him that John Lewis stores did not stock the particular product he was requesting.

"What about another brand. Do you have anything in the same price bracket?" The salesman, who was really no more than a teenager was looking really worried, and noticeably out of his depth with the techno demands of this savvy customer.

"I'm sorry sir, this is about it for our store. We could always try another store. I'll just see if I can ring through and check with another store."

He was off like a flash towards the immunity of the back office. Declan continued to climb all over the furniture, and the father continued to fidget with the sockets of the audio equipment. I moved on then to the next section of the floor, looking for a new phone charger. As I'd predicted the phone section was very crowded, and I didn't really fancy waiting too long to be served. If I left buying it until later on in my trip, I would probably go to an actual mobile-phone shop where there might be a wider variety to choose from. I spent about another half hour in the Department store, and when I finally emerged, laden with plastic bags full of presents to take back to Australia, it was much cooler and overcast again. It didn't seem like it was going to get any brighter, so I raced across the road to the bus stop where I could see the 111 bus was about to leave from. It was crowded as usual, but I was practically a local by now, and It didn't bother me. I knew my way, and I knew I'd be safe and sound in the lounge room before too long, sipping sherry and recounting my day to Alice or Patrick or even Joan, if she were interested.

When I arrived home, Patrick was in the lounge room reading, but Alice had not yet appeared. Patrick informed me that Joan was due any minute and that he would leave Joan with me whilst he went down to collect the fish and chips.

We sat there chatting for a little while, and after about ten minutes, there was a frenzied rapping on the front door, and we could hear Joan's shrill voice calling out, "Yoo hoo. It's me, Joan. Anyone home?"

Patrick and I smiled at each other, and Patrick called out generously "The door is open Joan, come in."

Of course, she couldn't hear him, because Joan didn't appear, and it went very quiet. Patrick waited a couple of minutes, and then he got up and opened the front door. Joan was there alright, but she was just standing on the step. (I had followed Patrick out to the foyer)

"Joan what are you doing, come inside." Patrick was usually quite gentle with Joan, but I could hear a slight irritation in his voice. I couldn't really blame him though, as this behaviour was fast becoming the norm for Joan, and I had only been here for five days.

At the sound of Patrick's voice, Joan snapped to attention, and started babbling away, "Oh Patrick, I'm so glad you are home, I haven't had any tea yet, and I can't remember why I came over."

There was real anxiety and panic in her voice, and any irritation or annoyance at her antics that either of us had harboured, melted away. Patrick spoke first. "Joan it's Fish and chips night and you're here to eat them, remember."

Then I piped in with "And it's my shout!"

Joan must have found these two comments to be easy processing, and she shuffled her way into the lounge room and plonked herself on the very chair on which I had been resting. I ran to my room and retrieved the two twenty-pound notes I had been saving. I handed them to Patrick, assuring him that I was happy to shout us all tonight. He took the notes reluctantly and called to Holly and Looby to accompany him to the car. Just before he left, he turned to me, and stressed that I was to keep a close eye on Joan, as she was having a wandering week. I assured him I would strap her into the chair immediately. He laughed and departed with the dogs. That left me and Joan. There was very little opportunity for me to do much of the talking, as Joan was in fine spirits to start with, and in even finer spirits after two glasses of sherry which she dutifully skulled in quick succession. She was telling me all about how hard it was to get her car insured – and she was only eighty-eight.

"I know I can drive, because I have a ruddy driver's licence. I Know it will cost me a thousand pounds to get my car insured, but what is money for anyway? I love going to the bank. It's my favourite outing after the pictures."

I just sat there opposite her in Patrick's chair, willing Alice to pull up outside the bay window and save me from Joan. I didn't really need saving, as Joan was very sweet and extremely likeable, but it was just hard to know what she was going to do next. True to form, Joan jumped up excitedly after a few minutes chattering, and informed me that she needed to pop back home to get a cardigan. I offered to give her one of my jumpers, but she declined my offer. "Australian wool makes me itch and it's far too warm. I'll be back before the Fish and chips Australian girl. Now how do I get out of here? Oh yes. Through the door. If I'm not doing anything else, I'm having a laugh. I'll be back in two shakes of a jiffy. Do you know what a jiffy is?" With that she was gone, leaving the front door wide open. I closed the door after her and wondered what I was going to tell Patrick about Joan's escape. I should have tied her down after all. To pass the time, I laid out the table for the four of us, carefully positioning Joan as far from the door as possible.

I'd just finished arranging a little bunch of flowers I'd taken from the larger vase of flowers Alice had in the lounge room, when Joan popped her head through the front door. "Yoo-hoo Australian girl, I'm back."

I can't say I wasn't relieved, as her speedy reappearance meant Patrick would never know Joan had escaped my clutches. I hurriedly sat Joan down in the seat I had ear-marked for her and continued on with our conversation as if we had never left off.

"Joan, tell me more about the fairgrounds you lived at when you were growing up." Mention of the word fairground was manna from heaven for Joan, and she happily carried on with her soliloquy with gusto. The gist of her one-sided conversation was that she had moved from fairground to fairground with her parents, who were performers, and that they had sent her to Catholic schools whenever they were in a town for long enough. Despite her religious upbringing, Joan had turned her back on God and the angels in adulthood. She stressed upon me, in no uncertain terms, that she was an agnostic. "I'd like to think that there is somebody up there helping us, but I don't know who. The bloody nuns told us about the angels. I would love to think that there are angels, but I haven't seen any yet. It's too late now."

At that very moment, the front door opened, and the dogs came bounding in, heading straight for Joan. I cheered her up with my next comment. "Here are the angels Joan. Not white, and no wings, but just as angelic."

Joan laughed and Patrick and Alice both appeared at the door.

"Greasy grub's up!" Patrick piled our plates high with the fatty fish and chips, and Joan squealed with delight.

"Oh, goody goody-gum-drops! I love Friday nights!" We all agreed with her for once.

After tea, Patrick escorted Joan home, and Alice and I reclined on the sofas. "Good day Alice?" I wasn't going overboard with my small talk to Alice, as I could see that she was pale, tired and a little withdrawn. I imagined that it had been a rough day, being a Friday, but it was better to phrase my interest positively.

"It was fine. Just tiring you know, like some days are."

I was hearing her loud and clear. Doing Richmond and Kingston, and then Joan in one day had been a little optimistic on my part.

"I know what you mean Ali. Tomorrow morning, we can all have a sleep-in, as the show doesn't kick off till three."

"Hah, hah Fil. I get it."

Alice and I were off to *Kinky Boots,* the musical, the next day. I had presented her with a voucher for a musical of her choice as a "thanks for the hospitality" gift, and she'd chosen Kinky Boots. I didn't know much about the show, but I liked the title, and it was a musical so what was not to like?

We made plans for tomorrow, and when Patrick came in, it was well and truly bedtime for me.

# Chapter 20
## Saturday Matinee, and Up in London at the Theatre!

The morning whizzed by in a merry-go-round of washing, cleaning and gardening. Getting all dolled up for the theatre was the fun part. When we were suitably glammed, we tottered out to the car (I had borrowed high heeled shoes from Alice and they were slightly big on me) and headed towards Twickenham. We, being Alice and myself, as Patrick had meetings all day, and he had impressed upon me that he wasn't the slightest bit interested in Kinky Boots – or travelling into London for any reason. Patrick had survived a career in banking, and had without doubt, endured his fair share of daily jaunts in cities all over the world, squashed to a pulp in the tube, or exhausted beyond measure after a twenty-kilometre bicycle ride. When he and Alice had lived in Dublin, they had rented a glorious second floor apartment, complete with a concierge, overlooking grandiose gardens in a fashionable area near the Liffey river, and Patrick had walked to work every morning, along the canals and into Dublin proper. I had stayed with them in the apartment for a month, and Patrick had impressed upon me that walking to work in Dublin had been a highlight of their five-year sojourn in Dublin city. That was Dublin. This was Twickenham. A similarly affluent suburb to Ballsbridge where the apartment had been, and it looked like Alice and I were also in for a walk this morning. Being a Saturday, there was a glut of sport indulgence, and parking spaces in side streets were at a premium. We finally found a park and began the two-block walk to the station. It was a beautiful, crisp afternoon and the breeze was a touch on the chilly side, but not biting enough to warrant wearing a jumper. Alice was excited, because she didn't get into London as much as she would have liked to have and going to see a musical was an added bonus. Like Patrick, Alice had walked to work from the nearest tube station when she'd worked at 'Great Ormond Street' in Central London. She had told me, on many an occasion, that she missed the hospital, but not the tube and the walking.

It was about a twenty-minute walk to the station, and we arrived in plenty of time for the London train. Alice suggested extending our walk when we arrived at Waterloo, as it was such a crisp afternoon, and we set off across the bridge at a cracking ace. We still hadn't eaten lunch, and although the intention had been to have a light lunch before the show, time was ticking on, and we only had about an hour to spare before the curtain went up.

Many other people were indulging their own personal fitness routines by walking the bridge, and we were surged along merrily with the crowd, not really noticing our pace, and eliminating the need for over exertion.

Once off the bridge, we jumped on a bus which was headed in the direction of the theatre, and stood there facing each other, trying to decide what would be the quickest meal to partake of, given that we only had fifty minutes till the show. We alighted from the bus directly opposite the theatre, and we were in luck, because there was a Portuguese café right in front of the bus stop. It was a no brainer. We were eating there. I had lined up and paid for the order even before Alice had time to decide what she wanted to eat. I knew she loved chicken and rice so that's what I ordered, along with a large diet coke, which was also on her favoured list. I can't abide the taste of the sweetener they put in diet soft drinks, so I bought myself a bottle of water and a chicken burger.

The food was crisp, fresh and plentiful. So plentiful that neither of us could finish our meal, and we had to leave with food on our plate – something quite foreign to both of us. I could see the crowds gathering outside the theatre across the road, haphazardly lining up, and jostling their way into the foyer. We had our tickets, so there was no rush, but Alice was anxious to line up and make sure we were admitted. Across the road we tootled. We waited outside for around three minutes, and then, like toppling jelly beans, the crowd spilled into the foyer. We were carried along with the momentum, a bit like that of an hour before when we'd been carried over the bridge at a cracking pace.

The foyer was grand, but slightly on the faded, jaded side, and it looked as though it had seen better days. The carpet was worn, and the decor shabby. I was disappointed in the foyer, as it sets a precedent of things to come. The steps up to our seats were squashed in and extremely steep. Alice and I were trying our best to negotiate the steep steps, when suddenly Alice was propelled forwards by a pushy woman in a purple outfit. She had a heavy deep south of America accent. Not that she spoke much. All she shouted was "Look out y'all. Let me through", and then she pushed Alice.

I could have told her not to tangle with Alice, but there was no time to do so. One minute, Alice was climbing up the stairs, and in the next instance, she was falling back – down the stairs. The American lady tried to get past us, but the passageway was too narrow to walk three abreast. Alice gained her composure and raised her voice slightly to the woman. "I'll move then, shall I?" The sarcasm was thick in her voice, but the woman seemed not to pick it up and "Yes" was her monosyllabic reply. She pushed on as if mountain climbing for USA in the winter Olympics.

"Well, the cheek of her!" Alice was none too pleased. I wanted to speak up in defence of the millions of Americans who would have politely waited their turn on the steps, but I remained silent. It was Alice's day, and the woman had been rude.

"Come on Alice, we're nearly at the top." My words did nothing to encourage Alice to move faster, in fact they seemed to slow her down, as she was still miffed at the American woman. The musical was a happy affair, a clever mix of bitter North of England drama and humour, and the songs were catchy and entertaining. The cast were true professionals, and I was glad that Alice had opted to see a musical and not something like Richard the Third at the Globe theatre. After the musical, we 'ummed and erred' about where we should go for dinner, and in the end, we decided to go home and have baked beans on toast. It was already getting late, and we didn't want to be in the city too late on a Saturday night. It took about an hour to get to Twickenham where we had left the car, and then about another twenty minutes until we reached home.

Opening the cans of beans was easy and cooking the toast even easier. Because I was still wearing my theatre outfit of mostly black, I snatched up a white apron from the back of the kitchen door and fastened it around my waist. I figured it would save me washing the outfit tomorrow in preparation for my little trip into London. If some more half price tickets were to pop up at the half-price 'tix' booth, I would be ready with my outfit.

We were just organising trays so that we could flop down in front of the telly with our cowboy meal, when Alice noticed a car which was stationary in the court with its lights on high beam. She had been drawing the curtains in the living room when she'd seen the glare.

"Fil, come in here, what do you think is going on with that car?"

"I haven't got a clue Alice, I am ignorant regarding cars. Last week that boy Daniel on the cliff top at Barton asked me what I thought of his motor, and I told him that I knew nothing about motors. And I still don't!"

"But Fil, you must know that a car shouldn't be sitting out there in our court at 8 o'clock on a Saturday night with high beam on. Who do you think it is?"

"I really couldn't say Alice, why don't you go out and see what is happening? It could just be someone lost and looking at a map. Or maybe someone is having a party and they are the first guests to arrive."

Alice looked at me as though she didn't think much of my suggestions and marched over to the coat rack to put on her raincoat.

"I'm going out to see what's happening. Lock the door, and If I don't come back in five minutes, ring Patrick, and then the police."

I thought that Alice to be over exaggerating when she added the police bit, but then maybe they called the police for small matters in England. In Australia, you would just sort it out yourself – or be killed in the process.

After five minutes Alice still hadn't returned. The toast and beans had gone cold and soggy, and I was sitting in the lounge room peering out the window and waiting. I could just make out Alice's silhouette, but so far no one had got out of the car. Maybe someone was ill? That would explain a lot. I was just about to phone Patrick, when the doorbell rang. I was reluctant to open it without knowing who it was, so I called out softly, "Who is it?"

"Fil, it's me, open the door please! You've locked me out!"

Alice sounded irritated, so I hastily opened the door. Alice was there alright, but so were two other people. They looked very old and frail. Strangers to me, but I wasn't sure whether Alice knew them or not.

Alice was speaking. "Fil, this is Clarissa and Frank. Their car broke down and they turned into our court. I've invited them in to wait for the AA. I'll ring them on my mobile. Could you please make us all a cup of tea?"

Clarissa and Frank were gazing at me in astonishment, probably thinking I was a good age for an au-pair girl or nanny. (I was dressed in all black, with the whiter frilly apron. Alice must have told them that I was in the house preparing the evening meal, and that I was Australian. Putting two and two together would have had me as the au-pair girl. More like the au pair girl who was past retirement age, and who was unable to cook anything other than beans on toast.)

Clarissa was admiring the watercolours and oil paintings in the foyer, but Frank was still staring at me, presumably perplexed over my standing in the household. He just stood there shaking his head. There was something about him that reminded me of the other Frank from the beach, but I just couldn't put my finger on it – whatever it was. Alice ushered Clarissa and Frank into the lounge room, and it took both of us to settle Frank comfortably in Patrick's armchair. Patrick wouldn't be home until after eleven, so it was fine to position Frank there. I retreated into the kitchen to make a pot of tea and rummage for biscuits, while Alice rang the AA. Whilst Alice was on hold, Clarissa was telling her that she couldn't remember the number plate of their car, because she was so flustered, and that they were both so hungry, because their son had sent them away without any supper. It turned out that they had been invited to their son's house for an early supper, where there was to be talk of their will, and proposed inheritance for their son and daughter. The daughter lived in France, so she would need to be informed of the outcome of the dinner-party meeting. In no uncertain terms, Frank had put his foot down to the outrageous suggestion that he and Clarissa were to be moved into a nursing home, and furthermore had insisted that neither the son, nor the sister would be squeezing a penny out of them. The dreadful son had promptly thrown them both out of his house, yelling that he never wanted to see them again, and Clarissa had driven off sobbing. Frank had been seething at his son's inappropriate and insensitive behaviour, and they had both been so genuinely distressed that they had not noticed the car spluttering, stalling and faltering on their way home. Clarissa finally realised that something was badly amiss with the car, and had turned off the main road, making a sharp left turn into Alice and Patrick's court. They had been so grateful that Alice had spotted them, and they felt very safe with us.

    Alice had finally made contact with the AA, and after much prodding and questioning, had managed to force Clarissa to remember her address and phone number. (They had both left their mobile phones at home) The AA switchboard operator had informed Alice that the mechanic would be at least an hour, so we settled back and chatted. I quizzed Frank on the history of London, and he happily answered any questions he could. Alice and Clarissa were getting on like a house on fire, as they shared a common interest in needlework, and Clarissa was keen to see some of Alice's work. We had finished the tea and biscuits, and the AA service mechanic still hadn't arrived. Alice suggested something more substantial to eat for our guests, and they both hungrily agreed that it would be a good idea to eat, as who knew how and when they would get home? They lived in the King's Paddock, which was just behind Hampton Court Palace. I knew the exact location of the housing estate where they lived, as I had trudged past there when I'd missed my Hampton Palace stop.

"I'll go and heat up our meal, and then I'll divide it up for the four of us." (Possibly twenty syrupy beans and half a piece of sodden toast each.)

I could see Frank licking his lips in anticipation of a gourmet meal a-la-Heston, and I didn't have the heart to let him know what to really expect when I emerged from the kitchen. Earlier on in the week Alice had prepared nightly meals to rival a Master Chef contestant – and tonight we were having baked beans on toast. Alice must have entirely forgotten that I'd spent hours in the kitchen slaving over a hot stove, opening cans and cooking toast. I had no choice but to make more toast and divide the beans amongst the four of us. I was done in five minutes.

"Here we go Clarissa and Frank. Eat up. Unfortunately, it's only baked beans on toast, but it will keep you going till tomorrow morning." Clarissa was very grateful, but Frank was turning up his nose again.

"Not too keen on baked beans." I remembered the countless full English breakfasts (mostly full of baked beans as they were cheap) I'd partaken of in Hotels and Bed and Breakfast establishments all over Britain on past trips, and I had to agree with Frank that beans on the rocks weren't my favourite either.

Clarissa was used to Frank complaining, and she piped in with, "Well, if you don't like what you are being offered Frank, you'll just have to go hungry tonight." Frank looked back at her sheepishly and he suddenly snatched the plate of beans and toast from the tray I was balancing. He polished off his portion in an instant, and then had little choice but to sit back and watch the rest of us delicately digest our meal. Clarissa was proving to be a slow eater, so I sided with her, and slowed down my pace. We had almost finished eating when the doorbell rang, and Alice jumped up to let the AA man in. She seemed to know it would be the AA even before she opened the door. (She told me later that she'd seen the yellow lights of the van flashing through the gaps in the lounge room curtains.)

A young mechanic decked out in over-sized grey overalls and clutching an enormous yellow torch appeared at the doorway for a few seconds, introducing himself as Jamie and letting us know that he would be outside taking a look at the car, if any of us wanted to join him. Frank got all excited and tried to struggle to his feet in anticipation of an opportunity to mentor the mechanic who could have easily been his great grandson. He had mentioned to me in the course of our pre-dinner conversation that he had "tinkered with motors as a young lad".

Watchdog Clarissa intervened even before Frank could reach his walking stick. "No Frank. You're not going anywhere. Leave the young lad alone to do his job. You'll be more trouble than you're worth."

Poor Frank sunk back into Patrick's plush armchair, deflated for the second time in ten minutes. I felt sorry for him and pulled my chair closer to his, so that we could continue our conversation about London. He really was very knowledgeable and had some intriguing tales to tell about Old London town. Clarissa and Alice also took up where they had left off, and we were all happily conversing when Jamie reappeared at the doorway.

"All fixed. Your motor is ready to go." He seemed proud of himself that he had managed to get the car going again, and we all praised him on his speed and efficiency. Frank started sitting up straight again and extended his veiny hand towards Jamie to accolade him with a handshake. Jamie, with the exuberance of youth, high fived him back instead, and Frank looked pleased as punch. Clarissa was anxious to leave now that the problem had been rectified, and all three of us helped Frank find his feet, and escorted (dragged) him to the door. I stayed in the house, but Alice and Jamie made sure that Clarissa and Frank were safely seat-belted in their car. Clarissa put her foot down, and off they sped. Alice and Jamie just stood there shaking their heads at the way Clarissa was flooring the accelerator, but the Bonnie and Clyde couple made it to the top of the court and disappeared around the corner. By the time Alice reappeared, and related to me how Clarissa had taken off like a bat out of hell, I had stacked the dishes in the dishwasher, and wiped down the benches in the kitchen. Another eventful evening in the Hampton household. We both went straight to bed, and I was so tired I didn't even hear Patrick come in, well after eleven.

# Chapter 21
## Meet You at the Archway

The arrangements I'd made to meet friends for lunch in Archway, North London were quite casual, consequently, I wasn't really exerting myself to race for the train this morning. I had mapped out my route across London in my mind's eye, whilst listening to the airbuses thundering overhead, and after breakfast, I'd confirmed the route with Alice and Patrick. Alice offered to drive me to Richmond station, which had a direct connection to Gospel Oak, where my friends would pick me up to go back to the Archway. I simply loved the sound of the English suburbs. Archway was quite close to Hampstead Heath, which in turn was close to Primrose Hill. In Australia, we tend to name our streets and suburbs after English towns and cities, but for the most part, the names are overused – to the point that there might be fifty Kent roads. (Knowing the Monopoly Board off by heart always helps.) Suburbs with aboriginal names feature well in the large Australian cities, especially in Canberra where I grew up. My favourite place name, within close proximity of my hometown is Tidbinbilla – a notable Space Tracking Station in the heart of the Brindabella mountains. Everyone knows about the existence of Tidbinbilla Tracking Station, but hardly anyone can pronounce the place name, so they refer to Honeysuckle Creek as being the space tracking station associated with Australia. But I can pronounce 'Tid...bin...billa', and I know it to be the real mcCoy. (Admittedly I am still stumped on the pronunciation of the longest place names in the world – 'Llanfairpwllgwyngllgogerychwyrndrobwllllantysiliogogogoch.' And no, I didn't just accidently lean on the keyboard whilst reaching for my coffee. (If you do that you get 'djvjfjrjrvnndncn' or a similar string of letters.)

Because I'd insisted to Alice that I would catch the bus to Richmond station, I needed to leave a little earlier than I'd anticipated. Being a Sunday, there was quite a bit of pedestrian and road traffic, and I ended up standing in the bus aisle, clinging on for dear life all the way to Richmond. When I climbed aboard the train to Gospel Oak (minding the gap of course), it was the completely opposite scenario. The carriages were half empty, and despite the fact that the train sat stationary and silent in the station for at least ten minutes, my carriage stayed more than half empty until we left. Quite a few families alighted at Kew Gardens, all set for an afternoon of acres of delightful gardens to visit. I made a note to find some time to re visit Kew Gardens this trip, if time permitted. I was keen on Kew, as it had a quaint little train which circumnavigated the gardens, and you could hop on and off if a flowering rhododendron or exquisite palm caught your eye. The tourist gimmick was a similar set up to the London Tourist bus, which wound its merry way around Ol' London town for twenty circuitous miles on the half hour – allowing tourists the opportunity to alight and re-board at their discretion. I found the Kew Gardens train to be infinitely preferable to hopping on and off the London bus with all my worldly goods. 'Toy-training it' was my kind of garden touring!

It was a fair hike to Gospel Oak, and because it was not a route I had ever travelled before, it seemed longer. I kept studying the map on the carriage wall, which depicted the stations on a train route – (all lined up like rows of squeaky-clean Dutch houses.) More often than not, whenever the train slowed to a halt at the upcoming station, the station name was obscured by the carriage walls and people bustling along the platforms, so I had no idea where I was. The station name was announced over the loud speaker, but it was mostly a muffled and tinny voice-over from a breathless station-master with a frog-in-his-throat. Consequently, I could neither hear, nor process what was being announced. I finally worked out a system to ensure I made it to Gospel Oak. My method was to locate a station on the line, three stops before Gospel Oak. I then counted forwards, until we reached Gospel Oak. It worked a treat, and along with two other people, I hurried off the train. (I could cope with the strange looks I was getting from other passengers when I moved up closer to the doors, and stood there slowly counting the stations as we pulled into them but I wouldn't want to use this primitive abacus counting method on all my train trips.)

For a few seconds I was disoriented. The source of my befuddled state was the elevation of the platform on which I was standing, as I couldn't for the life of me work out how to reach ground level. I scanned the deserted expanse of uneven concrete for some indication or sign as to which way to proceed, but there was not a soul in sight nor any signage. With no clue, I turned left, and ended up on the overpass bridge on the other side. I then asked a gentleman who was rushing past me on the bridge for directions on how to exit the station. He looked exasperated at having been obliged to abandon his frenzied pace for small talk, but at least he had the graciousness to propel me in the direction of a series of steps to rival the Spanish steps in Rome. Thankfully it was all downhill. When I finally reached ground level, I did one of my little jigs through the turnstiles, so pleased was I to have made it to Gospel Oak, and to be standing on terra-firma. A gangly station attendant, leaning on a broom, was watching me curiously as I pranced around, and I smiled at him. Reaching into my backpack I handed him one of the koalas. It was his turn to smile, and he hurried off to show it to his co-workers in the booth. Not a word had been spoken, but he seemed to know that the koala was a gift, and that I had been dancing and cavorting around because that's what tourists do!

They may do their fair share of dancing and cavorting, but they also do whopping amounts of waiting – whether it be for buses, taxis, ferries, planes, shows to start, museums to open or hotels to be ready for occupancy. That's what we tourists do best. We wait! Which is what I did outside the Gospel Oak station. My friends, Suzy and Finley only lived twenty minutes away, but it was a holiday after all, and both were prone to the odd weekend-morning-sleep-in. I'd rung to let them know that I was on the train about an hour ago, and Finley had assured me that they would be outside the station to pick me up around twelve thirty. It seemed to be taking them ages to get to me, and I was a little worried that I wasn't supposed to get off at Gospel Oak after all. There had been some talk of me going cross-country though London to get to Archway station, but I couldn't remember what the final decision had been. Just as I was reaching for my mobile to press redial, I recognised their car as the insane vehicle hurtling down towards where I was loitering, outside a waste recycling area. Finley was driving, hunched over the wheel like he was a starter in the English Grand Prix, and Suzy was waving madly, indicating for me to cross over to the other side of the road so that they might turn into a one-way street and pick me up there. I made a foolish dash across the road, ignoring the oncoming traffic, and scoring three blasts of a horn from a startled truck driver for my trouble. I was so focussed on getting across the road to Fin and Suzy, that I hadn't even bothered to look either way. The angels that Joan had denied existence to the day before, must miraculously have been granted substance and form. I was most definitely being harboured, protected and shepherded by scores of them on the busy road. Suzy opened the back door of the car for me, and I tumbled in.

"It's so good to see you Fil. How are you? You haven't changed a bit since last year. Did you have a good trip over?" Suzy was twisting around to get a good look at me, patting me on the head because she couldn't reach any other part of my body. (As a teacher she was well rehearsed in head-patting.) Finley was smiling at me in the rear vision mirror and agreeing enthusiastically with Suzy. "Yes, it's great to see you Fil. Grand!" Finley was of Irish stock, and fiercely proud of all things Irish. I would have to make sure he and Joan never clapped eyes on one another, or it could have been a re-run of the Irish War of Independence. Suzy was Australian, the eldest daughter of a close friend of mine.

She had come to England as a teacher and ended up marrying an Englishman who was really an Irishman. Very complicated, as most families are. Finley co-owned three black cabs in partnership with his brother, Gary, and he often took us touring around the countryside in his favourite black cab, which was in slightly better nick than the other two. He had a wicked sense of humour and could talk the hind leg off a donkey. He was an ideas man, and his current favourite pearl of wisdom was, 'What would you do if you knew you could never fail?' I could never work that one out no matter how hard I tried. Suzy was quieter, studious and very clever. They were both very clever. As I was thinking about both of them being so clever, I had Peppa Pig going around in my head, when the narrator dryly lets it slip that "George is a clever-clots". It always made me laugh to hear it when I was happily watching the show on the pretence of keeping the under-fives of the family company. (They could never work out why I was laughing)

Now I was sitting propped up in the smart, designer vehicle of a pair of clever-clots people, waiting to be reintroduced to the delights of North London. (There was even sunroof.) "We'll just swing by Tesco's to pick up some cakes and bread, would you like to come in and check out Tesco's Fil?" Tesco's was a food store dear to my heart. In fact, all English food stores were dear to my heart. And they were dear as well, especially if one bought the number of packets of biscuits that Finley did, on a daily basis. I loved all the English grocery chain-stores equally – like a mother wolf with her cubs. Tesco's, Sainsburys, Waitrose, Little Waitrose and Little Sainsburys, Aldi, Asda, Iceland, Marks and Spencer's, Harrods – you name it – I loved them all.

"I'd love to come in with you Finley." He could never know that my heart was palpitating madly, and I was finding it extremely difficult to contain my excitement. It turned out to be a short-lived glory. Suzy doused my fire 'well n' propa' with her 'right back at you Finley' reaction.

"Oh Fin, do we really need to go to Tesco's? Can't we just go home and have a cup of tea and some digestive biscuits? You like them don't you Fil?" Score one for the plaintive. I could hardly let Suzy know that I was itching to go to Tesco's with Finley, or that I didn't particularly relish the thought of tea and digestive biscuits. But I could hear the fatigue in Suzy's voice, and I was determined to be the model guest whatever the planned surprises they had in store for me, so I agreed complacently to the amended plan. There would be other Tesco's on this trip, and I would make sure I visited one with plenty of time to spare for food gazing. We had slowed down for the lights, and Suzy was pointing out a gentleman waiting at the bus stop. He looked as though he had been waiting for some time, as he looked none too pleased to be kept waiting. "Oh, did you see that guy at the bus stop Fil? His face was something savage." I smiled at Finley in the mirror. Suzy really was becoming anglicised if she referred to people as savage! Beastly would be next! Finley was on a roll with his jokes as he drove, pointing out landmarks of Northern London privy only to dinki-di Londoners. "See that big red bricked house on the hill over there Fil, the one with the fence around the front?" I craned my neck to see which house Finley had singled out, but we were whooshing past rows and rows of massive triple storied red brick houses with fences at a breath-taking pace. (Finley had just finished studying for 'The Knowledge', and he had memorised the streets backwards – complete with their pot holes, ditches, uneven gravel and steep inclines.) "I must've missed it five miles back Finley, you're too quick for me!" Suzy was giggling and snorting at our playful teasing from her front passenger seat. Finley wasn't going to give up though, until it was advantage Finley, and I knew from past experience, that would be at least three serves away – that's if I didn't react. "What was so special about the house you wanted me to see Fin?" Now Finley was grinning at me in the rear vision mirror again. "Oh, nothing special really. It's just that Gerry Hall used to live there. But she's not there now – moved out a few years ago." I knew the English loved to see where celebrities lived, and I supposed that being one of the Spice Girls constituted celebrity status, but Gerry Hall was not of my generation, so I wasn't feeling cut to the quip that I'd missed the house equated with her career as a Spice Girl. Now if

Finley had taken me to the childhood home of Julie Andrews, or Elaine Page, or even Michael Crawford, I would have been sitting up straight as a giraffe, binoculars and camera at the ready in a flash. Finley was prattling on, in his idiosyncratic English/Irish accent. 'Fil, if you're really interested in celebrities of North London, we'll go for a tour on our way home, and I'll point the houses out to you. But you'll need to sit up straight and pay attention.' Suzy was groaning by now. "No Fin. Not now, please. I haven't even put any make up on, and what if we see someone we know? I can't be seen in public like this. Can you please just drop me home first?" Finley appeared oblivious to the high-pitched disgust in Suzy's voice, and he just turned to her, patted her arm comfortingly and uttered, "Could do."

A mini-me for Patrick, and I was sure there were more than a few million men like Finley and Patrick roaming the streets of London. The could-doers, as opposed to the do-gooders of the world. I have a few male friends in Australia who would definitely be boasting simultaneous membership of both groups.

Suzy was dropped off at the end of their street in the Archway, and I jumped into the warmed-up seat she had vacated. I would get a better view of the promised houses from this dress circle, and it would be easier to hear Finley, as the car was quite a noisy blighter. Finley waved Suzy off with a scout's honour promise that we would be back in an hour to pick her up to go to lunch, and to make sure she was ready, and that she didn't ring her mother (my good friend) in Australia for the regular Sunday morning news updates from London. Suzy pledged that she would not go near her phone until we returned. She was off at once, skipping along the tree lined street where they had lived for four years. I think I glimpsed her in the side rear-vision mirror gleefully reaching for her phone, but she may have been searching for her keys, so I kept quiet. We had also sped off, and Finley was informing me (with great reluctance in his voice) that we would probably only have enough time in the allocated hour to visit ten or so celebrity houses, and would that be enough for today? I didn't have the heart to tell him that five houses would have sufficed, but if going with him meant no digestive biscuits for me, and the opportunity to relax in the plush front seat of the car and be shown the sights of North London, then ten it would be. My 'glass-half-empty' attitude had left me a trifle sceptical as to whose homes we would be visiting. I knew that one of Finley's grand plans had been to plan and deliver black cab tours of London with different themes. One idea had been a celebrity houses tour, so maybe today was a trial run, and I was to be the token tourist guinea pig. I hoped not, because it would have been easier on me to have had a companion with me to double-mark the houses. I was, after all, of a certain vintage, and if Finley (who was forty) took me to a rapper's house, or a golfer's abode, or even to the residence of a young singer who may still have lived at home, I would be grossly disadvantaged, as I could not even distinguish M from M – if we'd happened upon the home of Eminem. In Melbourne, where I live, some genius entrepreneurs have been running tours of celebrity houses for quite a few years now. The buses dive deep into the suburbs and end up touring around and around a court in a little-known suburb, fictional home to the cast of Neighbours – an Australian drama which the Brits simply cannot get enough of. I whipped out my phone and noted down "Neighbours-tell Finley". I would bring it up over lunch.

We were approaching our first port of call – Rod Stewart's childhood 'mansion' above a shop on Archway Road. A humble abode. A non-descript, bland two-bedroom flat above a Newsagent's shop. Not many people must have known about the celebrity status of the flat, as it was practically deserted on the street below. Finley was pleased as punch, to have a celebrity neighbour's residence so close to his own. He was holding up the traffic so that I might get an 'up close and personal' view of the flat, or perhaps even in the hope that a relative of Rod's might appear at the rabbit's hole doorway to the flat in the side alley. All I could really see was a plain looking, slightly dated and grimy flat above a shop. Still, it was a promising start, as we had filled in fifteen minutes doing the block three times. Finely had convinced me that his circumnavigation was entirely necessary, as I would be ensured of a view from different angles and vantage points. I wanted to ask him if the shadows would have lengthened in the time we were there, but I decided against any wisecracks until we had finished lunch. Then it would be open slather between us over puddings and port. The honking and tooting from frustrated drivers forced to manoeuvre around our vehicle, finally stirred Finley to advance onto house number two. Only it wasn't really a house this time. More like a grave site, and it was also a 'grave sight' for early Sunday morning cemetery goers to witness Finley and I standing in awe at the foot of the tomb of Karl Mark. I think I preferred the flat Rod Stewart had lived in as a lad to the gravestone in front of me with the dusty dead plastic flowers and weeds galore. Finley had taken me to Highgate Cemetery. He was busy giving an account of Marx's tomb site. "Did you know Fil, that this cemetery is part of seven cemeteries which were opened up around the outside of central London? They were called the Magnificent Seven." Finley really was a clever-clots if he knew that little gem of information. With my paltry general knowledge, and smattering of interest in Show Business and geography, I could just vaguely recall the Magnificent Seven as an American Western film with Yul Bruner, and that was only because I liked Yul Bruner's sterling performance in *The King and I*. The only other magnificent Seven on my mind were the Seven hills of Rome, which one could see clearly from the plane on descent into Fiumicino International airport.

After the doom and gloom of the cemetery, the next bundle of houses we visited were positively breathing fresh air. We parked outside George Michael's house, a few streets away from Highgate Cemetery, and we weren't the only ones to do so! There were at least thirty onlookers there, leaving flowers and just house gazing. It was a grandiose mansion, and there were keen fans walking up and down outside the house snapping away. The last time Finley had taken me to see George Michael's house had been when George was still in the land of the living, and his black Range-Rover had been parked in the driveway. No one else had been there, and we actually caught a glimpse of George as he ducked out of the house and jumped into his car. (We had only waited five hours for that appearance from George.) Today the driveway was devoid of any cars, and the majority of the onlookers were gathered on a tiny green island-escarpment opposite the house. The road was a beautiful tree lined avenue, brimming with wealthy four-storey houses. There was a sadness about George's house, and I urged Finley to move onto our next vista, as we only had twenty minutes until we were due to pick up Suzy.

"Let's just do a couple more on the way back to Archway Fil." Finley probably realised that all three places he had shown me were no longer occupied.

We left the little crowd at George's place and travelled for about five minutes in the direction of the Archway. (I had been there enough times to recognise landmarks such as Dick Wittington's bridge at the top of the hill.) Then Finley brought the car to an abrupt halt. "Guessing time Fil. It belongs to a man and his name starts with B." I looked at the house directly in front of me for some clues. I had an inkling that we must have be somewhere near Camden, or Princess Hill, as I'd seen the canals on my left, but no bells were ringing for me. An actor might have lived in a grand house on an expensive street such as this, but then so too might have a singer or an author or a cricketer or a politician. My last thought was a politician, so I went with my gut feeling that a genuine polie lived there.

"Is it a politician Finley? Is it Boris what's-his-name?" Finley burst out laughing.

"No. But I'd like it to be Boris. And it's not Jeremy Corbyn either – although we are quite near where he lives. It's Alan Bennett. You know, the playwright?" Coincidentally, I had brought a book by Alan Bennett with me, alongside of Ulysses to read on the plane. I chose it because it was on the slim side, and of no consequence in terms of weight in my hand luggage.

"Yes Finley, of course I've heard of Alan Bennett. I have his book, *Lady with a Van,* next to my bed in Hampton. Don't you think Maggie Smith played the old lady well? She's such a good actress. I can't see the van anywhere. It should still be in the driveway. They must have left it on the set." I was disappointed that the iconic van was nowhere to be sighted, but the house looked exactly as it had in the film. At least we had stumbled upon an abode where a British celebrity actually lived. I was enthralled by the walled garden at the front of the house (I love walled gardens.) We parked and waited expectantly for around five precious minutes, but Alan must've had a late Saturday night, as he didn't appear for a midday wave to any soul who may have been stationed outside. Finally, Finley gave up. Here was a quiet house with very little action, and even Finley had to admit that it was probably best to let Bennett be, in the solitude of his own home. There were two rubbish bins at the front of the house, and with playwrights on my mind, I wondered to myself whether Samuel Beckett had feasted his eyes upon two such bins when he had written 'End game' – a philosophical discourse between two dustbins unable to survive without each other. I had no control over my mind, as I quickly slipped into a daydream about living with or without people or possessions, and I only really came to, when the engine stopped, and I could hear Suzy appealing to Finley that she wanted to tell him upfront that she had conversed with her mother in Australia, but that her mother had rung her, and not the other way around. "I had to cut her short though, because she was going on and on about all the flower shows she was doing tours of." I smiled to myself as I opened my eyes. That was Jenna for you. Flower-power mad. The insane crush for all things flowery had lasted longer than usual for my friend. Previous phases had included Chinese cooking, pottery and calligraphy. Unfortunately for me, it was currently plants which had invaded her universe. I had promised to bring back one thousand plant plastic 20-centimetre-long plant labels from England, in my suitcase. (which was yet to be purchased.) Apparently, the particular labels I would be bringing home could only be purchased in England, and undoubtedly, I would have room in my suitcase to carry them back to Australia. It wasn't the room so much as the weight of the plastic sticks that I needed to worry about. I fished out my phone again, while the labels were on my mind, and scratched out a new note under the Neighbours note, to remind Suzy to give me the package. One consolation was that I would not be stopped at Customs and forced into declaring plants and seeds – as had happened on my last trip, when I had unsuccessfully attempted to bring back some poppy seeds into Australia. Not that I had been covert about it. There was absolutely no smuggling involved! We had searched widely online for the rules on bringing seeds back into Australia from England. As far as we could tell, some varieties were fine to bring in, but others were on the banned list. We couldn't seem to find out if the particular seeds we had purchased were kosha or not. Of course, we realised we would be taking a chance, as it depended on which customs inspector you struck on the day of travel, and his or her disposition at the exact time of searching.

We were further advised that after lunch was always a good time, as the customs crew were fed, and on the final stretch of their shift. But it didn't happen that way. In short, I was stopped, my bags were searched, I spent two hours in the detention room, and the seeds were supposedly destroyed. Except I don't really believe that they were destroyed. My belief is that they somehow found their way into the satchel of a green thumbed Customs officer, and the fully blooming poppies now form a substantial spread in his or her front garden or allotment. Admired and envied. Or, for another fanciful theory, check out the lapels of the war veterans at the next Remembrance Day gatherings. My bet? Those poppies are rightfully ours.

"Did you get to see many celebrity houses Fil? Did you see Patsy's house up on the hill over there?" Suzy was pointing up towards the church on the hill, but I wasn't really sure who Patsy was, so I just nodded and said, "I don't think so."

Patsy could not have been that famous an actress as Suzy had dismissed our celebrity houses tour, and moved on to the next conversation, which involved lunch. I suddenly remembered that I had read about an actress named Patsy who was one of the main characters in 'Emmerdale', an English 'soapie' to rival 'Days of our Lives'. She went up ten notches in my esteem when I remembered that fact as I love English 'soapies'.

I was still occupying the front seat, so I turned around to face Suzy, and question her on where we would be lunching.

"Yes, Suz, did you remember to book?" Suzy had not remembered to book, and an hour later we were still letting Suzy jump out of the car and race into any pub we drove past, in the hope that there would be a table for three going begging. Finley and I would do the block, in the hope that Suzy would be ready for pick up on our first rotation. Sometimes it took three circuits of the block to pick her up. We could tell by the look on her face whether or not she had been successful in securing a table. We had almost decided to opt for takeaway, when Finley remembered a pub back in Archway which had extended lunch hours and did a mean roast on a Sunday. We proceeded there, post-haste. Yes, they were still serving lunch. Yes, they could accommodate us, and yes, they served roast chicken as well as lamb. (I was in luck, as I ate chicken but not red meat)

I jumped out of the car to join Suzy on the pavement outside the pub, and Finley zoomed off up the hill to park the car. That was one thing at which Finley excelled. He would have risen quite rapidly up the ladder of any Rental car firm, if he chose to spend his days backing out and parking customer's rental cars. We only had to twiddle our thumbs outside the front of the pub, which was adorned with beautiful hanging baskets of rich red geraniums for five minutes or so, and then Finley came racing around the corner, on foot now, and in a different direction from which he had disappeared five minutes or so earlier. He was puffing and panting with the exertion of it all. Even though it was afternoon tea time when our meals arrived, we tucked in hungrily. It had been an exciting two hours since the train trip from Richmond, and it was a pleasant and quintessentially English pub in which we found ourselves eating lunch. All the conversation we had put on hold until lunchtime flew out the window, as we munched and crunched our ways through the roasts with Yorkshire pudding. After the meal, we were ready to talk, and Finley began telling Suzy about how we had traversed the streets of North London seeking celebrities. He was in mid-conversation, animatedly waving his arms around as he described our route, when he suddenly stopped dead in his tracks, and pointed towards the door. He couldn't or wouldn't speak, when Suzy asked him to tell us what was wrong with him, and why he had stopped dead halfway through a sentence. "Shh!" was all we could get out of Finley. "Shh! Shh!"

Neither Suzy nor I were speaking, and since all the other customers had long finished their meals, the dining room was deserted. Finley was still pointing towards the door through which we had all walked in, and I looked over in that direction to try and work out his sign language motions. Suzy had given up on him and was earnestly studying the dessert menu.

"I think I'll have some plain ice-cream. I'm so full, but I can't leave without dessert."

I was also as 'full- as-a-goog' but I was enjoying the meal, so I threw caution to the wind, and also ordered some plain ice-cream. Finley hadn't moved, and was still staring towards the door, squinting and then looking away. He spoke at last.

"Don't you two know who that is?"

"Who?" Suzy and I were simultaneous in our retorts. "Dr Who. That's Dr Who sitting over there, in the corner of the pub, near the door in that big green armchair." Both Suzy and I half stood up, to get a better view of the Doctor. I recognised the man in the arm chair near the door holding court with a group of young men as one of the actors who played Doctor Who. I wasn't sure which one (David I think) but I was certain Finley knew all about him. Finley was beside himself. "See Fil, I told you we would see a celebrity today and there he is!"

We stayed until Suzy and I had polished off our dessert, and then decided that it would be a good idea to drive me back to Gospel Oak before it got too dark. As we left the pub, Finley tried to linger behind for as long as he could without appearing too obvious, but the good Doctor had not drawn a breath, and hadn't even noticed us leaving. He seemed to be delivering a soliloquy of some sort, and the group around him were hanging on his every word, as if he were the Dali Lama himself. Suzy and I were not fussed with having seen the Doc, but the encounter had placed Finley in seventh heaven for the duration of the drive to Gospel Oak.

We swung into the station around 5 o'clock and I felt slightly remorseful that our time together had been so short. As I was shutting the car door, and about to swagger off into the sunset, I remembered the plastic sticks that I needed to hand-deliver back to Australia.

"Oh Suzy, the plastic sticks! We forgot to get them." Suzy looked aghast that she had forgotten to bring them with her when we'd picked her up earlier.

"We'll just have to come out next weekend, and you can collect the goods then. Or maybe you'd like to come over and stay for a couple of nights after your time in London? Just let us know, and we can make a weekend of it." Finley was quick to suggest an excuse for another food outing, and Suzy and I smiled at each other.

"That sounds great Fin. Thanks. I'll give you a ring during the week, and we can arrange a rendezvous. Thanks again for today." I could hear a train rattling overhead on the overpass. Time was of the essence if I were to catch the approaching train. I hugged them both and raced off up the station ramp.

A train was pulling up just as I reached the elevated platform. It was my train. I jumped on the first carriage to stop in front of me and sunk back into the bench-seat. Not quite the upholstery standard of Finley's motor, but not too bad. I settled back with my guide book of London and tuned out. It wasn't so much the muted conversation that made me open my eyes, but rather the type of conversation I had become aware of. There was a lot of high pitched 'clicking and clacking' and 'oohing and cooing' oozing from the seats opposite me. I wasn't really sure of the ethnicity of the sounds, but I was sure that it wasn't English that I was hearing. It reminded me of the taped sounds I had heard, emanating from Alice's study when she had been watching videos on her iPad on educating deaf students. Of course! That was it. The couple across from me were deaf, and they were deep in conversation with each other. They were gesturing to each other like the traffic police on the Champs-Elysee at lunchtimes.

They noticed me looking at them, and they both nodded enthusiastically, motioning for me to cross the floor and sit next to them. I hesitated, but then realised that it would have been rude to ignore them. I waited until the next station and jumped up to join them. Having a smattering of sign language in my bag of tricks turned out to be very fortuitous, as I was able to communicate with the couple most of the way back to Richmond, where they lived. I couldn't wait to get home to tell Alice that I had spent the last hour on the train with a deaf couple, and that we had hit it off on like a house on fire.

Despite the late hour, Richmond was abuzz with people when we swung into the station around six thirty. The crowds were everywhere, racing along the platforms, strapping babies and toddlers into pushers, sipping coffees and hauling suitcases along the platforms and up the wide steps to street level. It was a different pace to the madness of the 6 o'clock commute, but it was still all systems go. Because of the great number of passengers who had alighted in Richmond. the buses outside were filling up quickly, and I had the wait around ten minutes for my bus to Hampton. When it did come along, I was scooped up in a surge of raucous women who boarded the bus noisily and en masse. I somehow managed to entangle myself in the group, and I was so far from the driver that I had no hope of swiping my Oyster card. Because I had become part of the group by default, I had little choice but to sit down with them, and inevitably, one of the ladies struck up a conversation with me.

"Are you a tourist dear?" She seemed pleased with herself to have made the connection that I was a tourist, given that I had not said a word to her, nor did I look particularly foreign.

"Yes, I'm Australian. I'm staying with friends in Hampton. What sort of group do you all belong to?" I looked around at the other women as I spoke. They had paired up, as there were only two seats in each row. They were all talking ten to a dozen to each other and did not appear at all concerned that the women sitting beside me would have been ostracised form the conversations, had she not been next to me. The woman introduced herself as Mavis and proceeded to tell me all about the Woman's' Book Club group she belonged to, and how they had just been out to lunch to celebrate twenty years as a group. She told me that the makeup of the group had changed a bit in the last decade or so, as people had either got sick and died, or moved away from London. I wasn't too keen on hearing about the dying members but moving away seemed a plausible reason to leave a group.

"How long are you here for pet? We are meeting next week to begin discussing our September Sizzler. It's 'Fifty Shades of Grey', do you know the book?" Yes, I knew the book, but no, I had not read it (although most of my friends and family had done so) I declined the offer to join the club, but not because I was prudish about the steamy, raunchy book, but more because I only had another week in England, and I would not be able to make it past the first meeting. Mavis patted my knee in a motherly gesture and called out to one of the women across the aisle.

"Sarah, this lass is from Australia. She goes home next week." At the mention of Australia, the entire group turned their heads, and chorused, "Hello, and welcome to England." It sounded like they were welcoming me to an Alcoholics Anonymous meeting. Were they also expecting me to stand up tall and profess my addictions? I wouldn't know where to begin. I stood up anyway, as we were coming up to my stop, and I didn't want to miss it. Mavis also stood up, to let me pass, and one of the ladies from the Book Club followed suite.

Mavis sat down again, as it must not have been her stop, but the taller woman followed me down the steps. I remembered that I wanted to give Mavis a koala.

"Will you be seeing Mavis this week. I wanted to give her one of these koalas from Australia, and here is one for you too." The woman accepted the koalas graciously without a word of surprise at the small token, and turning left, moved on out of my sight. I watched her disappear and then set off in the opposite direction, towards Alice and Patrick's. You never knew who you were going to meet on the buses and trains in England!

Alice and Patrick were sitting in companionably silence in the lounge room when I arrived home. The television was on but neither of them were watching it. Patrick was glued to his book, and Alice was stitching. The dogs were snoring away in the corner of the room, ensconced in their day- baskets. Patrick smiled at me, and Alice looked up from her needlework, greeting me enthusiastically with, "Did you have a nice time Fil? Do you want any tea? Do you want to go straight to bed?"

I answered her slowly and briefly. "Yes. No. Yes."

I then said my goodnights and retired immediately to the sanctuary of my bedroom. Recounting the encounters of the day, including the sightings of the morning, the signing on the train, and the almost-signing (up to the Book Club) on the bus, would have to wait till morning. I was officially zonked.

# Chapter 22
## Hampton, but with London Calling!

Today was penultimate Monday. I spent nearly the entire morning sorting and sifting through my possessions, wrapping and labelling gifts, and generally lamenting over the amount of English memorabilia and gifts still to be purchased. In between these arduous tasks, I filled in the time with home duties – cleaning, cooking, washing and ironing. I had a severe case of both housemaid's knees and arms by the time I collapsed in readiness for lunch. I desperately wanted to be super prepared for my anticipated big week in London.

My last full week in England, and there was so much footprint yet to be explored in this fathomless city. Devoting four days to the intended central London expedition would be a luxury and a privilege. My 'excitement build-up' was at a premium level. London was calling, loud and clear. As I dreamily offered my washing to the erratic English sun Gods, my thoughts turned to those English explorers with whom, in my youth, I had lived through explorations. Many of these explorers had embarked on their tumultuous sea-crossings from the very soil on which I was standing. Most of them would also have set sail from either Southampton or Plymouth, both close neighbours of Barton on Sea. Being here in England cemented my affinity with these early explorers, and I occupied my tedious cleaning hours pondering the necessary provisions and cherished personal items they may have carried with them on their seven seas mission, in search of the great South Land. My country and my heritage. It was the cycle of life. Australia was already occupied, granted, but the aborigines who had inhabited the land for thousands of years would always be the first owners, and the true Australians. Subsequent generations, those born of English, Irish and European stock (myself included) would always only hold day passes. It was still an enormously contentious issue in Australia, and the divisions over land, flag and monarchy would never be resolved with token valedictory services around the country, but much of the dust had settled into an amicable state of affairs in the last decade. We all had some breathing space. Small steps.

The packing was complete. Clothes washed, clothes dried, clothes ironed, folded and packed to perfection. I had read recently about cutting edge brain research which asserted that folding clothes methodically and monotonously was found to be precipitous of a state of wellbeing and serendipity in the brain. Research I had a lot of time for. Once the brain patterning performance was completed, I was ready to be presented to the world of Carnaby street and the halls of Harrods. A London fashion-plate was about to be revealed. Gone the travelling attire, gone the 'skechers' walking-shoes, and gone the backpack. This little caterpillar was about to undergo a radical metamorphosis. Four outfits for four days, and extra bits and bobs such as my trusty travelling alarm, mini torch and the latest edition – the Richmond green poncho. My decision to set up camp in London for the best part of the week pleased me no end. In a moment of madness, I had added up all the hours spent cooped up on trains and buses and discovered that almost two days and two nights had disappeared. The idea of a home base would be the ideal solution. Cheaper, and less taxing. A couple of day trips from London were up for consideration – Bath and Brighton being hot favourites on my list, but I would be just as happy to mooch around London until either darkness or exhaustion muscled in on me. The frequently quoted quip 'He (she) who is tired of London is tired of life' kept repeating on me, and although I could admit to slight fatigue after all the action of late, I knew that I could never be tired of London. I lived in Australia by day and London by night, as my dreams were nearly always London based. I often supposed that I was leading a dual existence and I guessed I was not the only living soul who harboured such a secret. There is that well-supported Jungian theory that we are all part of an enormous collective unconscious, and that when we dream, we tap into this collective unconscious, which can take any form in space, place or time. Quantum mechanics – to the initiated. If this resonates with you, I'm certain you'll agree that it's hard not to know about it. Perhaps this notion of 'bilocation' was the good doctor's Keynote to his comrades in the Archway pub yesterday.

Finally, close to almost two thirty, I was able to stretch out on one of the comfy deckchairs on the back deck, munch my sandwich, nibble my apple, and sip camomile tea. (Patrick had inspired me to take up drinking camomile tea) I thought about camomile lawns and camellia hedges. Random happy thoughts, bliss in happy Hampton. I was luxuriating in my serendipitous state, when I heard frenzied banging, coming from the front door. Alice was at work, and Patrick had gone off on one of his sojourns for the day. That left me to investigate the source of the racket.

Of course, it was Joan! True to form, she had again locked herself out of her house and couldn't remember where she had left the keys. I didn't even flinch when she told me. Taking immediate control, I ushered her into the lounge room and grasping both her shoulders, gently pressed her down into the voluptuous body of the sofa. "Take the weight off your feet for a little while Joan." Making her feel comfortable and at ease in the face of the impending disaster in Joan's mind, was a small price to pay.

"I'll just go and retrieve the spare keys Patrick keeps for your house, and well go off together and let you back inside."

Joan hadn't listened to a word I'd said. She was staring at me, still in 'Stage One' of remembering whom I might be. And then there was light! "I know you. You're the Australian girl who was over here last year. Do you remember I was telling you all about my brother who married Queenie? Thought she was the bees knees she did. Had my brother twisted around her little finger, the daft cow."

I wasn't really au-fait with the daft cow expression, but I sensed it was a derogatory slight toward Queenie.

I hurried off to the kitchen and took down the spare keys to Joan's house. Patrick had shown me where they were hidden, in the back of the panty on a large brass hook. (When they weren't in Alice's handbag.) Back in the lounge room, Joan had decided to make herself comfortable, and she was rummaging through a pile of newspapers which Patrick had put aside to sort through, when time permitted, or he felt in a culling or categorising mood.

"Bit of a rubbish heap of newspapers you've got here! Saving them for a bonfire on Guy Faulks night are we?"

Joan chuckled and clicked her tongue loudly as she realised that she had made another of her little jokes. I smiled back. Guy Faulks night was not something we took notice of in Australia, but I did know that bonfires were lit all over the country in commemoration of an attempt to blow up the Houses of Parliament in London. I also knew that Patrick valued and prized the particular pile of newspapers Joan was squinting at, and that he would have a pink fit if he knew that Joan was alluding to burning them.

"Joan, the papers are Patrick's not mine. He's in the process of culling them, but it's not up to us to do it." Joan started sulking then, unaccustomed to being reprimanded. I felt instantly sorry that I had snapped at her, but I couldn't take it back. Instead, I changed the subject as quickly as I could. "I'm off to London tomorrow for nearly a week. Do you get into London much? Know any good places to go?" Despite my rapid-fired questions, Joan was not easy prey. Her dainty little heels were well and truly sunk into the sofa, and she had turned her barraged body inwards. I really was in the bad books. I persisted with my cajoling. "Joan you have some wonderful paintings in your home, do you have any suggestions for galleries I might visit in London?" The mere mention of Artworks struck a resounding chord and Joan lifted her head with a half-smile.

"Go to the National Portrait Gallery. Not the Tate. The Portrait Gallery is much more interesting, and they have a marvellous souvenir shop." Jackpot! I had stumbled on a passion for Joan, other than banks, riding red buses, and her dogs. We chatted on about the great artists of the world for a while, and Joan really came alive. I made her a cup of tea and some biscuits. I remembered reading about the British hierarchy of needs as 'a cup of tea, biscuit and a sit down'. I was scoring well with Joan, and we had a really memorable afternoon together. Joan's favourite painter was Degas. She told me that she just loved the way he painted his dancers, and because she had been a dancer herself in her younger days, she could admire his paintings for hours and hours.

"Look Australian girl, sorry, Fil. I can still do the splits at eighty-eight." That said, she jumped up off the sofa, sunk cobra-like to the carpet, and splayed her legs in a V position.

"See! I told you I was still agile. Only I can't seem to get up!"

I heaved her up as best I could, but despite her small stature, she was a dead weight. After the exertive cleaning and packing of the morning, my strength had dissipated, and I ended up dragging Joan back to the sofa and hauling her onto the cushions. (I was tempted to use the cushion for another purpose, but that was only a fleeting thought.) She was limp and heavy as lead. My suspicion was that Joan was playing tricks on me, because as soon as she fell back into the sofa, she was right as rain. It was me who was suffering by then. My back had gone, and my head was thumping. This was a wake-up call to me that my nursing days were well and truly over. Firstly, I had insulted Joan, and now I had manhandled her. The first aid training credential I had recently completed could possibly remain on my resume, but the half page 'Nursing Experience' boasting would need to be scratched. It would be a shame to suppose that I could save anyone.

Let alone secure a position in an Old Age home, or as a carer to a rich old biddy.

Another adjustment that would need to be made would be ruling myself out of the class of airline passengers possessing the strength to "throw the door" when seated in an exit row. I fly frequently between Melbourne and Canberra these days, and if I find myself seated in an exit row, I am generally happy, because exit rows mean extended space and leg room. I need to bend the truth ever so slightly when the over-eager flight attendant stands in front of me, asking if I am in a fit state to throw the door in an emergency. Of course, I did not have the strength to send a plane door hurting back down to earth. Who was I, Sampson? But, for the sake of the roomy seat, and the devoted attention, I stretched the truth time after time, assuring the flight attendant that I was in top shape (despite my persistent deep chest cough, and gammy leg.) Next time I flew, I would need to come clean.

Joan didn't take long to spring back into action. As soon as she felt that she could attempt the splits again, she resumed her position on the carpet, and began extending her legs. I shrugged and left her there to her practising. I had packing to complete. After about half an hour, Joan came toddling along to my bedroom to inform me that she had finished her warm ups, and that she was off to take her dogs for a walk. Would I like to join her? My aching legs let me know that a strenuous walk with this sprightly soul would be wonderful at the time, but that I would pay for it tomorrow when the muscles seized up. I wanted to be in top shape for London, so I declined Joan's kind offer on the pretence that I had too much to do before Alice and Patrick arrived home for tea. "Jolly good Australian girl. I'll say goodbye for now then. Too roo, tickety boo."

That was Joan gone. I promptly rested until the others got back, and we scoffed down leftovers for tea. I wanted an early evening, as I was starting to feel a little fretful about leaving Hampton and venturing out into the big wide world that was London.

"Just get a good night's sleep Fil, and you'll be right as rain in the morning." Alice, the pragmatist had spoken. Patrick, the realist, added to her advice. "If you feel agitated, drink a cup of hot camomile tea. It works wonders on slowing down your brain and inducing sleep." I considered both options and was propped up in bed with my chamomile tea and Guide -book of London before 9 o'clock.

# Chapter 23
## In London and in the Thick of it!

We had endured our extended goodbyes the previous evening. Today, Alice had another of her in-camera early morning meetings, and Patrick had an equally early morning walk planned. The girls were on Patrick's team. It was all quiet on the Western front. No Alice, no Patrick and no girls! I lugged my small black borrowed suitcase to the door and nudged it down the three steps to the garden path.

The morning of my great expedition into London was chilly, windy and bleak. I almost turned back up the path, with the intention of an extended dose of bedroom hibernation. I could do with a 'slimdown', and there were always those bars of chocolates, lollies and tins of shortbread I had bought to take back to Australia – should I feel peckish. But, ever the stoic, I pushed on. Chickening out of the London leg of my trip at this late stage could only confirm one thing to the casual observer – that I was fickle, demanding and untrustworthy. I was demanding, granted, but the other two traits – well it would have been harsh judgement. Seated on the bus, station-bound, I was still unconvinced that I was doing the right thing, and by the time we reached the station, I was sweating profusely, and my heart was thumping ten to the dozen. Time for the backup puffer which so far this trip had lain dormant in the bottom of my backpack. The gratification was instantaneous, and I was able to keep calm and carry on. Once comfortably settled back in my old familiar window seat in carriage number three, I reluctantly parted with my puffer, carefully placing it within easy reach in the corner of the backpack. I then bravely traversed the Hampton train overpass bridge. I did so with the anxious mindset of an early explorer, so determined was I to make it into London and get myself ensconced in my new digs. Deep down, I was scared stiff at being alone in a city of millions, but my urge to explore London was stronger than my fear, and here was my chance. I would not be entirely alone, so I should not have been worrying at all. I would be staying in a Convent in Pimlico. Four of my friends from Melbourne had already checked in, and I'd be meeting these friends for a lunchtime pub meal, and other planned excursions. We had it all figured out and judging by the huge amount of mobile calls we had been making to one another of late, we were all set to go. The plan for me was two days in London and surrounds with my friends, and then off to Archway for another couple of days with another group of friends (also Australian and known to each other). Finally, the entire contingency would congregate at Alice and Patrick's in Hampton, for a valedictory meal of pizzas and wine. Then that would be it! Game over.

There was the possibility that my Melbourne friends would be leaving London before the planned farewell dinner, but I wasn't sure of their flight details, and these days I had difficulty even remembering what day of the week it was. A holiday does that to you. All the routines of working, eating and sleeping fly straight out the window. Hedonism prevails! Regardless of the 'guest list', the dinner was planned, and it would be my last opportunity to see Alice and Patrick, as my plane back home was booked for the next morning. That much I was sure of. Up until a few days ago, I had planned to go home via Ireland, and meet up with my Melbourne friends over there, but my plans had changed a little. I had received more news from Australia (thankfully no bomb alerts), that the settlement date for my new apartment had been brought forwards, and that I needed to be home to finalise the settlement. I was excited beyond measure to be moving into the new apartment I had purchased last year off the plan, complete with resort style features, and the biggest gymnasium in the Southern Hemisphere. Purchasing the apartment had been part of my new fitness regime, and I was looking forward immensely to waking up at the crack of dawn and racing up to the fitness centre on the fifth floor of the complex to complete my two kilometres on the treadmills. So, even though I desperately wanted to do Ireland as well as England on this trip, it would have to wait until next year. I would go in the summer. When the inevitable rain would be warm.

Clapham junction was busy, but nowhere near as crowded as it would have been in peak hour. A West Indian gent and his black curly haired son sat directly opposite me in the carriage. The pair had been with me all the way from Hampton, and Clapham must have been home as they wandered off hand in hand down the covered arch which led out of the station and into the Clapham Streets. I was aware from conversations with Suzy that the West Indians had arrived in their drones in England in the nineteen thirties, and that they'd been brought over to fill the gaps in the work force. Recent changes in Government policy had them being deported, as they were not deemed to be English citizens. Not all of them, but a fair whack (apparently many of them could not afford the citizenship costs at the time.) Many of those being deported were elderly citizens. It just wasn't right! Seeing the young man and his son reminded me that I wanted to further investigate the plight of these older West Indians who had been classed as citizens when they'd come to England, but who had now lost that citizenship. It was disgraceful.

I really was becoming an expert at changing trains in the big stations. The trip into Victoria station was over in the blink of an eye, and the hardest part of the entire bus and train journey into London had been convincing myself not to turn around and walk back up the garden path two hours before.

It was about 11 am when I stepped out of the grand Victoria station and onto the makeshift barricaded footpaths outside. The road and building works around Victoria were in a perpetual state of repair and renovation. I could have sworn I had walked the exact same make-shift muddy path two years ago. So, it seemed, had the other one thousand commuters, who had miraculously materialised outside Victoria station. I just hoped we were not all headed in the same direction. They didn't look like pilgrims seeking a 'Convent sojourn' – but truth is often stranger than fiction. From the map Alice had hastily drawn for me, and from the laboured thickly accented directions from Sister Barbara on my mobile two nights before, I would only need to walk about two blocks before I arrived at the Mother house. That's what they called some Convents nowadays, and these nuns were Maltese, so they had 'Mother Houses.' One of my friends in Melbourne had discovered the prime-land bolthole in Pimlico when she had travelled to London s few years back without any pre-planned accommodation. Prue had remembered that one of the nuns on staff at the school where she was a principal, had boasted about the 'no frills but in a prime position' Convent in Pimlico, just around the corner from Victoria station. She had stayed in the Convent for a week, and then, as if by osmosis, teachers and Principals from all over Melbourne kept arriving in their drones, eager to experience the hospitality of the Maltese nuns, the convenience of a central London address, and most importantly, the prestige of having resided in posh Pimlico, rubbing shoulders with the best of the British elite. Last but not least, it was super cheap, and included breakfast. What more could one ask for on a teacher's wage? I loved Maltese pastries, and it wasn't far to walk. That's why I was convent-bound.

We were surging along the covered walkways, all one hundred or so of us, when I glanced up and glimpsed the very street name Sister Barbara had been impressing on me. It looked to be a long street, but maybe the convent was looming up on my left, as I could vaguely make out a neon sign with letters. As I got closer to the wording, I did my usual chuckle to myself. What was I thinking? Red lights and a sign directing pedestrians to a 'coveted-strip' was never going to equate with a convent full of nuns. (Unless of course it was the UK's answer to Sister Act.) I scuttled along the posh, pristine street, dragging my borrowed suitcase behind me. It was causing me much grief, as I had packed it full of appliances, the four good outfits, more travelling clothes, and of course, the koalas. Consequently, it was really quite heavy.

I came upon the Convent by accident. Rather like Alice in Wonderland, I stumbled into the hole in the wall which was the door to the convent, when a young wide-eyed nun, clutching a set of enormous wooden rosary beads finally came to answer the bell I had been furiously pressing. To the uninitiated and the short in stature, not to mention the short sighted, the convent door was practically cloaked. It was built into the wall, and there was no number indicating the Convent's position in the street, let alone a plaque of any description which might have given the much-needed clue as to the occupants of the building. There was no garden, no porch, no plaque and no person in sight. The nun who had appeared to investigate the source of the incessant ringing was looking at me curiously. She had witnessed me stumbling into the wide foyer of the Convent, dragging my suitcase in behind me, and was now backing herself up against the wall – obviously unaccustomed to strangers and disruptions to her daily routine. I reconfigured myself and extended my hand gently to the young nun. "Hello Sister Barbara. My name is Fil. I'm from Australia and I'm expected. I spoke to you on the phone the other evening, and you said it would be alright to leave my suitcase downstairs until my room was ready. Do you have any idea when that might be please?"

I thought I had given her plenty of opportunity to interrupt me and inform me that she was not sister Barbara, and that she had never been expecting me, but she stuck to her vow of silence and uttered not a word. Just as I was about to further explain that I was with the group of female travellers from Australia who had checked in yesterday, a second, older, much sterner nun appeared in the doorway. This one was a different kettle of fish altogether. In fact, she would possibly be classified in the piranha group without too much fuss. "Are you registered to come into our convent young lady?" I lost my bravado just looking at her, but I held my head up high and nodded. "Good. Then we are on the same page. Please walk this way into my office. Oh, and Sister Christine, you are dismissed!" Off scuttled Sister Christine. She hadn't even had one line to blurt out, but she played her part well. I gazed towards the doorway through which the older nun had disappeared, debating whether to make a run for it myself, or whether to imitate her waddle all the way to the office. She had, after all, urged me to 'walk this way'. Second smile to myself at the old joke I was dredging up. I couldn't manage to 'penguin waddle' and drag my suitcase at the same time, so I reverted back to the shuffle and drag motion I had employed whilst wandering the streets on my quest for the convent.

The office was beautifully furnished, with the enormous mahogany desk, behind which the nun positioned herself, taking pride of place in the room. It was light and filled with lusciously verdant, lovingly polished aspidistras, positioned delicately on little wooden plant stands. There was also a good supply of huge vases of roses, plump and pink. An intricately designed Persian rug in blues and pinks hugged the polished oak floor. I loved the nun from the minute I laid eyes on that room. There was also a fresh deep smell of earthy nature and delicious cooking, and I prayed it would be a plethora of pastises (I was very, very, hungry)

It wasn't pastises cooking after all. The tease of a nun had a deadpan face when she informed me the smell was cabbage. "Today is cabbage Tuesday. Will you be staying for lunch?" I detest cabbage at the best of times, especially cabbage as an accompaniment to tripe, and I guessed this would be the kind of pairing that went on in Maltese convent kitchens. That or cabbage with brains.

"No thank you Sister, sorry, Mother. I'm meeting my friends for lunch at a pub not far from here. I think it has royalty associated with its name, but I can't actually remember the exact title. I've got the directions on my phone." The light suddenly dawned on Mother that my friends were the group of Australian women who had arrived last night. "I believe you are with the other Australians?" Thank heavens. The penny had finally dropped, and she had realised who I was, and who my friends were. I was in.

"Fillet Sister Christine will show you to your room, and you can leave your suitcase there." I let her think my name was Fillet, as it didn't really matter. Some of my friends called me Filia, and Filly and even Filladelphia, so I guessed I could cope with Fillet for a couple of nights. (As long as they didn't extend the pseudonym to 'fillet of fish'.) Sister Christine must have been snooping around the door to Mother's office, as she jumped back when I opened it. She reached past me for my suitcase and grappled with the handle, pulling it clumsily towards herself. The suitcase somehow toppled over, and Sister Christine also lost her balance. I tried to help her back up to her feet and we both started giggling. Mother was not amused. "Do hurry up ladies, you are blocking the doorway, and I am expecting an important parcel to arrive this morning. Sister Christine, please return to your post near the front door. You are dismissed. Fillet, you'll have to leave your suitcase downstairs until later. We have a very busy morning." That was the first and last time I had the pleasure of Mother's company. I regarded her as a person of intense scruples, and I admired the fact that her leadership qualities were so finely honed. That was more than obvious in her delegation of duties for Sister Christine, the missing-in-action Sister Barbara, and the cabbage-cooks in the kitchen awaiting their next instructions. It seemed to me that her eye for detail and juxta positioning of colours and objects of great beauty would have impacted on many, more people had she been the chief auctioneer at Christie's Auction House, urging bidders to purchase and nurture plants, paintings and furniture seeped in stature and style. But for now, she remained be-speckled behind her mahogany desk in Pimlico, steering her convent with steely reserve from within the thick white walls. To the outside world, the thousands of commuters who scurried past the Convent doors every evening on a short cut to Victoria station, the Convent did not exist. The door was so small, it was hardly noticeable, and the nuns were safe and sound inside. I wondered who else knew about the nuns – besides Australian and Maltese travellers. It must have had something to do with strong religious ties and a deep sense of community which thrives in convents and monasteries. That need for solitude, the safety and security of the convent parameters.

Since the suitcase belonged to Alice, and since it had been an old one that she was on the verge of throwing out, I wasn't alarmed by the fact that I would be unable to covert it in my bedroom straight away. It would hopefully be safe in the convent, and I had my money, glasses and passport with me at all times – so nothing of any real value – nothing that could not be easily replaced, was in the suitcase. Sister Christine was gesturing to me to follow her towards the over-powering source of the cabbage smell. I wished I had popped one of my paper masks into my backpack, as it would have come in handy, just about…now! We had stopped outside the open door to the kitchen, and the smell was all consuming. I could hardly breathe, but that was probably because I had been holding my breath for so long. Sister Christine's face was purple. (matching the cabbage?) Neither of us could hold out for much longer. I peered into the kitchen and observed two small rotund hobbits in habits and blue striped butcher's aprons stirring and chopping away as if it was the Last Supper they had been ordered by Mother to prepare for.

Sister Christine had finally found her voice. "Follow me, through this dining room, and I'll show you where you can leave your suitcase. We need to put it somewhere safe. Some of the older men who have rooms upstairs have the light-finger." Oh yes. The light-finger. I'd heard about that particular stigma. Better hide my suitcase well. But, as I've stressed, I wasn't particularly fussed if it did the disappearing trick. My mother always used that phrase, the 'disappearing trick' when we were young. It was always one sock which did the disappearing trick on its mate. As we grew older, it was perfume and select items of clothing which were disappearing at an alarming rate. Finally, as teenagers still at home, we who would be chastised by Mum for doing the disappearing trick, when it was time to wash or cook or clean. It was a comforting phrase, a little slice of nostalgia for ill-spent youth which kept popping in and out of my head. Possibly classified as daydreaming. Recent statistics have us daydreaming for fifty percent of our day. I think I might even verge on seventy percent, so practised was I at the occupation.

We had reached the broom cupboard in the alcove beyond the dining room. Sister Christine was whispering to me to stash my case into the cupboard behind the brooms, and that she would then push something heavy up against the cupboard door as a barricade. I feared that if her idea went to plan, then I would be wearing the clothes I was in for the next two days. There is camouflage, and there is camouflage. I took one last look at the suitcase, thanked Sister Christine and turned back towards the dining room, trying to recall where the front door had been located. Sister Christine called out to me to wait, but I just had to make a run for it. The cabbage smell had won out. I badly needed fresh air.

Another observable difference between England and Australia is the position of the horizon. It is much higher in Australia, and that's what makes you think of wide-open spaces and marine blue skies. As I stood outside the convent door, deliberating over my map and the iPhone directions, I was struck by the low horizon, and the lack of any real sky in the city. The air was plentiful though, and I took great heady gulps of it as I set off in search of a bus which would take me to the pub where I was to meet my Australian friends.

Sitting next to me on the bus was an older woman, dressed to the hilt, and clutching a small tapestry embroidery bag. She caught me looking at the bag. "If you can guess what is in my bag, I will give you a pound. I neither wanted nor needed a pound, but I had a shot anyway."

"Is it a jacket, or some sort of clothing?"

"Not even warm."

"OK, I give up. Tell me." I wanted to devote all my attention to looking out for my stop, and the proposed game was nothing but a distraction. The lady looked at me indignantly, as if I had crossed her by not playing along. I had a last stab.

"Is it food?"

"Yes. Second guess luck. Entirely correct. Here is your pound." I looked closely at the women, and I concluded that she would have had less money than any of us on the bus, and that I couldn't possibly take the note.

"No. You're alright. I thought that using an English turn of phrase might help her to think of me as a fellow Brit, but the ploy backfired on me."

"You're Australian?" I informed her I was indeed an Aussie and pulled one of the koalas out from my backpack. "This is for you. A memento from Australia." She looked very pleased to receive the tiny grey koala and assured me that it would be placed on her bedside table when she returned home, so that she might be able to look at it in the small hours when she couldn't sleep. She then asked me if they had any glow in the dark versions of the tiny koala, and I had to admit that I didn't know. In the back of my mind, I was remembering that someone had already asked me that same question on this trip. Perhaps there could be a lucrative market in glow in the dark koalas.

The woman told me that she was on her way across town to Marylebone, where she would be feeding her friend's cat. The friend was in the Maldives, and the cat liked the comfort of home, so she had been trekking over to feed the cat every lunchtime for the past three weeks. Her friend was due home next week. I listened to her story with one ear, reserving the other one for the driver. I had asked him, when I had finally found a bus which was to pass the Royal pub, if he would call out to inform me of the correct stop. The 'lady-of-the-cat' was still unravelling her story to me when the driver screeched back to me, "'Ere's your stop girlie. It's the pub 'n all." I thanked him as I hurried off the bus. I don't think the cat-lover lady even noticed that I had left the seat next to her. The streets were beautiful. Thick green tree-lined avenues with stately homes and well cared for gardens extended as far as the eye could see. On nearly every corner I approached there was a pub, and on every second corner there was a Convenience Store. I ventured into the first convenience store I came upon and asked for directions to the pub where I was to meet my friends. The shop assistant was Pakistani or Indian, and very friendly. Like the shopkeeper on the cliff top in Barton on Sea – this man was over the moon when he heard my Australian accent. I didn't think it was that strong, but he kept urging me to repeat my questions so that he could hear my voice. That was all very well, but at some point in time, it would have been helpful for him to have supplied me with some useful information as to the location of the pub I was seeking. After about ten repetitions of the phrase. "Excuse me, but I'm looking for the 'Pig and Swallow', he came up with the goods."

"Ah yes, the 'Pig and Swallow.' It is two blocks up. Not far. They do a good pork roll, but then yer' afta swallow it whole!"

I got it. The swallow joke. But he had moved onto the next customer, probably hoping for someone who would actually buy something in the shop, and not just stand there asking inane questions. I cursed myself for not having had the foresight to have purchased a packet of polo mints before the twenty questions. I thanked the back of his head, placed a koala on the counter, and scuttled out of the shop. I would just nod from now on, and keep my eyes peeled.

"Fil, Fil, where have you been?" How many times had I been questioned about my whereabouts on this trip? One implored explorers, prisoners, hunger-strikers, astronauts and lost dogs to explain or bark back their movements after having been lost or detained for months on end. Questioning a person who had regained consciousness after six months in a coma might have been justified (and may also have provided some useful scientific breakthroughs), but not humble travellers, who barely moved a kilometre an hour. "I've been coming, I'm just slow." Maryanne, who knew me too well to continue to question, grabbed my hand and dragged me into the pub without a word. As surely as night follows day, as soon as we approached the table there was a loud sing song rendition of the dreaded phrase from my five friends. "Fil, where have you been?" I was quick to retort, "Why I've been to London to see the queen!"

We all had a good laugh at my little dig about our being in London, and after a few drinks and a hearty English pub meal, we were in full-flight with our catchup conversations. Whilst we were still eating, the publican had approached us with a jug of warm beer. "On the 'ouse," was all he mumbled. Charlene answered for us all, "Thanks mate!"

We all nodded in appreciation, and I produced a koala for him. The koala population in my backpack was depleting thick and fast. Beer was not a favoured beverage amongst our group at the best of times, but it had been a magnanimous gesture on the part of the publican, and we dutifully gulped down the warm beer, and promptly ordered another bottle of Australian Chardonnay which was more to our taste. The publican was pleased with our patronage, and the revenue we were bringing into his pub on what might have been a quiet-midweek lunch hour, had we not swelled the numbers. He even managed to find his voice and slip in an Ausssie-ism when he brought the bill over to our long table. "Fanks ladies. It's bonza ta see yer all 'avina laugh like vat." We stayed on in the pretty little, typically English corner pub until about three thirty, relating stories and making our plans for the next day. Finally, Charlene instigated our leave by suggesting that we all move onto Harrods for afternoon tea. One by one we all put in a protest vote at more food and drink, and outnumbered, Charlene good-naturedly conceded that she would drink from her own well and explore Harrods on her own. The idea of an afternoon to ourselves appealed to the rest of us, and the decision was made to paddle our own canoes until around 6 o'clock when we would reconvene at the finish-line, outside the Convent for our evening tour of the city with Finley and his black cab. That worked in beautifully with the plans I had already made with Fin, as he was expected at six thirty. A half hour window for the late comers and the dawdlers of the party would surely suffice. I had two places of interest that I'd been eager to visit for ages. I had a desperate urge to explore the riches of the National Portrait gallery and I was dying to visit St Paul's Cathedral to experience the 'Whispering Wall'. We said our goodbyes, and set off towards central London, each one of us with a secret yearning to see a part of London not yet uncovered, or perhaps to rekindle an old flame. It was good for us to have time to ourselves, as often, two can be company, but three is a crowd. Best that we all had some down-time.

I easily found the National Portrait Gallery, and the first thing I noticed was a plaque on the outside wall which stated that the Gallery had been founded in 'Eighteen Fifty Six', exactly a century before I was born. I wouldn't have been surprised to have seen the date as the 16th as well. My birthday, and the date on which the greatest number of people in the world are born (nine months after

Christmas, or so it goes.) There was no date included, so I had to be content with the one-hundred-year connection. The second thing I noticed (felt) was the deluge of rain, which had decided, selfishly, to pour down in bucketloads, sending locals and tourists scuttling into the closest buildings for shelter. Since the Gallery was positioned within the surrounds of Trafalgar Square, the sudden outburst of heavy rain meant overcrowding in the foyer and Tourist shop of the Gallery. In an attempt to avoid the dripping crowds, I made my way directly up to the top floor of the Gallery.

This section housed fascinating portraits of the Tudors, and I could easily have spent the next two hours studying their facial features, and the intricate way in which the artists had depicted their finely chiselled noses, lips and foreheads. The headpieces and frilly neck-bands were also fascinating. I was on a short fuse though, and after about half an hour of drooling and racking my brains to recall the Tudor Kings, queens and dignitaries we had been forced to commit to memory in our far-removed Australian bush schools, I left the rooms, and took the lift back down to the ground floor. I knew I wouldn't have time to explore the other floors, and luckily the crowds had melted away and left the Tourist shop relatively empty. There were no windows inside the shop, and the air conditioning (or boiler?) was extremely loud, so I wasn't really sure if it was still raining outside. It didn't really matter, as I wanted to peruse the postcards of current celebrity portraits which were housed on the floors I had skipped. If I found a postcard-portrait I really liked, I would make my way back upstairs and have a good gander at the original. After about ten minutes in the shop, I had accumulated a pile of postcards and boxes of coasters and placemats which I had selected for purchase, with the intention of taking them back to Australia as presents.

I hadn't been really moved to race up the stairs for a private viewing of any of the postcard portraits I intended to buy. I also included a poster-size image of Shakespeare, with a gloss finish. (This poster came complete with thick cardboard cylinder for easy carrying and stowing. That was it for me! I would frame the poster when I got back home. The National Portrait Gallery was the only place in the world with an original portrait of William Shakespeare, and I now had an image of the portrait on my poster. Not a bad afternoon's work! With my purchases completed, and a further one hundred virtual pounds vaporising into the ether, I made a hasty retreat out of the Portrait Gallery and headed back up towards Trafalgar Square. The last place of interest on my 'to do' list was the

'Whispering Wall' in St Paul's Cathedral. Whilst researching places of interest worth visiting in London, I had come across the 'Whispering Wall' of St Paul's, and ever since then I'd wanted to traipse up to St Paul's and have a soft natter to myself.

When I reached the Cathedral, it was literally crawling with tourists. (Probably the same group who had been sheltering from the rain in the National Portrait Gallery.) I wouldn't have had a hope of hearing any whisperings, or any grand political or royal London secrets. The best I could achieve, after having climbed the two hundred and fifty-seven steps, was to stand with my back to the curved wall, and whisper to the wall that I had once taken my mother's pretty jade – necklace out of her top drawer and worn it to the school disco. Not that I was convinced anyone would hear my paltry confession some thirty metres around the curved part. It was a bit of fun, and had I been with Maryanne or Charlene, we would have gone 'hells bells' with the secret whisperings. I now understood where all the whisperers such as the 'in-demand' baby, dog and horse whisperers got their break. The Master course in whispering would, without doubt, be at the Whispering Western wall of Jerusalem. I thought I might try my luck there on my next trip to the Middle East.

After my whispering, I felt hoarse and parched. No one had whispered back to me, and I was done with remembering secrets. I found a small café outside St Paul's where I purchased an unhealthy can of Coke and a packet of crisps. Totally indulgent afternoon tea! The coke was sweet and thirst quenching. I knew I was swallowing three cups full of pure sugar – but I didn't care. My thirst came first. As usual, I had left it until the last minute to find a bus to take me back to Pimlico. Then there was the added concern I had, over the threatening rain, and whether we would actually be taking the tour with Finley in his black cab tonight, or whether we would all end up with pizzas and a rowdy game of Bridge or Charades. Only one way to find out! Leaving the steeped in history St Paul's and the Whispering Wall behind, I began the long arduous task of finding the correct bus to take me back to Pimlico to meet the others. It was going on five thirty, and the rain had resurged with a vengeance for Act Two.

As I was rummaging in my backpack, trying to avoid getting the poster and the postcards wet, I realised that my treasured and well-travelled umbrella was missing in action. I mentally retraced my steps, back to the last time I had used the umbrella and recalled that I'd thrown it out of the backpack onto the counter in the Tourist Shop at the National Portrait Gallery to make room for my ten boxes of coasters with famous faces on them. (They had been on the specials table, a section in any shop towards which I consistently tend to make a bee-line) The umbrella must have been out of my sight on the counter, and I had probably left it there. I knew how to get back to Trafalgar Square from St Paul's as it was the trip I'd just endured. There was nothing for it. I'd just have to trudge back to the scene of the crime If I wanted to claim my umbrella. I was taking a chance that the shop wouldn't have already closed, but I needed my umbrella if this rain persisted – and it looked to be setting in fast. The bus trip didn't take more than fifteen minutes, and the time flew by for me, caught up as I was chatting to an English schoolgirl of around twelve who was sitting next to me. The girl informed me that she was coming home from school (late because of lacrosse practise) and that she lived in central London. (No address disclosed, but it must have been somewhere posh by the look of her clothes and school bag, haircut and polished nails.) She was meticulously dressed in a private school uniform, highly polished shoes and a colourful striped tie. Her blazer was too big for her, and she looked a little sad. I tried to cheer her up by prattling on about Australia, and how lucky she was to pass so many of London's iconic buildings and streetscapes every day. The young girl looked at me in agreement.

"I suppose so but it sorta puts a damper on it when your mum and baby sister come to pick you up from school every day. I've been at that school for four years now." I was a little confused with the implications of her statement, but as she was talking, she kept glancing over at a 'thirty-something' woman and a small child in the seat opposite us. They waved back at me.

"Yes, I mean them. They are my family. My mum and my sister, but I don't really like to have them sitting next to me. They cramp my style. My mum is such a worrier. She won't let me breathe." I looked over towards the mother and the sister. They looked perfectly fine to me, but then I wasn't a 12-year-old girl with an over-possessive mother. I remembered my own mother driving down to pick up one of my sisters from the bus stop at the Shopping Centre, and my sister frantically urging Mum to hide behind the bus shelter until her friends had gone. She was my youngest sister-sixteen years my junior, and her excuse was that Mum looked too old. Mum was barely forty at the time.

The girl by my side added that she had been making the same trip every day for the past four years. I felt sorry for her, and digging into my backpack, past layers of postcards and placemats, I unearthed a trio of koalas – one for each member of her family. Then, as we had almost reached Trafalgar Square, I jumped off the bus.

And I was in luck. The Tourist shop was still open, and my umbrella was still laying silent on the counter where I'd left it. I thanked the shop attendant and raced back out into the rain. Up went the umbrella. On went the Richmond green poncho. Out came my Oyster card, and on to the next bus I jumped. (The Victoria station signage had been my clue.) As I mounted the last step before I reached the driver, sitting up like the Queen's personal chauffeur in his driving-capsule, I slipped. The man behind me caught my elbow as I tried to maintain my balance.

"Steady on vere my girl, you'll end up under the bus next, if you lose your balance again." It was the dead weight of the ten boxes of placemats I had foolishly purchased. How on earth did I think I was going to be able to pack them all into my suitcase? And did I even have a suitcase? Ponderings for later – because at this exact moment I had much bigger fish to fry. The fish (more of a stingray as it turned out) was the driver, and the problem was that I had tapped my Oyster card, and it did not have enough credit to make the trip to Pimlico. And the rain poured down, and the passengers behind me called out urging me to hurry up and move on. The surly driver fixed his black beady eyes on me and snapped, "No credit. Off yer git." I couldn't believe that I didn't have enough credit. It was impossible. I had topped the card up with twenty pounds that very morning, and I hadn't done that much travelling. "There must be a mistake. I topped it up today. Can't I just hop on the bus and get off in a couple of stops? It's pouring rain and I'm very late for an appointment."

"Suit yerself, but you'll afta stand."

I pushed my way past the throngs of people and ended up towards the back of the bus near the rear exit. It was hard to hang on to the rail above my head and look out of the fogged-up window at the same time, but I was desperate to get my bearings and jump off the bus as soon as I recognised a familiar landmark. I kept my head down in case the driver was looking to see if I had jumped off the bus, but there were so many people crammed into the steamy space that I couldn't possibly see him. I started to relax when I saw a sign to a well-used lane I remembered from my walk around the Pimlico neighbourhood that morning. Good. From memory it was only two stops to Victoria. It was well past six thirty by then, and I knew the others would be all dolled up, fed and watered and ready for the big black cab. I willed the bus to pick up speed so that I wouldn't be late and give them all cause to employ their usual greeting to me of "Where have you been Fil?"

There was a firm hand on my shoulder, and a man in a crumpled, rain-sodden transport uniform at my side. The hand belonged to him, and he belonged to the British Transport Association. Or so he claimed.

"Excuse me madame, can I see your Oyster card?" The man looking straight at me was small, mean and unforgiving.

I handed my card over to him, and he produced a little machine from the satchel over his shoulder. He shook it, and the machine whirred into life.

"Why do you need my card?"

I knew the answer even before I asked the question. Suddenly the bus stopped dead. One and a half stops from Victoria Station, ten minutes from my friends.

The man was officiating on. "If you have no active card, you are breaking the law riding the buses. It is illegal. You will be fined on the spot, and the bus will not be able to continue on its route until you have paid. No one is going anywhere until you have paid the fine."

I was aghast. Nothing like this had ever happened to me before. I cursed the bus driver, who must have alerted the authorities that I had no credit on my card. This nasty individual must have already been on the bus to have singled me out so quickly. I wondered if it was a scam, and if there were a few people involved in it, but I was late and becoming increasingly upset with this man bullying me into handing over eighty pounds as an on-the-spot-fine. I had one hundred pounds in my wallet, and I was so agitated and upset that I handed four twenty-dollar notes to the man. He took the wad, and then insisted that I leave the bus immediately. I was so embarrassed, I jumped off as quickly as I could, landing heavily on the wet pavement a few blocks up from the station. The official followed. He proceeded to write out a receipt for me, and as he was doing so, another uniformed man came up and stood beside him. They exchanged a few words, and then the first man slipped two of my twenty-pound notes into the hand of the newcomer. I tried not to look, but they caught me glancing, and the first man turned to me, and said in a low voice, "Off you trot now girlie, and don't try that trick again." The condescension in his voice, mixed with the sincerity of a rattle snake triumph at having caused me such belittlement, was all too obvious. In retrospect, he did me a favour, toughening me up to the world of the single traveller and teaching me that when in a strange country – do as the locals do. Walk. I should have hopped off the bus as soon as the surly driver had given me that look. But it was wet, and I was late, tired and getting hungry, and expected, so I just didn't. This was learning the hard way. As I had no real idea which way to run, but I was in such a state of disdain, I just bolted. When I got my bearings again, I realised I was literally around the corner from the Convent where the others would be waiting. The sheer relief of knowing that I wasn't alone, caused me to burst into tears. Again!

I started running down the hill towards where the little group were congregated. As I got closer, Charlene called out, "There you are Fil, we were getting worried. Are you OK? You're soaking wet, and you look very dishevelled. What's been happening?"

Astute and uncannily intuitive. That was Charlene for you. Traits she had inherited from her maternal Irish grandmother, which she had cultivated to her advantage in allowing her to always say the right thing at the right time.

"I'm sorry I'm late, but I've just had a harrowing experience on the bus." Charlene took my backpack full of the presents I had purchased at the National Portrait Gallery, and gently led me over to the others, who were looking very concerned – presumably at the state of me!

"Fil, are you ready to go? Do you want to go up and get changed?" Maryanne had rushed up and pulled me away from Charlene. I felt like a tug-of-war rope, with both of them pulling from both ends. The rest of the group were the onlookers, not really knowing what was going on, but happy enough to sympathise. I put a stop to the pulling by calling out loudly to both of them. "Yes. I'm alright. I just lost track of time, and the amount of credit I had on my Oyster card." They both stopped dead in their tracks then and gave me some space to get my breath and decide whether I had time to rush upstairs and change out of my wet clothes. The problem was solved by Finley who came tootling around the corner in his black cab, topping his chauffeur hat towards us, and calling out in a loud cockney voice "'Ere, anyone call a cab?"

Unaware that I was dripping wet, Finley jumped out of the cab, and in a mock fanciful bow – opened the back door for all of us to clamour inside. it was quite spacious in the cabin, with two cushioned benches facing each other, and plenty of the room on the floor for our bags. We could all stretch our legs out, and the roof was high enough for the claustrophobic members of the group to breathe easy. Finley had repositioned himself in the driver's seat at the front of the cab, and as there was a glass partition between him and us, he had rigged up a little microphone so that he might be heard in the back cabin. He was heard alright.

As loud and as clear as the president of the Olympic committee announcing the city which would be hosting the next Olympic Games.

"Is that OK for you in the back?"

None of us had the heart to burst his bubble and inform him that he was a trifle loud. Maryanne, who was closest to the glass partition, came to the rescue, and slid the glass across, assuring Finley that everything was wonderful in the back.

"Right you are. Off we go then!" He didn't seem to notice in the rear vision mirror that we all had our ears covered every time he spoke.

I had issues of my own with which to contend. The brown leather seat I was sitting on was getting wetter by the minute, and I needed to get out of my wet slacks. Water had started to drip onto the floor of the cab, and it definitely wasn't a good look for me. My top was relatively dry still, as the Richmond poncho had done a good job of covering it, but the bottom legs and the knees of my slacks were soaking from when I had stormed through puddles when fleeing from the bus inspector.

"Does anyone have a spare pair of slacks, or a skirt I could wear? These slacks are soaking wet." Not one of them was able to help me out, as they'd all had time to change before the promised night tour of London, and had all brought small glitzy handbags with them. "In case we stopped somewhere nice for a cocktail or two." Well, if they stopped, I wouldn't be getting out of the cab. I'd stay and keep Finley company. Annoy him, as Alice would have said, had she known of my intention to stay put. Maryanne had an idea.

"Fil, why don't you have a look in your backpack, and see if you have hidden any spare clothing in the bottom of it. Remember you used to do that when we went bushwalking?" I could barely remember the bushwalking days, at least twenty years ago, when a group of us had decided to form our own bushwalking club, walking in mountains and on coastal trails every first Saturday of the month. The club lasted for about three years but died a gradual death when the numbers dwindled to three, on account of members falling off like flies with bad knees and bad backs. Sitting in the back of this cab, experiencing London city without having to move an inch, was far less exerting. I humoured Maryanne by rummaging around in my backpack and was rewarded with a pair of knee-length shorts which I must have stuffed in the bottom of the backpack for a sunny day. Ironic, that today was a rainy day and I was desperate for some dry clothes. They wouldn't pass the dress code for Harrods, but they would be fine for the back of the cab.

"Found something I can wear!"

I pulled the crumpled shorts out from their lengthy slumber and held them up to the others. "Look. My sunny day shorts! I think I also have one of those roll up micro towels here somewhere. Yes. Got it!" I was excited with my find. The others looked doubtful, and Maryanne urged me to change quickly, as Finley had just announced that we would need to get out at the next stop to view a peculiar English eccentricity in a wall. (Humpty Dumpty?) I struggled out of my wet slacks, and used the micro towel to dry my legs, arms, face and dripping hair. Maryanne kept guard by doing some serious out-of-the-window gazing for the upcoming wall. The others just laughed and told me to hurry up. I made it just in time. Finley had stopped the cab and was walking around to the back passenger's door to help us all out.

"This is what I wanted to show you." We were close to Wellington Arch, and the others all piled out of the cab. I pleaded tiredness, and stayed where I was, draping the towel over my bare legs, in case Finley peered into the cabin. They weren't gone for long, but I could hear exclamations of surprise and disbelief. My curiosity was piqued, but not enough to allow me to appear in public in crumpled shorts. I had my standards to uphold – even in the semi-darkness.

"What did you see? What was so intriguing?"

What they had seen was a tongue in a wall, reputedly that of Napoleon, and cemented into the wall about two metres from the ground. No one knew if it was a real tongue, or just clever clay modelling, but it was a great tourist draw-card, and Finley had been pleased to show them his surprise attraction. The rest of the tour was pretty standard, with no more tongues or murder scenes down by the Tower to view. We were given the deluxe tour by Finley, viewing iconic tourist landmarks such as: Marble Arch, The Houses of Parliament, Lord's Cricket Ground, Shakespeare's Globe theatre, West End, Hyde Park and many more. Between the six of us, we managed to take fields of photos, and luckily for me, there had been no need to leave the cab after the tongue stop.

Two hours later, Finley deposited us outside the convent where he'd picked us up. I had found a muesli bar and some dried apricots and nuts in my backpack, and had munched on them throughout the tour, so I wasn't going to be needing any tea after all.

We thanked Finley for the excellent tour, his jokes, and the smoothness of the ride. We had one hundred pounds to give him, but he wouldn't hear of taking any money from us. "Just do the same for me in Australia, and I'll be happy. Night now." He had zoomed off before Charlene could throw the money through the window at him.

And it was off to bed for the lot of us.

# Chapter 24
## Brighton

'Didn't we have a lovely day the day we went to Brighton?' I couldn't quite make out where I was. Ever done that thing where you open one eye, have no idea where you are, and quickly shut both eyes as tightly as you can, willing yourself back to sleep so that you might wake up in a different place? Not exactly a 'bilocation'-trip, but something remarkably close. I was just about to drift off into a luxury micro-sleep when I remembered where I was, and why it was imperative for me to jump out of bed that very second. It was Tuesday, I was in the convent in Pimlico, and we were off to Brighton for the day. Not the whole gang of us, but three musketeers, the triad, desirous of a day trip to Brighton to experience the sights and smells of the sea. All three of us owned a beach house in Australia, but there is something untenable about the English seaside. I'd experienced this essentially English quality in Barton on Sea, but my companions had only arrived from Australia early yesterday morning, and for two of them, the sea was already beckoning. Although we had decided last night to split into two groups for the day, those doing Brighton and those doing Bath, we all set off for Victoria station together. We must have looked a real sight for sore eyes, seven women slipping and sidling out of the convent door at seven thirty in the grey misty morning, complete with back packs and sunhats, beach towels and umbrellas headed for Victoria station. We caused more than a few of the London early morning commuters to stare and stumble, especially those bustling past the convent door, who may have been privy to the fact that a convent (brimming with nuns) lay behind the thick grey stone walls.

'Nuns on the Run' would no doubt have been at the forefront of their minds.

We weren't hurrying because we were attempting to escape, but rather, because we didn't want to be late for our trains. None of us had any desire to change our plans for the day. Charlene, Maryanne and I streaked (not literally) on ahead of the other four, as we were uncertain which platform we needed for Southern rail, which would take us to Brighton. The other four were more casual in their pace, as Betty, the squadron leader of the group had already organised the times, platforms and tickets required for the Bath interlude. I had been to Bath several times before, but never to Brighton, so I had no qualms in opting for the seaside. I was certain that Terrie, Meg, Margot, and Betty would return with tremendous tales of Bath and Roman architecture. None of them had been to Bath, so they were all very excited.

Victoria station loomed larger than life as we raced up the steps to the little mini mall which led to the escalators. There were people everywhere, and everyone was racing. They couldn't all be late! It was quite confronting, as none of us had ever really been sucked up in the wave of commuters at an enormous train station like this before. At one stage in our lives, all three of us had lived in the same leafy suburb in Melbourne, and we had often met up at the sleepy local train station to journey into the city to see a show. We would be lucky to see three other people at the station.

Here, there must have been at least two thousand people all in a desperate hurry. Inevitably we were separated in the seething surge, and I could feel myself being swept along towards the steep 'descent-escalator' perpendicular to the huge piazza of the station. I felt like Annie Taylor, the fed-up North American school marm, who in nineteen hundred and one huddled herself inside a barrel and hurtled off the top of Niagara Falls. To top it off, it had been her birthday. If you've ever stood anywhere near Niagara Falls, and experienced the sheer force of nature that is Niagara, you will have nothing but the utmost of admiration for this 'pushed-to-the-limits-by-teaching' woman. I was heartened to remember that Annie had lived to tell the tale. My own fate was in the hands of the Gods this morning. I discovered that if you closed your eyes, and cast them downwards, it wasn't so bad a ride. At the bottom of the escalator, there was no time to stand and get your bearings. People poked and trampled over me with little regard for my distress and separation anxiety. I kept asking anyone who was stationary for long enough if they knew where I could purchase a ticket for Brighton. I had my fingers crossed that Charlene and Maryanne would be waiting for me at the ticket office (assuming there was only one office). Eventually my crocodile tears impacted on a kindly old lady who was sitting squashed on a bench near the entrance to the Ladies toilets. "Are you lost dear, can I help you?"

"I'm looking for my friends. We got separated in the peak hour rush. I'm trying to find the ticket offices, as I think they might be there waiting for me." It was difficult to hear the old woman's response, but I thought she was pointing to the corner, and telling me to go around it. I handed her a koala for her troubles, and she looked delighted.

"Are you from Australia? I have a great niece who lives in Sydney called Sharon. Do you know her?" Another misguided Brit. I didn't want to give her any hope that I might have chanced upon her relative, so I pretended that I hadn't heard her, and moved as quickly as I could through the central piazza and over towards the corner, she had pointed out to me. As soon as I rounded the corner, I felt less frenzied, and a calmness overcame me. I wondered if the old lady on the bench might have been a traveller, as she had put me in a good place away from the madness of the main piazza. The gang were waiting for me. They couldn't have known I had been lost, or surely they would have demonstrated more sympathy towards me? "Where have you been Fil? We've been waiting for you for ten minutes. Hurry up or we'll miss the train. We've bought you a ticket. You owe Charlene sixty pounds!"

Maryanne was an Alice clone. Never one to mince her words, and always annoyingly correct. Charlene was less inclined to boss but more inclined to talk to all in sundry, so it was no surprise to me that Charlene had already teamed up with a woman travelling to Brighton by herself and had invited the woman to sit with us in our carriage.

"There you are Fil. This is Lyla. She is travelling to Brighton today the same as us, so I've invited her to tag along. Haven't I Lyla?"

Lyla was a woman of about sixty, slight and dark. She was eccentrically dressed in a white cotton shift with a violet silk shawl draped carefully and elegantly around her shoulders. Her outfit was complemented by a huge, chunky, orange-beaded necklace. She also wore a large wide-brimmed lemon straw hat, and open lemon plastic sandals. Lyla would have been perfect on the set of an art deco film set in Portofino or the Amalfi coast chatting to Monsieur Poirot, but in sooty, tired, crowded Victoria station at 8 o'clock in the morning, she looked decidedly out of place. I thought she was sweet though, the way she smiled gratefully from beneath the rim of the hat, and the way she extended her slim brown-as-a-berry ring laden hand towards me as a form of greeting. I thrust my one free stubby, sweaty, red-chaffed hand towards her, and we clasped palms tightly. Perhaps this was what Charlene, Maryanne and I needed to have done outside the station-linked hands and hung on for dear life. But then we might not have been separated, and Charlene may not have befriended Lyla.

So now there were four of us. Lyla was English, but not a Londoner. She lived alone in a small cottage in Barnstable (her words) and worked long hours in a nearby hospital. Lyla was holidaying in the capital for a week and had decided at the last minute to do Brighton today, as it was promised to be warm and sunny, and a marvellous opportunity for an outing to the seaside. Lyla looked as though she took herself off to the seaside every second day – so tanned was her skin, but maybe she was lonely, and in need of company. Charlene, with her generous heart, and equally smart dress-sense would serve her purposes nicely. If nothing else, she would give Lyla a decent run for her money in the fashion stakes.

The train trip on Southern rail was wonderful-refreshingly green and scenic. I loved the fact that we were actually headed for a legitimate destination, and not just travelling the favoured circuitous routes with ad hoc shopping and sightseeing. In Australia, distances between capital cities and regional centres are often endured by rail, but fewer people tend to utilise the trains for day trips or short holidays. Our most iconic train is the Indian Pacific transcontinental from Sydney to Perth, so named because it links both mighty oceans. Four full days of steaming, horizontal train tracks, a joyous choice for digesting the red earthed terrain that is central Australia. The Ghan rail train is hot on the heels of the Indie, trekking even deeper into the desert. She is a spectacular steam specimen, if you have weeks and wads of cash to spare. Proud as I am of Australian trains, first prize in steam train travel will always be rightfully with England. The name George Stephenson is still hot on our lips, alongside of the lathered-on-zinc cream needed for a day at the beach in the hot Australian sun.

As if we were a quartet of royal princesses off to the seaside for the day, we were blessed with an entire carriage to ourselves, and four seats facing each other. It looked like a set from a movie. Charlene was engrossed in a conversation with Lyla, impressing upon her how much she loved Cornwell, and how she and her husband, Ted, had spent a week in Cornwall last September with hilarious tales to tell. Lyla was happy to listen, and by the end of the one-hour trip, their friendship was firmly cemented. They had a great deal in common, so it was a fortuitous meeting. Maryanne confessed to being bone-tired from the long plane trip from Australia, so she dozed on and off for much of the journey. I daydreamed, guzzled coke, and munched on popcorn – leopards find it hard to change their spots.

Brighton station was grand, yet countrified. Twisted wrought iron canopies, and white-washed palings with beach colours. French doors and long sash latticed windows were everywhere, giving the whole place a feeling of grandeur and glory days. I could smell the salt of the sea as soon as we disembarked, and the hot dogs and oily hot chips wafting from the cafes and food vans around the station added to the seaside sensations. There were shops with similar names to those in Australian beach hamlets such as 'Beach-Shack' and 'Surf Shop'. Establishments I would not be entering, unless I was overcome with the recollection of a promise to buy a particular gift which could only be purchased at the English seaside. Rock candy perhaps? The recollection was hazy.

"We need to find the ladies before we hit the beach!" Since Betty was in Bath, Maryanne stepped up and assumed the sous-squadron leader position. Neither Charlene nor I bothered to contest her self-imposed status, and Lyla, being a late addition to the group, remained status-less in these stakes. "Good idea, Maryanne, tally-ho then." I slipped in the tally-ho bit because it gave me a little edge with the English vernacular. I had gradually built up my supply of English phrases over the weeks I'd been in England, and I was happy to initiate the others into English-speak in the most surreptitious ways possible. Slipping apt phrases into the conversations here and there such as, "Aren't I marvellous! I can converse like the natives," seemed like a humble way of boasting.

After our trip to the ablutions block, which was more than completely satisfactory for a train station, and five pence cheaper than Victoria or Waterloo stations, we all gathered outside the station entrance for a group photo. Above our heads was a flashy purple and pink comic-sans font sign displaying the diagonal greeting, 'Welcome to Brighton.'

The station master was our photographer, and somewhat of a 'ladies' man' as after he had taken a couple of shots, he embraced his feminine paparazzi side, and began ordering us to strike up different poses under the snazzy welcome sign. I was doubtful that we would be featuring on the promised life-sized poster outside the regional tourist bureau on our next visit to Brighton, but I did an Elsa and let go of my glass-half-full pessimism. The others were happy to oblige him, and it was really all just a bit of fun.

Ten minutes later we were ready to paint the town red. Layla had come alive with the photography session. "He was dreamy wasn't he, Fil?"

Dreamy? To whom might she be referring? She couldn't possibly mean the campy, balding station master, who had to be pushing seventy-five, and although twinkle-eyed, agile and jovial, would never make it to the top one hundred hunky English bachelors. "Err, I suppose he was OK Lyla. What did you like most about him?" Shouldn't have asked and shouldn't have been impartial to her description of the man as 'dreamy'. My fence-sitting blunder came at a high price. In one foul swoop I had unwittingly nudged Charlene off her perch alongside Layla, who continued to barrage me with gooey sentiments about Mr Station Master for three blocks of Brighton vintage shops and quaint pastel-coloured boutiques.

These Brighton merchandising establishments would never be just any old shops. They were well fit to rival Fifth Avenue, Maddison Square Gardens or Rodeo Drive, only they were mostly seedy, grimy, grungy and squashy. Americans would be claustrophobic in the tiny vintage glassed vestibules the English referred to as shops. Even as Australians with acres of English heritage, we found the crammed conditions challenging. My discomfort was doubled by the fact that I was now officially Lyla's second-best Australian friend. Giving her one of the koalas had been meant to help her come to terms with the fact that we all lived in Australia, and that she lived in England, so the likelihood of any of us becoming her best friend was slim. But Layla didn't take the hint and stuck to me like glue.

The koala was left to suffocate in the bottom of her tightly zipped handbag.

We had come to a pit stop outside a semi-deserted tattoo parlour for a well-earned breather. I hoped no big, bald tattooist was looking out his shop window in anticipation of a group tattoo. That would be the exact kind of documentary Louis Thoreau would kill to make. "Three Aussies and an English (burnt) rose, seeking Zen tattoos in Brighton, England." Nice one Louis. We moved on quickly as Charlene spotted the very tattooist I had visualised approaching.

Luckily for us, the tide was in, and we were immediately sucked in by the swell. There were tourists by the hundreds, even though it was a week day, and it was getting harder to stay together. Maryanne and Charlene had paired up when my new-found relationship with Layla dawned on them, and Charlene, ever the teasing monkey (her Chinese birth sign), suggested that we all go back to the bruiser for a small tattoo as a memento of our trip to Brighton. She even suggested we get a letter each, and collectively we would spell the word 'pals'. Needless to say, she had no takers for her tender.

Me and my memories.

All the while we were making our way down towards the beach, I was thinking back to two years before when we'd all been staying in the Mercy nuns' convent in Ardmore Ireland, for a month's holiday. One of my friends (another monkey trickster) convinced us that she'd had herself tattooed whilst in Belfast, and that the tattoo symbolised truth. (She was sixty-seven at the time) The tattoo looked genuine enough. We were all stupefied. It was so out of character, and not something Clare would stoop to in a month of Sundays! It turned out that despite the tattoo espousing 'truth', she herself hadn't been telling the truth, and the tattoo on her left upper arm was a transfer which would rub off in the shower or bath. Clare kept up the charade for three days, and it was only when we forced her to take an ocean dip, that the truth was revealed. That would have been OK in itself, but it was the fact that Clare had held a highly professional job as matron of hospitals her entire life, and her dress, abode and lifestyle were not to be sneezed at, that had caused a few of us to smell a rat. We all had a good laugh afterwards.

We had arrived.

That was what Siri told Charlene after she had asked Google for directions to the promenade. No pussyfooting around with Siri. 'You have arrived at your destination' was the sum total of her offering. No mention of where the best place to eat might be, or the temperature of the water should we desire a swim or a paddle. Short and sweet and to the point. That was Siri for you. I remembered back to the days when I had been hopelessly lost in English cities, the Edinburgh wind whipping up my crumpled oversized map, or the Cornish sun so blinding and fierce that it was impossible to locate any landmark without sunglasses and a magnifying glass-and I bestowed blessings on Siri. So, what if she sometimes got it wrong, and we ended up back where we had started? Siri was the best thing since sliced bread in my book, and nothing would sway me back to the days before Siri had started calling me 'Dumble-head fillo'. It wasn't Siri's fault that she'd got my name wrong. Back in Melbourne, I mind two children once a week. The oldest one, familiar with me since he was able to recognise faces and is quite a character. They both are. Jack has a fascination with iPhones and iPads, as do most children nowadays. Last Christmas, he somehow got hold of my phone, and informed Siri that my name was 'Dumble-head fillo' and it stuck. It was cute at the time, but since Siri, along with my pseudonym had followed me to England, it was getting a bit embarrassing.

"I think I'll sit on the beach for a while and take in the air. Anyone interested?"

I was feeling sweaty and dishevelled from the constant weaving through the crowds and back-streets to get to the promenade, and a bit of a stretch out on the sand appealed to me. The other three opted for a meander along the ever-popular Brighton Palace pier, and Charlene said that she would ring or text me as soon as they'd found a sunny spot for lunch. I was to join them at the lunch location. It sounded like a plan to me, so I sauntered off towards the water's edge, kicking off my shoes as I moved. The sand was nothing like the texture of Australian sand. It wasn't even sand at all, but thousands upon thousands of pebbles. I had read somewhere that Brighton was known as the poster beach for pebbles in the United Kingdom. Being used to laying out my towel and smothering my exposed limbs in sun-cream, not forgetting the zinc for my lips – I had absolutely nothing to do but plonk myself on the pebbles and stare out to sea. Not many people were sitting on the beach. Apart from myself, there was a group of five teenagers, earnestly digging into the wet foreshore, carrying small buckets and spades. I wondered if they might be on a school excursion as they were in a uniform of sorts, but I couldn't really tell because their shirts and trousers were rolled up to their knees, and the girls had hitched up their skirts. Whatever they were doing, and for whatever reason they were on the beach, they were having bucket loads of fun, and it was pleasant to sit back and watch them frolicking. Eventually they moved on up towards the pier, and I was left sitting, cross-legged on the beach, the sole sun seeker of the morning. I still hadn't heard from the others, and I'd been on the beach for at least an hour. Maybe it was time to make tracks and see if I could spot them in one of the little bars, sipping pineapple juices, or in the pinball arcade, whistling to the music-box sonatas and winning Star Wars prizes to take back to the nuns.

Wandering up and down the pier proved to be a futile move, as Charlene, Maryanne and Layla were nowhere to be found. Missing in action. If push came to shove, and I had to phone the police to report missing persons with passports, I'd cope providing a description of Charlene and Maryanne, but I'd probably struggle with describing Layla. I had a clear recollection of what she was wearing, but her face had begun to fade from my memory. Maybe I was a trifle sunstruck? Or just not good with faces. Another hour had passed, and I still hadn't found them. I'd tried ringing both Charlene and Maryanne, but they must have had their phones turned off. I left messages on the answering service just in case. Even though they had gone walkabout, I wasn't panicking, as I knew they'd be somewhere close by. I had exhausted all avenues and alley ways along the pier, twice. Just as I was about to give up and seek some food and fortification, I heard shrill high-pitched laughter coming from the back corner of the poky, slightly jaded little bar I was passing. I poked my head inside, fighting off the long, plastic, pastel-coloured tentacles which framed the doorway, and sure enough, it was Charlene, lolling back on a pink lotus flowered beachy chaise-lounge, in fits of laughter. The other two were there as well, but they were seated sedately and straight-backed in striped-blue deckchairs. They appeared to be in the role of the audience, just gazing Charlene as she laughed out loud and continued to entertain them.

I approached the little trio happily, bearing no grudges at the fact that they'd left me to burn to a crisp on the pebbly beach. I had always yearned for one of those hot pebble massages, where hot stones are placed on your back, and rotated around on your skin. They are quite popular in Australia, but also quite expensive. I'd missed my chance of a hot pebble indulgence today on the beach below. I should have cajoled the frolicking youth who had shared the beach with me to smother my back in pebbles, and the hot midday sun would have done the job of warming them up. But that would have meant stripping down to my swimsuit which I had worn under my track suit today – just in case. I was never going to do that on a public beach, so the hot pebble massage was a non-event. "Well, well, well, oo do we 'ave ear now?" I greeted the three of them as one would greet any group of steadfast friends. Having been friends for more than thirty years, we were so familiar with each other that there wasn't any real need for formal conversation. "Well, well, well" had that slight hint of sarcasm, but it was embedded into the cultural nuances we had built up amongst ourselves over the years, and Charlene and Maryanne understood the exact contextual implications of the phrase: 'What 'av we 'ere?' Layla, the yet-to-be-initiated, was the only one looking confused and apologetic. The other two just carried on as if I hadn't interrupted, and Charlene pushed her drink towards me.

"You must be thirsty from that fierce English sun, have a drink." Layla was beginning to look a little more relaxed when she realised that neither Charlene nor I gave their being missing in action and ending up in this bar of questionable repute, another thought.

"Where to next? Do you want to wander up and down the pier with us and see if we can win some prizes?" Charlene loved seaside piers and fairs.

Incongruous really, when one thought about her exquisitely decorated and furnished river-side townhouse in Melbourne-full of antiques and wonderful green plants. The 'so-called' prizes would be rubbish, but if it made her happy.

"Love to. Let's go." We were out of the bar in two minutes flat, and Charlene led our little group directly to a colourful stall with little tyres stacked up in rows, and baskets full of soft balls to throw at the tyres. The aim of the game was to aim the balls at the piles and knock them down. The more you knocked down, the bigger the prize you could choose. Charlene and the others had already sussed out the stall on their way to the bar, but Charlene had insisted that they wait for me to turn up, so that we could all have a shot at winning the prize. The prize she had her heart set on was an enormous yellow teddy bear, with a stature to challenge Big Foot.

"That's the prize I want Fil. I'll show you how it's done. I don't care how much it costs. I want that yellow teddy bear for 'little Meggie'."

Meggie was her youngest grandchild. I thought Meggie would be around nine months by now, and not even a quarter of a size of the bear Charlene had her heart set on. The stall attendant was no court jester, and he rapidly replenished the little basket of balls with one hand and grabbed the pond notes Charlene was thrusting at him with the other. He was surly to start with, but quite animated at the twenty-pound mark. Charlene finally cracked it after parting with thirty-three, pound notes. (We had to change a couple of five-pound notes for her when she ran out of pound notes) Ridiculously expensive bear, but at least we could now move on. I hadn't been offered a shot after all, as Charlene had gone into fight or flight mode as soon as she positioned herself with the soft balls.

Maryanne and Layla were wandering around the immediate vicinity, and that had left me as the lady-in-waiting to Charlene. I suggested to her that we leave the enormous glassy-eyed prize at the stall until after we had visited the Brighton Pavilion which had also been on our agenda for the day. The pavilion was a former royal seaside residence built over two hundred years ago, and well worth a visit according to the Guide- books. Charlene reluctantly agreed that it might be better to leave the bear at the stall, rather than lug it into the Pavilion.

"You might need to also pay a child's admission price if you bring the bear in." The pound-depleted Charlene was forced to agree with me. After we'd all had our fill of the pier (to last us ten years at least), we took our lives in our hands and scuttled the wide road to where rows and rows of grand Brighton terrace houses lined the esplanade. We found a pizza eatery and enjoyed an early lunch.

Then it was time for some serious sightseeing. I had wanted to see the exotic Royal Pavilion for years, as it bore a striking resemblance to the main railway station in central Melbourne, all curves, turrets and rounded domes. An eclectic mix of Indian, Chinese and Gothic architecture. Spectacular architecture, a product of the times, and I was dazzled when we rounded the corner and feasted our eyes upon the imposing sight. Inside did not disappoint either. We purchased the audio-tour headphones, and although we kept together for most of the time the headphones allowed us the freedom to linger or surge ahead as the mood took us. 4 o'clock was our rendezvous time, at the front entrance, should we miss each other. Then all we needed to do was to catch a taxi back to the pier, collect the prized yellow teddy bear, and be back at the station for the five thirty train back to London.

I ended up spending most of my time in the grand kitchens. I was fascinated with the cutlery, crockery and the utensils in general. I kept imagining the cooks whipping up Christmas dinner for the royals, and the love and pride which would have gone into the preparation. There were even samples of food platters and baskets of lush looking fruit. All plastic of course, but the crowd got the picture. 4 o'clock came in no time, and I considered lingering, but we really needed to stick to our schedule of the five thirty train. Layla had decided that she wanted to stay on in Brighton for a couple more days, so we would leave her at the pier and she'd find herself a Bed and Breakfast for two nights. She'd been in her glory meeting and traipsing around with us and had promised to look us all up on her planned visit to Australia in a couple of years. Charlene had stored her mobile number and email address, and Layla knew that we all kept in regular contact with each other. A soon as we were all present and accounted for outside the main entrance to the Pavilion, Maryanne hailed a taxi, and in we all piled. I scored the front seat, which was where I liked to sit, due to my propensity towards motion sickness. Most of the medication the passport control workers had sniggered at back in Melbourne, had been strong motion sickness tablets. This driver was a woman, so there were five women in the taxi. She was a very capable and experienced driver, and we wove in and out of the streets towards the pier in record time. Her name was Concetta, and she told us that she had come from Central America last year, to make a new life for herself and her son in England. There was no father, and no other family. While Maryanne and Charlene went in to collect the teddy bear and give the stall-boy a tip for having minded the bear, Concetta and I had a little chat. Layla had disappeared with

Charlene and Maryanne, and as I had hopped into the front seat when Maryanne had hailed the taxi, it made sense for me to stay put and keep an eye on the metre. It probably wasn't the best choice to have me as the metre girl, as the metre was too far away from me to see it clearly, and I would have had to change glasses to see that far. That would have looked too obvious. I did squint at the metre a couple of times in the course of our conversation, but it was just a blur. I decided to stop looking and just cough up at the station. There were three of us, so I would only need to find a third of the money to pay Concetta.

"What is your child's name, Concetta?"

Concetta's face lit up when I mentioned her offspring, and I was glad that I had made a wise choice with my questioning. I could have asked her about her immigrant status in the UK, and her response might not have been so favourable. She might have taken offence and driven off in a fit of rage at an Australian quizzing a South American about a dicey issue. (I wasn't even certain of the South American country in question) I was happy for her that she'd managed to start a new life in the United Kingdom, I was just curious about how difficult it might have been to obtain British citizenship. For my trouble, and genuine interest in children, Concetta handed me her mobile phone, urging me to look at some of the photos of little Donato before the others returned. I kept up my smile and dutifully scrolled and scrolled and scrolled. I was still scrolling when Charlene, the enormous teddy, and Maryanne opened the back doors and slid in. Teddy was placed in the middle seat, and we were now four women and an enormous bear in a taxi.

"Did Layla get off alright?" I handed the phone back to Concetta, smiling and gesturing to one particular shot of Donato on a ferry. He was very cute, all five hundred images of him which I had swiped through for the last ten minutes were proof to his cuteness.

Concetta didn't even wait for the two back seat passengers to buckle up. She floored the accelerator, and we were off like a cannon, sticking to the side streets she knew like the back of her hand. It crossed my mind that the 'Knowledge Test' for taxi driving in Brighton might not have been as difficult as it notoriously was in the Capital. London was a whole different story, with the thousands of streets and obscure laneways. I couldn't wait to tell Finley my ingenious observation. It didn't take us long to reach the circular taxi rank at the Brighton station. It was peak hour, and commuters were swirling around like blowflies, trying to find their trains, or just generally clogging up the doorways. We divided the fare (including a handsome tip and a koala each for Concetta and Donato). It was very reasonable, given that there had been three of us in the car. I was glad that we hadn't tried to walk back to the station, as it really was a hike from the pier.

All three of us dozed for most of the hour-long journey, and we were back at buzzing Victoria station before we knew it. Charlene had placed the prized teddy bear beside her on the train, and initially we received quite a few strange looks from other passengers in our carriage, but once we were all asleep it didn't matter. We could have had half the train coming in for a viewing and would have been none the wiser.

Back at the convent, we collapsed in the sitting room, totally drained and worn out from the long day. I think I may have had a slight touch of sunstroke, as my face and arms were bright red, and my head was thumping. The Bath group were still not back, and darkness was encroaching. We decided to have a sandwich in a café around the corner from the convent. When we returned the others were waiting for us in the sitting room.

"How was Brighton?" Betty spoke, but Terrie, Meg and Margot all wanted to know how we'd fared. Of course, Charlene raced back up to her room to retrieve the beloved bear. When Betty and the others saw the size of the teddy, they couldn't stop laughing. Charlene was unfazed and insisted that she was going to cart the bear around Ireland with her as a good luck charm. Betty joked that she may have to tie the bear to the roof, or they might have to get a bigger car, what with the amount of luggage and wild animals which needed to be included. We laughed and bantered with each other over a cup of tea and sweet, crumbly convent biscuits, and finally decided to call it a night around nine. I was just grateful that none of the Bath four had commented on the redness of my face. It would have been poor form to have stayed up any later, as there were other travelling guests in the convent, and none of us had the desire to wear the reputation of being loud Australians. It was highly probable that there were scores of loud Australian tourists roaming the streets of London, but they weren't us. Besides, we wanted to be able to return to the convent on future trips. It was clean and comfortable, beautifully furnished, laden with hospitable nuns, and almost in the centre of London. It couldn't get much better. Later that evening, cocooned in my tiny bedroom with the lamp dimmed, soft mood music from my phone, and the window slightly ajar, I lay on my bed and rewound the day. Layla and Concetta were a high priority on my list of musings, but I also included my friends, and I said some quiet prayers that they might have a safe trip around Ireland. All six of them. Well, seven now, with the bear.

# Chapter 25
## Palaces and Pantomimes

Sometimes we are granted a second chance – the opportunity to make things right, when we clearly got it wrong the first time. Or, we never got wrong the first time, but the all-knowing universe had intervened, and we had found ourselves uncomfortably positioned on the tail-end of the plane – hanging on for dear life, and not understanding why on earth we were there in the first place.

Today was my second chance at visiting Buckingham Palace, after the ill-fated attempt on the day of the Parson's Green train bombing. One notable difference in my favour was that, unlike that morning when I had come into London on the train, I was already nesting in London central, and there was no necessity to venture anywhere near a train. The convent was positioned perfectly within walking distance of the palace. Leisurely perambulation would be the preferred method of transport today. The others were leaving for Ireland this morning, and I would be staying in the Archway with Suzy and Finley for the next couple of nights, so it was goodbye to the convent digs. It had been an eye opener, staying in a convent in Pimlico – not really something your average tourist would ever consider. Although rare, I knew it not to be entirely an enigma, as other members of my immediate family had also experienced convent life. Not that they were nuns – just out to experience life to the full. About five years ago, my sister Julie and her husband Bernie embarked on a trip to Italy, leaving their five young children in my trusty hands. The trustworthiness of my hands was a contentious issue, as they were subject to daily temptations to throttle, but I somehow managed to survive the four weeks, and emerge with a steely, unwavering resolve that for me, adoption would never be an option. On a more positive note, it was probably quicker and less taxing on the purse strings to have undertaken the 'try before you buy test' than to have made endless trips to other continents, as some of my friends did, desperately seeking babies. The convent connection with the tale of Julie and Bernie's Italian voyaggio, was that I had convinced them to stay overnight in a monastery outside of Rome perched high up in the hills. A priest, with whom I had worked in Melbourne, had recommended the abode, and they were expected. Countless emails had flowed between Bernie and the abbot, and it was all arranged. Signed off! They were to be there for the evening meal on the designated date. Typically, Julie and Bernie wandered around the Vatican for the most part of that day, leaving it till almost nightfall to make their weary way up into the hills towards their pre-arranged accommodation. There are reputedly seven hills of Rome, and they had not a clue on which hill the monastery was situated. Six hours later, at daggers with each other, and in darkness as pitch as any native Sicilian, they fell upon the enormous monastery double-doors. The 'gents' were all up even though it was around 4 o'clock – and the next day, Julie and Bernie had fallen on their swords just in time for morning prayers. How fortuitous! As the story goes, the exhausted pair fell asleep on the hard, narrow wooden chapel pews, and the kindly priests covered them with 'swaddling clothes' and returned to their chanting. So, even though convent-crawls might not have featured high on the agenda of the typical tourist, they were something to be considered. Something of a gold mine really, when you stopped to think about the number of convents and monasteries in the Christian world.

We were partaking of our last meal together in the convent dining room. It didn't feel all that different to breakfasting in a Bed and Breakfast establishment. The only really striking difference was the gallery of religious pictures and icons which lined the dining-room walls, and the religious knick-knacks in pride of place on little tables tucked into corners and in the hallway. One of the nuns must have been on twenty-four-seven feather dusting and polishing duties, so intense was the sheen on the artefacts.

"What time does your plane go Charlene?" I was sitting next to Charlene, munching on my hardened toast, convinced that the nuns would scuttle around the breakfast room when we left, collecting scraps of bread to pound into hosts, which would then be couriered on to Westminster for the following morning's mass.

"Not till after lunch, but we want to get to the airport early to organise our luggage. We seem to have accumulated so much already."

I could have pointed out to her that if she left the great enormous teddy bear she was so emotionally attached to with the nuns, she would have no luggage issues at all. But in fairness to Charlene, she did have quite a solid investment in that bear. It was also a genuine bear, not a koala which had been named a bear by the British. I kept quiet on that one. I knew she would work it out. Charlene was a seasoned traveller with a sharp wit and even sharper tongue. She could talk her way out of almost anything. Carting a bear, the size of a small child around Ireland would be a piece of cake for Charlene. Added to that, she had tried so hard to win it for Meggie, the intention being that the bear would somehow become a sort of family heirloom. A heroic tribute to family solidarity on Charlene's part. We all finished breakfast in good time and moseyed off to our rooms to finalise packing. As I only had a small suitcase, the bulk of my luggage being back at Alice's occupying almost the entire bedroom as I still didn't have a large suitcase, I was first downstairs and eager to leave. I rang the bell near the front door, and Sister Christine appeared from the kitchen, beamed at me, and asked me if I would like her to stow my suitcase in its usual hiding place. I agreed that it would be safe there, and she picked it up effortlessly and bustled off, swishing her skirt in a happy little jig. She had found her calling. 'Valet services by Sister Christine of Pimlico convent' had a nice ring to it. I sat on the little polished wood bench near the front door, twiddling my thumbs and eying off the closed door opposite my bench, deliberating whether or not to go and knock and thank the Reverend Mother for her hospitality. Five minutes passed, and the others still hadn't appeared, so I jumped up before I could change my mind and rapped on the door.

"Come." That icy, monosyllabic utterance was enough to torpedo me back to my bench, and hastily retrieve my Giude-book to London, burying my entire head in it, should the Reverend Mother suddenly fling open her door to expose the phantom door knocker.

The door never opened, and I guessed Sister Christine would probably be the scapegoat for me some time later in the morning. I was still cowering on the bench, cut to the quip with the sombre response, when the old wooden stairs to my left started groaning and straining with the weight of six women and their bulging suitcases. All half-a-dozen of them were tackling the stairs at once, and it looked like the scene from a movie, with them all edged in on the creaking stairs. I thought *Ghost Busters* straight away, then *Calendar Girls* but they were all fully clothed, so Calendar Girls wouldn't work.

"What have you all been doing up there. I've been waiting for hours!" Slight exaggeration on my part, but it had felt like hours waiting in the torture chamber directly opposite the Reverend Mother's office. I was so relieved to see them all I hugged the nearest woman as they congregated on the last stair only it wasn't any of my friends, but Sister Christine, who had materialised in the hope of more work experience for her valet job. She seemed pleased with my unexpected display of affection and hugged me back fiercely. She then offered to help with the luggage and we all lugged the cases towards the door. We needed to wait the mini cab to arrive and Maryanne suggested that we wait outside as it was a little crowded in the foyer outside Mother's office. I wholeheartedly agreed with her, as I was still a little scared of Mother.

"Come on then, out we all go." Barb took charge of where we were to stand to wait for the mini cab. She gave us all a position on the street where we might be most obvious to the driver. We could not have been any more obvious had we been dressed in clown outfits. Seven women huddled together on the street outside a convent. I took the opportunity to say my goodbyes and slip away. I could have waited for the mini-cab to arrive, but it was getting on, and I wasn't sure how far it would be to walk. The last time I had tried to make it to Buckingham palace, I had been leading the group of women I had met on the bus from Waterloo on the morning of the bombing. Today I would be alone.

"Well, bye everyone. Enjoy Ireland, and don't forget to send lots of pictures on Facebook." Most of them had not yet been converted to Facebook, Instagram or texting, but it was a work in progress-and they all had mobile phones with internet access. We completed the group hug, air-kissing and blowing kisses ritual in record time, and I was off down the street without turning back. Those first five minutes of being alone after having been surrounded by people for days on end can be disconcerting, but I soon settled into the crowd of walkers rushing around the streets of Pimlico. Just where they were all headed, I wasn't really sure, but I kept my head down and continued walking in the direction of the palace. I remembered some of the streets from years ago when I had first witnessed the spectacular 'Changing of the Guard' at Buckingham Palace. By the time I arrived a crowd had already assembled but being on my own meant that I could squeeze in next to big groups of bus tourists, or tag onto the end of a family group, or even climb up on the statues as some of the more agile onlookers were doing. No, on second thoughts, I wouldn't be climbing anywhere. I am so accident prone I probably would have interrupted the whole performance by falling from the top. I would need to be extra careful as I was by myself. It didn't take me long to find a family to latch onto. They were Italian, and they reminded me of Chevy Chase and his family from their vacation movies. The wife, Maria, dripping in Italian gold looked excited, the son looked bored and the teenage girl looked at her phone. Papa was off buying water for them all. They struck up a conversation with me, and when it was discovered that I had an Italian background, I was unquestionably welcomed into heart of the family. The bosom of the wife actually, as she clasped me towards her cleavage upon hearing that my father was from Bari.

"Mi piace Bari. Molto bene," was all she said, but I was 'in like Flynn'.
We watched the parade as a family. The backdrop of the Palace was magnificent, and I had to keep reminding myself that the Queen and the Duke of Edinburgh may have been breakfasting behind the palace walls. I did have some knowledge of the spectacular gardens beyond the walls, as I had watched a travelogue in the Queen's gardens.

I also knew the queen loved trees. Always an admirable streak. But today they were in absentia, so my hopes of ever actually glimpsing the Queen in the flesh were once again dashed. To make up for my disappointment, I posed for a selfie on the wall outside the palace, in the hope of a prince riding by on one of the mounted horses and sweeping me off my feet. Although this may have worked for Meghan Markle, who, as a teenager on a trip to London, had been photographed with a friend in the very same spot, it was never going to happen for me. A. I was too old and B, I was too heavy for a prince galloping by to drag me up onto his horse (unless it was a draft horse) and ride off into the sunset. The best I could hope for would be for some kindly tourists to throw money into my purple sun hat, which had fallen onto the ground while I was setting up my retractable 'selfie stick'. In my well-worn travelling clothes, I would not have blamed the coin-throwing tourists for mistaking me for a royal vagrant. Fidgeting with my selfie stick reminded me of a news item I had heard before I'd left Australia for this trip. Apparently, in Sydney last year, there had been an inundation of Asian tourists taking selfie photos with glorious Jacaranda trees as a backdrop. (The Jacaranda is a brilliant purple Christmas bloomer.) It was reported that these tourists were setting up their tripods on main roads. Some of the 'selfie seekers' included brides and grooms lying down in the middle of the roads in attempts to secure the best angle. What was the world coming to?

The Italian family were moving onto their next tourist attraction – Madame Tussaud's Waxworks in Marylebone, which I knew from experience, attracted more than its fair share of visitors. It would not be a hyperbole to suggest that the wax dummies attracted millions of visitors a year. The Italians had been light-hearted and funny. A typical Italian family, comfortable with effusive hand-gesturing, screeching and squealing, and that was from the parents!

The morning passed in whirl of regalia and horses (sadly no prince appeared.) I couldn't help likening the whole scenario to an audience participation play complete with crowd cues of gasping, groaning and hooraying at the exact right moments. Outside Buckingham Palace for the Changing of the Guard was certainly the place to be on a summer's morning.

It was sad bidding farewell to my Italian family, but if I was to make the opening act of 'Evita', I would need to move quickly. I jumped onto the nearest bus headed for central London. I think I only had to ask five people for directions before locating the theatre. Just as I was approaching the heritage building where Evita was playing, I noticed a bustling sandwich bar two doors down. After the incident of the egg sandwich, I had resolved to boycott sandwich bars, but time was of the essence once again. Throwing caution to the wind, I raced into the shop and politely requested a take away coffee, and cheese and salad roll. (I was adamant in my avoidance of the whole row of egg sandwiches.) Guzzling down the coffee in record speed and burning the roof of my mouth in the process, I slowed things down with my roll munching, and took small steps down Charring Cross road towards the Phoenix. With ample time to spare, I settled myself in the Noel Coward Bar with a 'G and T' and a bag of crisps. (The bower bird in me had returned with a vengeance, and I stowed my half-eaten roll in the side of my backpack.) I was tempted to set the phone alarm for half past six with a memo to myself to finish eating the roll for tea, but I figured that hunger pains would do the same job by tea-time.

This was certainly the life! One of my favourite musicals, my favourite mixed drink, and my beloved crisps. The only thing that could have topped my euphoric state, would have been for Noel Coward himself to appear behind the bar in a cameo appearance. I had heard about Cecil B De Milne and Charlie Chaplin making impromptu appearances in the films they directed, so it was not entirely implausible. (The fact that Noel Coward himself had been dead for almost half a century may have been a slight hitch, but I'm sure he had relatives somewhere in a London who could have obliged.)

Eva Peron did not disappoint, and a New Argentina was born! We were all singing away by the end of Act Two, and this time I was sitting next to someone who could actually sing, unlike the foghorn I'd endured by my side at 'Les Mis'.

It was a very pleasant afternoon, and there had been no time to miss my troupe of friends who'd left for Ireland, or even Alice, Patrick, Finley or Suzy who were all just a train journey away from me.

After the thrill of 'Evita', I ventured across the road from the theatre to a little cafe which was mainly reserved for theatre goers and was mainly manned by theatre hopefuls. When I'd purchased my ticket to 'Evita', there had been a voucher attached which entitled me to a cup of tea and cake at the arty theatre cafe. When I walked in, a young boy resplendent in an orange jumpsuit, came flouncing up to me and thrust a large menu on my face. I set him straight immediately that I had a voucher which specified the partaking of tea and cake. When I say I set him straight, it was only in a metaphoric sense, as I don't think setting him straight was his heart's desire. He told me he was a performer, and that he was auditioning for a chorus part in a new West End Show tomorrow afternoon, hence the glitzy headband which was holding his gelled down hair firmly in place. The new show involved a fair share of dancing, and he was training his hair to stay back so that his vision would not be impaired. He was hilariously funny, and very boyish and sweet, and we chatted away amicably, exploring our mutual love of theatre. The cake was mouth-watering, and he plied extra cream onto the top of the passion fruit icing just because he found me 'divine'. It was getting better and better for me. First the boy in the Japanese restaurant in Kingston had called me beautiful, and now I was divine in the eyes of this young actor/dancer. After I'd stuffed myself full of cake, I visited the Ladies, and the doors to both the Ladies and the Gents were plastered with signatures of famous West end performers and classical English actors. The signatures were surrounded by 45-inch records, and the whole door scenario was very retro. I took a photo for my Facebook page. All in all, I left the cafe in high spirits, and with a very positive attitude about myself. It had been another exhilarating day. I planned to go to the Tower of London tomorrow, and then to comb the shops in Oxford street and Knightsbridge. I felt happy with my plan, and suddenly tomorrow couldn't have come quickly enough.

By the time I wound my weary way back to the convent, it was nearly dark. Almost in automatic pilot, I rang the bell, and instantly, Sister Christine appeared. I perked up when I saw her. "Sister Christine, I'm back!" Sister Christine did not look all that pleased to see me. She screwed up her rounded face and looked me up and down. (I did look a bit like the Wreck of the Hesperus by then.) Finally, she spoke. "Fil, you were supposed to come and pick up your suitcase. I waited all afternoon. Why are you so late?"

Her personality changed from this morning when she'd bear-hugged me almost to death was very puzzling. I racked my brains for an inkling as to this bizarre behaviour, but I was clueless. Sister Christine had found her voice again. "We have no room for you tonight Fil. You told Reverend Mother that you would only be staying for a couple of nights. We have a men's bowling club from Brazil here for the next week. There's ten of them and they're very sprightly for their ages."

The light went on. I thumped my forehead in disgust at myself. I was not meant to be in Pimlico tonight! I was expected in Archway with Finley and Suzy. I was so exhausted I couldn't think straight. One thing I did know was that it was too late to be travelling around London by myself tonight. The last time I had ridden the night trains had been in Paris some years ago, when I'd left my two friends in a hotel near the Guard de Nord to skip off and have a meal with Amant – another Australian friend who worked in a language school in Paris. Amant wasn't his real name of course, but he was determined to transform himself into a true Parisian, so he procured a black bow tie and a black curly poodle, swatted at French until he was perfectly fluent, and changed his name from Lenny to Amant (pronounced Amon, like "amen" only you needed to change the e to an o and leave off the n.)

Amant was taking me to a Vegetarian Restaurant tucked in behind Notre Dame, and wonderfully positioned in the First arrondissement. He lived quite close by in a small studio flat, which had been the utility room of a French townhouse in a former life. It was tiny, but home is where the heart is, and he was gloriously happy there. A huge solitary spreading chestnut tree providing shade and bird-song, stood in stately sojourn in the courtyard outside his nine-foot sash window. The last time I had been in Paris, we had feasted on bacon sandwiches in the tiny flat, and the scene had stuck in my memory. Tonight though, I would be meeting Amant alone, as my friends were feeling queasy from the Euro Star train trip. I had set off by myself, assuring them I would be back at the hotel before nightfall. Navigating my way to the prearranged rendezvous spot under the gargoyles of Notre Dame was easy enough and eating the plateful of earthy French artichokes even easier. It was only when the time came to make my way back to the hotel that things got a little sticky.

I should have agreed with the chivalrous Amant when he had insisted on escorting me all the way back to the hotel. Instead, I compromised, and allowed him to accompany me to the station, and bid me farewell at the top of the entrance to the underground. I stood facing him and repeated his instructions verbatim before I raced down the stairs. "Down the stairs, turn left at the bottom, go along a bit and down a further flight of stairs. You'll then be on the correct platform for your train." I managed the first instruction, but at the bottom of the stairs I was stumped by a barricade and a huge pile of concrete rubble (which, Amant could not have known about) and a sign entirely in French. I'm not too bad at basic French, but I could not decipher the lettering. There was an arrow pointing to the right, and it looked like the intention was for all through traffic to make a right turn. No one else was around where I was standing. No guard, no one! Panic was raising its ugly head again, and I was suddenly terrified. Up ahead I could see a group of young boys pointing me out to each other. I prayed for the train to arrive before they had a chance to reach me. It did arrive, and I was on it in a heartbeat.

Unfortunately for me, it was the wrong train, as once I'd found a seat (and there was a whole carriage to choose from), I asked two young girls in the carriage if it was the correct train for the station near our hotel. They were French angels. Not only did they both speak English, but they took complete control, and dragged me off at the next stop. They then calmed me down, and the three of us trudged up what seemed like a hundred steps to the overpass, and down to the other side of the platform, where we boarded another train which had just pulled into the station. The girls made sure I was OK, before leaping back off the slowly moving train to retrace their steps to the former platform which was now on the other side. Presumably they would wait there for the next train. I couldn't believe their kindness. No fuss. No expectations. French hospitality at its finest. Once I had settled in on the correct train, I attempted to ring my friends to let them know I would be late, but there was no reception in the bowels of the French underground. I just had to wait till I got back to the hotel to relate my sorry end to what has started out as a pleasant evening.

Therefore, not tonight, not on any night, would I be riding the trains alone, even if I could speak fluent Swahili. As a last resort with Sister Christine, I tried the plea-bargaining "Please Sister Christine. Couldn't I stay here one more night? I'll go straight to bed, and I'll be gone in the morning. I promise. You won't see me for dust."

Sister Christine looked doubtful, but she must have remembered how good the hug had felt this morning, and how complimentary of her I had been with Revered Mother. Maybe Mother had reprimanded Sister Christine for the door rapping incident this morning, and the cluey young nun had put two and two together and worked out that it was me who had cowardly run from the door.

"I suppose we could sneak you up to one of the higher-floor rooms for the night. Reverend Mother mustn't find out, and you must be gone in the morning. O.K.?"

I gratefully agreed to her terms, and we both crept along the downstairs dimly lit corridor to where she had stashed my suitcase. "Mother asked me why the suitcase was still here when she saw it this evening. I had to tell her that you'd forgotten to pick it up, and that you were coming back later tonight to do so. If we see her on the stairs, that's the story, right?" Sister Christine seemed to be enjoying the cloak and dagger scenario, and I played along with her for the sake of peace. I was beyond exhaustion by then. My head ached, my bones throbbed, my stomach was rumbling, and I had difficulty getting my breath on the stairs which led up to the second-floor home to the witness protection suites. Picture of health at 9 o'clock, that was me. Sister Christine was the complete opposite. Fuelled and invigorated with the whole charade and convent cabbage, she helped me hobble to the room, fussing over me as if I'd just come back from the front. We passed a little alcove/sitting room, and I could make-out about five men in there, sitting at a round table playing cards. There was a lot of shouting and clapping of hands going on. The bowlers! They looked old and harmless enough, but I would be locking my door and barricading myself in my room, just in case. One could never tell what fast moves these bowlers had up their sleeves. I remembered that Charlene had impressed upon me to me to avoid the bathrooms at night, as she had been aghast at finding a pair of black men's underpants on the shelf in the bathroom, when she had visited there one night. Her very words to me were, "Stay clear of the bathrooms, Fil. Just wait for daylight."

I forced Sister Christine to accompany me to the bathrooms – just in case. She kindly waited for me to complete my bed readying ritual. Then she showed me my room. It was simple, yet adequate for my purposes. It contained a single bed with a puffy white doona, a cupboard, a window and a small basin. I think they refer to rooms such as these as cells, and I think I know why. Still, I was in no position to quibble, and I graciously took the towel and little green bar of soap Sister Christine handed me.

"For your morning shower. Don't forget, you need to be gone early – at least before Reverend Mother rises. Remember, under no circumstances are you to go down to the dining room for breakfast." She gave me a quick, shy double pat on the arm, and was gone. I could hear laughter and guttural coughing and spluttering from the floor below, and I quickly bolted my door.

Perched on the side of my bed, I phoned Finley. Suzy always retired early, but I knew Finley would still be up reciting the Knowledge or making plans for his next renovation project. Finley wasn't in the least fazed that I had mixed up my days and missed my curtain call in the Archway. They had just thought I'd got held up, and that I would ring when I was ready to be picked up from the station. Once he understood that I was not coming, Finley promised me he would explain to Suzy what had happened, and that I was alive and safe – back in the convent. I did not mention that Sister Christine had smuggled me into a different room to the one I had been staying in, nor did I hint at the arrival of the boisterous bowlers on the floor below. We made arrangements for Finley to pick me up outside the main entrance to the Archway station the following evening around six. Normally I would have walked the three street-scenic route to their home, but it was all uphill and I would have my tried and trusted suitcase to contend with. Before turning in, I wrapped up one of the koalas in some tissue paper I always carried with me, and carefully composed a short note to Sister Christine, thanking her for my extended stay and her skulduggery. (Obviously I didn't use the word skulduggery, but it was implied.) I placed the koala and the note on the tiny bench above the sink. Sure-as-eggs Sister Christine would be inspecting my room with a double strength Geiger counter for any traces of me in the morning. The koala would be a lovely surprise for her, and proof that I, like Elvis, had finally left the building.

# Chapter 26
## Leaving the Convent Take Two

You would not think there would be birds in the centre of London, singing their lungs out at 7 o'clock. But there were. A whole orchestra of them by the sound of the racket. It sounded like the heats of Eurovision, so off-key were the majority of them. It wasn't only the public who were frequently inconvenienced by being awoken in the early hours of the morning by serenading birds. I had recently read in an article on our revered leader – Queen Elizabeth Second, relating the incident of when she had been engaged in reading aloud her annual Christmas message from her desk, when an avalanche of birdsong from the Buckingham Palace garden ruined the recording. The frustrated producer asked her to "redo it from the top". Reputedly, the queen shot him a steely gaze and asked: "From the top of the second page?"

To which he nervously replied, "From the very start, if possible, Your Majesty."

Brave broadcaster! It gave me a good laugh when I read the article. This morning, I was identifying strongly with the Queen. I was not about to make a second exit from the convent though. Stealing away at this ungodly hour had been a struggle enough, especially given that I had to somehow managed to heave my brimming suitcase down two flights of stairs without hauling it over the banister, and with no Sister Christine to barrage me. She was no doubt still fast asleep and dreaming of unicorns, polishing silver, ballerina dancing and opening doors for dignitaries. Despite the brevity of our friendship, I was really going to miss her shy, cheeky ways. To look at butter wouldn't melt in her mouth, but last night I'd sensed an alter ego. I wondered what her name had been before she'd entered the convent. I thought her lucky to have had Christine accepted as her religious name. I'd known many nuns in my lifetime and most of them started out religious life with men's names like Sister Julian or Sister Antonio or Sister Thomas Aquinas.

I supposed it was the Christ part of her name which appealed to the authorities of the church.

I hadn't really thought about what I would do with my suitcase for the day. My current plan was to wheel it along behind me and weave my way up to Victoria station. There were always lockers at the larger stations, and I intended to hire a suitably sized locker for the day. Fortunately, the suitcase wasn't too big, and it would possibly fit. Otherwise I would need to investigate leaving it in the luggage room, where it could be stood upright. I'd seen documentaries on stations and train travel, and people were always leaving their cases in the holding zones. Thinking about the great stations of the world distracted me from the weight of the case. I thought of Gandhi, and how there is a railway station in South Africa, famous as being the place where the great man himself was thrown off a train for riding first class in 1893. This was categorically not the done thing! Apparently, visitors to that railway station find it difficult to locate the small plaque erected in memory of Gandhi. Just a simple snippet of trivia, but a claim to fame for railway stations.

No one took the slightest bit of notice of me as I made my way uphill, dragging my case behind. It was going to be a challenge, carrying the case up the stairs at the entrance to the station. I could see that I was in for a jostle and a struggle, when out of the blue, a knight in shining armour materialised in front of me, offering to carry the cumbersome suitcase up the stairs. "Allow me to assist you. That case looks heavy, and I would be happy to carry it up the stairs for you. May I?"

I liked the way he asked for permission to help me out, and I especially liked his tanned, handsome face, sea-green eyes, and blue pin-striped suit. He was gorgeous. Dreamy as Layla had described the balding station master-photographer from Brighton the other day.

"Th…thank you, that's very kind of you." I stammered, but managed to look straight at him, and he smiled and effortlessly lifted up the case. He then extended his free hand to me, in a gesture which indicated he was about to help me up the stairs. Did I look that old? I knew it was early morning, and that I had slipped out of the convent without any makeup, and in my non-descript travelling clothes, but I couldn't have looked so bad that he'd mistaken me for someone old-could I?

Clearly yes, because this time, he was not asking my permission to pull me up the stairs. He just hauled me in! When he'd deposited us both at the top of the stairs, he tipped his hat, and was off like the 4.50 from Paddington. My fleeting brush with a beguiling businessman was over before it had begun. I was glad the others were far away in Ireland, but I could have done with Charlene, because I was certain that had she been with me, she would have feigned a gammy leg or some debilitating heart condition, and the green-eyed gent would have stuck around. Too late now. He had ridden off into the sunset on the scaled back of a slim, silver escalator.

From memory, I had seen an imposingly bland steely locker section adjacent to the ablution blocks and bathrooms, so I had an idea how to kill two birds with one stone head down there to stow the case and freshen up at the same time. I also needed to reconfigure my backpack, and check that I had the necessary provisions for the day, including my umbrella of the nine lives, and the green Richmond rain poncho, as it had looked very much like we were in for another punishing deluge when I'd left the convent earlier.

The bathrooms were underground down three flights of stairs. I had some difficulty negotiating the suitcase on the steps. It was small, slow steps forward, like shuffling along the Great Wall of China. I imagined my feet to be bound, and hence my small, laboured steps. No wonder the Chinese banned the barbaric practice of foot-binding more than a century ago. My feet were aching, and I had no bandages suffocating them, only a mega suitcase to slow me down to a snail's pace. Had I packed my backpack last night in readiness for today, I could have saved myself the ordeal of bumping the suitcase down every single step. I wished Mr Businessman would reappear and offer to help, but as I was in the Women's' ablution block, it was highly unlikely. There was an agitated queue of women and some young squealing children in pushers or in reigns at the bottom of the steps when I finally thumped down onto the last step and turned the corner. Assuming my place at the end, I wriggled around impatiently, leaning my leg on my suitcase from time to time for a bit of a rest. I was watching the anxious women in front of me, fumbling around in their pockets and purses for the correct change to feed the turnstiles. I knew it would be futile to search through my own pockets, as I was coinless. A wave of uneasiness threatened. The tired-looking young girl with limp blonde hair who was manning the turnstiles was gazing at me, my suitcase and my stricken face. She must have surmised that I couldn't speak English, as she approached me, and spoke to me in halting Polish. (I recognised a few basic Polish words)

"No. No. I am not Polish, I am English, and I don't have the correct change. Actually, I don't have any small change. I have a credit card though!" I whipped my credit card out of my wallet and held it up to her.

"See!"

The girl shook her head, laughed and rushed over to tell her friend that she'd mistaken me for a Polish tourist. She then grappled in her pocket and held up a couple of coins which she inserted into the slot, and I was able to pass through the turnstiles as easily as I had entered the UK weeks before. My case was ceremoniously carried through a little silver-grilled side gate by the philanthropic offsider. Then the gate was shut firmly and noisily, barring anyone else from trying to sneak through. Some of the women and children on the other side of the gate glared at me, but I put my head down and ignored them. I couldn't blame them for their anger and dismay, but I stayed stoic on my side of the tolls.

Before I marched off to attend to my secret woman's business, I thanked the two giggling girls who had helped me, opened my case, and handed them a koala each.

"Tu jest misio dla ciebie przysługę."

It was the first time I had recited one of the Polish phrases I had committed to memory before leaving Australia, in case I were to meet Polish girls such as these two – and hand them each a tiny koala. Both girls burst out laughing again, and I wasn't sure whether or not it was my Polish accent or my mixing up of the Polish euphemisms which caused their mirth. They appeared delighted with the little tokens of appreciation, and I could sense the bathroom brigade of onlookers straining and glaring even harder, in an effort to glimpse what sort of bribe I had handed to the two attendants. Emerging from the ablution block ten minutes later, I felt like a new person – more than ready to tackle the swanky shops of central London. Record and book shops featured high on my wish list, but I thought I might pop in and have a gander at Top Shop, to buy some clothes for a few favoured teenage nieces and nephews. (The bride and groom from Westminster had raced off there to buy clothes, and I was curious to see what sorts of clothes were sold there.)

My thirst for a book-shop was quenched almost immediately, as there was a 'Fisher's' book shop when I reached the top of the stairs. I still had my cumbersome case with me, but I tucked it in neatly behind the front counter and moved over towards the autobiographies section – my favourite place to be in a bookshop anywhere in the world. I was happily flicking through the first chapter of Dawn French's "Dear Fatty" having a little chuckle to myself at her clever witty writing, when I noticed a man staring at me and making an irritating "ttt" sound. I smiled at him anyway, but he just scowled back, and moved closer towards me. I could see then, that he had a name tag on his collar, as well as the shop logo. Drats! He must have been a shop employee. He wasn't a very happy chappy. Here's what he hissed at me, verbatim: "Madame, it is highly improper to dawdle, and read any book you pick up. You cannot just stand there for hours digesting the books. I suggest, as is our policy here at Fishers of Victoria, that you read only one page of a book to judge if you like it. Then either put it down or buy it. This is an express bookshop, and people have trains to catch." I couldn't read his name. The print was too fancy, too purple and too small, but it began with a T, and I am willing to bet he was called Tristan, or Tarquin or some other of Hyacinth Bouquet's relatives. (No. Not Onslo.)

I carefully placed the books I had been browsing through back on the shelves (arranging them purposefully on incorrect shelves) and hurried over to pick up my suitcase, fearing that it wouldn't be there, and that there was also a time limit imposed on leaving suitcases, in addition to the unwritten browsing rule. The suitcase was still there, but I could feel the accusing eyes of the 'puffed-up-pigeon' of an employee boring into me. I closed my eyes and wished him to become entangled in his swarmy waistcoat.

Time to leave.

Outside the shop, in the gigantic old-world main arena of Victoria station, hundreds upon hundreds of ant-like people darted, and zig-zagged in a frenzy to catch trains or get to work. I had read somewhere that the population of London swelled by three hundred thousand each morning, as tourists and commuters from all over England made their way to work, rest and play. I was now officially one of the three hundred thousand. I took a deep breath and plunged headlong into the crowd, riding along with the rest of them towards the lockers. It was a hurtling journey, with people dropping off like flies to bungy-jump onto the escalators at a phenomenal pace. If you were not quick enough, you could easily miss your window, and end up deposited opposite the exit to the Northern or Southern line railroad-never to be seen again. Hundreds of the public must have been disadvantaged by this peculiar escalator practice. Namely the elderly, the very young, the agoraphobics, the disabled, the schizophrenics, the short sighted, the long sighted, and the simply 'slow' citizens and tourists. It reminded me of childhood games we had played in our front yards – rushing across the stretches of yellow dried Australian lawns to avoid being squirted full force by the boiling hot water from the hose. You had to be quick, or you'd be soaked and scorched. These shoppers, or commuters or travellers – whoever they might have been, were as busy and focussed as ants building their empires. It was a sight for sore eyes, and one I could have feasted upon all day. (had I been able to remain stationary for long enough.)

I needed to hop off the merry-go-round, because I had reached the lockers, and I also needed to focus myself, and find out about leaving my case. The Gods were again smiling on me, and a smartly dressed grey haired man, with an official railway jacket, and a multitude of army badges, came up to me and asked me if I was lost.

"Uh, no, I'm not lost, I want to leave my case here, I just don't know how to go about it."

"Not to worry lass, come with me, and we'll do it together. Now, there's nothing explosive in the case is there? Only, you have to declare the contents."

The man was very old and very earnest and very honest, and he didn't bat an eye-lid at helping me.

"I love an opportunity to assist a damsel in distress."

I felt mediocre about being called a damsel in distress. I had preferred being called 'beautiful' in Kingston. It had a much nicer ring to it.

I'm sure the station assistant (Geoff) had my best interests at heart, because he was quick and deft in his assistance routine. I handed him my credit card, and he expertly inserted it and printed me off the receipt. He then escalated my suitcase to top locker status, as easily as if he were swatting a fly. And handed me the key.

"Don't go losing the key now, will you." (I'm not reliable with keys, but he wasn't to know that, he must have been a bit psychic.)

I thanked him for his help, handed him a koala, and headed up the steep escalator towards the South exit. Off to the thousand-year-old Tower of London at last! Today would be my third visit to the Tower, and each time I make the trek across the river, I find it to be new frontier. Situated on the muddy banks of the mighty Thames, this iconic London landmark started off life as a castle for medieval kings and queens. Over the years it has evolved as a 'sometimes confronting tourist attraction' – an authentic taste of the England of old. If you suffer from vertigo, stay home, because the Tower visit involves much circuitous climbing, and most people find that they can enter easily enough, but escape is not quite as facile a venture. The first few rooms I poked my head into were so noisy, and so crowded with tourists, that I didn't even bother to get my toes wet. I wasn't in the best of moods, as the beefeaters (in costume) had been quite beefy in their handling of the multitude of bags and suitcases when I had placed my backpack on the table for the searching and rifling routine. They'd singled mine out because it was so heavy, but that was only because I had been proactive to the point of hyperactivity when I'd frantically prepared for all manner of weathers.

Disappointingly for the bored beefeaters, nothing of any interest was found. I was allowed to continue surging with the crowd. My inside knowledge of the Tower gave me the edge over most other tourists, and knowing which doors to slip through, and which doors to avoid, saved me a great deal of time. My relationship with the Tower was most defiantly one of love/hate. I loved that it was medieval, and I hated that it was mostly associated with deaths murders and hangings, with the odd case of poisonings, beheadings or hurling of traitors over the balconies thrown in for good measure. I remembered from a previous trip to the Tower – a story about dramatic escapes by members of the Royal families by tying strips of sheets together and shinning down the sheets to the safety of the ground. (Well, maybe not shinning, but moving as quickly and as silently as possible.) The 'piecede-resistance' of the Tower had to be the Crown Jewels. They were even smaller than I'd remembered, and quite a distance from the eye in their glass cases, but never-the-less, magnificent in all their glory – there was no denying it. Interestingly, they are not all jewels as one would suppose. The Crown Jewels are in fact, one hundred and forty royal ceremonial objects coveted proudly in the Tower. They include the regalia and vestments worn by British kings and queens at their coronations. If you had the idea that you would just drop by the Tower to view glistening shining jewels similar to those stashed in a pirate's treasure chest – think again!

There were more outrageous costumes and outfits in the glass cabinets than in Elton John's wardrobes, and one would need to devote days to the viewing. The most magnificent of all the head pieces had to be the imperial state crown, worn by British monarchy for eons and featuring more than three thousand precious gems. That's a lotta loot!

After I'd digested the Crown Jewels and the Tourist shop for the third time in my travels to England, there wasn't really all that much left for me to do. I ambled up and down the protected medieval courtyard, munching on a yoghurt muesli bar, sipping water, and checking my phone to see if there were any messages from my friends in Ireland. Siri informed me that there were three messages. All were from Charlene, and in triplicate: "Quick Fil, get over here ASAP. Do not go straight back to Australia on Monday, I repeat – do not go straight back to Australia! Abort flight! You are needed in Ireland." I had a little chuckle. Yeah! Sure Charlene!

I was in the cobblestoned main courtyard, racking my brains to come up with a witty retort to text back to Charlene, when a frizzy-haired, middle aged woman with a red beret, large red hooped earrings, and a light blue scarf draped loosely over her shoulders, came up and just stood silently in front of me, waiting until I had finished texting. I am the slowest texter of all time. I felt her standing there next to me, waiting, but I just wanted to finish the sentence. As it was, every second word was misspelt, despite the fact that I had my glasses on. Finally, I could stand it no longer.

"Did you want something?"

It was not my intention to pursue a deep and meaningful conversation with any stranger at this stage of my tour. I was almost at the exit gates and on a mission. I had places to go and people to see, and by now, I was over the Tower for another five years.

The women, holding a guide book out in front of her, was pointing to a faded picture of the Tower, and looking doe-eyed at me. When she spoke, it was with a heavy French accent. "Mon Dieu, I am looking for zee bloody tower. Can you please elp me to find zis bloody Tower?"

I suppressed a giggle and pointed in the direction of the Tower-to my left. The woman shook her head and pushed her guide book into my face pointing to the wording below the picture of the Tower which read: "The Bloody-Tower is to be found in London on the banks of the river Thames."

I tried to make the French woman understand that the Bloody-Tower, and the Tower of London were one and the same place, but she would not be convinced. She grew tired of my gesturing and elongating my vowels pretty quickly after I failed to convince her.

"Ooh lahlah, zee Engleesh, zay are impossible to understand!" She then flounced off in a hissyfit, helbent on thrusting the guide-book in the face of the next unfortunate tourist to whom she took a fancy. I called out to her retreating back, "Au revoir! Bon fortune!"

She took not the slightest bit of notice and I was left wondering whether she had been French after all, or just someone with a thick accent proficient at annoying other tourists. My mission after the Tower was to find the nearest train station and make my way up towards Oxford street on the tube. There was a tube entrance on the next corner, and on impulse, and with no real sense of direction, I skipped down the thirty-nine or so steps to the platform below. I was a youngster without training wheels. (no suitcase to trip me up.) Quite a few people were on the steps, but they were all much faster than me, and I was quickly left behind. I didn't mind. This smidgeon of peace from the throning crowds of central London was priceless.

Down on the platform, in the bowels of the earth was an entirely different story to the solace of the stairs. So that's where they were all headed. Platform surfing, planking and pacing looked to be the new craze down here. I was surprised to see so many school children, bounding up and down the platforms, giggling, smirking and jostling each other. The poor teachers were doing their best to round them up and keep them grazing in one spot, but I could see hordes of them scattered up and down the platform. A sheep dog or two might have been the go at these tube stations on excursion days or school holidays. I found a seat about five metres back from the track, and plopped down, tired out by the steps. The flashing light and the resounding rumbling from deep inside the wide tunnel told me that a train was approaching. (as did the nasal voice announcing the imminent arrival of the train to Piccadilly.) I had no idea which train I wanted to take, but I was sweating, and starting to feel very claustrophobic, being so far down. The doors of one of the carriages suddenly opened directly in front of me, and like a zombie off on holidays, I walked straight onto the train. The annoying voiceover continued to replay the recording, "Mind the gap, mind the gap." But I was in a trance and it didn't register.

If I'd thought the station was crowded, this carriage was so jam packed, it was difficult to breathe. I immediately snapped out of my zombie persona, and in a panic, jumped back through the still open doors to the now deserted platform. Hobbling back to my seat, I took deep breaths and decided that I would need time to psych myself up to the point where I'd feel comfortable about jumping onto the next approaching train. I had a tube map with me, and I worked out that it wouldn't really make much difference which train I took, I would still end up in central London. Somewhere!

The nasal voice was in full throttle again. "The approaching train is for Leister Square. Step away from the platform!"

I normally don't get voices in my head directing me to act in a certain way, but they were coming as thick and fast as pelting drops of rain this morning. "You can do it! Get on that train! Do it!"

I half-closed my eyes and jumped onto the carriage. Thankfully, there wasn't a wall of people flush with the carriage door. There were vacant seats, and I could see people's faces, and not their squashed-up limbs and backs of their heads, as had been the case in the Piccadilly carriage five minutes beforehand.In fact, it was so quiet in the carriage, I almost fell asleep. There was a young girl sitting next to me, clutching her hand bag to her chest, and looking at me suspiciously – as if she thought me to be the leader of an elite underground pick-pocket gang. I smiled at her, but she didn't reciprocate. We both got off at Oxford street, and as soon as her feet touched the platform, she was off like the wind, looking back over her shoulder to me to see if I was following. (There would be no koala for her today.) I wasn't. Following her that is. I had stopped dead to consult my map, and the crowd on the new platform had surged past me. When I looked up again, the girl had disappeared, as had the crowds. I was alone in a platform-wasteland, with the wind from the tunnels whipping up at my feet. It was so strong that my flimsy tube map was lifted from my hand and whooshed into the tunnel. I wondered how many maps and assorted wads of paper-work ended up in the Lost Property department of the London Underground. Either that, or squashed to a pulp by the sheer force of the next train.

Map-less, I tackled yet another 'straight-as-a-die' escalator and distracted myself from the height of the contraption by studying the West End posters plastered over the walls on my upward journey. Outside, the sky was typical London-grey and spitting. Up went the umbrella. By the looks of things, umbrellas were the norm up here in the daylight, as the streets were a sea of mushrooms, with faces and legs popping out at different angles. The rain didn't bother me. I found it refreshing and cleansing. The pavement was quite wet and shiny – a clear indication that it must have been raining for most of the time I had been bunkered below.

My priority was to find a record store. I knew Oxford Street was the best place to find out-of-print labels, and I thought I would probably have something to eat in the enormous music shop once I'd found it. With the help of three kindly strangers and a Polish street vendor who sold me a London inscribed tee-shirt, I easily located the enormous record shop. Once Inside, it was a quick bite to eat before I rode the escalator up to the third floor – the Folk and classical section, where I intended to make my purchases.

The sales assistant was half English and half Aussie. And possibly half boy half girl. He was a hoot, and we had a good chat about Sydney, where he'd been born. Travis was his name, and he bounced and flounced me along the rows of record – racks until we found what we were looking for. I ended up with some choice CD's. That's what I love about England. You can generally put your hand on whatever your heart desires. I wanted a certain CD and hey presto – Travis found it!

"I'm so thrilled I could find this for you." Travis thrust the CD I'd been searching for across the kingdom for the past five years, every time I'd had an overseas trip. "I knew you'd be gutted if we couldn't find it. But we have."

The streets of London were a treasure trove to me that afternoon. After the success of the record store, I moved onto bookshops and Knick-knack stores.

I avoided the clothing sections of the big Department stores, because I knew it would be midnight before I left if I ventured into one of them.

By 5:30 I was rubbish! (picked up the phrase from English television) Totally exhausted, feet and back aching, and ready for bed. Harrods had been on my list of 'to do's', but that adventure would have to wait until next time. The main reason I'd wanted to do Harrods was to stand and gaze at the food in the food halls, but I wasn't hungry, and not one hundred percent sure of the dress code for Harrods these days. I'd need a day for Harrods on my next trip. I wished I had not left the Convent and that I could see the nuns one last time. Not that I wasn't excited to be going to Archway for a couple of nights! I was. Just zonked with the big day. After I had picked up my rested suitcase from Victoria Station, I stumbled upon the Northern line, which would take me to Archway station in time to meet Finley as per our arrangement.

It was the usual fun and games of trying to find a seat for myself and my suitcase on the train to Archway. I obviously had not planned things carefully enough, as I found myself wedged in under the smelly armpit of a burly businessman who was not only blocking the doorway, but simultaneously blocking anyone from exiting the train at the stations along the route to Archway. I spent the time shuffling backwards and forwards, and by the time we reached

Archway, I had invented a new barn dance which involved shuffling backwards and forwards, and coming face to face with a new partner at each station stop. I had just about got the hang of the steps when my station was announced. We tumbled off!

On the Archway platform, I had a moment of disorientation, as I knew there to be at least four different exits at Archway station. You know what I did! And it worked. There was Finley, snoozing and chortling away in his black cab outside the station. People were looking enviously at me as I made my way around to the driver's side to rouse him from his slumber.

"Fin, Fin, wake up Fin. I'm here, and if we don't hurry up, you'll have a cab full of commuters, trying to get home for their tea." Fin opened his eyes slowly, Ike a lazy crocodile, and whispered to me, "In the back me lady."

I shoved my suitcase into the back seat and made my way around the cab to the front passenger side. Finley must either have been talking to the suitcase, or he had remembered a story I'd told him about a taxi driver we had encountered in Los Angeles a few years ago. I have only visited the United States once. The trip from Australia is entirely over ocean, so I was quite highly strung by the time we set foot on solid ground again after so long in the air. Outside the airport, my friend hailed a cab to take us to our accommodation at the Biltmore – our splurge hotel for our first night. (It was downhill digs after that.)

There were three of us, and the other two selflessly jumped into the back of the cab, leaving me to the dreaded front seat. I opened the front passenger side door to sidle in, and the driver, who had been slumped over the wheel with a baseball cap pulled low over his face, and looking like he had just been shot, called out sharply, "In the back ma'am!"

I hastily slammed the door, and squashed into the back seat, on top of my two friends and our three large suitcases. (The driver had not popped open the boot/trunk for us either) We couldn't breathe, and the driver (another of the elective mute breed I have encountered in my travels over the years) took off at such an unexpected and ridiculously reckless speed that we were all throw backwards and took quite a battering. I ended up on the floor, and no amount of pulling at my arms and legs by my friends could move me. I kept calling out from the floor, that I wanted to get out, and to stop the cab, but my friends kept pushing my head back down and putting their hands over my mouth. They could still see the back of the driver's head and were terrified! The driver was possessed, and sped headlong onto the elevated, steely tangles of Los Angeles freeways on what felt like one wheel. This went on for an eternity.

When we pulled up at the Biltmore, he screeched to a halt in the circular driveway, and almost ran over two bell boys decked out in their double-breasted jackets with the shiny brass buttons. They ducked out of the way, and we tumbled out of the car, dragging and bumping our suitcases out onto the driveway. The taxi disappeared in a squelch of tyres, and we handed the bell boys two fifty dollar notes to pay the driver when he returned for his fare, urging them to keep the change as a tip for themselves, and the high insurance premiums they must have had to pay for their own protection – with the likes of our driver to contend with on a daily basis.

For years after that, whenever we were piling into cars to go to the races or on a road trip, one of us would imitate that L.A driver with,

"In the back ma'am!" Finley knew the routine well.

Had I been in the back with my suitcase here in the Archway, I may not have had such a perfect view of the hustle and bustle of Archway road at knock-off time. There were, again, people everywhere. It was much busier than Hampton had been, on the two occasions I had been shopping there in Tesco's, around dinner time.

"Why are there so many people Fin?"

Finley was concentrating hard on weaving the cab in and out of the traffic, trying to avoid hitting pedestrians and babies in pushers. He turned towards me with a smile, and replied sarcastically, "All the better to practise on my dear, all the better to practise on." He was joking of course. Finley is an excellent driver, and very patient with the traffic, as we had experienced on the London night tour.

The street where Finley and Suzy lived was lined with cars when we pulled up, but Fin managed to manoeuvre the cab into a tiny strip of asphalt about five houses down from their place. We sauntered back up the road, with Finley effortlessly lugging my case and giving me a running commentary on the occupants of every house, and little juicy tit-bits from their lives. He was an excellent raconteur, and I was really enjoying hearing about the street sagas. When we arrived home, Suzy was just finishing setting the table. I noticed there were five places set, and I asked Suzy if we were having any other visitors besides myself. She didn't answer me, but just took my hand and guided me into the lounge room where I was pleased to see Paddy and Meg, two of Finley's siblings, propped up on the armchairs watching telly. They had been invited over for dinner as a surprise for me.

"Hi Paddy, Meg. What a lovely surprise. How have you both been?"

The catch-up surprise dinner was delectable (Suzy and Fin were both great cooks) and the company wasn't bad either. Paddy had some entertaining stories about the colourful characters in the council flats where he lived about three miles up the hill towards High Barnett. Meg chipped in with stories of her own about life in Nottingham, where she lived. (Meg was holidaying in London with Paddy for a week)

I talked about life in Australia, and Finley and Suzy mostly waited on the three of us. I could get used to this being a guest and waited upon caper.

All too soon it was 'all aboard the black cab' for Paddy and Meg, and in a whirlwind of hugs, kisses and promises to meet up in Melbourne in the very near future, they were off. Suzy went along for the ride, leaving me with instructions not to start blowing up the blow-up bed until they returned – only they might be around an hour, as Finley wanted to get petrol for the cab, and she wanted to pick up a few groceries in Tesco's.

"Are you sure you don't want to come and have a look at your favourite shop Fil?"

Ordinarily I would have loved the opportunity of Tesco's at 10 o'clock at night, but, like clockwork, at this hour, I was just too tired to move.

"No thanks Suz, I'll be fine. I'll just rest in the sitting room till you get back, and then I'll hit the sack."

We could hear impatient honking outside, and Suzy grabbed her bag and fled. The metre was ticking.

It was quiet in the house when they all left. I tidied up as much as I could and laid out the lifeless lilo-mattress flat on the floor where Suzy has indicated I would be sleeping. My territory was shaping up to be what they called 'cramped quarters' but I was grateful for their hospitality, and the whole apartment was really quite small. I spent about ten minutes in the ring with the lilo, but no amount of grappling, twisting or flattening would allow me to get it into a position where I could pump it up by myself. Exasperated, I gave up and after brushing my teeth and slipping on a comfy tracksuit, fell asleep on the couch in the living room. Finley and Suzy weren't away all that long in the end, and once they'd seen I'd done the groundwork with the lilo (literally), the two of them managed to pump it up and then make it up with sheets, doona, and a fluffy pillow, even before I was awake.

Someone was shaking me, urging me to wake up. I thought I was still in the convent, and Sister Christine had sneaked into my room to tell me that Reverend Mother had summoned me to discuss my immaturity at such an advanced age. (Knocking on doors and running away caper.)

"Wake up Fil. We're back, and your bed is all pumped up and ready for you. Sweet dreams. See you in the morning." She tiptoed away to her bedroom and softly closed the door. I assumed Finley was already in bed, and she didn't want to wake him.) Dragging myself over to the lilo I collapsed on top of it, before I could drag the doona over me. I must have fallen asleep again in record time, because I have no recollection of anything beyond that point, other than that I was wedged in between the table and the wall on the blow-up bed. It had been a long, long, day.

# Chapter 27
## Waking Up in Archway

It was the whirring which woke me. Pitch dark, a little on the chilly side, and a strange whirring, resounding echo of Chitty-Chitty-Bang-Bang engaged in a sluggish morning start up. Whirr, clang-clang, whirr, clang-clang was the emerging pattern. I feared I was drugged, and alone in the darkened cellar of a factory in the seedy docks of the Thames. Nothing was surer. I struggled with sitting up. I struggled even harder with remembering who had captured me and why, and finally, I struggled with the big white metal whirring ghost to my side. In frustration at my inability to focus, I pushed roughly on the large rectangular shape and suddenly, crash, bang! The 'ghost' which was carrying some weight, suddenly toppled over and crashed into another piece of furniture I could not recognise in the darkness. I fumbled for my mini-torch, grateful that I'd had the foresight to include it in my luggage and snapped it on. Instant torchlight, bright and purposeful, exposed a huge, rock-solid-ghost. AKA the fridge. I breathed a sigh of relief that there were no ghosts or captors and tried to figure out how to single-handedly manoeuvre the fridge back into a vertical position. Guided only by weak torchlight, I eased my way carefully towards the lounge-room door opposite, where I had flicked off the light-switch some hours before.

It all came flooding back to me. I had been sleeping on the dining-room floor, flush up against the cold uninviting wall on a blow-up mattress. The large white fridge had been to my left, and there was a high wall on my right. A table piled high with books and assorted items was at a diagonal to the fridge. How I came to be sleeping in the dining room for the night, was a story in itself, but at least I had regained my bearings, and I was not the unwilling geisha of some drug lord in a dungeon under the river Thames. Every time I pushed on the fridge to move it back into position, a loud scraping noise followed, and I was fearful of waking

Suzy and Finley. I kept the light on, in order to see what I was doing. It didn't help though, as the fridge was too heavy for one person to move.

Finley and Suzy did not appear, and I could only assume that they had slept through the whirring, the clanging and the crashing. It may have been that they were accustomed to the noise of the idiosyncratic fridge in the dining room, but the crash would have woken Rip Van Winkle it was so loud. Some years ago, we had a history-making overnight storm in Melbourne. The freeways were underwater, and there was storm-damage to thousands of houses. I spent the entire night huddled under the stairs in the dark, too afraid to open the front door of my townhouse for fear that water would gush into the living room. Not that we were all affected. A friend of mine who lived in a suburb also deluged by the storm, slept through the whole event, waking in the morning to a blue sky and puffy white clouds. She tells the story of how she looked out into the backyard and did not even notice that the wrath of the storm had taken the entire roof off the patio, and the whole back area was now exposed. When questioned at her workplace about the severity of the storm, she replied optimistically, "I didn't hear a thing, but the whole of the patio roof has disappeared!" That was typical Jennifer. Not the most observant bird watcher in the wetlands.

It took ages for me to get back to sleep after the fridge incident. I think it must have been around 5 o'clock when I last looked at my phone. The next thing I heard was Finley's voice, screeching out that we'd been robbed in the night and that they had probably taken all the contents from the fridge. He didn't seem the least concerned that he had woken me with his war-cry, or that I might have been killed when the fridge intruder entered the dining room for a midnight feast and tripped over my blow-up mattress.

In a voice thick with sleep, I wheezed out to Finley that there had been no intruder. "It was me Finley. I am solely responsible for the fridge toppling over."

"Fil, why didn't you tell us you were hungry last night? I would have made you a toasted sandwich to see you through till morning." Again, that difference in what the English consider to be a midnight snack and Australian snacks of the wee small hours. We tend to stuff ourselves full of potato chips, ice-cream and chocolate bars when feeling peckish after midnight. The sensible English would have no tolerance for such foolhardiness. Food is very much associated with the culture of places, and multicultural Australia has evolved ethnically over the past century from 'three veg and meat', to the most exotic of cuisines. Being such a hot country, we tend to feast more on fruit and light salad vegetables, which are easier to digest, and lighter on the stomach.

I assured Finley that I wasn't hungry last night, and that the chef-style meal he had prepared for Suzy and myself had been nutritious and very filling.

"What happened then Fil, did you have a bad dream and knock the fridge over with that mean left hook of yours?" Finley stood there at the top of the five stairs leading into the one and only bedroom, in his boxers and a faded Christmas tee-shirt, punching the air with his left fist clenched, and a big beam on his face. He could be a bit of a trickster, even this early in the morning, and I had to smile back at him for his perseverance with the humour. "Ha-ha Finley, what time does your gig start this morning?"

Finley had big dreams, and the latest of them was of becoming a stand-up comedian. However, there was very little dosh to be made grubbing about in the industry, unless you were fast tracked to Benny Hill status by adoring fans in the flush of first love with your comedy. Finley wasn't into the smutty British humour, more like everyday nuances and little twists of life upon which he applied clever contemporary social commentary. He was extremely well read and informed in varied walks of life. Finley was a people watcher, and he gleaned his material from the everyday. He had enjoyed the sweet taste of success of late, with a first-time gig at a local pub which hosted an amateur comedian's night once a month.

"It was brilliant," was his only comment when quizzed by Suzy on how the performance had panned out. Suzy took this reply as a resounding measure of success, immediately face-timing all in sundry in Australia to relay the good news. In our minds Finely was, from that moment on, a reputable comedian, and the pride of Ireland and the Archway. Cracking the English comedy scene without packing the punches with smutty inuendoes was not to be sneezed at. That one-night stand had been a few months back now, and since then Finley had unfortunately developed cold feet, and was, in Suzy's words, "reluctant to put himself out there again".

It was a pity, because he had a lot of natural raw talent. It was just the nerves that tended to get the better of him. I decided to have a deep and meaningful conversation with him, regarding his stage-fright, and see if I could convince him to get back on that horse! The D and M would have to be tonight though, as I had another action-packed day to live through, and I was excited beyond measure to be going to the 'Oxo-Tower' on the Thames near the London Eye, for a slap-up lunch with Finley and Suzy. My plans for the morning included a meander with Suzy up to the church, past the posh houses I so loved to drool over, and then a mid-morning swim in the indoor-pool at Crouch End, where I had swum on my last visit. It was a fair hike to Crouch End, but the pool was worth it. After our swim, Finley would pick us up, and we had arranged to go to 'Muswel Hill Organic', where we would be stocking up on enough organic fruit and vegetables to see Finley and Suzy through the following week. They had been on a health kick for a couple of months, and organic beetroot and cucumber juices laced with pineapple, ginger and kiwi fruit were the order of the day. That would take us up to midday, and our lunch reservations were for one thirty.

It was all going according to plan – the organic juice and wholemeal toast with fetta and smashed avocado breakfast, the brisk walk up to the church where we lit a candle for Finley's mother, Kathleen, who had passed away last year, and finally the long trek by foot to the Crouch-End indoor pool. It was at the swimming pool that things began to go hay-wire. I take full blame for the disturbance. Suzy was in a world of her own, lapping up and down in the crystal green warm water about three lanes away from me. In retrospect this was a good thing, because she was spared the embarrassment of having to say that she knew me, even though she had signed me into the swim club in the front entrance about twenty minutes before the incident. My affinity with water runs deep, and as a child, I spent most of the summer months in my local outdoor pool, and quite a few of the winter months in the heated Olympic length pool in a close by suburb. We swam at school, and we swam in the ocean on our beach holidays. I think it would be fair to say that, had I been previously incarnated, it would have been as a mermaid, so strong were my ties to water. Consequently, over the years, I had mastered many aquatic tricks, and my prowess in the pool had not gone unnoticed by many a judge in the swimming carnivals Water prowess was very much a part of my entire youth. My signature trick was my ability to hold my breath under water for two entire lengths of the pool. (No, not the wading pool.) I have a few humble trophies on my mantle-piece as testimony to this talent.

Back to the Crouch-End pool. There I was, happily lapping along beside Suzy, when my leg started cramping.

"Suzy, Suzy! My leg is cramping, I've got to get out of the pool." There were only about four other swimmers in the water at this hour of the morning, so I ducked under the thick coiled ropes and crossed three lanes to reach to the metal rung ladder, in order to elongate my leg on dry land. It took a few minutes to stop the cramping by stretching my leg out against the wall running alongside the pool. Once the pain had dissipated, I cautiously lowered my body back into the pool, and floated lazily on my back. The other swimmers had abandoned the pool, but I could see Suzy soldiering on, gently lapping her way to Scotland by the look of it. I could also see the pert little pool official in his little yellow cap and red life-jacket, prancing and pacing up and down the side of the pool, keeping up appearances with his checking of water levels and temperatures. He looked beyond-bored, and ready for some action. I hoped more people would arrive to keep him occupied in his pseudo-important supervisory role. It wasn't really my business though, so I decided to enjoy the space and solitude, and practise my underwater swimming skills, which I had temporarily neglected (for the past forty years.) I waved good-naturedly to the supervisor, and nose-dived under the water, straight down to the shiny, smooth floor of the pool. I then began coursing through the water, safe and sound on the cool concrete. Back where I belonged at last. It was so calm and deep and soundless down there. No wonder dolphins always appeared so happy and relaxed. I was approaching the end of the pool, and I felt confident that I still had enough breath to keep going. (Those scales in my singing lessons in the months before I'd left must really have strengthened my lungs) Tucking my legs in under my knees was easy enough, but once I was into the second lap, I started to wane, and realised that I was not going to make it to the end of the lap. Up I spouted, more whale than dolphin-like.

    I realised almost immediately that all hell had broken loose. The supervisor I had waved at as I'd duck-dived down into the water was running along the side of the pool with a long stick, rippling the water and calling out frantically. "I can't see her, I can't see her anywhere!" Suzy was also up there on the side of the pool, wrapped in a huge white towel, and looking extremely worried. Making up the rescue team were at least four other swim-staff, positioned at both ends of the pool alternately blowing shrill whistles and yelling out my name with megaphones. (Suzy must have told them my name.) One of the swimmers whom I remembered from before I'd periscoped into the deep, was now in a state of half-dress and filming the scene with his iPhone. Everyone is a film-maker these days! I swam meekly over to where Suzy was standing.

    "Fil, you disappeared. We all thought you'd drowned!"

"No, I'm still alive. I was just reliving my childhood on the bottom of the pool. I used to love it down there, and I've won lots of trophies for holding my breath under water for more than four minutes."

Suzy did not look impressed, and neither did the life guard/supervisor when he finally caught up with us. He was livid!

"'Ear, whacha fink yer playin at lady?"

I realised that this boy was also unimpressed with my underwater skills, and that I was not about to receive a trophy today. I was 'not bovered', as I had no room in my suitcase for huge trophies. Suzy was trying to placate the irate supervisor. "So sorry. We are so sorry to have caused a disturbance. Aren't we Fil?" I supposed we were, but I hadn't intentionally set out to waste any one's time.

"Yes. I'm truly sorry, I had no idea anyone would even realise I was under there. It won't happen again."

We didn't hang around for long after that. Suzy was very quiet in the dressing rooms, and I was remorseful that the incident had happened at her swimming club. I hoped it wouldn't put a dampener on her membership status with the club. With a bit of luck, the club officials and supervisors would forget all about the misunderstanding in a few days, and they may even have had a chuckle about how they had lost me, over a cup of tea or a pint at the pub.

After we had showered and dressed in tracksuits and sweaters, we made our sorry way outside to wait for Finley. I was racking my brains to find a way to make it up to Suzy, when she suddenly turned to me and started chuckling, then laughing, then full blown bellowing.

"Oh Fil, it's funny in retrospect isn't it? You on the bottom of the pool, and the whole pool in an uproar looking for you. At first, I was upset with you, but now I can sympathise with how you must have felt when you resurfaced. What did you think was going on?"

What I'd thought when I'd surfaced like a hunted down Nessie, or a giant whale in Japanese waters was "I mustn't have heard the fire alarm, being so far underwater". That wasn't what I told Suzy though. I made out to her that I was sorry beyond measure. And I was. Extremely sorry had managed to put a dampener on the day. The swim had been intended to put us both in a relaxing mood, and the rattling experience had done nothing to put us at ease. I was glad that a meditation at the World centre for Christian meditation was on the agenda for today. It would give me the opportunity to appraise my actions, and ask myself questions such as, 'Why do I think only of myself, and not the other people in my immediate environment?' A contemporary educational writer gaining weight in her field of positive psychology, is Carol Dwek. She has a "Not yet" theory, which in a nutshell proposes that we can all achieve a state of perfection or high achievement, but just 'not yet'. It is a mindset thing. This afternoon I would go deeper with that notion for myself.

Finley was pulling into a car space just outside the pool. I gave Suzy a surreptitious glance, trying to suss out whether or not she would be betraying me and relating the pool adventures to Finley. She caught my glance and with well disguised exasperation, reassured me that she would wait until tonight to tell Fin, and that with a bit of luck, it might make a good routine for Finley's comedy. I remembered that he was looking for new, fresh material and knowing how clever he was at voices and accents, I felt sure he could pull off a spiffing one act monologue, set in a fictitious swimming pool – possibly somewhere in Spain, as the Brits loved to holiday in places like Ibiza or the Spanish Riviera.

"Top swim was it, girls?"

I thanked my lucky stars Finley had not arrived early. Had he done so, he would have been sitting outside the front of the complex, impatiently waiting for us to finish our swim. Undoubtedly, he would have heard all the racket. It was a wonder the fire brigade hadn't been alerted, and the High Street cordoned off. My fantasising about what might happen was unnecessary after all, as Suzy redeemed herself and blurted out for both of us, "Yes. It was very refreshing. I did about thirty laps, and Fil was going so well until she got cramp." I breathed a huge sigh of relief. I'd thought Suzy was going to spill the beans when she began her sentence with "Fil was going so well until…"

"Are you able-bodied enough to come shopping with us Fil, or do you want me to drop you home so that you can rest that cramping leg of yours?"

There was nothing wrong with my leg, but it was worth playing along with Suzy, in the hope that my recklessness and disregard for others would never be exposed.

"I'm fine now Fin, and organic food shopping is exactly what I need to cheer me up and get some iron into me."

"Oh well, that's settled then. Off we go. Hold onto your swimming caps!" Finley floored the fiat, and we were off up the hill to the discretely tucked-away Muswel Hill shopping hamlet before either Suzy or I had time to secure our seat belts, let alone fuss with headgear. The little villages and hamlets of North

London are contentedly nestled in a world of their own. A British Brigadoon. The fact that most of these villages lie within a radius of roughly thirty kilometres of the city is an added bonus for the commuters. However, many of the residents both live and work in these affluent areas, some of them never having set foot in the centre of London their whole lives, and others who may have lived in the inner city were now embracing a dedicated lifestyle change. In Muswel Hill the roads were extra wide, and the houses nearly all had that 'WOW' factor and that was just the facades and the gardens. I would have loved to have seen inside some of those houses. Television's dynamic duo Kirstie Allsopp and Phil Spencer-Property experts extraordinaire would possibly give their eye teeth to make it inside some of them. (As would I, if I still had my eye teeth.) We parked directly outside the barn-like, brightly painted organic shop, Fin and Suzy having discovered in a popular London epicure magazine, that this particular shop had made it to the top ten of organic shops in England – and that it was classed as a London store. Finley, Suzy and I gathered up the calico and cotton shopping bags they had brought along for the fruit, grains and veggies. The shop was heavenly, and the aromatic smell of fresh fruit and vegetables, musky candles and oils permeated the wooden interior. I wished I were staying all week with Fin and Suzy – I would have been buying up big with the vegetables and whipping up some awesome organic gourmet meals for when they arrived home from work, tired and seeking comfort food. Alas though, my days were numbered in this fair portion of the land. Come Term Four in Australian schools, I'd be well back n' working again. I remembered Margi and felt enormous envy that she would still be traversing Norway in search of the Northern Lights.

We decided to split up with separate lists, which we promptly listed on our phones. Time was flying by, and Suzy had booked lunch for one-thirty. I had been entrusted with the grains and bread list. (The assumption being I couldn't go too far wrong with dry packaged food.) We always shop organic at home, so I knew exactly what I was searching for – I just didn't know where to look. Finley had the 'cream-of-the-crop' for his list-fruit. That left Suzy with the vegetable category. I had no end of trouble finding the grains on my list, even though there were only three on my list. I ended up asking a shelf-packer to help me locate the grains, and when he was able to do so, I produced a koala for him. The boy was very chirpy and went about his work whistling even louder after he'd received the small token of appreciation. Finley Suzy and I reconvened in ten or so minutes, and pooled or loot. The whole expedition only took half an hour, and we were home in plenty of time to spruce ourselves up for our posh lunch in the city.

We all looked pretty swank by the time we left the house for the restaurant. I had brought my best outfit with me, as well as my one pair of high heels. Suzy and Finley were also all dressed up in their finest regalia. Suzy informed me later, that they had decided last night, after I had surrendered myself to the bosom of the blow-up-mattress, to wear their wedding outfits to the restaurant the next day. (Not the tandem bridal gown and suit outfit – but their going away outfits which had included an expensive vintage floral dress and high heels for Suzy, and a navy-blue tailored suit with pink tie and loafers for Fin.)

Finley and Suzy had dined in the extravagant riverside restaurant on a previous occasion, but that been a while ago now. The restaurant had been recently renovated, and the decor and views of the river were reputedly to die for. (Many people did die in that exact same spot, as it was very close to the Tower of London, and people would take boats to the Tower, often not making it.) An Australian friend of mine owned an apartment in Vauxhall, abutting the river, and the last time I had visited London, three of us had stayed with him for a couple of nights, whilst the others in the group had ventured across the river to stay with the nuns in Pimlico. Brett, the owner of the apartment, had taken the other two on a sightseeing tour of London for a day, and I had stayed behind, languishing on the balcony with my river, a book and an over-supply of crisps, for the better part of the day. It was a long labour of love, but my fascination for the Thames was born that day. Now, like a criminal returning to the scene of the crime, I kept coming back to the Thames.

We stepped out of the lift on the third floor of the building, and there she blew! Grey and glorious! My appetite was roused at the sight of my river, and we were all speedy in our decisions over what to order. The beautifully prepared food did not disappoint. Our waiter was Polish (what's new in the world?) and he took great pains to explain the daily tapas menu to us. After lunch, we sat out on the exposed patio draping the river, enjoying coffee and cake. The Thames was still one of the mightiest bodies of water I had ever clapped eyes on. A veritable vestige of the British empire in all its glory! We have rivers in Australia the width and depth of small county towns, and granted they are spectacular, but this river swamping me, belied so much history that it was beyond taking in. Londoners tended to take this vestibule of history for granted, but I spent most of the hour we were outside ingesting the expanse of water, gasping and exclaiming in delight every time a boat or a barge passed us by. I hadn't felt this much rapture when I'd been in Kingston or Richmond-on-Thames. It was the backdrop of historic buildings, steeped in history which did it for me. I extended my head as far as I could towards the south to see if I could make out Brett's apartment, but to no avail, as there were too many tall buildings in between. It would have been great to have had the time to catch up with Brett and his balcony – but I knew there would be other trips in store for me in years to come.

It was 4 o'clock before we knew it, and the best laid plans of mice and men – the plans of a meditation and a visit to Camden market-relaxing with either a beer or fruit-juice in the thick of the market, would need to be rain-checked until tomorrow. (or scratched entirely.) Camden, with its locks and antique stalls by the score, was very popular with tourists and locals alike. It was also jampacked with shops and stalls catering to a wide section of customers with their slightly unconventional dispositions and disparate dress-sense. I was disappointed that we could not fit everything in, but Finley suggested a walk on Primrose hill, which was quite close by. Suzy and I both agreed to the compromise.

"You'll love the views of the city Fil, they're panoramic!" I recognised the phrase Finley had used from one of his skits, where he described a view of somewhere dreary as being as "panoramic as prison bars".

It was a promising description, and a view and a walk sounded like the very tonic we all needed after our rich and filling lunch. It was threatening rain when we reached the car, but we stuck to our plan, and diverted our route back to the Archway for a spot of mountain climbing on Primrose Hill. Accustomed as he was to the streets of North London, Fin managed to manoeuvre the fiat into a poky gravel pit in one of the side streets. The rain had really set in, and we were still quite a few blocks from the park.

"I keep a spare rain jacket in the boot Fil, you're welcome to wear it to stop you getting soaked." Suzy and Finley had come prepared with rain jackets and umbrellas, old hands that they were with the London weather. I, on the other hand, had put vanity before sensibility and comfort, and as a consequence, was valiantly attempting to tread my soggy way up Primrose Hill, complete with high heeled shoes, my best purple dress under Finley's checked lumberjack rain jacket, and a plastic bag over my head to stop my hair from getting soaked. (My mascara was already running the length of my face.) A pair or two of cross-country skis would have come in handy at this point in time. If you took into account the first morning of my trip when I had fumbled around in the dark at 5 am, feeling for clothes to wear up to the beach, and the fact that I had selected the very same outfit to wear today, this would be the second time I'd felt embarrassed by my attire. Maybe it would be better from now on, to restrict my wardrobe to jeans and a sweater. (With loafers on my feet for unexpected walking episodes.) I might have brought a change of clothes and shoes, had I known that we would be walking and 'singing in the rain'. Finley liked to sing as he tackled steep inclines (the Irish in him), and Suzy and I made sure we lagged several metres behind him when he burst into song. (The Australian in us.)

The sweeping views of London from the pinnacle of Primrose hill were superb, even in English rain. I was glad I had forced myself to hang onto Finley for dear life and allowed him to virtually pull me up the last part of the hill. Suzy managed quite well by herself, accustomed to deluges and steep inclines. Despite the rain there was quite a crowd of walkers and sightseers, and the whole scene, dotted with colourful brollies and kites was typical England. We do have parks in Australia, thousands of them, and I don't know what it is about our parks and recreation spots that makes them nothing like the ones here in England, but they just aren't! Some years back I watched an English series entitled 'This is England!' and I was very impressed with the keen eye of the director in his depiction of England. It was a bitter-sweet, raw edge post-Falkland-war drama, with many uncomfortable and confronting scenes, but it was so recognisably this country. The wasteland T.S Eliot so aptly described, as well as the England of Dickens and Pinter – that dark side that begs denial yet manages to flaunt itself brashly, with little regard for consequences.

We stayed on the soggy hill and surrounds for about an hour, as the rain had dissipated to a fine drizzle not long after we had conquered the hill. Naturally, once at the summit, I longed for my pastels and easel, but I had to make do with my iPhone and my mind's eye. There would be plenty of time to paint when I returned to Australia.

"I suppose we'd better mossy on down the hill before it starts getting dark." Finley sounded reluctant to leave, and Suzy and I felt it too – the pull of Primrose Hill. It was a beautiful parkland, almost within hiking distance of the centre of London, but still very natural and untouched. People demonstrated respect for the land, and this was reflected in the way everyone went quietly about their business, whether it was picnicking, kite-flying or dog-walking (on a lead of course, and there was a lot of that going on, given that it was the weekend.)

I was really grateful to Finley and Suzy for taking me to this panoramic, peaceful reserve, and I wanted to find some way of repaying them for their kindness. An entire day of their precious weekend had been centred around sourcing things for me to do as a tourist in London, and apart from the awkward half hour at the pool this morning, it had gone very smoothly. I would need to have a good think about it tonight and see if I could conjure up an unexpected surprise for my friends.

When we arrived back at the house, it was around seven thirty, and all three of us collapsed in front of the television in the lounge-room watching the news. None of us could face any more hot-food, so we compensated with tea and biscuits. Finley loved his tea, boasting to ten strong cups a day in thirsty weather. However, he had little idea of thirsty weather, as for him, twenty-three degrees was a 'scorcher.' The decision to 'call it a night' at eight thirty was unanimous. Finley, ever the dreamer, had a solo dawn motorbike ride planned, and Suzy would be leaving around seven to travel across town by train to her school, where their annual September fete was taking place. She had invited me to the fete way back in April when we had been planning my trip, given that I was to be visiting around the fete time. I'd said that I would see how things panned out, and now that the time had come, I just didn't have the strength to sit propped up on a plastic school chair with Suzy, for five hours on the crotched dolls stall. Suzy understood completely.

Apart from my severe case of TL (Tourist lag), I had no other valid reason for casting my vote in favour of an early night, other than it had become my pattern of late to go to bed with the chooks. This meant that I woke early, at around six thirty each morning, leaving ample time for a morning meditation.

My blow-up double-bed lilo was still securely positioned between the fridge and the wall in the dining room. So acute was my fatigue, that I didn't even notice it had shrunk to almost half the size it had been the previous night. When I finally laid my head upon the pillow, I did think the mattress was sinking faster than Venice, but I was asleep before I could look for the pump.

My iPhone alarm woke me at 4 am.

I was fuzzy for a few seconds, but once I'd orientated myself, I realised my mistake. My intention had been to set it for seven, but without my glasses, and my state of extreme tiredness, I must have mistaken the luminous four for a seven. As I lay there, trying to reclaim my sleep, I heard a loud banging noise, and then muffled male voices. The disturbance was coming from the front of the house, and I wasn't sure if it was just inebriated neighbours coming home very late and tripping over what sounded like dustbins, or if it was genuine burglars. After the fridge incident of the night before, I was reluctant to creep up the stairs to Finley and Suzy's bedroom and wake them up. I tried 'solution focus' and buried my head in the doona, placing my hands over my ears for good measure – but I couldn't breathe and had to up-scope for air. The noises were louder the second time, and I realised that I'd have to get up and investigate. At home I keep a baseball bat under my bed for such occasions, but thankfully as yet, I hadn't had the experience of using it. I knew plenty of people who had though, and they had impressed upon me to always sound confident and affronted – that would give me the upper hand. Hannah, a social worker friend in Melbourne had a memorable, if not overexaggerated story to tell about attaining the upper-hand in situations of fight or flight. She was shopping one day just before Christmas, when the shops are packed, and tempers frayed. As she neared her car (which she'd had to park on the top floor of the centre car park), laden with heavy boxes and a pencil-thin two-metre tall, white plastic Christmas tree, she could see three balaclava clad youths attempting to break into it. She was instantly petrified and started shaking, dropping the tree and the boxes in frenzied alarm. Then (as she tells the story) she was overcome by a presence the size of a tsunami. Possessed, Hannah hurled herself towards the young offenders, screaming out every profanity under the sun, at the top of her lungs. It went something along the lines of, "What the…do you think you are doing?"

You can guess the rest!

I had Hannah's story fresh in my mind, but I wouldn't be playing the lead role in her script tonight.

Who knows what reaction I would receive? Hannah had been successful in scaring off the Melbourne Shopping-Centre thugs, but things may have been different in London. Images of the Cray brothers, Lizzy Borden with her axe, and the Fred West murders were always fresh in my mind in England. I couldn't put it off and longer. It was obvious that Finley and Suzy could have slept through an air raid, and even if I managed to rouse them, what could they do? I wasn't even sure if the commotion was coming from outside our house – but it was certainly loud enough. Suddenly it went quiet, and I summonsed up the courage to skulk up the stairs and into Fin and Suzy's room to look out towards the front courtyard. I had to go into their room, as there was only one large bay window at the front of the house, and it was in their bedroom. Once inside, I hid myself behind the thick, red, velvet curtain in case Fin or Suzy stirred, and put my hands and face up to the window in an effort to detect any movement or shadows. It was quiet and still in the courtyard. I stayed hidden behind the curtain for about five minutes, but apart from the odd snort from Fin, there was no noise. Not even the birds had yet woken. Satisfied that everything was OK. I crept back towards the bedroom door, and softly closed it behind me. What with the elaborate plans that had been made for the day ahead, it would be no use disturbing the happily sleeping couple at his stage. Morning would be here soon enough.

# Chapter 28
## A Lost Bike and Some Lost Hours

Morning was here soon enough! Too soon and too early for me. I must have accidently moved the deflating lilo closer towards the kitchen with the early morning goings-on, and my second awakening of the morning was not again courtesy of the mis-set alarm, but the huge bikie-clad boot of Finley, up for his early morning bike ride. He mustn't have seen the end of my lilo jutting out into the kitchen, as he stepped right onto my outstretched legs and tripped, landing right beside me on the lilo. It hadn't hurt all that much, but I had still squealed in pain, alarmed by the fact that a big hairy bikie was in my room and on my bed. Finley had lost his balance entirely then and landed heavily beside me on the lilo. Did he apologise for nearly breaking my legs? I think not, since he was Finley, and he was not going to miss the opportunity to crack a joke (after having successfully cracked a leg or two)

"Well, well, if it ain't you Fil. We'll have to stop meeting like this."

He grinned and pretended to shake my hand. I played along and shook his outstretched hand with gusto. I then dryly retorted back to him, "Well, well, if it ain't you Fin. Sadly, either you or I will have to go!" (Courtesy of the wit of the great Oscar Wilde, and in reference to wallpaper, but it still fitted the moment.) Finley wagged his finger at me, and joked, "Ya got me this time Fil. I'll chalk one up for you on our slate. I think I am still twenty quips in front though. It'll be hard to come back from where you are."

I lay back on the lilo, which by now was no more than a thick rubbery film over the polished wood of the dining room floor, with a smidgeon of air thrown in for good measure. It was hard on my back, but at least I was horizontal and not vertical. These interrupted sleeps were taking their toll on my body. I allowed myself the luxury of quiet meditation-mood music from my iPad and was almost in a delta state when I heard Finley shouting out from the courtyard in a very distressed voice. He was very clear, because he was so loud, and also, because he was repeating the same phrase over and over, "My bike. My bike!"

I jumped up off the floor and pulled on my kimono over my flimsy nightie. It was inside out, but I had no time to grapple with it. Finley was in trouble, and although he had been solely responsible for waking me from my second round of sleep for the night, I still reacted when he was in dire straits. Suzy was also up by now. She must have been in the shower, because she appeared in the doorway, clad in a terry towelling pink dressing gown and her hair coiled up in a matching pink turban, dripping wet, wanting to know what was wrong with Finley's bike.

"I'll go and find out what's happened Suzy. You just get ready for the fete or you'll be late." Suzy looked up at the clock on the wall and let out a yelp of her own. "Oh, is that the time? I really will be late. Can you go please Fil?"

I could still hear Finley calling out, but he had added a clue to the initial dialogue. "Someone's stolen my bike!" I thought I must have misheard, because although I knew next to nothing about motor bikes, I did know that Fin had a massive motor bike, and that it claimed most of the courtyard, vying, on most evenings, for a place alongside the two garbage bins and a large crate full of bottles. I found Finley huddled over the spot where his motor bike was normally parked, searching for clues. "Finley! What's happened? Where is your bike?" Fin looked crestfallen. He was gritting his teeth – a thing he did when he was highly stressed.

"Gone. Stolen. Did you hear anything last night? I can't believe there wasn't any noise getting a big bike like mine over the concrete wall."

I realised I had too much information stowed away in my head. Information which included vital snippets like, Yes, I did hear noises, and no, I didn't realise that Finley's bike was being stolen. I answered him cautiously. "I may have heard something, but I thought it was just the neighbours coming home late from the pub."

Finley was so distraught that he didn't seem to be listening to me. I gave up then and suggested to him that we take the car and start looking for the bike. He seemed to cheer up at my 'brill plan', and I quickly raced back inside and changed into my tracksuit. I would have my shower later. Suzy offered to stay home and help Finley look for the bike when she found out what had happened, but he would not hear of it. So, it was Finley and I who ended up tripping the highways and byways of Archway and surrounds, looking for the bike. We had almost given up hope when Finley spotted two dishevelled looking teenage boys pushing a motor bike up a hill near the Crouch End shopping centre. We were about fifteen minutes from Fin's house. When they saw us approaching, they flung the bike onto the side of the road and fled over a nearby fence. (I don't think they knew who we were, only that we were suspicious of them.) We couldn't believe our luck. It was Finley's bike, and despite being covered in mud, it looked to be intact. "Fil, why do you think they didn't ride off into the sunset with the bike?" I had no idea, but I was very happy that his bike had been found. Finley phoned Suzy, who was still on the train to tell her the good news. Suzy was suitably enthusiastic. I could hear her high-pitched voice coming through the phone. "Oh, that's fab Fin. Now you can still go for your ride. Are you going to report the incident?" Finley replied that he would think about reporting it, but that he wasn't really all that fussed now that the bike had been returned in one piece. I wanted to point out to him that the bike hadn't really been returned, but that we'd had to go out and look for it, and that he had been in a very agitated state when we hadn't been able to find it anywhere. Still, he was happy now, and it was still only 9 am. The day had not been entirely ruined. I managed to convince Finley to go for the anticipated ride into the country, and we decided that I would drive the fiat home, and Finley would follow on his bike. It sounded like a good plan to me, and as soon as I made sure that the bike started, I positioned myself in the driver's seat of the Fiat and started crunching the gears until I found one which would allow me to take off. I had driven in London plenty of times, so I wasn't fazed at the prospect. Even though I drove slowly, we were home in fifteen minutes, and Finley and I were sitting in the lounge room sipping tea and munching on chocolate biscuits before nine thirty. After that he was off like the flash, and I had the house to myself all day!

It was going to be a wonderful Sunday morning, luxuriating in the Archway, tripping down to the High street, pottering in the garden and re-packing my suitcase. Maybe a little cooking as a surprise for Finley and Suzy. All of my favourite things.

Sadly, I accomplished none of these dreams. When Finley left, I showered and dressed, and then felt like a little lay down. Pacing myself – I called it. I had the house to myself, and nowhere to be until 3 o'clock when I was due back at Alice and Patrick's, so I let my hair down and flopped on the lilo. It was also let down – flat, and at floor level again, but I wasn't perturbed, as I knew I'd be back in my own bed in Hampton for the last night tonight, before the big trip home. My sleep last night had been so broken, that a wee shut eye was practically the only thought I could entertain. On the hard floor, in broad daylight, with the typical Sunday morning bustle on the streets and in nearby gardens, I slept!

It was past 2 o'clock when Finley woke me. Back from his jaunt in the countryside, and ravenous. The only reason he knew I was still there was because he again tripped over my outstretched leg. I woke with a start and a disoriented yell, and Finley also let out a scream, only he attached a profanity or two to his outburst.

"Fil, what are you still doing here, I thought we weren't going to see you until tonight!"

Finley and Suzy were invited to Patrick and Alice's place in the evening for a farewell dinner to me. "I fell asleep Fin, I was so tired. I guess I've missed my morning of doing nothing in particular. I must have slept through it all. Did you have an eventful morning on your bike?"

Finley looked pleased enough to see me, once he had recovered from the shock of finding me sprawled out on his dining room floor. We had the inevitable second round cup of tea and biscuits, and Finley ate at least ten biscuits, on account of his "voracious appetite from all the fresh air". By then it was past 3 o'clock. Finley offered to drive me over to Alice and Patrick's, but since it was quite a distance across London, I suggested we wait for Suzy, and the three of us could travel together in a couple of hours. Fin seemed relieved that he would not have to leave straight away. He was yawning and rubbing his eyes.

"I think I might take a leaf out of your book Fil and go and have a kip. Suzy will be home at four, and we could leave shortly after. That suit you?"

I was more than suited with the plan, and as soon as Fin had retreated to the bedroom, with a sandwich, milk and more biscuits, I grabbed my purse and backpack and headed off down the street to the High street, where I knew there would be an outdoor market with fresh fruit and veggies. My plan was to buy a whole heap of salad veggies, as well as some fruit for a fruit platter. We would be ordering pizzas for tonight, and I wanted to make sure that no one paid for anything. I had that sixties song in my head 'It's my party and I'll cry if I want to, except that in my head it was playing as, 'It's my party and I'll buy if I want to!' I found two fair-sized crisp pale green iceberg lettuces, some juicy tomatoes, a plump fleshy avocado, some chunky broccoli, a long stick of celery and a bunch of sweet spring onions. It would be a salad fit for a king (or queen).

The fruits I selected for the platter included juicy oranges and pineapple, crunchy apples and pears, and three ripe peaches. I deliberated over a dressing and decided at the last minute to throw in a couple of lemons and a fresh bunch of both mint and coriander. I knew Alice had a marvellous Nigella Lawson salad dressing she kept made up in her fridge which would enhance the flavour of the fresh market vegetables. For good measure, and because I was feeling hungry, I picked out a small bunch of grapes which I duely devoured.

My backpack was brimming, and I wished I had brought an extra bag to lug all the produce home. The Sunday market had been set up down the hill from the station, and I planned to make for the station, and then rest on the seats outside the main entrance and recover my breath before tackling the next rise in the road. I realised they didn't call the cemetery 'Highgate' for nothing and judging by the sheer abundance of graves and mausoleums in the actual cemetery further up the hill, it would not have been implausible to assume that a few of the resting souls had put themselves there through over-exertion climbing these very hills. A pit-stop would be precautionary and for the best. I was reclining on the bench, alone and sipping from my water bottle when I heard someone calling my name. "Fil, Fil, what are you doing sitting there all by yourself. Did you miss the train back to Hampton?" It was Suzy, on her way home from the fete. I'd forgotten that she needed to be picked up at four, after the long day on the stalls.

"Suzy. Thank heavens. I've gone and bought all this fruit and veggies for salads and a fruit platter tonight, and now I'm having trouble getting it all home. Have you rung Finley to pick you up yet?"

"Yes. He's on his way. We'll just stay put until he gets here."

I was so delighted to hear that Finley and the cab were on their way to fetch us, that I jumped up too quickly, and half of the contents of my backpack escaped and started rolling back down the hill. Being a Sunday, there were no commuters, but a few people were out for a stroll and an ice cream, and amidst much laughter and squealing, the whole group of us managed to collect most of the fruit, which had been bulging in the neck of the backpack. Only one orange managed to escape for good, cleverly rolling under a large parked truck. We watched it roll and left it there. Ten points for ingenuity. In the middle of all the confusion caused by the runaway fruit and veggies, Finley pulled up in his cab, and swung into the very spot he had been waiting in when I'd arrived in Archway two evenings ago.

He started laughing when he saw the chaos I had caused, and called out to me through his open window. "Archway won't be the same without you Fil."

Suzy was laughing too, and as soon as we got home, she flopped on the couch and told Finley of how she had come upon me sitting alone and forlorn on the seat outside the station.

"Fil, we are going to miss you when you hop on that plane tomorrow. It will be very quiet around here." I was going to miss them too. Especially Finley's black cab, which had already saved me from hours of waiting around for trains and taxis. (Not to mention the monetary savings)

"How about you two go and relax for a while, and I'll make the salads and fruit platter for tonight. We can pick up some cold wine on the way, and I'll get Alice to order the pizzas. Do you guys have a preference?" They didn't, so I phoned Alice, and let her know of my change of plans, and that we would be arriving around seven. I also asked her to order the pizzas for delivery around the same time. (I would reimburse her later with the last of my English pounds.) Lastly, I told her that we had wine, fruit and green salads. Alice assured me she would request a 7 o'clock arrival for the pizzas.

Once the plans had been finalised, and Fin and Suzy had disappeared into their bedroom to prepare and dress up for the big pizza party, I threw myself into preparation-mode, and chopped, sliced, washed and dried the fruit and salad vegetables. Suzy had left me two large plastic bowls, and they were perfect. I intended to transfer my creations into the pottery bowls I had seen at Alice and Patrick's.

Everything was working out perfectly. The salads were completed, the fruit for the platter was sliced and cubed, and my suitcase was packed and ready to be carried out to the car. I micro-showered and dressed and shoved my hill-climbing outfit (jeans and a tee shirt) into a plastic bag. Unless I got the chance to wash them tonight, they would just have to stay in the plastic bag unwashed until I got back to Australia. (I wasn't going to let Alice know I had dirty washing in my suitcase.) It suddenly hit me that I might need to borrow another suitcase from Alice, as we still hadn't managed to buy a new one. It wouldn't be a problem though, as I could give it back to Alice when she came to Australia at Christmas time to visit her father. He was on his own now, and Alice was the apple of his eye. She was right up there in equal first place with Trixie – the beloved canine member of his one-person household. Patrick would not be accompanying Alice to Australia, as he had commitments at home over Christmas with his political Party. It was all so serious – Patrick and his politics.

So, the suitcase dilemma was sorted, the salads were sorted, and the pizza was sorted. I started feeling a little maudlin and nostalgic as I counted the number of hours until my flight the next day. Sixteen hours to go, and I would be sitting on the plane-bound for Melbourne. What a trip it had been, and what a collection characters had crossed my path. I wished they could all be present at the farewell dinner party tonight. I was ready and waiting, and Suzy was still in the bathroom, finishing off her makeup. She looked very tired, and I was very grateful that she was coming tonight. I would have understood if neither she nor Finley were able to make it, as it really was an hour or so of travel, but they had both insisted that they wouldn't miss it for the world. With ten minutes or so to kill, I found a cool spot sitting on a wicker chair at the bottom of the garden I had promised to weed and began making a list of all the people I would have invited to my party tonight had there been time and a suitable venue. I counted up thirty in all. Ian, Jean, Harold, Maurice, Christine and her bouncer husband, the two teachers and Frank and his wife who lived in Alice's court in Barton, the beautiful people from the café in Barton on the cliff top, and the Pakistani shop keeper and his extended family, the two men who had been fishing in the New Forest, plus the two fishermen from Limington, the bus driver from the New forest, and the two teachers from the open top bus, and finally from Barton, the gaggle of Polish girls who worked in Lidl, and who would have loved a Sunday evening party up in London before they started their shift on Monday morning. That was Barton done! I would probably have to rethink the venue if all the people I had struck up an acquaintance with in London and surrounds were to be invited. "Are you ready Fil, it's almost six, and it'll take us a good hour to get to Hampton." Finely and Suzy stood side by side at the back door, both in clean casual attire, and both hopping from foot to foot, because I was dawdling and daydreaming as usual.

"Coming. I'm ready." I took a last look at the overgrown, very English shaped garden, and zipped up to the back door. (English back gardens are generally so miniscule, you can cover the entire space in three or four paces.) I knew this to be a fact, as I had seen Miranda Hart's minute back garden in suburban London on a gardening show she co-presented with her mother, and Miranda, being Miranda had mistaken a rare flower for a weed and yanked it out with one callous pull.) Finley had already packed the car, so there was nothing left to do but lock up and venture out into the cool evening to the waiting cab. Bye-bye Archway. Adios amigos!

Possibly because it was after 6 o'clock, and a Sunday evening, the roads to Hampton were very quiet, and we made it in good time. Suzy and Fin had politely emphasised to me that they wanted to get away by eight thirty or 9 o'clock at the latest as tomorrow was Monday, and a working day for both of them. I agreed wholeheartedly and let them know that I also wanted an early night, as I still had packing and cleaning to do, and I needed to get in a good night's sleep in anticipation of the long flight back to Australia.

When we pulled up in Alice and Patrick's driveway, having only made one stop along the way at an off-license to pick up two bottles of Australian chardonnay, Alice, Patrick and Joan were all standing on the front porch, waving tiny Australian flags and singing the National Anthem, 'Advance Australia Fair.' It was touching (especially as they had been waiting for us to arrive for almost an hour), but it sounded dreadful – mainly because Alice was shouting to compensate for Patrick not knowing the words, and Joan was off with the fairies, laughing and singing 'God Save the Queen'. The resulting rendition was hilarious, and it gave the three of us a good laugh. It was a salubrious start to our last evening together, and I did my level best to entertain them all with stories of Australia, and how different it was in the bottom half of the world to the English way of life.

The pizza and salads were rapidly devoured, and I just managed to pour Alice's dressing over the green salad in time. It was late to eat, but we all thoroughly enjoyed ourselves. All too soon Finley announced that he needed to go and rev up the engine. Ever the gentleman, he offered to drive Joan home – having no idea that Joan lived next door. Suzy, Alice and I were in the kitchen finishing the dishes, and Patrick had taken the dogs for a brisk walk around the block before they were secured in their night cages. That had left Finley and Joan in the lounge room together. Joan must have readily agreed to being driven home in the black cab, as when Alice and I helped carry Suzy's plastic bowls out to the cab – there was Joan, buckled up in back, feet curled up under her posterior (usual position) ready to be driven home.

Alice was laughing so much she couldn't speak. I chipped in with "Have a great trip out of the driveway Joan". Fin looked at me quizzically, and I leant in towards him and whispered, "She lives next door." Finley looked over his shoulder at Joan, ensconced in the back seat of the cab, and chuckled loudly.

"I'll just take her around the block, and then I'll turn into her driveway. She'll be thrilled, and probably won't even realise what's happening. Alice agreed the

Joan could be very vague, and Suzy took the opportunity to hug us both and jump into the cab herself."

"There's no punch without Joanie." She sang back to the two of us – and they were off, waving and blowing kisses till they reached the corner of the court.

Patrick and the dogs were just rounding the corner as the black cab hurtled up the deserted road. The first thing he said when he got close enough for either of us to hear him was, "Who was the third person in the cab?"

We both looked straight at him and started laughing, falling over each other and pointing towards Joan's house.

"Oh no. Don't tell me! Where are they taking her? This could actually be a good thing." Patrick was laughing by now as well. We decided not to wait outside for the cab with Joan propped up in it to return, and Patrick said that he would nip over later to see if Joan was home and tucked up in bed. Alice and I went inside to look for a suitably large suitcase for me to borrow, and Patrick went off to do some bedtime reading. In my bedroom, Alice and I both flaked out on my bed. I wanted to go to sleep there and then, but she refused to let me off lightly, and told me to look under the bed, where she kept an old suitcase which I was welcome to borrow to take home with me. I fell on my knees to the floor and poked my head under the bed. Sure enough, there was a suitcase hiding under there, but it was neither old nor battered. It was brand new!

"It's your going away present Fil, from Patrick, Joan and me. Please, please, please don't sit on it, or hurl it over any banisters. Promise?"

I hugged her and promised, and then rushed out to thank Patrick. I think he was a little embarrassed with my gushing over-enthusiasm, as he just looked at me and muttered, "That's fine, and…Joan's gone to bed."

We all went to bed then. My last night. My last glimpse of Suzy, Finley and Joan. My holiday was over. Almost!

# Chapter 29
## That's a Wrap!

Usually, when you are off on an adventure, you wake up early, abandon your bed, and prepare for take-off. Usually when you are at the end of an adventure, you wake up late, struggle out of bed, and prepare for the worst. Neither of these two things happened to me on my last morning in England. It was just as if nothing out of the ordinary was about to happen today. It was just as if I opened my eyes, remembered what day it was, and what was about to happen, and then indulged all morning routines on automatic pilot.

Alice slept in. Patrick was off walking the dogs, and I was sitting glumly in the lounge room with the empty dog cages, wondering whether to awaken Alice, or just to keep sitting there, waiting for her to wake up. Inertia had set in. Deep inertia.

"Fil, why didn't you wake me? We'll be late for the airport. Are you ready to go?" There was anxiety in her voice, and I could detect a decibel of alarm at the fact that we might not make it on time for the plane. What Alice didn't know was that I had the joker up my sleeve regarding the flight. Alice and Patrick were under the impression (from me) that the plane left at midday, but the actual flight time was two thirty-five. I always like to be at airports early, and I have learnt the hard way that it is better to be two hours early than two hours late. If you can't find anything useful and exciting to do at an international airport for a couple of hours, then you must be a very dull and unimaginative person. The shops, the bars, the restaurants, the restrooms, the duty-free zones and the lounges- a plethora of possibilities. I was actually looking forward to hanging out in the QANTAS lounge before my flight, knowing that there were hot showers with the cream of shampoos and conditioners, as well as a bountiful buffet. I would follow my usual routine of changing into my travelling clothes, to ensure maximum comfort on the plane. I started cheering up when I thought of the potential airport offerings. My mood instantly morphed.

"Rest assured my good friend Alice, all is well. I am packed, preened and positively pumped in readiness for the airport." My over-the-top verbosity did the trick with Alice, and she raced off to her boudoir to shower and dress. I was about to go into the kitchen and make some toast and a cup of tea for Alice when Patrick poked his head around the kitchen door.

"I'm back. Is everyone ready for the airport?" I was ready. The dogs were ready. Patrick was ready.

That left Alice, who was probably ten minutes off being ready.

"Are you making Alice some breakfast to eat on the way to the airport Fil?"

Patrick obviously knew Alice like the back of his hand and had worked out that the two slices of bread in my hand were not for me.

"I've brought her a croissant to eat in the car, and there are some little plastic bottles of orange juice in the fridge. That'll have to do for her, or well be late. And by the way Fil, I know what time the plane really takes off." He winked at me and went out to the foyer to bring my suitcase outside.

That was Patrick to a tee. The last one standing with the quips and winking routine. He and Finley could have had a really good double act if they didn't live on either side of London to each other. I followed Patrick out, dragging the smaller case straining with presents and tins of shortbread. I had bought ten tins of shortbread with varied members of the royal family on the lids, because it was impossible to find that exact brand of shortbread in Melbourne. (Not because we were all royalists in Australia, although I did know a smattering of hard-core followers of the Royal family.) The dogs were already sitting up expectantly in the back seat, strapped into the seat belts for added safety. Since I would be sitting in the back with them, I was relieved that they were secured.

"Just waiting on Alice now."

Patrick was drumming his knuckles on the roof of the Jag, and the secured dogs started yelping, thinking it was a game. After a couple of minutes, Alice came rushing out of the house, and she threw her arms around me, exclaiming sincerely. "We'll all miss you Fil. It's been quite a holiday." I hugged her back, and then gave Patrick a quick peck on the cheek. Patrick walked calmly back to the front door which Alice, in her haste, had left wide open. He locked it carefully and gave Alice one of those 'do I have to do everything?' looks. Then it was goodbye to the house, goodbye to the court and goodbye to Hampton. We sailed up the ramp onto the freeway with Heathrow in our sights.

It had just gone 10 o'clock.

Patrick tried his best to bring the Jag to a rest as near as possible to the airport terminal, but it was the usual chaotic Monday morning at Heathrow, and the closest we could get to the main entrance was about fifty metres away. Alice jumped out of the car and helped me pull the two cases out of the boot. They were both on wheels, so it wasn't going to be very difficult for me to manoeuvre them towards the big glass doors.

"Well. This is it Fil. See you in the land of Oz."

"Ye. See you Fil. It's been very entertaining listening to your stories every night. We'll miss you, wont we Alice?"

A final hug from both of them, and they were gone. I stood there alone for a few minutes, taking it all in. I was going home. The holiday had finished. It was the end of my adventure.

The people I'd met, the landscapes I'd traversed, the food I'd eaten, the friendships I'd cemented. It was worth it all for the pleasure it had given me. I would like to think that I'd dished out some pleasure too and had not just been a passive recipient. A traveller's tale!

This was living life to the full.

I couldn't even begin to think of what might be unravelled on my next adventure. I gazed up at the low English horizon, with one solitary expression, multiplied into thousands of tiny cells exploding my entire mind, 'This is England!' Then, I heaved my cases through the Heathrow double glass doors.

I was on my way home.